Contents

KU-635-116

Frommer's®

Mediterranean Spain

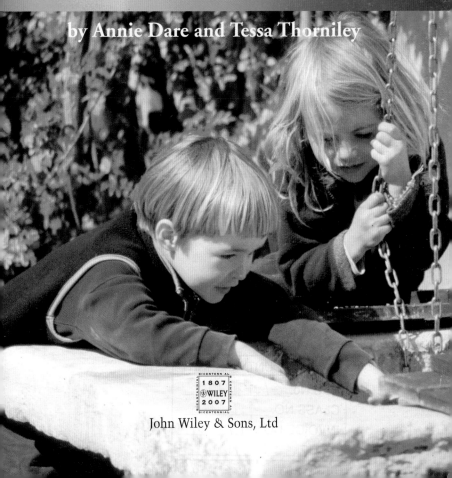 with your Family

From tranquil villages to the bustling Costas

by Annie Dare and Tessa Thorniley

BICENTENNIAL
1807
WILEY
2007
BICENTENNIAL

John Wiley & Sons, Ltd

Published by:
Wiley Publishing, Inc.
111 River St.
Hoboken, NJ 07030-5774

ISBN: 978-0-470-05528-1

UK Publisher: Sally Smith
Executive Project Editor: Martin Tribe (Frommer's UK)
Commissioning Editor: Mark Henshall (Frommer's UK)
Development Editor: Anne O'Rorke
Content Editor: Hannah Clement (Frommer's UK)
Cartographer: Tim Lohnes
Photo Research: Jill Emeny (Frommer's UK)
Wiley Bicentennial logo: Richard J. Pacifico
Production by Wiley Indianapolis Composition Services

For information on our other products and services or to obtain technical support, please contact our Customer Care Department within the U.S. at 800/762-2974, outside the U.S. at 317/572-3993 or fax 317/572-4002. Within the UK Tel. 01243 779777; Fax. 01243 775878.

Wiley also publishes its books in a variety of electronic formats. Some content that appears in print may not be available in electronic formats. Printed and bound by Printer Trento in Italy.

5 4 3 2 1

About the Authors

Annie Dare is a freelance journalist and subeditor. She lives in North London.

Tessa Thorniley has worked on the city and finance desks of *The Daily Telegraph* and *The Daily Mail*. She lives in Rome.

Acknowledgements

Thanks for contributions and help to Malcolm Moore, Jessica Rainey, Ayesha Mendham, Guy Hunter Watts, Giles Birch, Anthony Jefferies, Jean Fabrice Vernet & James Rickards, John Lahr, VW Camper Sales, the Spanish Tourist Board, P&O Ferries, *La Luz* magazine.

An Additional Note

Please be advised that travel information is subject to change at any time and this is especially true of prices. We therefore suggest that you write or call ahead for confirmation when making your travel plans. The authors, editors and publisher cannot be held responsible for experiences of readers while travelling. Your safety is important to us, however, so we encourage you to stay alert and be aware of your surroundings.

Star Ratings, Icons & Abbreviations

Hotels, restaurants and attraction listings in this guide have been ranked for quality, value, service, amenities and special features using a star rating system. Hotels, restaurants, attractions, shopping and nightlife are rated on a scale of zero stars (recommended) to three (exceptional). In addition to the star rating system, we also use 4 feature icons that point you to the great deals, in-the-know advice and unique experiences. Throughout the book, look for:

FIND	Special finds – those places only insiders know about
MOMENT	Special moments – those experiences that memories are made of
VALUE	Great values – where to get the best deals
OVERRATED	Places or experiences not worth your time or money

The following **abbreviations** are used for credit cards:

AE	American Express
MC	MasterCard
V	Visa

A Note on Prices

Frommer's provides exact prices in each destination's local currency. As this book went to press, the rate of exchange was 1€ = £0.67. Rates of exchange are constantly in flux; for up-to-the-minute information, consult a currency conversion website such as www.oanda.com/convert/classic. In the Family Friendly Accommodation and Dining sections of this book we have used a price category system.

An Invitation to the Reader

In researching this book, we discovered my wonderful places – hotels, restaurants, shops and more. We're sure you'll find others. Please tell us about them, so we can share the information with your fellow travellers in upcoming editions. If you were disappointed with a recommendation, we'd love to know that too. Please write to:

Frommer's Mediterranean Spain with Your Family, 1st edition
John Wiley & Sons, Ltd
The Atrium
Southern Gate
Chichester
West Sussex, PO19 8SQ

Photo Credits

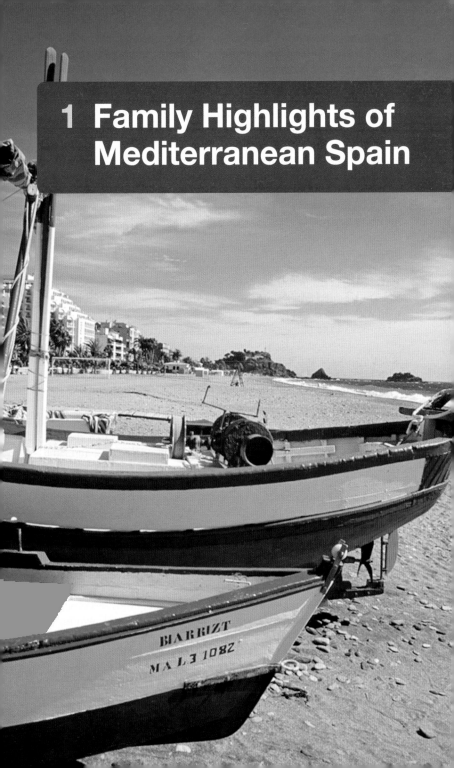

1 Family Highlights of Mediterranean Spain

Spaniards absolutely fall over themselves for children, whether it's their own or other people's offspring: their love for youngsters borders on a national obsession. Bringing up baby in Spain is a big undertaking: shops are packed with elaborate swaddling clothes and families shell out for christening outfits that cost the earth. Children are adored and fawned on, but are very far from being wrapped up in cotton wool: hardly anywhere is out of bounds for Spanish youngsters. Any English notions of bedtime and 'no-go zones' should be gloriously abandoned at immigration: taking your family to Spain is something of a holiday from rules.

Restaurateurs will look at you blankly if you ask whether it's okay to bring children to the table – in Spain, it's akin to asking whether breathing is a good idea. Not that you should expect a huge number of facilities. Some restaurants, almost always those run by expats, sometimes have the odd high chair or two, but it's rare you'll find children's menus. Childrens clubs haven't caught on here enormously and crayons and clowns at dinner-time are the exceptions not the norm. What it lacks in planned entertainment and facilities though the country more than makes up for in its absolutely whopping warm welcome.

As one of the oldest countries to really absorb mass tourism, Spain has an excellent and cheap tourist infrastructure to take the headache out of planning and getting around. In spite of chartered tourism, with just a little bit of imagination and, probably most critically, access to a car, you'll get the chance to explore some remote areas of this fascinating and fast changing country. Spain, is a mountainous and vast country, its geographical variety almost rivalling Australia and is in parts as empty of people, who like Oz, are concentrated chiefly round the coast. Inland life is more remote and unchanged, and rural Spain, its beautiful mountains and natural parks, the Sierra Nevada, and towns such as Aracena are great antidotes to 21st century city life. Whether your children are at the age of chasing butterflies or hiking, there's enough to wear them out over 10 years of holidays on the trot.

The beaches of the Mediterranean, Costa Del Sol, Costa Tropical, and the natural park of Cabo de Gata, meanwhile, all have brilliant sheltered shores perfect for paddling. The windy bays on the Costa Brava have slick watersports schools where older children can be taught surfing, wind or kite-surfing and sailing. Every town in Southern Spain comes with swings and slides and almost every second town has a giant water park with lots of decent municipal swimming pools in between.

The guaranteed sunshine, which is such an irresistible draw to Spain actually becomes quite a serious drawback if you intend to make forays inland with children – particularly Andalucia – in August. It's wise to trim back any ambitions you have for city sightseeing not just because of attention spans, but that searing heat, too. Granada, Cordoba and Seville can all feel hotter than a brick oven at the height of summer.

For adults Spain is fascinating, and there's absolutely masses – historic sites, swashbuckling stories, outdoor adventure, live culture, street performances – to keep your little one amused at the same time. Spain has so much going for it for families – lots of unspoiled areas and cheap food and accommodation, plus short flight times, readily available children's necessities, and no need for inoculations. Having children shouldn't mean the end of adventurous travel. If it isn't too much of a paradox, with a little bit of planning, you can be a spontaneous as you please together.

BEST FAMILY EXPERIENCES

Best Family Events You'll have to exercise some guile to actually avoid the fiestas, romerias and paella eating free for alls that are the bread and butter of Spain's community calendar. Seville's Semana Santa is one of the few carrying a parental guidance caution – its solemnity is a little off-putting for most – but otherwise there are mini events strewn the length of the coast and dotted throughout the year, almost all carrying special childrens features. Fallas is a Valencian bonfire night stretched over five days, with papier-mache effigies ablaze (you vote to save your favourite – be it Bart Simpson or Francisco Franco, or George W. Bush), fireworks, bullfights, beauty pageants and paella cook-offs. See p. 25. Catalan festivals are famous for their human towers tradition, in which strongmen stand on each others shoulders to form six and seven storey human Towers-of-Pisa, with the top spot saved for a light little boy or girl. Valls, 100 km south of Barcelona, is 'the cradle of castles', but you can catch the human towers at festivals everywhere from Tarragona to Barcelona. See Chapter 10.

If you want something a bit more educational, the town of Alcoy near Alicante holds a three-day Moros y Cristianos (Moors and Christians) festival, a re-enactment of the conquests and re-conquests done in full historical dress. See p. 26.

Barcelona's Fiesta de la Mercé (Weekend around 23 September) features free concerts in every square and the streets are peopled with outsized statues. The Correfoc (fire run) is when fire spurts from 'dragon's mouths' and families can 'dance with the devil' under sparklers and huge revolving fireworks. See p. 28.

Although the event isn't geared to children, bear in mind Valencia does host the America's Cup in 2007.

Best Cities Valencia scores top marks in terms of family diversions. Even the process of getting around the city is family friendly. Traversed by a dry river bed serving as a pedestrian thoroughfare, the historic walled city is linked to the world-class City of Arts and Sciences, Spain's rival to

April Fair, Seville

Disney's Epcot Center. The sea enclosure here alone is likely to sweep your children off their maritime feet, with penguins, whales and an amazing dolphin show that's a sure hit with children, who can take turns in feeding the sealife. There's also the Gulliver Park where children can play at being a Lilliputian. If your youngsters are likely to enjoy paella, then Valencia is the home of the dish, and you can eat it down on the beach while they roam across miles and miles of sand: perfect sandcastle territory. See p. 215. **Malaga**, meanwhile, is quite simply one of Spain's coolest cities, for adults and children alike. Slap in the centre of the Costa Del Sol you are within striking distance of the most amazing theme and water parks. Just a scoot along the coast lies all the entertainment of Marbella and Torremolinos – fair-rides,

Cirque de Soleil, magicians, toy trains, incredible shopping malls, sailing schools, English-speakers and, for fussy eaters, any food you might be missing from home. But best of all is that Malaga has remained really genuinely Spanish. The El Palo suburb of Malaga has one of the nicest family beaches along the whole coast, grassy plots by the beach and cheap chiringuitos serving up sardine skewers, plus back in the town centre there's cracking shopping and the wonderful Picasso art museum for teens. Great flight links, the high footfall making for extremely competitive services such as car hire and its position as the gateway to the interior attractions like El Chorro and the White Towns earns Malaga its place in the Frommer's Family top three. See p. 105. **Cartagena's** an unsung hero on the coastline, but if your children have any leanings towards historical boffinery it has child friendly museums coming out of its ears, and great beaches within easy reach. See p. 208.

Best Natural Attractions For outstanding natural beauty travel to the zones of Sierra Nevada, the mountain outdoor playground, and Cabo De Gata, a windswept sun-parched zone of precious few roads, and jaw dropping beauty. Both are best explored by foot, on horseback, or in the case of the former on skis, and the latter, with paddles and fins. See p. 180 and p. 202. Other attractions include the Cave of Marvels, a fairy-tale underground parallel universe outside Aracena, featuring stalactite and stalagmite fretted grottoes, sparkling rock pools and ceilings of mineral spears. See p. 80. Closer to Malaga are the Caves of Nerja, again, stalactites and stalagmites with prehistoric artefacts and Paleolithic paintings. See p. 122. El Chorro, inland from Malaga en route to Ronda, is a jaw-dropping dam locking in the water to Embalse de Guadalhorce, a series of amazing bright blue mineral coloured lakes to swim in and canoe around, and next door, the LSD-landscape of El Torcal, is an otherworldly natural park of strangely shaped limestone rocks. See p. 146. The municipally minded Spanish tend to stock their parks with well marked look outs, plus picnic tables and barbeques.

Best Aquarium Barcelona Aquarium holds an 80-metre long chute, which lies between schools of moray, giltheads, sunfish, ray and sharks. It's children first, here, with interactive displays and workshops. Best of all though is that children between eight and 12 can stay overnight, the highlight of the Friday and Saturday night sleepovers being the scary night-time shark activities. See p. 256.

Valencia

Cordoba

Best Beach Resorts The trick is to avoid the densely packed tourist traps and find the real beauty spots. At it's best that means long, clean, white sandy beaches, shimmering blue water and pine-tree backed sand dunes. The lively seaside town of Sitges, a day trip from Barcelona is replete with beaches. For most visitors the seafront is the main attraction, with families flocking to the eastern beaches where full facilities from bathing cabins to watersports rental kiosks make for an easier, albeit less secluded seaside experience. See p. 281. For a more chi-chi beach resort, Marbella, the heartland of the Costa del Sol, is hard to beat.

Although the town itself wouldn't make the top picks for families, two good beaches either side, El Fuerte and La Fontanilla, are excellent spots. Along the east coast, the beach resort near the port area in Valencia, El Saler is a beautiful, sandy beach sheltered by sand dunes and pine trees.

While further along Devesa beach is a wilder alternative for the adventurous family willing to load up with supplies. See p. 226.

Best Sports There's a wealth of traditional sports such as tennis, golf, swimming, horseriding and the newer, gorge walking, canyoning or even sky-diving.

Spain's ski resort, **Pradollano**, in the Sierra Nevada mountains, is another gem for energetic travellers. Thanks to lighting along the El Rio slope, night skiing is an option and the resort itself is very well equipped including a child day-centre. There are 51 runs to enjoy, more hours of sunshine than almost any other European ski resort and you can even see the sea while swooshing down the slopes. See p. 180.

Best Museum Barcelona's **CosmoCaixa** is a beautifully designed science museum with lots of interactive fun for children: electrostatic balls and swinging pendulums and experiments to be conducted first hand. The highlight is The Flooded Forest – a rainforest with towering trees, exotic birds, fish and even alligators. A tunnelled entrance into the forest gives you the macroscopic view of an ants nest, poison-arrow frogs and lots of snakes. See p. 254. Lots of smaller towns have their own brilliant, idiosyncratic museums on famous sons or historical happenings, including Ronda's **bandit museum**, a dinky site that delves into the lives of the some of the country's best-known baddies, and Cartagena's excellent, and very child friendly, **Civil War Museum**. See p. 137 and p. 210. Barcelona has the lion's share of good art galleries, but Malaga's Picasso Museum is worth an hour or two of even the most impatient teen's time.

Best Spectacle Andalucia is famous for its horses and extraordinary tests of equine control. Catch an immaculate show of horsemanship in Estapona. You'll leave thinking horses really can fly. See p. 144.

Best Castles and Palaces
From the 8th century most of Spain was under Moorish rule. The **Muslim palaces** constructed during that time remain some of the country's finest. Seville's **Alcázar**, although built in 1364 by Pedro the Cruel sometime after Christian reconquest, is one of the finest examples of Mudéjar, or Moorish style – an architectural homage to Muslim design and decoration. For children, the palace's labyrinth of gardens, with fountains, pools, a maze and a water organ provide a shady playground and a bit of balance to the high culture of the palace rooms. See p. 59. Granada's **Alhambra**, on which the Alcázar is modeled, was originally constructed as a Muslim pleasure palace and despite undergoing some heavy-handed restoration, and the decidedly Christian palace that was later plonked into the grounds, it is an awesome sight. See p. 161. Visitors to Seville should also take in the **Cathedral** – Europe's

Alcázar, Seville

third largest. Children delight in climbing the attached bell tower, La Giralda, with views across the entire city. See p. 59.

Best Theme Parks Thrill-seeking children can flock to theme parks when the temperature gets too high in town as many have a water park – or water rides – plus the usual selection of hairy rollercoasters. Seville's **Isla Mágica**, one of the few parks to be found within city walls, is well worth a detour. Its sprawl of water and jungles, with zones each based around Spain's globe-trotting past, plus regular shows, provide plenty to dazzle, dizzy and exhaust energetic youngsters. See p. 61. An hour south of Barcelona in the resort town of Salou, is another amusement gem, **Port Aventura**, one of Europe's largest. It's a similar size to Alton Towers but the main themes here are Mexico, the Far West and China. Think Polynesian water rides and an awesome 8-looping Dragon

Khan rollercoaster. There are gentler rides too, to ensure a day here can be as relaxing or white-knuckle inducing as you wish. See p. 286. For an altogether quirkier time, head to the roasting desert around Almeria. The little town of Tabernas, clinging on to life in the barren landscape, is home to **Mini-Hollywood**, the one-time film set where some of the world's biggest A-list stars have shot movies. Built around a typical Spaghetti-Western town, the place is wonderfully authentically false with its sheriff's office and saloon bars. Stick around for the hammy but entertaining shoot-em-up that happens twice or thrice daily. See p. 200.

Best Art Picasso, Dalí museum, Parc Guell. Southern Spain was home to some of the most radical of 20th century artists, in Gaudi, Dali and Picasso, each of whom have excellent museums or sites in their adopted/home towns of

Parc Güell

Barcelona, Figueres and Malaga respectively. Parc Güell is architecture made fun with typical Gaudi aplomb: houses look like they've plucked straight from a Hansel & Gretel fairy story. The whole thing is like Disneyland on LSD, studded with mosaics of reptiles and trademark Gaudi swirlings and flutings, lying on a hillside above Barcelona. See p. 257. The Dalí Museum in Figueres (towards the French border) is almost as idiosyncratic as the surrealist himself, of which the Mae West room has to be one of the wackiest. As befits the uncontainable artist's personality, Dalí's works don't fit into the former theatre, and spill out across the town. See p. 279. Finally, Malaga's Picasso Museum is the most recent art site, only opened in this, the town of the artist's birth, in 2003. See p. 254.

BEST ACCOMMODATION

Best Rural Retreat A place to let the children run free, the **Alojamiento Rural Cortijo del Pino**, just outside Granada provides a blissful get-away-from-it-all farmhouse setting. Lush surroundings and a pool, plus a self-catering house sleeping six make it a great spot for a family wanting to explore nearby Granada but not stay in town. See p. 175.

Best Breathtaking Views
With some of Spain's clearest,

cleanest seas, the **Cabo de Gata** nature reserve is unparalleled. In the tiny town of Agua Amarga, lies Charo's Houses, where families can hire either or both of the two farmhouses. While the adults soak up the super-chilled atmosphere of the place, lolling by the pool, the children can explore hidden corners and acres of organic fruit groves. Back in the nearby town of San Jose is Hotel Cortijo Solitto, a ranch-style four star kitted out with South American rugs and boarding a stable. The emphasis in this more central hotel is on the facilities, including a tennis court, archery, swimming pool, table tennis and pool table. The nearby beaches are some of Spain's finest. See p. 202.

Best Boutique/Design Hotels
Mas de Canicatti. For some serious pampering with a serious price tag, it doesn't come more hip, funky, or lavish than this design hotel set in sprawling gardens surrounded by more than 100-acres of citrus groves. Several of the suites have private pools. For a seriously groovy stay, the vast new rooms, with floor-to-ceiling windows are decked out in zinc, glass and copper. The botanical gardens are an excellent place for children to explore and there is also a pool and tennis court. Valencia, one of southern Spain's best cities for families is a 20 minute drive away. See p. 229. **Mass Passamaner**, 15 minutes from central Tarragona is a rural five-star set inside a blue-shuttered,

Town of Agua Amarga

yellow mansion, enclosed within a field of hazelnut trees. The building itself is an amazing place decorated with stained glass windows, sculptures and ceramics. Comfy sofas, a vast garden, tennis, a spa and a pool provide ample distractions. The other big draw is the restaurant, overseen by a double Michelin starred chef. There are two self-contained family villas off the lovely spa and staff are happy to fix your tickets to the Port Aventura theme park nearby. See p. 286.

Best Campsites Tarifa, **Camping 'La Caleta'** (Cabo de Gata). This campsite is one of the most beautifully situated in all Spain and if you're in the area for its nature then there's no improving on actually sleeping out in it. There's nothing fancy to the facilities here: showers, shop, phone, etc, but it really is the lovely cove it's beside that makes this worth pitching camp.

It's a semi-private, secluded cove surrounded by beefy limestone cliff formations, all hollows and jags, with ledges to use as diving boards, for those with the pluck, into clean water. For children there is a playground, garden and swimming pool. See p. 206.

Best Alternative Apartment Casa Los Naranjos (Apartment cave, Granada). For a break from convention, pretend you are a gypsy family and spend a few nights sleeping in the Sacromonte caves. The comfortable modern self-catering apartments sleep four and they share a sunny terrace. Inside, simple furniture rests on the terracotta floors and sitting rooms are draped with Moroccan hangings and rugs. See p. 174.

Best Luxury Family Villa Rental Casa de la Morena (Outside Ronda). Swishing through the iron gates, past palm trees, visitors to this luxury villa will find a slice of rural Arcadia.

The sturdy whitewashed buildings are draped in jasmine and vines, with a vast Mulberry tree towering over the central courtyard. Orchards roll down to the river and the organic gardens provide guests with armfuls of fresh vegetables. The rooms are vast and plentiful – the site sleeps 12 – with some of the best-equipped kitchens for self-catering you are likely to find. For youngsters there are two pools, a private cinema, table tennis and football, pool, and in the games room, board games and a karaoke machine. A chef, maid service and babysitting is all on-hand at 24-hours notice. See p. 148.

Best Farm Retreat On a ridge just outside Orgiva, Granada Province is the organic olive, orange and lemon farm of the Cortijo de Los Piedaos. Four of the estate's ancient, thick-walled farm buildings have just been converted into lovely self-catering holiday cottages (but if you don't want to cook, curries, Thai and vegetarian food can be ordered in). It's very eco here too: water is recycled, the A/C and heating is from low-energy heat pumps, solar-panels heat the water and swimming pool are chemical free. Each casita is quiet and private, but close enough together for big family groups to spill out over: there's lots of toys and games for children, and top notch English language baby-sitting for €7.50 (£5) an hour, everyone – from toddlers and teens to grannies – is welcome here. You can walk straight out from the door of your apartment, past the two fishponds, through poppies, borage, clover and grass, through the orchards to the Guadalfeo river. Swimming and private yoga classes, plus treatments like acupuncture can all be arranged. All four cottages are safe and have space for children, but Villa La Rama is probably the best – it sleeps four in a double and a twin, and has its own washing machine. The other cottages share a laundry room. Book well in advance. See p. 185.

Best Whole House Trasierra. A 16th century olive mill set in thousands of acres of orange, chestnut, cork and olive groves, Trasierra – idiosyncratic, elegant and bohemian family home to its English owners – is a real piece of Sierra Morenan utopia for guests, who can take over any of the seven guest rooms, the cottage, or the whole place. It's relaxed but refined, the interiors are artfully thrown together (owner Charlotte Scott is an interior decorator). Walks along the nearby river are staked out with ribbons tied round trees, there are waterfalls to find and picnic by, you can swim in the pool or nearby lakes and rivers, or there's riding, walking, painting, yoga, massage, ping-pong, bicycles and flood-lit tennis court too. Food is Mediterranean but of the type to write home about, and served all together or at private tables. Babies are free, but if you have young children it's best to take over the whole house. See p. 75.

BEST EATING OPTIONS

Best Paella More democratic, and downright fun, is eating all the different varieties of paella you can share as a family: Valencia really is the home to the dish and the best Valencian restaurants are on the harbour, where the old Hemingway haunt of La Pepica is neck and neck with La Rosa. See p. 230.

Should your family venture up into Las Alpujarras, nestling in the foothills of the Sierra Nevada, the Café Libertad (Orgiva) is a popular expat café-cum-restaurant. Owners Sally and Andrew use organic produce where possible (the menu is seasonal) and are happy to serve half portions or make something from scratch for fussy littluns. In case one of your party prefers meat at mealtimes, a very popular pork and chips has been added to the menu. See p. 187.

Best Views Ronda is one of Andalucia's most spectacular

Sardines

towns and because it stands on a towering plateau in the mountains of Malaga Province it has some of the most inspiring views in Spain. **Del Escudero** is the more affordable sister restaurant to Ronda's famous Tragabuches. Either from the elegant main dining room or the gardens below, diners can gaze out for miles over the surrounding valley below, while savouring the chef's modern Andalucian cuisine. See p. 153.

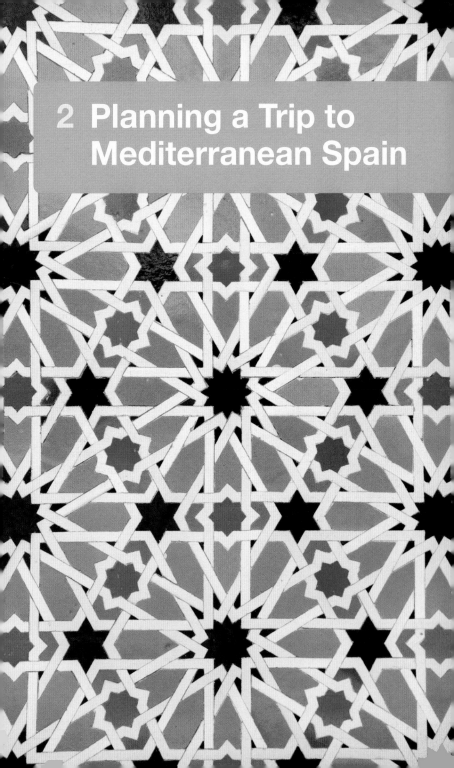

2 Planning a Trip to Mediterranean Spain

MEDITERRANEAN **SPAIN**

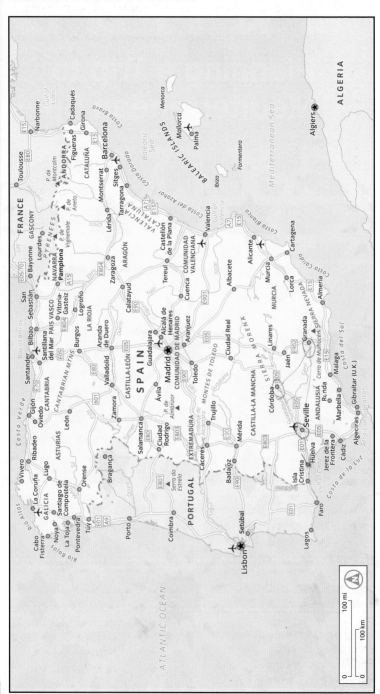

S pain keeps on surprising us. It remains a luminous place to visit for UK families; a fast changing and effervescent culture bubbling with possibilities and landscapes to savour. The number one destination for Brits didn't make it there by fluke – the reason the UK says *Viva Espagne!* is because Spain is still burning bright. Even though it may be best known for its popular beach resorts, there's so much more to Spain for families to discover. Mediterranean Spain provides a wealth of experiences for UK families to enjoy and part of its allure lies in the range of attractions on offer from beautiful beaches and rural villages to wonderfully weird and haunting architecture, fast and furious water parks and intriguing history – then there's the food and weather...

Planning a family trip can be a testing experience: plan too rigidly and you'll get stressed out trying to keep to the schedule, or underplan and you'll miss some wonderful sites by making rash decisions. The most important thing with planning is to get the *children involved*, talk about what you'd like to see and do, and take everyone's wishes into account. A holiday in Mediterranean Spain can be an unforgettable adventure and if you build in flexibility to your plans then you'll be in for an exciting trip to create some memories to last for a lifetime.

ESSENTIALS

Regions in Brief

Spain is divided into 50 provinces, which in turn lie in 17 autonomous regions. Malaga, for example, is a province within the autonomous region of Andalucia. Malaga city is the capital of Malaga province, while Sevilla, in Sevilla (or Seville) province, is the capital of Andalucia and of its province.

The Andalucian coastline extends from the Portuguese border in the west to halfway between Almeria and Cartagena in the east. There's more than one Costa here; the remote stretch in the west is the **Costa de la Luz**, named after the quality of its light, while the **Costa del Sol** extends from the eastern border of **Gibraltar**, past **Malaga** and as far as about Alumnecar, after which it becomes the **Costa Tropical**.

Seville is quite possibly the quintessential romantic Andalucian capital and its place on the itinerary of any Andalucia-bound family is well deserved. All the clichés of Andalucia – orange trees, the pealing of church bells, classic giant Mudejar architecture, the clip clopping of horse-drawn carriages and flamenco singers breaking out into spontaneous song – are all found here in plentiful supply. It's like the characters in a tourist board brochure just walked straight off the page into one of the prettiest stage sets you could imagine.

Aracena natural park, to its north and west, is a misty

mountain-side of dells fluttered through by butterflies that's almost entirely car free. If the pre-packaged fun of Seville's **Isla Magica** leaves your children cold take them to the **Cave of Marvels** here, a dank rocky vault packed with crazy-shaped stalactites and stalagmites. Further along this string of charming villages is the town of Jabugo. This is the capital city of ham country and you'll see the world-famous pata negra species snuffling around for its diet of acorns at the forest floor.

Take advantage of your position at the top of the food chain with some incredibly good rustic dishes you can get to at the cheap restaurants here after a ambling hike through this gentle hill country. Due south of Seville sits **Cadiz** province, which is famous among gourmets too, but this time for its sherry (fino) and its excellent fish.

Sanlucar de Barrameda, a charming town of old relics that's bursting with burly modern Andalucian characters, is firmly etched on Spain's domestic tourists' itineraries for its Manzanilla brand of the wine, and gets pilgrimages for its famous lobster, too. The annual horserace, one of the few in the world to still be conducted on the beach, is well worth heading for if you are in the area come August.

The provincial capital Cadiz is a lovely underexplored city, with plazas that bubble with Spanish families come dusk. The churches here are packed with the paintings of old masters, the edifices grand testament to the riches of the new world. For children, there are beaches and tall watchtowers to climb. Inland, the sherry capital **Jerez** is where you can wow the flock with the incredible precise floor show of the dancing Andaluz horses that are put through their paces once a week. For most holidaymakers, however, all these towns are the side dishes to the prime piece of vacation beef that is the **Costa de la Luz**. Although steadily growing in popularity and fame in Blighty, and with a legion of year round British émigrés now settled about its pretty towns, this stretch of Andalucia's coast is still gloriously uncommercialised. The Atlantic sea puts some off because of it's a bit nippy and the wind that lures the kite and windsurfers to these shores beats back the sun worshippers, but there are lovely sheltered bays, pine forests, dunes; you can go dolphin spotting in the straits of **Gibraltar** and see Africa, just nine km off the tip of **Tarifa**.

It would be nice to think that Costa de la Luz's arrested development might have been caused in part by looking along the coast at the Costa del Sol as a cautionary tale (but it probably isn't). In fact, you can have a great time on a few of the beaches along Malaga's coast line, and the capital city itself is somehow entirely immune to the sometimes negative aspects of mass tourism in both directions from its coasts, in charter heartlands like Torremolinos and Torre del Mar. If you're a bit flash, and like to show it, stick to Puerto Banus, otherwise spend a few days in the capital then go inland to the bonkers landscape of **El Torcal**, **Embalse De Guadalhorce** and **El Chorro**. Go further inland still, west from here into the high Serrania de Ronda, for Malaga's **White Towns**, Gaucin and Ronda, which are well linked to the sister province of Cadiz's versions, like Arcos de la Frontera. These are villages set on hilltops with miles of agricultural land sweeping out like carpets at their feet. They make great places to base yourselves, and share yarns of the old clash of civilizations that was the Moorish occupation of Spain, and there are beautiful natural parks on your doorstep here, and lakes and streams to swim in and ancient cave art to delve through. Carry on the Islamic education with a stop off at **Cordoba**, 10 centuries ago, the capital of Muslim Spain, whose buildings was once on a par with Damascus and Constantinople. The Mezquita is an amazing edifice, and the whole old town is beguilingly fossilized.

Next door, the province of Jaen, has the Sierra de La Cazorla park, Spain's largest protected area, but often loses out to Sierra Nevada in foreign tourist affections. Although its mountains are dazzlingly rich in wildlife, you can see the argument: the crux of which is

Granada city itself sitting at Sierra Nevada's foothills. Granada city is really three steep hills eyeing each other up across the Daro River each with its own strong stamp of character: the Alhambra hogs the limelight but the less showy domestic architecture of the Sacramonte cave district gypsy quarter and jumbled Arab Albaycin hold their beautiful own. Few views match a sunset from San Nicholas plaza, with the snow capped Sierras behind. Those of a rural bent will be equally swept away by the giddying vistas from the rooftop of the mountain range itself. On its southern flank lies the Alpujarra, boasting some of the level best rustic cottages and where you can go for really long walks, giant hikes or tiny rambles, depending on your ability, age and inclination. There are lots of hippies and bohemians who've set up home in these hills, so any alternative therapy you can imagine is readily available too. Just half an hour by car is a really peaceful gentle Spanish holiday stretch of coast in the **Costa Tropical**. It has ragged cliffs at its edges and none of the glitz preen or show of the Costa del Sol. It also has a fair amount of not too pretty agricultural development, with miles of plastic greenhouses, but there are pockets of charm along the coast. Further east is **Almeria** and the rugged, bone dry beaches of Cabo de Gata, an empty protected wilderness of shimmering waters and hardly any housing. The heat wall here is fierce and sends your head foggy: the hot-burning passions that fuelled the murder that inspired Lorca to write *Blood Wedding* happened here. Lots of the beaches are inaccessible by road. Inland are the Spaghetti Western landscapes, and Mini Hollywood, the theme park devoted to the tumbleweed movies made in the area in the 60s. East further still is **Cartagena**, a bite size town of mighty historical import with a giant port. **Alicante** is a bit like the Costa Blanca's answer to Malaga – surrounded by a moat of anabolically enhanced seaside resorts, it has somehow managed to retain a real charm. In the final balance, though, it has little for families, and **Benidorm** is really only good if you like your holidays to be high-rise. **Cape Salou**, in a pine forest to the south of Valencia is a real treat for families, and **Valencia** itself has a giant dolphinarium and the splendid and ultra-modern City of Arts and Sciences. Better still, it's the home of the paella and has a gem of an old town. Finally, there's **Barcelona**, which is one of the most unique and exciting cities in the whole of continental Europe. For all the Catalan reputation for grouchiness, Barca knows which side it's bread is buttered, and it's party side up. There are beaches, the rather high culture but somehow very excessive meanderings of architect Antoni Gaudi, lots of parks and museums, and on its heels is the high camp of **Sitges**, plus the biggest theme park in

Spain, Port Aventura is just down the way. Head north, though and you'll get miles of bluffy coastline along the **Costa Brava**, and the jagged border with France that is the Pyrenees.

Visitor Information

The **official Spanish tourism board website** can be found at *www.tourspain.co.uk*. This site has links to all the regional offices. The Spanish National Tourist Office in the UK is located at: 22–23 Manchester Square, **London**, W1M 5AP (☏ *0207 486 8077*) (Monday to Friday, from 9.15am to 1.30pm). The amount of online information on Spain has blossomed and now there is a glut of websites to help you plan your trip and prioritise what to see and do while you're there. For general information on the **Internet** try: *www.spain.info* or *www.red2000.com*. The website *www.idealspain.com* was once a personal opinion site, but is now much expanded. For a subjective overview of the country try *www.travelinginspain.com* – courtesy of Jerrold and his wife from the US. There is a fair bit of detail at *www.livinginspain. co.uk* mainly aimed at English-speaking expats. Of the more regional sites: *www.andalucia. com*, *www.andalucia.org*, *www.aboutgranada.com*, *www. almeria-turismo.org*, *www.about sevilla.com*, *www.cadiznet.com* and *www.costadelsol.com*, *www.malaga.com*, *www.turis cordoba.es* are good starting points. For a virtual brochure on Spain's paradors *www.paradores.es*.

Entry Requirements, Customs & Bringing Pets

Passports & Visas

If you hold a passport from the **European Union** (EU), Norway or Iceland you do not require a visa whatever the length and purpose of the visit. Holders of Canadian, Japanese, or US passports do not require a visa for stays of less than 90 days. A special visa is required for longer visits. Prior to October 1998 many children (under 16s) were included on adult passports. If that is already the case then they can continue to travel in this way until they reach 16, or the passport they are listed on runs out, or is changed in some way. If you renew the passport or change it, or your child does not yet have a passport, you will have to apply for a first **five-year passport**. To check the current rules go to *www. passport.gov.uk*. For more see *www.ukpa.gov.uk* or call the 24-hour a day, seven day per week staffed advice line (℡ *0870 521 0410*). For further queries about visas for Spain the UK Consulate has a 24-hour information line (℡ *090 65508970*).

Taking Your Pet

An Export Health Certificate issued by an official British Veterinary Inspector is required to import pets into Spain. Most pets will need at least a special tattoo or microchip, a passport and a rabies vaccination certificate. It is worth noting that many tourist sites and restaurants do not allow pets.

To obtain a certificate contact your nearest Animal Health Divisional Office in the UK. (℡ *08459 335 577*) *www.defra. gov.uk*.

Owners who want to bring their pets back to the UK must comply with the Pet Travel Scheme (PETS). Check *www. defra.gov.uk/animal/quarantine/ index.htm*. Also, *www.ukin spain.com,* the website of the British Embassy in Spain has further details.

Going to Spain

Travellers from the EU countries can bring most personal effects into Spain duty free. That includes any luggage items provided they are not considered to be for commercial use in nature or quantity. This is determined by officials at the border checkpoints. However, the EU bans any animal food products being taken into the country, including: meat or meat products, milk and dairy products. The only exception is baby powdered milk, as long as it is sealed in its original package. For other foods the maximum is one kilogram. Under Spanish import and export rules, visitors are permitted to bring in: 800 cigarettes, or 400 cigarillos, or 200 cigars or 1kg of tobacco. For alcoholic drinks the limits are: 10 litres of spirits or 20 litres of fortified wine or 90 litres of wine, of which 60 litres can be sparkling or 110 litres of beer.

Coming Home

HM Revenue & Customs has revised the guidelines for the amount of tobacco British citizens can import into the UK, from within the EU. However, Spanish law has stricter rules on the quantity of tobacco that can be exported (without additional paperwork) and sets a cap at 800 cigarettes. Under UK rules, you can be stopped and fined for carrying more than 3,200 cigarettes, 200 cigars, 400 cigarillos, 3 kg tobacco, 110 litres of beer, 90 litres of wine, 10 litres of spirits, 20 litres of ortified wine, into the country. Check further details at *www.hmrc.gov.uk*.

Money

The Euro

SINCE 2002 when the peseta was outlawed, the euro (€) has been the official currency of Spain. As with many other EU states, prices in Spain started rising back in 1999 when the euro was first tentatively introduced and haven't stopped since, much to the chagrin of the country's inhabitants. There are 100 cents in a euro. There are eight different coins 1, 2, 5, 10, 20 and 50 cents, plus €1 and €2. There are seven different notes: €5, €10, €20, €50, €100, €200 and €500. Prices vary hugely across Spain depending whether you are traveling in the big cities or towns or in the more remote areas. As a rule, children – usually aged between six to 17 – pay less than adults in entry fees. Under that and they largely travel or stay for free. The currency exchange rate at time of writing from sterling into Euros is £1 = €1.479. To check the latest currency fluctuations or to use a currency converter log on to *www.xe.com*.

Euro(€)	UK(£)
1	0.67
5	3.36
10	6.70
20	13.48
50	33.70

Credit & Debit Cards

It is worth taking some foreign currency to get you started. Most of the high street banks in the UK including Barclays, HSBC, Lloyds TSB as well as the Post Office, Thomas Cook and Thomson offer commission free currency. But beware as they often make up the difference by offering a less competitive exchange rate. For online commission-free currency try Travelex *www.travelex.co.uk*. Once in Spain, almost every bank has a 24-hour ATM that can be used to withdraw cash. Most accept credit and debit cards. You will need your four digit **PIN**. One of the simplest ways to pay for goods when away is with a credit card. They are accepted in all major hotels and restaurants and most supermarkets and petrol stations. In Spain you will frequently be asked for **photo ID** to use the card – a passport or photo drivers license is fine. Check how much your credit card provider charges for converting currency before you travel, it can be expensive. Withdrawing cash on your credit card from an ATM is even pricier. Withdrawing £100 can cost more than £5 when the cash handling fees and currency conversion fees are added up. To check for your nearest Mastercard (Cirrus or Maestro) ATM see *www.mastercard.com* (📞 *0800 964767*) for UK queries or (📞 *900 971231*) from Spain. Again, using a debit card abroad is not necessarily cheap but it is convenient. You probably won't

TIP ▶ Keeping Costs Low ◀

Spain is no longer an out and out budget destination but there are plenty of ways to keep costs down. When eating out, the *menu del dia* is usually around €8–€15 (£5.40–10) and represents the best value. Avoiding the most central, touristy spots is smart too as they are usually pricey and rarely serve the best food.

Taking a picnic is a great idea if you driving through one of Spain's many national parks or spending the day on the beach. Fresh fruit and vegetables can be found in abundance across Spain. Food in supermarkets is pleasingly cheap for anyone used to shopping in the UK.

When driving, avoiding the 'AP' routes will not only cut costs, it will also steer you towards the far more scenic coastal or mountain roads.

Camping is a great budget accommodation option. Some campsites are better equipped than the budget hotels, with swimming pools, tennis courts, laundry and other facilities. They frequently have a prime location right by the beach.

Campsites offer an ideal opportunity to save money and base families in a safe environment. Children will love barbeque food – so money can be saved shopping at supermarkets – and having friends of a similar age to play with, while adults can relax knowing children are in a secure area. The facilities such as swimming pools, shops and launderettes on site also lend themselves to a great family break. Leading UK operators include Keycamp, Eurocamp, Hoseasons and Canvas Holidays. www.abta.com.

Staying in *casas rurales* – Spain's equivalent to B&B's – is another option although quality varies widely. Hostals – not to be confused with youth hostels – are budget hotels in Spain. Prices in general for goods and services and accommodation tend to be less expensive inland than along the built-up coastal areas.

It is worth noting that hotel room rates in some of the smaller business destination towns such as Valencia or Cartagena drop their prices significantly at the weekends to attract tourists.

For families travelling extensively by train, a rail pass will certainly save money (see Getting Around section). Many sights in Spain are free on Sundays and they often have special rates for families. Children under six do not usually have to pay to sightsee.

What Things Cost in Mediterranean Spain

- Admission to a museum €1–10 (£0.67–6.75) (except the really big attractions or water parks)
- A paella for two €20 (£13.40)
- Breakfast (coffee and roll) €2–4 (£1.35–2.70)
- Menu del dia in restaurants €8–13 (£5.40–8.80)
- Double room in a three star €60–100 (£40.20–67)
- Bus rides €1–1.20 (£0.67–0.80)
- Copy of the *Daily Telegraph* €3 (£2)
- Dodot Etapas nappies – €16.99 (£11.40)
- 60 Huggies nappies – €14.95 (£10)
- Nestle Nativa Start **baby milk**, 900 g – €11.50 (£7.70)
- Hero Baby milk, 900 g – €8.99 (£6)
- 1 litre of milk starts at around €0.55 (£0.37) for your bog standard cow. Up to €1.10 (£0.75) for super deluxe organic with added vitamins.
- The average price for products and services varies depending on the province you are visiting and the season.

Expect to pay anything from €7–15 (£4.70–10.05) for a three course meal including wine or drinks and dessert but normally excluding coffee. Childrens' menus are rare, but at that price you can afford to leave some for later and asking for a doggy bag will not be frowned upon.

know the exchange rate and most banks charge at least 15% (with a minimum £1.50) plus a 2.75% conversion fee.

Travellers' Cheques

These are still popular with older tourists but are becoming somewhat obsolete given the large number of 24-hour ATMs dotted across Europe plus the need to show ID every time you cash one. They tend to be more expensive than using debit or credit cards. If you do choose to take some, if only as a back-up, you can get them at banks, building societies, travel agents and the Post Office, among other outlets. Keep a record of their serial numbers in case of loss or theft, and carry them separately from money and/or cards.

When to Go

Southern Spain's climate is such that it can be enjoyable at any time of year. If roasting in 40 degree heat on a beach is your thing then July and August will certainly oblige.

Otherwise, for the more active family and to avoid the crowds, the best times to visit are without a doubt April, May, June and September and October when it is a good few degrees cooler. The

Average Daytime Temperature & Rainfall in Mediterranean Spain												
Barcelona	Jan	Feb	March	April	May	June	July	Aug	Sep	Oct	Nov	Dec
(°F)	48	49	52	55	61	68	73	73	70	63	55	50
(°C)	9 9		11 13	16	20	23	23	21	17	13	10	
Rainfall (cm)	1.7	1.4	1.9	2.0	2.2	1.5	0.9	1.6	3.1	3.7	2.9	2.0

Malaga	Jan	Feb	March	April	May	June	July	Aug	Sep	Oct	Nov	Dec
(°F)	54	54	64	70	73	81	84	86	81	73	68	63
(°C)	12	12	18	21	23	27	29	30	27	23	20	17
Rainfall (cm)	2.4	2.0	2.4	1.8	1.0	0.2	0.0	0.1	1.1	2.5	2.5	2.4

Seville	Jan	Feb	March	April	May	June	July	Aug	Sep	Oct	Nov	Dec
(°F)	59	63	68	75	81	90	97	97	90	79	68	61
(°C)	15	17	20	24	27	32	36	36	32	26	20	16
Rainfall (cm)	2.6	2.4	3.6	2.3	1.6	0.3	0.0	0.2	0.8	2.8	2.7	3.2

Costa Del Sol is, in fact, a year round destination and winter is regarded as a peak season for golfers and the many conferences that take place here.

If you are tied to school holidays and must travel in the peak summer months, it is advisable to stick near to the coast, or retreat to the high mountains to escape the excessive heat. With small children, a day trip to an inland city in July or August will really be too much because of the heat. Seville has the dubious reputation of being one of the hottest places in Europe at certain times in mid-summer, which can detract significantly from the delights of strolling around the Alcazabar.

Public Holidays

The Spanish calendar is scattered with holidays of all kinds. **Local and national breaks** take place for fiestas, religious celebrations, concerts, dances and more. Visiting Spain during these times is a great idea but many people flood to the towns for the celebrations and prices usually skyrocket.

Public holidays include:

6 January, Epiphany

14 April, Good Friday

1 May, May (Worker's) Day

15 August, Assumption of the Virgin

12 October, El Pilar

1 November, All Saint's Day

6 December, Spanish Constitution Day

8 December, Immaculate Conception

25 December, Christmas Day

Fiestas, fairs, pilgrimages, carnivals and religious processions are an integral part of Spanish life. Andalucia alone celebrates more than 3,000 events each year. For families, the local summer fairs – or ferias – are the best celebrations to attend, particularly those in the smaller towns, which will be far less daunting for children. Equally inviting are many of the smaller Romerias, when a town or village makes a pilgrimage to a local religious shrine. These are packed with colour. Everybody dresses up in their finery and beautiful Andalucian horses are paraded through the town, with an effigy of the town's saint leading the procession. The Romeria ends with a huge cook-out in a rural spot outside town. Dancing and partying go on late into the night.

Carnivals Part of the Catholic calendar, these are usually celebrated before the 40 days of lent. They centre around Shrove Tuesday (5th February 2008, 24th February 2009). In the larger towns festivities last the whole week. During the Civil War, General Franco abolished carnivals in rebel areas and after the war the custom was outlawed completely for many years. However, in Cadiz and some other towns the tradition continued and is once again thriving today.

Summer Fairs or Ferias

Celebrated in every town across Spain, ferias close streets to traffic, businesses shut down and the local bars and restaurants serve food and drink in the open air as music blares from every corner. Come nightfall, the fairs shift to a 'recinto ferial' or fairground on the outskirts of town. An amusement park is usually

set up for children, and visitors should expect plenty of singing, dancing and fireworks. Tents or 'casetas' are erected by local clubs or political parties, although some will be invitation only. Ferias usually start midweek and finish on Sunday night.

Semana Santa or Holy Week (Easter)

A more reverent celebration than Carnival but a no less splendid spectacle. Towns across Spain compete to put on the most elaborate processions. They tend to start in a local church and wend their way through the streets, bearing effigies of Christ on the Cross and the Virgin Mary in mourning. The procession is led by *penitentes*, who are dressed in the same conical white hoods worn by the Spanish Inquisition (and the Klu Klux Klan, but not related). Seville, Malaga, Cordoba and Granada have some of the most outstanding celebrations in the week leading up to Easter Sunday (23rd March, 2008 and 12th April, 2009), but Seville is without a doubt the most famous *www. turismo.sevilla.org*.

Corpus Christi

A Catholic feast celebrating the presence of the body of Christ in the holy water. It is held in June, starting on the Wednesday after Trinity Sunday. The consecrated host is carried aloft through the street in a solemn and splendid procession. Balconies and buildings are usually bedecked with flowers. In Granada, the celebration lasts three days and visitors can enjoy the Granada Festival of Music and Dance. Seville, Ronda and Vejer de La Frontera also have significant celebrations.

Town Patron's Day No matter how large or small, every city or town in Spain celebrates its own patron saint (or saints), usually with a bank holiday and a party.

Romeria This is a community pilgrimage to the local shrine that tends to take place in May before Pentecost. It takes its name from the pilgrims, or romeros, who walked all the way to Rome. In the smaller towns, the processions are usually made on foot or horseback behind a decorated horse and wagon, and end at a shrine some way out of town where a picnic and general merrymaking get underway. The biggest and most important of the year converges on the Huelvan hamlet of El Rocio. Nearly a million people make the long journey under the glare of Canal Sur's TV cameras.

Special Events For Families

January

Granada Reconquest Festival The town celebrates the Christian conquest of the Moors in 1492 with colourful processions led by folk in period dress. Held on 2nd January. For more information call the tourist office ☎ 0034 958 22 59 90.

Fiesta de Los Reyes Across Spain, parades are held on the eve of the festival of epiphany (5th January). The three kings of the Orient ride about the town, dispensing sweets to children.

February

Bocairente Festival of Christians and Moors (Valencia). A re-enactment of the struggle between the Christians and Moors. Expect parades, fireworks and colourful costumes. Beginning of February. Call the tourist office ☎ 0034 963 986422 www.spanishunlimited.com.

Carnavales de Cadiz The oldest and one of the best attended carnivals in Spain, it was modelled on the Venice event. It is a boisterous and dazzling street party with troubadours, drummers and satirical song groups providing entertainment. Children and 'juniors' win prizes for the best costumes. Call the carnival office ☎ 0034 956 211 313 www.cadizayto.es/turismo.

March

Las Fallas (The Fires) de Valencia. Without a doubt one of Spain's craziest festivals, celebrated on the day of St Joseph, the patron saint of carpenters. Vast papier mâché effigies – known as *ninots* – are set on fire, fireworks explode in the night sky, bangers are let off in the streets and an air of anarchism and rowdiness takes hold of the town for five days. At 8am every morning '*La Despertá*' happens.

The fiesta's organizers wake the towns-folk by throwing down firecrackers, to make sure no one misses the day's entertainments. Throughout the day visitors can see bullfights, parades, paella contests and beauty pageants around the city and children have their own events. Every day at 2pm in the Plaza Ayuntamiento the '*mascletá*' happens – a pyrotechnic earthquake that shakes the city. Call the tourist office ☎ *0034 963 153 931 www.turisvalencia.es*.

April

Feria de Sevilla (Seville Fair) All-night flamenco dancing, entertainment booths, bullfights, horseback rides, flower-decked coaches and dancing in the streets are just a few of the highlights. The partying is centered around the Barrio de los Remedios. Expected start dates of the **nine-day party** in the coming years are: 16th April 2007, 31st March 2008 and 20th April 2009. See *www.turismo.sevilla.org* ☎ *0034 954 595 288* or *www.andalucia.com* for more details.

Moros y Cristianos (Moors and Christians) For three days in April, Alcoy, a town near **Alicante**, hosts a re-enactment of the centuries old battle between the Moors and Christians, in full historical dress. The simulated fighting and anachronistic Moorish costumes are worth seeing. Alicante tourist office ☎ *0034 965 20 0000 www.alicanteturismo.com*

The 32nd Americas Cup (Valencia 2007) From this

month and well into the summer, Valencia will become a **sailing mecca** as 12 teams prepare to battle the Swiss defenders, Alinghi, for the trophy. *www.americascup.com*

Concurso Nacional de Arte Flamenco (Cordoba) This flamenco festival is held every three years, with the next event taking place from April until May, 2007. ☎ *0034 957 480644 www.flamencocordoba.com*

May

Feria del Caballo (Jerez de la Frontera) This major equestrian event is held in the first week of May each year in the Gonzalez Hontoria Park. Some of the world's finest horses and riders compete in the dressage shows and endurance trials.

Las Cruces de Mayo (Festival of Crosses) – Cordoba. Usually held on the 1st, 2nd and 3rd of May (Santa Cruz day) each neighbourhood in town decorates its own cross with flowers. The best dressed crosses are awarded prizes. Music, dancing and drinking are all part of the festivities. People drink Montilla-Moriles wine and dance to '*sevillanas*' – a type of folk music. ☎ *0034 902 201 774 www.turismodecordoba.org*

Festival de los Patios (Cordoba) The festival gives anyone the unique opportunity to stroll into the private homes of Cordoban residents and admire the ornate, floral decorations especially created for the

celebration. 📞 *0034 902 201 774*
www.turismodecordoba.org

June

International Music and Dance Festival (Granada)

The festival is traditionally based around classical music, ballet and Spanish dancing but it also features contemporary music and dance. 📞 *0034 958 221 844 www.granadafestival. org*

Las Hogueras de San Juan

(St John's Bonfires) – Alicante. During the summer solstice, 20–24th June, bonfires blaze through the night. The celebration is like a mini Las Fallas, with firecrackers, sparklers and fireworks and the burning of the wooden and papier mâché effigies.

Verbena de Sant Joan

(Barcelona) A Catalan festival lights up the city until dawn with an array of bonfires and fireworks. The fireworks show at Montjuic Park is exceptional. For an account of the night see *www.barcelona-on-line.es* 📞 *0034 932 853 834*.

El Mercat Medieval de Alicante

Held in the old quarter of Alicante, behind the town hall at the end of June every year, the market is choc with stalls selling all kinds of handicrafts from ironwork and glassware to pottery. Dancers, falconers, jugglers and musicians in period costume provide further entertainment.

📞 *0034 965 143 452 www.alicante turismo.com*

July

The European Balloon Festival

(Igualada, 50 km, or 30 miles, inland from Barcelona) Thousands of spectators gather to watch as over 40 hot air balloons are launched into the sky, turning it rainbow coloured. Market stalls are set up to give visitors are taste of the local cuisine. 📞 *0034 938 042 202*

August

Feria de Málaga (Malaga Fair)

A test of any partygoer's stamina, this fiesta usually lasts for 10 days. It kicks off with a fireworks display and counts an Arabian horse and carriage parade as a highlight. There is a Magic Fair for children and unlike some of the other major summer fairs, all of the tents or casetas in the Malaga event are free and open to all. 📞 *0034 952209603 www. malagaturismo.com*

La Tomatina

(Battle of the Tomatoes) – Buñol, Valencia. Probably one of the biggest food fights in the world. Truckloads of tomatoes are shipped into the town where they become missiles for the warring towns and villages. Showers are brought in especially for the clean up. Singing, dancing and partying accompany the event. It is held on the last Wednesday in August. There are not many places to stay in

Buñol. 📞 *0034 902 123 212*
www.comunitatvalencia.com

September

Diada Nacional de Catalunya

(Barcelona) Catalans celebrate the region's autonomy from the rest of Spain, particularly after the years of repression under the Franco dictatorship. Expect to see many people waving the senyera – the official flag of Catalonia. 11 September 📞 *0034 932 853 832 www.bcn.es*

Fiestas de la Mercé (Barcelona)

From around 19–24th September Barcelona honours its patron saint, Nostra Senyora de la Merced, known for her compassion to animals. The events kicks off after mass at the Iglesia de la Merced with a procession of volunteers in animal costumes (tigers, lions, horses). It proceeds to the Cathedral of Santa Eulalia, then on to Plaza de Sant Jaume, Las Ramblas and Plaza de Cataluyna, as the crowds wave sparklers and set off fire-crackers in the streets. The four day celebrations also feature correfocs – or fire-creature costumes. Visitors already in Barcelona can find information in the La Merce booths near Plaza Catalunya.
📞 *0034 932 853 832 www.bcn.es*

November

All Saints' Day (Across Spain).

A public holiday that is reverently celebrated as relatives lay flowers on the graves of the dead. 1st November.

December

Día de los Santos Inocentes

(across Spain) Spain's answer to April Fool's Day, giving everyone the chance to do loco things. 28th December.

Festit íteres (Alicante) This is

annual puppet festival taking place at various outdoor and indoor venues throughout the town. 📞 *0034 965 143 452 www. alicanteturismo.com*

What to Pack

The lighter you are able to travel the easier your transit to Spain will be. That's not always possible with children in tow but remember that Spain is not a Third-world country. You can buy nappies, wipes, milk and baby food pretty much everywhere. Be warned, however, that if you arrive in Spain over the weekend, particularly Sunday, many shops will be closed, so have some spares to hand.

Health Insurance & Safety

Travel Insurance

Before setting off make sure that your travel insurance policy is up-to-date, valid for the entire trip and covers everyone who is travelling. Check exactly what is covered, particularly if you plan to do any dangerous sports or activities. For a family a comprehensive, family policy will ensure that you are insured for trip cancellation or interruption, default, delays and medical

Checklist for Babies and Toddlers

- A pushchair (try to balance weight with what it can hold)
- A baby monitor, plus an electricity adaptor
- High SPF sun cream
- UV protective clothing for the beach
- Nappies for swimming – not widely available, plus a supply of regular nappies in case you arrive and the shops are shut
- Arm bands and possibly a knee and elbow length high SPF swimsuit to protect against the sun
- Bottles and sterilizing equipment
- Insect repellent
- Baby banz – sunglasses to fit children
- Favourite books, toys, pens, crayons – distractions for journeys
- Comforters and dummies (more than one comforter as they tend to get lost)
- Calpol or other baby/toddler medication
- A car seat
- A lightweight chair seat – these can be cloth and tied to the back of adult chairs
- A potty

expenses. Double check for any exemptions in the small print. You should always tell your insurer about any pre-existing medical conditions before you buy a policy otherwise you may find that you are not covered. Less than half of all UK travel policies cover medical expenses caused by terrorism. If you plan to travel more than two or three times a year then an **annual policy** will be better value than several single trip policies. Check the Association of British Insurers' website for a wealth of information ☏ *0207 600 3333 www.abi.org.uk*. Always take your insurer's emergency contact and medical helpline telephone numbers and details of your policy number away with you.

The new **European Health Insurance Card – EHIC –** (formerly the E111) provides UK residents with free, or reduced cost state healthcare when visiting an EU country. The quickest way to apply is online at *www. dh.gov.uk* or *www.ehic.org.uk* ☏ *0845 606 2030*. Alternatively, you can pick up a form from the Post Office. You can fill out a form and put your spouse and children on it as well. This should be done as well as and not instead of taking out travel insurance as few countries will pay the full cost of medical treatment.

Staying Healthy

Spain poses few significant health risks for visiting families, quite the opposite. The **Mediterranean diet**, rich in garlic, olive oil, and wine has long-been associated with improved life expectancy and reduced incidence of heart disease in the population.

However, dodgy food and water are most common cause of travellers' diarrhoea. The best preventative measures are to drink mineral water and avoid any **un-cooked fish or shellfish** from the heavily polluted Med.

That said, **Spanish water** is safe to drink from the tap, even if does not always taste great.

Motor crashes are the most common form of serious injury among travellers in Europe, so at all costs avoid drink driving and make sure everyone in the car is wearing a seat belt.

During the hot summer months in Spain, limit your **exposure to the sun** and drink plenty of water. Keep children slathered with sun block or togged up in UV protective clothes when outside and make sure they wear a hat.

For general advice when travelling with children, read *Your Child Abroad: A Travel Health Guide* Dr Jane Wilson-Howarth and Dr Matthew Ellis (Bradt, £10.95)

If You Fall Ill

Spanish medical facilities are among the best in the world. If a medical emergency arises, hotel staff will quickly put you in touch with a reliable doctor. If not you can contact the **British**

Checklist for a Plane or Car Trip

- Babies under two years of age usually fly for free, but they will be sat on your lap.
- If you are travelling with toddlers, give them a lolly or sweet to suck at take-off and landing to reduce the effect of earpopping.
- For babies, take at least one day's supply of nappies and a changing pad in case the aircraft has no designated changing area.
- Take formula milk in handy carton form if possible or sippy cups and snacks for toddlers.
- Sterile bottles and teats should be prepared before you leave.
- It is worth taking a baby's buggy or pram to the aircraft door, where it can be stored in the hold.
- Have a bag of drawing pads and small toys to keep children occupied.
- Remember there will be some waiting about before the flight and possibly delays, so be prepared for the worst and pack enough distractions to keep children engaged.
- Pack a small comfort blanket for babies/toddlers, so they have chance to sleep.

Checklist for a Car Trip

- First and foremost you will need a child safety seat. Most car rental agencies have these available for around €3–5 (£2.02–3.37) per day.
- If you are hiring a car, opt for one with air conditioning to avoid roasting in the summer months.
- Pack window shades to block out the sun.
- Pack a potty for toddlers, plus a blanket in case they want to sleep.
- For a long distance journey have a cool bag of drinks, snacks, fruit and disposable wipes or tissues to hand.
- For older children take story tapes or CDs or a portable DVD player, books and colouring books.
- Try finding games/books relevant to Spain to engage the children – simple naming books in Spanish are becoming more widespread.
- Plan stops along the route before you leave, such as a trip to a municipal swimming pool, or park if you have young children and are driving in the summer.
- Just to be safe, take a first-aid kit, spare plastic bags in case of car-sickness and a change of clothes.

Consulates Madrid (see fast facts) for a list of English speaking doctors. Certain private sector clinics in Spain have been known to overcharge tourists for treatment. If you require medical attention always call the **24-hour medical assistance line provided by your insurer** first for advice on the best place to go.

Before You Go

If you or your child suffer from a chronic illness, consult your doctor prior to departure. Pack prescription medication in its original container to ensure it gets through airport security.

Travelling Safely with Children in Mediterranean Spain

Petty crime is no different in Spain, the UK, France or anywhere else. Muggers, pickpockets and scam artists usually target tourists in busy locations in the principal cities by distracting their attention and taking what they want. Keep your passport and money in a **money belt** if you are worried. Otherwise use common sense and keep all bags firmly shut and with you at all times. Be especially careful if you are carrying a new model mobile telephone: do not leave these out on café tables.

Spain has a **moderate crime rate.** Barcelona's El Raval district, as well as the Barrio

DID YOU KNOW? >> Driving in Spain <<

It is your responsibility as driver, to make sure that your vehicle complies with the laws in the country you are visiting. In a British car the key points to consider are adapting headlamps. You must have two warning triangles for Spain. A GB plate is required. Spare bulbs. First Aid kit and fire extinguisher. You must have a high visibility jacket in case of providing roadside assistance, or leaving a stranded vehicle. This MUST be kept in the front of the car.

Gothic, Parc Guell and Plaza Real tend to be the hotspots where you need to be extra vigilant. Central areas of Valencia, such as Plaza de la Reina and Plaza de la Virgen are currently being targeted by Romanian children. They approach tourists in cafes and wave newspapers as a distraction before making off with whatever they can grab.

Theft from **parked cars** is depressingly common so keep all items out of site or locked in the boot and keep any valuables with you or locked in the hotel safe.

Lost or stolen passports should be reported to the local police and your Embassy.

Sadly the Spanish capital Madrid was the victim of a massive terrorist attack in March 2004. Terrorist attacks are rare although ETA remains active in Spain.

What to Do If Your Children Get Lost

Most of this is common sense. Make sure your children know that they must not wander off and certainly not with strangers. If they are older and want to head off in a group, arrange a **rendez-vous** point such as the reception of a museum and time to meet them later on. Make sure they have your **mobile phone number** and **accommodation address** on them, with instructions to ask for a member of the **police force** should they not be able to find you. There name should never be visible on their bag/clothing, and tell them the importance of never divulging their name to a stranger. Beaches can be lethal: you lay back and close your eyes for what seems a second, and when you open them, your child is nowhere to be seen. With the sea close by, the potential for disaster is clear. The rule is to take turns to flake out while the other one keeps watch. If you're alone, you have no option but to stay hyper alert. Think about investing in a product such as wrist-worn monitors with adjustable distance alarms for children of varying ages. Should the worst happen it might not hurt to have a picture of your children handy. Also pack some **brightly coloured clothes** for them to wear and it will make then easier to keep an eye on, especially in busy squares or crowded areas such as airports. For very young children, a harness is the best way to keep them close. Otherwise keep hold of the hand of young children: they move more quickly than you think.

Specialised Resources

For families without internet access Samantha Gore-Lyons' book *Are We Nearly There?: The Complete Guide to Travelling with Babies, Toddlers and Children* (Amazon £7.19) or Helen Truskowska's *Travelling – Take the Kids* (Amazon £9.89) will start you off on the right track. Online, however, there are hundreds of websites dedicated to travelling with children, which are stuffed with tips, first-hand experiences, booking advice and more. One of the best is *www.babygoes2.com*. It features destination guides, equipment checklists and annual awards. At *www.forparentsby parents.co.uk* you will find suggestions and feedback on travelling abroad with your family. Alternatively, *www.takethefamily. com* allows you to book your holiday after browsing a selection of special offers for everything from mini-breaks to adventure holidays all at family-friendly resorts available to British travellers. If your children are under four years old *www.tinytravellers.net* is a good resource. For a straight from the horse's mouth account, the chat forum on Dea Birkett's (former *Guardian* journalist) website is excellent. Also try *www.family travelforum.com*, although you need to be a member to get the full benefit of the site. Website

www.themeparkinsider.com offers discounts and information on – you guessed it – theme parks.

For Single Parents

A quarter of all children now live in one-parent households, three-times more than in the early 1970s. While there are plenty of resources that offer advice for travelling with small families, it can still be expensive because of hotel surcharges. What's more, many of the 'free children' deals advertised in holiday brochures exclude single parents.

There are several organizations that can help. HELP (Holiday Endeavour for Lone Parents) is a charity that offers low-cost and subsidized holidays with major companies in the UK and Spain regardless of a family's income. [HELP, 58 Owston Road, Carcroft, Doncaster, South Yorkshire DN6 8DA ☎ *01302 728791* Janice@help.fslife.co.uk] Alternatively, try the Single Parent Travel Club ☎ *0870 241 6210 www.sptc.org.uk*, a membership self-help group offering low-cost short breaks and holidays. Gingerbread ☎ *0800 018 4318 www.gingerbread.org.uk* is a charity supporting lone parent families. For tips or to be put through to an online help desk call One Parent Families ☎ *0800 018 5026* or check *www.oneparentfamilies. org.uk*. The following is a list of tour operators specializing in the sector: Mango ☎ *01902 373 410 www.mangokids.co.uk*; Small Families ☎ *01767 650312 www. smallfamilies.co.uk* and One

Parent Family Holidays ℂ *0845 230 1975 www.opfh.org.uk*. Several of the other dedicated family holiday websites have links to ideas for single parents.

For Families with Special Needs

The following organizations offer advice and information for families traveling with a member with special needs.

Holidaycare: *www.holidaycare.org.uk*

RADAR (Royal Association for Disability and Rehabilitation): *www.radar.org.uk*

Tripscope: *www.tripscope.org.uk*

The 21st Century Traveller

Internet

The best place to head is an Internet café. The website *www.andalucia.com* provides a comprehensive list of cybercafés, province by province. The site also provides an extremely detailed account of how to set up a free internet connection in Spain (no monthly charge, calls at local rates) with one of the major telephone companies. Alternatively, it provides a list of Internet service providers (ISPs) in Spain, if you want to hook up that way. These include free connection using Wanadoo (*www.wanadoo.es*) connection by Uni2, or Arrakis (*www.arrakis.es*) ℂ *0034 902 020 100* for a low-cost

connection. It praises Metro Red Online (*www.metrored-online.com*) ℂ *0034 952 880032* or Mercury (*www.mercuryin.es*) ℂ *0034 952 837575* for their 'tremendous patience in English in helping customers set up a connection'. One international site that allows you to search for web cafes is *www.cybercafe.com*.

Computer Access

Without a doubt the quickest service is via a Wi-fi connection. Wireless 'hotspots' where you can get high-speed Internet connection without telephone line or network hardware are cropping up all over Spain. However, coverage in general is still very patchy across the country.

Again *www.andalucia.com* provides a list of Wi-fi Hotspots in Spain as well as details of sites under construction. Many hotels provide guests with a password for free access or you may have to buy a ticket or card (usually giving 1 to 24 hours surf time). Try the website *www.wi-fihotspotsdirectgory.com* for a broader list of coverage across Spain. Website *www.personaltelco.net/index.cgi/WirelessCommunities* gives a list of free coverage.

Mobile Phones

Most European mobile phones work in Spain but watch out because even if you make a local call you will be charged the international roaming rate. You will also have to pay for incoming calls. If you plan to be in Spain for more than two weeks, consider picking up a pay-as-you-go package for around €30 (£20.10), including the handset. These often include around €12 (£8) of free calls. You can then 'top up' the available minutes at most grocery shops and all mobile phone shops.

ESSENTIALS

Getting There

By Plane A vast number of airlines fly to Spain and Gibraltar from the UK and Ireland. The main gateway airports to the south are Malaga, Gibraltar and Alicante, with low-cost flights also operating into Jerez. Many charter flights fly to Southern Spain and no-frills or low-cost airlines are increasing all the time – making regional departures much easier – alongside the main scheduled flight operators. If you are staying at the western end of the Costa del Sol, or in the Costa de la Luz, consider flying into Gibraltar instead of Malaga and saving yourself a lot of driving.

Aer Lingus ℓ *0818 365 000* from Ireland or ℓ *0870 876 5000* from the UK *www.aerlingus.com*

Air Berlin ℓ *0 870 738 88 80* *www.airberlin.com*

Avro ℓ *0871 622 4476 www.avro. co.uk*

Bmibaby ℓ *0870 264 2229 www. bmibaby.com*

British Airways ℓ *0870 850 9850* or *www.ba.com*

easyJet ℓ *0871 750 0100 www. easyjet.com*

Excel Airways ℓ *0870 999 0 069* *www.xl.com*

Flybe ℓ *0871 700 0123 www. flybe.com*

GB Airways ℓ *0870 850 9850* *www.gbairways.com*

Globespan ℓ *08705 561522* *www.flyglobespan.com*

Jet2.com ℓ *0871 226 1737 www. jet2.com*

Iberia ℓ *0845 601 2854* *www.iberia.com*

Monarch Airlines ℓ *0870 040 5040 www.monarch-airlines.com*

MyTravelLite ℓ *0870 156 4564* *www.mytravellite.com*

Ryanair ℓ *0871 246 0000 www. ryanair.com*

Thomsonfly ℓ *0870 190 0737* *www.thomsonfly.com*

Flying for Less: Tips for Getting the Best Airfare

● Book tickets well in advance, stay over Saturday night or fly mid-week or at more anti-social hours. Be flexible with dates and times.

● Keep an eye on promotions in local newspapers, online or on Teletext.

● Join a frequent-flyer club and collect points that you can use to reduce the cost of any subsequent flights.

● Use a bucket-shop or consolidator to cut costs. But beware as these tickets are usually non-refundable or carry stiff cancellation fines. See below for a list of the reliable consolidators.

Best of the Net

The Internet has become the best place to search for bargain travel deals. There are thousands of different sites, which can make it daunting to sift through so much choice. The best place to start is with one of the big web-based travel companies: Expedia *www. expedia.co.uk* or Opodo *www. opodo.co.uk* to give you idea of the price of a ticket. They have different deals with the airlines so it makes sense to compare a few to get the best deal. Many of the larger airlines invite customers to sign up for weekly e-mail alerts giving details of any last minute deals. It is always worth checking the airline websites directly, particularly in the case of the low-cost carriers. Alternatively, log on to *www.ufly4less.com*, a site that scours the websites of the 13 most popular low-cost airlines to find the cheapest deal. The service costs £25 a year. Another website *www.skyscanner.net* does the same job in Europe. One of the original flight comparison offer sites (*www.cheapflights. com*) has a useful news section listing routes and sale offers for low-cost airlines. Or try DoHop *www.dohop.com* a quick service

flight comparison site that compares the prices of most major airlines. To search for charter flights *www.travelrepublic.co.uk* is a good bet with some great last-minute reductions.

By Ferry Crossing the Bay of Biscay and then hauling yourself across Spain to the south isn't recommended for families; it's too far, way too long and not very practical.

However, if you have more time and really want to embark on this kind of voyage then from Britain there are two car ferries that sail to the northern Spanish coast: Portsmouth to Bilbao and Plymouth to Santander.

On the ferry children are free to run around and there is often entertainment put on to amuse them, a crèche, plus a cinema and often a small swimming pool.

P&O operates the Portsmouth to Bilbao service ☎ *0870 240 0565 www.poferries.com*. It sails every three days and takes 35 hours, with two nights at sea, on the outward journey and a 29-hour, one night at sea, trip on the return leg. Observation platforms let you look out for sea life in the Bay of Biscay: from sperm whales to dolphins.

The Plymouth–Santander is run by Brittany Ferries ☎ *08705 360360 www.brittany-ferries.com* with twice weekly departures or thrice weekly at peak times. It takes 24 hours.

From Ireland there is no direct route to Spain. Brittany ferries sails to Roscoff in France and you can get a connection from there.

Flying with Children

Before you go:

- Check your airline's website for its policies and advice for flying with children.
- Always state the age of your child before travelling as children under two are classed as infants and usually fly for much less or for free provided they sit on your lap.
- Take a handy bag with the all the essentials as well as plenty of toys and games (see checklist on p. 30).
- Drinks are infinitely spillable so it may help to have small cartons of their favourite drink to hand.
- Consider taking a safety seat on board for your child, but check with the airlines about their rules first. Some require the child to have a full-ticket to use a seat.
- Let the children have their own small-wheeled cases – they'll love pulling them, and it reduces the load on you.
- Let the children have their own hand luggage – a backpack containing their survival kit should do it.

At the airport:

- Make sure you get to the airport in plenty of time.
- Consider using the automatic check-in – it saves on queues.
- Reins or harnesses for toddlers are essential for waits in the terminal – it only takes a second to lose a child.
- Ask if the flight is full. If not, helpful booking clerks might agree to block out the seats next to yours, to give you more room.
- If your children use a buggy, keep it with you for the long airport walks, don't check it in.
- Staff will sometimes allow families with young children to board first. If they don't, board last, when all the other passengers have stowed their luggage and settled down. Always disembark last, when the flight staff will be free to help you.
- Sit near the front of the aircraft so you don't have to fight past other passengers on the way in and way out.

During the flight:

- Warn cabin crew if you're going to change a nappy – they may be willing to help by, for example, lowering the changing table for you.
- If your children are fussy, bring your own food – airline meals are notoriously patchy.
- Scented nappy sacks are useful for all sorts of things – dirty nappies, of course, but also clothes that have been sicked on, used wipes and general rubbish.
- Despite pressurized cabins, ears can still be troublesome. Feed babies during take-off and landing. Ear plugs and sweets can help children who haven't learned how to 'pop' their ears.

By Car Driving in Spain is easy and should be stress free. There are main roads and more scenic routes usually running close to the motorway. However, due to the sheer scale of road building in Spain, there are frequent diversions. It is best to buy the latest maps, as anything more than three to six months old is likely to be out of date.

Drive distances

Seville–Malaga: 208 km
Granada–Seville: 250 km
Valencia–Alicante: 180 km
Seville–Valencia: 668 km
Malaga–Valencia: 622 km
Valencia–Cartagena: 280 km
Valencia–Barcelona: 350 km

By Bus Eurolines, part of National Express ☏ *08705 808080* or *www.eurolines.co.uk* runs services from London to Barcelona and Madrid as well as Malaga, Seville, Granada and Cordoba.

By Train It's unlikely that you will want to travel all the way to Spain by train, but if you do check out *www.seat61.com*. You should also consult the timetables and prices at *www.renfe.es/ingles*, the Spanish national rail site. RENFE can also be contacted through their UK agents in London at: Spanish Rail, Suite 2, 79 Baker St, London, W1U 6RG ☏ *0207 224 0345* enquiries@spanish-rail.co.uk
www.spanish-rail.co.uk

International trains into Spain run from Lisbon to Madrid and from Paris to Madrid and Barcelona and both take just over 11 hours. Overnight trains also run from Geneva and Zurich to Barcelona. Spains 's high speed trains, the AVE (Altitud Velocidad España) travels between Madrid and Seville, stopping at Cordoba, in less than three hours. Work is in-hand to extend the line to Malaga (finished by 2007) and from Seville to Granada. A further line from Perpignan in France, to Barcelona is due to open in 2009, but completion dates have proved flexible in the past.

Spain 's Talgo and TER services crisscross other parts of Spain, connecting major cities with smart, speedy trains. The expreso and rapido services are slower (but more picturesque) and tend to stop everywhere. Rail Europe *www.raileurope.co.uk* has regional passes covering Spain, Portugal and Morocco.

Package Deals & Escorted Tours

While the travel industry is booming, the number of people taking package holidays is stagnating due to the rise of cheap independent travel thanks to the low-cost airlines. Traditional package holidays on the Spanish Costas are in decline, faced with competition from new, cheap, fashionable destinations such as Eastern Europe. But, this can work in a family's favour. In order to compete, prices along the Spanish coastline will have to come down. It is also worth noting that package holidays have come a long way from shoe-horning people into the purpose built resorts in Spain, complete with high-rise hotels, full English breakfasts and Premier League football matches on the TV in every bar. Of course, if that's what you want, it isn't hard to find.

There's a lot to be said for package travel for families, where everything is pre-arranged and you have to spend less time planning. If you book through a travel agent, make sure they are a member of the Association of British Travel Agents (ABTA), the largest trade body for tour operators and agents in the UK ☎ 207 637 2444 www.abtanet.com to check. Always check for hidden expenses when making a booking. Ask whether the airport departure fees and taxes are included, plus transfers to a resort or hotel.

Escorted Tours

These are structured group tours, with a group leader. The price usually includes everything from airfare to hotels, meals, tours, admission costs and local transportation. Basically all the little details are taken care of. However they can be expensive and often leave little time for 'wandering off' because they are jam-packed with planned activities.

Getting Around

By Car Driving is without a doubt the best way to see Spain's rural areas. However, driving in many of the major cities and smaller towns can be tiresome as

the roads can be very narrow, parking is a problem and drivers are often thwarted by tricky **one way systems**. If you prefer to drive, make sure you know the location of a **car park** near to your destination in the towns. **Renting a car** in Spain is relatively cheap compared to the rest of Europe. There is plenty of choice, either via the big international companies or the smaller (usually cheaper) local outlets. For a comprehensive guide to the major car hire companies in Spain's airports go to *www. spanish-airport-guide.com*. Here's a few to get started:

Avis: *www.avis-europe.com*. From the UK ☎ *08700 100 287*.

Budget: *www.budget.co.uk*. From the UK ☎ *08701 539 170*.

Europcar: *www.europcar.com*. From the UK ☎ *0870 607 5000*.

Hertz: *www.hertz.com*. From the UK ☎ *0870 844 8844*.

Saving Money

The local car hire companies tend to be cheaper than the big international ones. It always pays to check for any hidden extras. Some of the airlines have special arrangements with the car hire firms, so it is worth checking this. When searching for deals, the website *www.travelsupermarket. com* is a handy price comparison stop.

Rental Rules

To rent a car in Spain you must be over 21 years of age, produce a valid licence (no copies) and a credit card when you hire the vehicle. Double check for young driver surcharges for anyone under 25. Seatbelts are mandatory and child seats are mandatory for children up to age 3. Children under 12 are not permitted to sit in the front seat of a car.

The major hire car companies will rent out child seats if necessary. Insurance: fire and third party liability insurance is mandatory in Spain and is included in all rentals. It is unlimited in case of damage or injury to people or property outside of the car.

Standard insurance does not usually cover the first €250 (£168) of any damage. Always check the position of insurance cover for drivers under 25. Collision Damage Waiver and theft protection are optional types of insurance. If you are driving your own car from the UK to Spain, your British motor policy should cover you while abroad. Always let your insurer know that you are going abroad.

Anyone driving their own car to Spain should take out breakdown cover (including Europe) in the UK. Check rates at the AA (☎ 0800 085 2721) *www.theaa. co.uk* or try the RAC (☎ 0800 828 282) *www.rac.co.uk*.

Maps

Map reading in Spain can be testing. It is absolutely essential to have an **up-to-date map**. The roads in Spain are constantly changing and being re-routed. The amount of road-building

going on is staggering. In particular many roads were renumbered in 2004, so make sure your map was printed after this.

By Plane Spain has a good network of domestic flight connections though this is not necessarily the cheapest way to travel. The three main operators are Iberia *www.iberia.com* ☎ 902 400 500, Spainair ☎ 902 13 14 15 *www.spanair.com* and Air Europa ☎ 902 401 501 *www.aireuropa. com.* The new Catalan airline ☎ 902 33 39 33 *www.vueling.com* provides some good internal flights and routes to Europe.

By Train Spain's occasionally confusing railway system is consolidated under the national train company **Renfe**.

One of the best services in Europe is the high-speed trains or **Ave**. The train between Madrid and Seville now takes just two and half hours.

If you plan to travel extensively on the rail networks buy a copy of the Thomas Cook *Timetable of European Passenger Railroads www.thomascook publishing.com.*

For economical travel Renfe trains, particularly the faster Talgo trains, are a good bet. Many of the main long-distance routes have overnight express trains with first or second class carriages and beds.

Interail passes are a good money saver on the railways if you plan to travel in more than one European country. Check the offers at Rail Europe ☎ 08708 371 371 *www.raileurope.co.uk*.

- Drive on the right-hand side
- To drive in Spain you must have a valid driving licence and third-party motor insurance. All UK driving licences are accepted although the older green licences and Northern Ireland ones can cause confusion. It is best to have a new European compliant photo-licence.
- The minimum driving age is 18 for cars and motorcycles over 75cc.
- Every car must carry a luminous visibility vest and a warning triangle to be set up on the hard shoulder in the event of a breakdown.
- Seat belts (front and rear) must be worn. There are exceptions for pregnant women or disabled persons carrying a medical certificate.
- Head light converters are compulsory
- Do not drink drive. Having more than 0.05% of alcohol in your bloodstream can mean a severe fine, withdrawal of your licence or imprisonment
- Children under 12 cannot travel in the front passenger seat unless a suitable restraint system is used.
- Fines are issued on the spot. Ensure you get an official receipt. Foreigners paying fines on the spot can qualify for a 30% discount.
- The use of mobile phones (or anything similar) is forbidden at all times when driving except via a hands free apparatus that does not require the use of ear pieces or head sets.
- Towing is not permitted under Spanish law unless the vehicle being towed is on a trailer.

Speed limits:
- Major roads and motorways – 120 kmph (75 mph)
- Built up areas – 50 kmph (31 mph)
- N roads, carretera nacional and certain others – 100 kmph (62 mph)

Road classifications:
- **E road** – European route. These are major highways to connect Spain with the continent. E1 from Seville to the Portuguese border. E5 runs from Cadiz to Seville and then Madrid and Burgos. E15 from Estepona and then north to Barcelona and on to the boarder with France.
- **A or AP** – Autopista. These are fast-track highways connecting the regions. The 'P' in AP stands for Peage, meaning a toll road. Frequently the E and the A or AP roads are the same.
- **A/C** – These are provincial roads. They vary in standard, but as a general rule the fewer letters that follow the letter A the better.

The rest are local roads, usually prefixed by two letters such as SE (Seville). Some of these are extremely narrow and in bad condition.

By Bus Spain's bus network is extensive, low priced, comfortable and often quicker than the train, depending on the length of the journey. In the rural areas, the bus networks are more extensive than the rail system. A bus ride between Cordoba to Seville or Madrid to Barcelona is about two-thirds the price of a train. The major bus company is Alsa ☎ *902 42 22 42 www2.alsa.es*. The Alsa website has an English translation option. Alternatively, Damas, for routes in the west of Andalucia *www.damas-sa.es*. Huelva – ☎ *959 256 900*, Seville – ☎ *954 908 040*. Socibus is for routes in Andalucia and connections to Madrid ☎ *902 22 92 92 www.socibus.es*. Alsina Graells is a Catalan bus company with routes from Granada, Almeria, Seville, Cordoba, Malaga and Murcia. *www.alsinagraells.es*. The website has an English translation option.

ACCOMMODATION

From castles converted into hotels to modern high-rise resorts overlooking the Med, Southern and Mediterranean Spain has some of the most varied hotel accommodation in the world – with equally varied prices.

One- to Five-Star Hotels

The Spanish Government rates hotels by according them stars. A five-star hotel is truly luxury, with matching prices;

a one-star hotel is the most modest accommodation officially recognized as a hotel by the Government. A four-star hotel offers first-class accommodation; a three-star hotel is moderately priced; and a one- or two-star hotel is inexpensive. The Government grants stars based on such amenities as elevators, private bathrooms, and air conditioning. If a hotel is classified as a *residencia,* it means that it serves breakfast (usually) but no other meals.

Hostals

Not be confused with a Youth Hostel for students, a hostal is a modest hotel without services, where you can save money by carrying your own bags and the like. You'll know it's an hostal if a small 's' follows the capital H on the blue plaque by the door. An hostal with three stars is about the equivalent of a hotel with two stars.

Casas Huespedes & Fondas

These are the cheapest places to stay in Med Spain and can be recognized by the light blue plaques at the door displaying CH and F, respectively. They are invariably basic but respectable establishments.

Renting a House or Apartment

If you rent a home or apartment, you can save money on accommodation and dining and still take trips to see the surrounding area. Apartments in Med Spain generally fall into two categories: hotel *apartmentos* and *residencia apartmentos.* The hotel apartments have full facilities, with dress down service, equipped kitchens, and often restaurants and bars. The residencia apartments, also called *apartmentos turisticos,* are fully furnished with kitchens but lack facilities of the hotel complexes. They are cheaper, however.

Rural Tourism

A comprehensive range of rural accommodation facilities are available throughout Spain. Farmhouses, country cottages (either lodging with families or on a self-contained basis), refurbished cave dwellings carved in mountain slopes, purpose built rustic complexes, splendidly renovated country mansions and palaces. By going rural, you can be certain that you will have the opportunity to enjoy some of the most beautiful and pure spots of the Spanish countryside. You will also have an ample range of activities such as horseback excursions, pony trekking, walking, cycling, canoeing, rafting often in the vicinity. Below are the key regional associations:

ASETUR deals with the whole of Spain. *www.ecoturismorural. com*

Red Andaluza de Alojamientos Rurales; Andalucia ☏ +34 902442233 *www.raar.es*

Federación de Agroturismo de Catalunya Interior; Cataluna ☏ 938691886 *www.faciagro turisme.com*

Asociación de Turismo Rural de Murcia ☏ +34 902 106600 *www. ecoturismomurcia.com*, *www. noratur.com*

FEVALTUR: Valencia *www. ecoturismovalencia.com*

Villas Turisticas

These small villa complexes, found in exceptional scenic locations in the Andalucian countryside, have been purpose built with scrupulous respect for the local architecture.

Villa Turistica de Bubión ☏ +34 958 763909 *www.villabubion.com*

Villa Turística de Cazalla de la Sierra (Seville). ☏ +34 95 488 3310 *www.villasdecazalla.com*

Villa Turística de Fuenteheridos (Huelva). ☏ +34 959 125202

Villa Turística de Grazalema (Cadiz). ☏ +34 956 132136 *www.tugasa.com*

Villa Turístcas de Laujar (Alpujarras, Almeria). ☏ +34 950 513027

Villa Turística de Periana (La Anarquía, Malaga). ☏ +34 95 253 6460

Villa Turística de Priego (Aldea de Zagrilla, Priego Cordoba). ☏ +34 957 703503 *www.villadepriego.com*

Caves

These troglodyte caves, refurbished to accommodate modern living facilities, are a simple but unique alternative to holiday accommodation in some beautiful spots in inland Andalucia. For Information and reservations contact:

Andalucia Authentica ☎ *+34 95 205 2560 www.andalucia-autentica. com*

Promociones Turísticas de Galera ☎ *+34 958 739068 www.casa-cueva.com*

Timeshare

Timeshare is huge in southern Spain. It's very common for families to use a system such as RCI to exchange their timeshare weeks elsewhere in the world and go to Spain. This is one of the most typical ways of travelling as an extended family, too, with grandparents, for example. ☎ *0870 60 90 141 www. rci.com*

Paradors

The Spanish Government runs a series of unique state-owned inns called paradors (*paradores* in Spanish), which are found across Med Spain. Deserted castles, monasteries, palaces, and other buildings have been taken over and converted into hotels. The Tourist Board has a booklet called *Visiting the Paradors.*

At great expense, modern bathrooms, steam heat, and the like have been added to these buildings, yet classic Andalusian architecture, where it exists, has been retained. Establishments are often furnished with antiques or at least good reproductions and decorative objects of the country. Meals are also served.

The government chain offers several incentives for family stays.

Keytel International: 402 Edgware Road, London, W2 ☎ *020 7616 0300 www.parador.es*

Planning Your Trip Online

Surfing for Hotels

Expedia *www.expedia.co.uk* provides a thorough run down on the hotels featured on the site, including their attitude towards children. Also try Travelocity at *www.travelocity.co.uk*. The Spanish website (with an English translation option) *www. rusticae.es* is an excellent resource if you are looking for upmarket hotels. It lists 160 beautiful handpicked bolt-holes, divided into rural and metropolitan. Other gems across Spain can be found at *www.secret places.com*. If your family is looking for a stylish hideaway try *www.i-escape.com*. It has pictures and indicates which hotels are child friendly. The *www. travelintelligence.com* site has an archive of reviews from more than 120 writers. For lower cost deals try *www.hostels.com*, *www.lowcostbeds.com* or *www.hostelworld.com*. Trip Advisor aggregates reviews by independent travellers *www.tripadvisor.com*. If you want to stay in a reliable hotel chain while visiting Spain search the *www.bestwestern.com* website.

Todo Turismo Rural is a national agency promoting rural tourism with a bank of places to stay throughout rustic Spain. ☎ *914 659 567 www.todoturismo rural.com*. RAAR is the Andalucian-specific equivalent, and represents a network of rural accommodation ranging from farms, country fincas to camping. ☎ *902 442 233*.

Rustic Blue is an excellent web-based lettings agency that benefits from being one of the very few to have a full-time staff on site in Andalucia (in the Alpujarran village of Bubion). They represent rural holiday homes and villas, little inns and country house hotels and also organize walking, horse riding and painting holidays in Ronda and Alpujarra. *www.rusticblue.com*

Also check out

www.littlehotelsofspain.co.uk

www.ownersdirect.co.uk/Spain.htm

www.coloursofspain.com

GETTING CHILDREN INTERESTED IN MEDITERRANEAN SPAIN

Involving children in planning your trip is the best way to get them interested. As well as using this book to show them what to look forward to in Mediterranean Spain, whether it's splashing about in water parks, being bedazzled by Flamenco or discovering natural parks, introduce them to relevant books, films and games to whet their appetite. Here's a few ideas.

● Ask the children to research cities and towns, language, best buys and so on. Have family quizzes based on this information.

● Encourage children to put together a scrapbook of pictures and text about the places you'll be visiting – there's lots of material available in travel brochures and on the Internet, and from tourist boards.

● Get the children to send to national and regional tourist boards for information – they love getting mail.

● Suggest they research the airline with which you are traveling, find out the type of carrier you're likely be going on.

● Let them practice currency conversion and language pronunciation.

● Get them to research any particular interest of their own: football, horse riding, tennis, wildlife.

● If possible, let each child have or try a digital camera, or the family camera – they love taking pictures.

● Take addresses with you, so that the children can play their part in writing postcards home.

Reading list

The Story of Ferdinand by Munro Leaf and illustrated by Robert Lawson. First published more than 50 years ago, this tells the story of Ferdinand the little bull who accidentally gets sent to a bullfight in Madrid. For babies and pre-school children. Published by Puffin.

Look What Came from Spain by Kevin Davis. This picture book describes the inventions, holidays, animals, foods, sports and music that 'came from Spain'. For children aged 4–8. Published by Franklin Watts.

With Love from Spain by Carol Weston and illustrated by Marci Roth. The book tells the tales of 11-year-old Melanie as she travels through Spain with her family. For ages 9–12. Published by Knopf Books.

Prince of the Birds by Amanda Hall. An adaptation of Washington Irving's *Tales of the Alhambra* tells the tale of Prince Ahmed who is born in Granada but locked away in a tower. He eventually escapes to find his love and flies away on a magic carpet. 4 and up. Published by Frances Lincoln.

Shadow of a Bull by Maia Wojciechowska, illustrated by Alvin Smith. Manolo Olivar is haunted by the legend of his world-famous bullfighting father and searches for the courage to pursue his own dreams. Ages 4–8. Published by Aladdin.

The Poem of the Cid by Anonymous, translated by Rita Hamilton and Janet Perry. A medieval Spanish epic poem telling the story of El Cid, a warlord of Herculean stature, plus devoted husband and family man: an example to us all. A blend of fiction and fact telling tales of his campaigns in Valencia and the crowning of his daughters as queens of Aragon and Navarre. Published by Penguin. Teens and upwards.

Into Wild Spain by Jeff Corwin. For children interested in animals, parks and wildlife in general. From the Rock of Gibraltar, up the Atlantic coast to Seville and the Doñana National Park, Jeff finds plenty of strange and interesting animals to describe. Ages 9–12. Published by Blackbirch Press.

Film Scenes Shot in Spain

● *Conan the Barbarian:* Andalucia

● *Die Another Day:* Cadiz and Seville

- *Doctor Zhivago:* Grenada, Malaga, Guadix

- *El Cid:* Andalusia

- *Empire of the Sun:* Cadiz

- *The Fall of the Roman Empire:* Andalucia

- *A Fistful of Dollars:* Andalucia

- *Indiana Jones and the Last Crusade:* Granada and Guadix for Morocco

- *Lawrence of Arabia:* Aqaba is really Playa del Algorocibo near Almeria

- *The Good, The Bad and the Ugly:* Andalusia

- *Time Bandits:* Granada

- *Star Wars Episode II: Attack of the Clones:* Plaza Espana, Seville is Naboo Theed Palace

- *Living Daylights:* Gibraltar

FAST FACTS: MEDITERRANEAN SPAIN

Breast Feeding Breastfeeding in Spain is less common than in the UK, some even putting it down to the legacy of Franco's dictatorship. Whatever the reason, you may get stared at, especially if you're feeding an older infant. Then again you may want to brazen it out, since breastfeeding is your natural right, or you might prefer to find a secluded spot.

Business Hours Banks are open Monday through Friday from 9.30am to 2pm and Saturday from 9.30am to 1pm. Most businesses are open Monday to Saturday from 9.30am to 1.30pm and from 4.30pm to 8pm. Shopping centres and department stores tend to open from 10am to 9pm or 10pm but are usually shut on Sundays. Shops in the coastal cities at high season often open past 10pm. Lunch is usually served from 1pm to 4pm and dinner from 9pm to 11.30pm. The rules for bars and tapas haunts are less strict. Many open at lunchtime at around 1pm and are open in the evening until 1.30am or later.

Climate See 'When to Go'

Currency See 'Money'

Customs See 'Visitor Information'

Driving Rules See 'Getting Around'

Pharmacies Pharmacies follow normal business hours although all major cities have a 24-hour pharmacy. To find an open pharmacy outside normal hours, check the list of stores posted on the doors of most pharmacies in a town. The law requires pharmacies to operate a rotating system of hours so that there's always a drug-store open somewhere.

Electricity Most hotels have 220 volts AC (50 cycles). Some older places have 110 or 125 volts AC. Carry your adapter with you, and always check at your hotel desk before plugging in any electrical appliance. It's best to travel with battery-operated equipment or just buy a new hair dryer in Spain.

Embassies & Consulates If you lose your passport, fall seriously ill, get into legal trouble or have any other major problems contact your embassy or consulate. Here are the Madrid addresses and hours: The British Embassy: Calle Fernando el Santo 16, ℂ *91 319 02 00*, Metro: Colón). Open Mon–Fri 9am–1.30pm and 3pm to 6pm. The Republic of Ireland: Paseo Castellana ℂ *46 91576 35 00*, Metro Serrano. Open Mon–Fri 9am–2pm.

Emergencies The national emergency number for Spain (except the Basque country) is ℂ *006*. In the Basque country it is ℂ *088*.

Etiquette In Franco's day you could be arrested in the street for wearing skimpy revealing clothes. Today it is still considered extremely rude for men to go bare-chested except at the beach or poolside. Even in the very hot weather it is courteous to cover up when visiting churches or cathedrals. Spanish speakers should address strangers with the formal '*usted*' instead of the familiar '*tu*'.

Language The official language in Spain is Castilian (or Castellano) and is spoken in every province. However, many local dialects have reasserted themselves since the restoration of democracy post 1975 and the end of Franco's dictatorship. Catalán is spoken in Barcelona and Catalonia and its derivatives are also spoken in the Valencia area. Most hotel, restaurant and shopworkers speak some, or fluent English.

Drink Laws The legal drinking age is 18. Bars, taverns and cafeterias frequently open at 8am and serve alcohol until 1.30am and later.

Mail To post a letter within Spain costs €0.25 (£0.17). To post a letter to the UK (normal weight) costs €0.50 (£0.34).

Passports To pick up an application for a standard 10-year passport (or 5-year passport or less for children) visit your nearest passport office or major post office. Alternatively, contact the United Kingdom Passport Service ℂ *0870 521 0410 www.ukpa. gov.uk*. For residents in Ireland: Go to the Passport Office at Setanta Centre, Molesworth Street, Dublin 2 ℂ *01 671 1633 www.irlgov.ie/iveagh* for a 10 year passport. Alternatively, go to 1A South Mall, Cork ℂ *021 272 525*, or a main post office.

Police The national emergency number is ℂ *006* in Spain, or ℂ *088* in the Basque country.

Toilets Called *servicios* or *aseos* or *lavabos* in Spain or labeled *caballeros* for men and *damas* or *señoras* for women.

Safety see 'Health and Safety' in earlier chapter

Taxes Spanish value added tax (VAT), known as IVA, is 7% when levied on food, wine, basic necessities and hotels. For most goods and services, including car rentals you'll pay 13% or 33% for luxury items – jewellery, tobacco, imported liquors.

Telephones If you make an international call from your hotel it will probably be very expensive because a surcharge is levied on every operator-assisted call. Phone booths (cabinas) on the street take coins (€0.25 (£0.17) for 3 minutes). For calls to England alternatively, buy a European phone card from almost any mini-market or tobacconist from €6 (£4) and upwards for much cheaper calls. Codes: Directory inquiries is

☏ 1003 in Spain; Operator assistance for international calls is ☏ 025; Freephone numbers in Spain are ☏ 900 numbers. Telephone numbers are usually nine-digits long and preceded by a provincial code for local, national and international calls. To call Spain from the UK dial ☏ 0034. To make international calls from Spain dial ☏ 00 and then the country code (44-UK, 353-Ireland).

Time Spain is one hour ahead of the UK. Daylight saving time runs from the last Sunday in March to the last Sunday in September.

Tipping By law, restaurants and hotels must include their service charge – usually 15% – in the bill. While tipping is less common in Spain it doesn't hurt to leave a few Euros extra on the table after a good meal and most waiters and waitresses have come to expect it from foreign travellers. For taxis tip an extra 10%.

3 Seville

SEVILLE

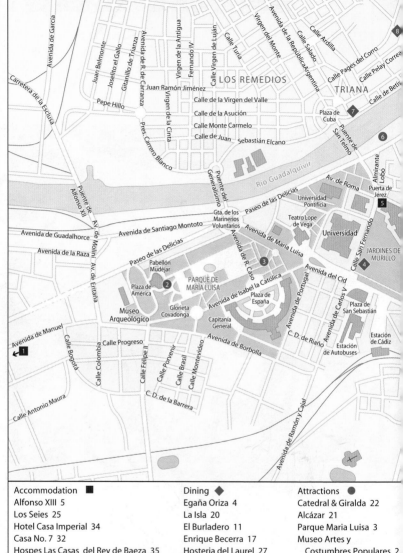

Accommodation ■	Dining ◆	Attractions ●
Alfonso XIII 5	Egaña Oriza 4	Catedral & Giralda 22
Los Seies 25	La Isla 20	Alcázar 21
Hotel Casa Imperial 34	El Burladero 11	Parque Maria Luisa 3
Casa No. 7 32	Enrique Becerra 17	Museo Artes y
Hospes Las Casas del Rey de Baeza 35	Hosteria del Laurel 27	Costumbres Populares 2
Taverna del Albardero 18	Barbiana 19	Isla Magica 10
Hotel Doña Maria 26	La Albahaca 29	Bullring (Maestranza) 14
Hotel San Gil Seville Parras 28 36	Taberna Sol y Sombra 9	Museo Taurino 13
Las Casas de la Judería 31	Poncio 8	Casa de Pilatos 33
Las Casas de los Mercaderes 24	Cafeteria Serranito 15	Torre del Oro 6
AC Ciudad de Seville 1	Rio Grande 7	
Hosteria del Laurel 28	Cervecería Giralda 23	
Hotel Murillo 30	Freidura Al Arenal 16	
Puerta de Triana 12		

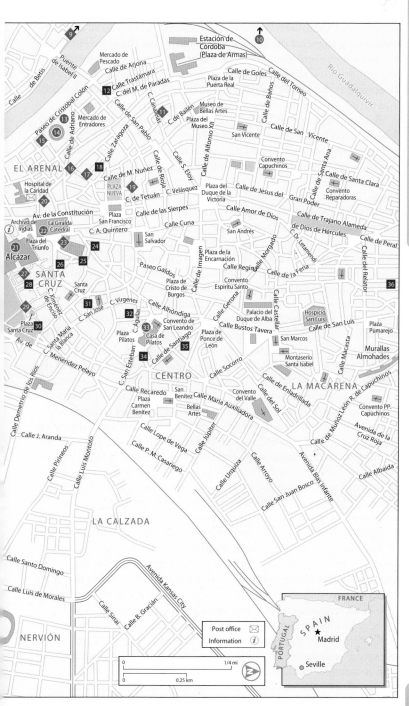

9

Estación de
Córdoba
(Plaza de Armas)

10

Río Guadalquivir

Puente
de Isabel II

Calle de Betis

Mercado de
Pescado

Calle de Arjona

Calle de Goles

Calle del Torneo

Plaza de la
Puerta Real

Calle de Baños

Calle Trastámara

12

C. del M. de Paradas

Paseo de Cristóbal Colón

13

Mercado de
Entradores

Calle de Adriano

Calle de San Pablo

Calle Zaragoza

C. Canalejas

11

C. de Bailén

Museo de
Bellas Artes

Plaza del
Museo XII

Calle de San Vicente

Calle de San Vicente

San Vicente

14

15

EL ARENAL

16

17

18

Calle de M. Núñez

Calle de Rioja

Calle S. Eloy

Calle de Alfonso XII

Convento
Capuchinos

Calle de Santa Ana

Calle de Santa Clara

Convento
Reparadoras

Hospital de
la Caridad

20

PLAZA
NUEVA

C. de Tetuán

C. Velásquez

Plaza del
Duque de la
Victoria

Calle de Jesus del

Gran Poder

Av. de la Constitución

Plaza
San Francisco

Calle de las Sierpes

Calle Amor de Dios

Calle de Trajano

Alameda

Archivo de
Indias

La Giralda
Catedral

C. A. Quintero

Calle Cuna

San Andrés

de Dios de Hércules

C. Di. Letamendi

Calle de Peral

Plaza del
Triunfo

21

22

23

San
Salvador

Plaza de la
Encarnación

Calle de Imagen

Calle de la Feria

Calle del Relator

Alcázar

24

Paseo Galdos

Calle Regina

26

25

SANTA
CRUZ

27

28

Santa
Cruz

Plaza de
Cristo de
Burgos

Convento
Espiritu Santo

Calle Gerona

Palacio del
Duque de Alba

Hospicio
San Luis

Plaza
Pumarejo

36

C. Ximénez
de Enciso

C. San José

C. Virgenes

Calle Alhóndiga

Calle de San Luis

29

31

32

C. Aguilas

Convento de
San Leandro

Calle Bustos Tavera

San Marcos

Calle Macasta

Murallas
Almohades

Plaza
Santa Cruz

30

Santa María
la Blanca

Plaza
Pilatos

33

Casa de
Pilatos

Plaza de
Ponce de
León

Montaserio
Santa Isabel

Av. de

C. Menéndez Pelayo

C. San Esteban

34

Calle de Santiago

35

Calle Socorro

CENTRO

Calle de Enladrillada

LA MACARENA

R. de Capuchinos

Calle Demetrio de los Ríos

Calle Recaredo

San
Benítez

Calle María Auxiliadora

Convento
del Valle

Calle del Sol

Convento PP.
Capuchinos

Plaza
Carmen
Benítez

Bellas
Artes

Calle de Muñoz León

Avenida de la
Cruz Roja

Calle J. Aranda

Calle Lope de Vega

Calle Júpiter

Calle Albaida

Calle Pirineos

Calle Luis Montoto

Calle P. M. Casariego

Calle Urquiza

Calle Arroyo

Avenida Blas Infante

Calle San Juan Bosco

LA CALZADA

Avenida Kansas City

Calle Santo Domingo

Calle Luis de Morales

Calle Sinaí

Calle B. Gracián

NERVIÓN

| Post office | ✉ |
| Information | ⓘ |

FRANCE

SPAIN

PORTUGAL

★
Madrid

● Seville

| 0 | 1/4 mi |
| 0 | 0.25 km |

If one city sums up the beauty and mystique of southern Spain, it's Seville. Like a theme park made real, the city stands proud over the plains of south-west Andalucia, its towers and spires and minarets threatening to pierce the azure skies. Hundreds of thousands of families flock here every year, intent on visiting its great monuments, eating and drinking the fine food and wines of the region and generally swooning at the aching loveliness of orange blossom-scented streets and patios, soulful flamenco songs and unmatchable urban vistas.

By comparison, Seville province is a poor relation – but then anywhere would be, by comparison. There are some fine towns and some stunning and tranquil natural parks and mountains where children can play and amuse themselves. But by and large, Seville is the place to be. Better to stay in the city then hop on a train to Cordoba, or south to Cadiz. Here the landscapes are more dramatic, the white towns more redolent of Spanish dreams and everything costs less, from hotel rooms to tapas and hamburgers.

The bottom line is that Seville (Sevilla in Spanish) is unmissable. Whether you are looking to spend a day cooling yourselves off and having fun at La Isla Magica water-based theme park on the 'island' of La Cartuja – the former Expo site – or visiting the myriad monuments, you will find plenty to satisfy curious young minds here.

The city itself, the most beautiful, inviting, haughty and romantic of Spanish cities, seems to delight in showing off its different faces. In spite of its sultry summer heat and its many problems, such as high unemployment and street crime, Seville regularly features in lists of the world's top cities to visit, so be prepared for crocodiles of fellow tourists easing around the great monuments. Visit the sites early or late to avoid the crowds – and the children will thank you for it. Seville's popularity also goes a long way to explaining the sevillanos' arrogance, but never forget this is Spain. Well-dressed locals parading during the evening paseo may seem aloof, but they will delight in a small child's antics and even the hardest señora's heart will melt at the sight of lovers strolling through the stunning whitewashed streets of the lovely Barrio de Santa Cruz or its more earthy neighbour, La Macarena.

Much of the city's romantic reputation is down to Don Juan and Carmen – aided by Mozart and Bizet. But the images associated with Andalucia – orange trees, flower-filled patios and castanet-rattling gypsies – come to life here. Driving is a nightmare: Seville was planned for the horse and buggy rather than for the car. But this is also a city looking to the future. A metro system is due to open in late 2007 and redevelopment continues along the Guadalquivir river.

Seville's climate is out of step with the British summer holiday timetable: in July and August temperatures can reach 50 °C to make the city as unbearable for adults as it is for children. The best time to visit is spring or autumn.

ESSENTIALS

Getting There

By Air Ryanair has flights to Seville from Stansted and Liverpool from £40 return (*www.ryanair.com*), British Airways (*www.britishairways.com*) and Iberia (*www.iberia.com*) fly from Gatwick and Air France (*www.airfrance.com*) from City Airport and Heathrow. Direct flights link Seville to most other British cities including Southampton, Manchester, Newcastle, Belfast, Edinburgh, Glasgow and the Isle of Man. The airport, San Pablo, +34 954 449 000 +34 954 672 981 Fax: +34 954 44 90 25 is 10 km north-east of the city centre, towards Carmona, Cordoba and Madrid on the A4. Internal flights link Seville to several key cities in Southern Spain. A half-hourly bus service (6.15am to 11pm) runs to the city centre (the Santa Justa train station; €2.30 (£1.54). The taxi fare the same distance is about €20 (£13.40). Car hire kiosks are on the ground floor of the terminal building, Atesa (0034 954 449 023), Avis (0034 954 449 121), Crown Car Hire (0034 954 980 214) Europcar (0034 954 254 298) and Hertz (0034 954 514 729), but it's better to hire a car when you want to leave Seville, otherwise it will only sit in an underground car park for the duration of your stay.

By Train Around 16 trains each day connect Seville, at the Estación Santa Justa, Av. Kansas City s/n (95-240-02-02 for information and reservations, or 95-454-03-03 for information) with Cordoba; the AVE train takes 45 minutes, and a TALGO takes 1½ hours. Three trains per day run to Malaga, taking three hours; there are also three trains per day to Granada (4 h).

By Bus Buses mostly run from Prado de San Sebastián, Calle José María Osborne 11 (95-441-71-11), with routes to Cordoba taking (2½ h), Malaga (3½ h) and Granada (4 h). For information and ticket prices, call Alsina Graells at 95-441-88-11.

By Car Seville is 217 km (135 miles) northwest of Malaga, 252 km from Granada, 97 km from Jerez de la Frontera, 129 km from Cadiz, 192 km from Algeciras, and it is well connected by several motorways. During periods of heavy holiday traffic, the N-V (E-90) from Madrid through Extremadura – which, at Mérida, connects with the southbound N-630 (E-803) – is usually less congested than the N-IV (E-5) through eastern Andalusia.

There are a number of underground car parks in the old town: at Plaza Nueva, Plaza de la Concordia, Plaza de la Magdalena, Plaza Ponce de León, Marqués de Paradas, C/ Sor Ángela de la Cruz, Plaza de la Encarnación, and Avenida Paseo Colón. 24 hours of parking normally costs around €20 (£13.40).

Visitor Information

The regional tourist office is on Avenida de la Constitucion 954 221 404. The tourist office for the province is in the Plaza Del Triumfal, between the Cathedral and the Al Cazar 954 210 005 www.turismosevilla.org. The city tourist office is behind the town hall, at Paseo de los Delicías 954 234 465 www.turismo.sevilla.org

City Layout

At 4 km by 2.5 km, Seville boasts one of the biggest walled areas in Europe, and fortunately for those with little legs, most of the places you'll want to get to lie within it. To its east are **barrio Santa Cruz** and **El Arenal**, which sit on opposite sides of the main thoroughfare, **Avenida de la Constitucion**. You'll only want to cross the river, from El Arenal at either Puente de San Telmo or Puente Isabel II, to reach the old **gypsy quarter of Triana**, or further out, the Puente de la Barqueta, for **Isla de La Cartuja**.

The Neighbourhoods in Brief

If you are here to soak up atmosphere, it makes sense to base yourself in the atmospheric **Barrio Santa Cruz**, although beware that because of the age of buildings here only a very few of the area's hotels have swimming pools or gardens to keep children happy. Other options are the up-and-coming district of **La Macarena** or even across the Guadalquivir, in **Triana**.

Getting Around

By Public Transport Seville has a good bus system and taxis are plentiful (Tele Taxi 954 622222; Radio Taxi Giralda 954 675 555; Radio Taxi 95-458-00-00) but there are lots of better ways to get about. More and more Sevillanos are coming round to the two-wheels = good, four-wheels = bad, way of thinking. If the children are old enough, hire a bike and ride the city's flat, cycle lanes which have been laid down on main routes and where a number of lock hoops are appearing. A few places now hire out bikes, folding ones cost €9 (£6) for three hours or €18 (£12) for 24 hours. 34619 461 491. www.rentabikesevilla.com run guided tours and can deliver and pick up bikes from your hotel.

Don't think about **hiring mopeds** – Spanish teenagers may make it look like a good way to get around but they've (already) had years of weaving in and out of traffic. You can't move in Seville for **horse and carts**, which will appeal to younger ones and more romantic parents, but if you can't find one they officially wait for custom at Cabo Noval, Plaza Virgen de los Reyes, Plaza del Triunfo, Avenida de la Constitución, Puerta de Jerez, Torre de Oro, Isabel la Católica, Plaza de España, Plaza de América and Adolfo Rodríguez Jurado. An hour costs €30 (£20.10). Also fun for children is the hop on and off, double-decker AC tourist bus which stops at Torre Del Oro, Plaza de España, Isla Magica and the Monasterio de la Cartuja. A ticket is valid for 24 hours, and the buses leave every 20 minutes taking one hour if you don't get off. ☎ 902 101081, adults €11 (£7.37), children €5 (£3.35). *www. sevillatour.com*. Waterbabes may prefer to do their sightseeing from the river; cruises leave from the dock by Torre Del Oro, Paseo Alcade Marqués del Contadero ☎ 954 561 692. There are also cruises to manzanilla-making Sanlúcar de Barrameda on Saturdays and Sundays May to October.

Planning Your Outings

Seville's best bits are all within a stone's throw of each other so there's no real reason to get your head around a public transport system, which is a bonus when travelling with young children. There are few queues for the key sights, even at high season, although you may feel you are moving in a crowd of tourists. Be sure to keep children hydrated.

FAST FACTS: SEVILLE

American Express Hotel Inglaterra, Plaza Nueva 7 (☎ 95-421-16-17), is open Monday to Friday from 9.30am to 1.30pm and 4.30 to 7.30pm, Saturday from 10am to 1pm.

Airport See 'By Air' earlier in this chapter.

Babysitters See individual hotel listings

Car Rentals See 'By Air', earlier in this chapter

Consulate the British Embassy is at Plaza Nueva, 8 ☎ 954 228 874

Emergencies ☎ 112. Seville has emergency care facilities or centros de urgencies: the nearest to the old quarter is the Centro de Urgencia el Porvenir, is just across from the Jardines Murillo.

Hospital Universitario Virgen del Rocio ☎ 955 012 000 Avda. Manuel Siurot, s/n Hospital Universitario Virgen Macarena ☎ 955 008 000 Avda. Dr Fedriani, s/n Centro de Urgencia El Porvenir ☎ 955 017 300 Marqués de Paradas, 35

Internet Correos, the cental post office 10am – midnight, Interpublic third floor, c/ O'Donnell, 3.

Maps See 'City Layout'

Newspapers & Magazines Mostly Spanish language, including the monthly *El Giraldillo* which carries cultural listings, the daily morning freesheets *Metro, 20 Minutos* and *Qué. Casco Antiguo* covers tourist and tourist area news, the *Tourist* and *Welcome Olé* are its free English language equivalents.

Pharmacies Spaniards love prescription drugs and Farmacias are plentiful (9am–2pm, 5pm–8.30pm). Each district runs a rota system to cover both siesta and the night shift: ask your hotel or ☎ *902 522 111*.

Police for petty crime ☎ *092*, for more serious matters call ☎ *091*.

Post Office Correos y Telegrafos, Avenida de la Constitución, 2, ☎ *954 224 760*, also sells mobile phones.

Safety As with most European cities, petty crime and theft is commonplace: and the normal rules apply, keep your wits about you and don't invite attack by dangling cameras or purses or leaving possessions visible in empty cars.

WHAT TO SEE & DO

Children's Top 10 Attractions

❶ Alcázar gardens and maze The Palace's lush gardens offer a great area for children to run around rows of pomegranate, jacaranda and bitter orange trees. See p. 60.

❷ Catedral de Sevilla For the sheer size and scale alone, children will love the world's largest Gothic church. Climb to the top (or use the lift) of the Giralda. See p. 60.

❸ Parque Maria Luisa Hire a rowing boat, ride some donkeys or just relax with a picnic in a leafy corner at this beautiful park. See p. 61.

❹ Isla Magica A great sprawling theme park with a zone corresponding to different parts of Spain's globe-trotting past. Take a train round a South American silver mine or get lost in an Amazonian jungle. See p. 61.

❺ Barrio de Triana Take a trip to the Gypsy quarter and grab an orange juice and pastry while watching the vibrant municipal market's wheelers and dealers in full flow. See p. 62.

❻ Torre del Oro Be dazzled by the 13th century, 12-sided Tower of Gold, next to the Guadalquivir River. See p. 64.

❼ Feria The most famous feria in Spain will appeal to all age groups with its lights, horses and magical array of brilliantly coloured, flounced gypsy dresses. The spectacle and spontaneity is intoxicating. See p. 64.

❽ Tapas Take on a tapas trail from the city that started it all. See p. 72.

❾ Ceramics Seville is famous for its Azulejo (decorated tile) trade and finding a few choice tiles to take home for the family as souvenirs can be good fun, with lots of hand painted tiles and animal figures. Make your way to El Postigo for some of the best. See p. 72.

❿ Flamenco From bars and windows you'll hear the sounds, and from street corners to plazas you'll experience the passion of Flamenco which once seen is never forgotten. Colourful costumes, castanets and dazzling dancing will captivate all ages. See p. 73.

TIP ›› **Don't Use the Car** ‹

Seville has narrow streets and insufficient street parking so explore the city on foot, or even better, if your children are older, rent yourself a bicycle. The historic area of Santa Cruz is small and largely pedestrianised, so you won't be daunted.

Barrio de Santa Cruz Santa Cruz was a ghetto for Spanish Jews until they were ejected from Spain in the late 15th century in the wake of the Inquisition. Today it's Seville's most colourful old quarter and home to its **two biggest monuments**, the **Alcazar** and the **Cathedral**. Winding medieval streets with names like Vida (Life) and Muerte (Death) – try testing children on translations – open onto pocket-size plazas. Flower-filled balconies with draping bougainvillea and potted geraniums jut over this labyrinth, shading you from the hot Andalucian summer sun. To enter the Barrio Santa Cruz, turn right after leaving the Patio de Banderas exit of the Alcázar.

Turn right again at Plaza de la Alianza, going down Calle Rodrigo Caro to Plaza de Doña Elvira.

Alcázar There are lots to amuse the children at this **14th century Moorish palace** if they look beneath the surface, although it's the gardens that are likely to hold more appeal. Let them see if they spot the two tiny dolls faces carved into the stucco arches on the right as they enter the Patio de las Munecas (the Patio of the Dolls). Or the spectacular **Salon de Embajadores** (Hall of Ambassadors) with its Mocárabe gold ceiling that looks like bubbling burnished stalactites.

Alcázar

After that, journey outside to the palace's lush gardens with its 300-year old magnolia tree, carp-pond, a **Grotesque-style grotto** to play in, rows of pomegranate, jacaranda and bitter-orange trees and an incredible, working **Roman-style water-organ** that plays a tune every half-hour – all good fun. Follow the punchy scent of myrtle bushes to the far end of the pavilion where you'll find a **maze**, which will provide even more hours of fun for young ones.

The palace itself is the legacy of Pedro I, the 14th century king of Castile who has gone down in history as Pedro the Cruel. He hired teams of artisans from Toledo and Granada to craft the ultimate homage to **Moorish architecture** at a time when Seville had long been re-conquered by the Christians. The palace is a blend of Moorish and Christian influences – known as **mudéjar style.**

Patio de Banderas ☎ 95 450 23 23. Admission €7 (£4.74) adults, free for children under 12. www.patronato-alcazarsevilla.es. Oct–Mar Tues–Sat 9.30am–5pm, Sun and festivals 9.30am–1.30pm. Apr–Sept Tues–Sat 9.30am–7pm, Sun and festivals 9.30am–5pm.

Catedral De Sevilla and Giralda Tower ★★

If the children loved St Paul's, they will marvel at the sheer size of this cathedral, which is the **world's largest Gothic church** and technically the largest church in Europe, beating St Peter's and St Paul's in terms of volume.

In fact, it took at least 17 architects to draw up the plans for the cathedral, giving some clue as to the scale of the project the church authorities took on in the 15th century. Their aim was to create 'a church which those who see it finished will think we were mad for attempting'. The chapels along the side of the dark and cavernous central cathedral contain **art works** including Murillo's Vision of St Anthony, Goya's Saints Justa and Refina and Zurbarán's retablo of the life of St Paul. Christopher Columbus's tomb is housed in the cathedral, borne by four statues of kings representing the rulers of Castile, Leon, Aragon and Navarre. Children should make for the top of the Giralda, **the minaret** which is all that remains of the mosque that used to be where the cathedral now is. The route up is a series of sloping ramps, originally designed to

The Giralda Tower

Will the Real Colom Please Stand Up

Spanish scientists have been testing the **DNA** of hundreds of Catalans with the **surname Colom** in an attempt to prove that **Christopher Columbus** was in fact a former pirate born in Catalonia. More than five hundred years after his death, they think they are on the brink of disproving that the explorer was an Italian gentleman from the port of Genoa. Historians point to the fact that Columbus never wrote in Italian, preferring to record his voyages in Latin or fluent Spanish. Success has many authors: conflicting theories over the centuries have argued he was Spanish, French, Greek, Corsican and Portuguese. In 2003, an international group of scientists took a sample of Columbus's DNA from his tomb in Seville. They compared the DNA to samples taken from the same tomb from Columbus's younger brother Diego, and his illegitimate son Hernando, to establish a genetic pattern. These are now being compared with hundreds of samples taken from people living in Spain, France and Italy with the surnames such as **Colombo, Colomb and Colom**. The team is hoping to find a common ancestor who may be the link between the Admiral and today's Coloms.

allow the muezzin – who called the faithful to prayer – access to the top on horseback. Today there's a lift for parents with pushchairs.

Plaza Virgen de los Reyes (Puerta del Lagarto). ☎ 954214971. Fax: 954228432. www.catedralsevilla. org. Mon–Sat 11am–5pm. Sunday and holidays 2.30pm–6pm. July and August Mon–Sat 9.30am–3.30pm, Sunday and holidays 2.30pm–6pm. €7.50 (£5) adults, free for children under 12 years. Free on Sundays. An audio-guide costs €3 (£2).

Parque Maria Luisa ★★ This beautiful park, given to Seville in 1893 by Isabella II's sister Maria who donated half the riverside grounds of her palace, the Palacio de San Telmo, is the place to **escape the hustle and bustle of the city**. Hire a rowing

boat and take the children for a trip along the canal or let them ride in one of the donkey carts around the stunning, central space of the plaza, which are available at weekends and during peak season. Then feed the snow white doves that flock here. The park is full of leafy corners and small grassy patches **perfect for picnics**, and you can also hire **family-friendly tricycles** with buggies attached or tandems, though leaving the park is off limits. Part of *Lawrence of Arabia* was filmed here – hardly surprising as the overall impression is of wandering through a film set.

Isla Mágica ★ It may seem anathema to head for a theme park when you're in a city far beyond the wit of anything the Disney Corporation might dream up but La Isla Magica is actually worth a detour. The Magic Isle is the only theme park in the world within a city's limits, and it's a **sprawling place of water and jungles** whose every zone points to a part of Spain's **globe-trotting past**: there's Seville, Port of the Indies (where youngsters can boat on the lake, or dare-devils can freefall through 70 metres on the Desafio), Quetzal and World of the Maya, which has a spinning top and the vertigo-inducing Ciklon. The Gateway to America has Potosí, a train that potters round a recreation of a South American silver mine, and a replica 16th century galleon. Then there's a jungly Amazonia, the Pirates' Hideout, the Fountain of Youth and El Dorado, which has virtual reality rollercoasters and 4D films, to explore. Children love the **viewing platforms** next to the water drops, where they queue to get soaked as the boats hurtle down steep tracks with a huge splash. Little ones are catered for with **small boat ponds** and radio-controlled boats, and there's often **live entertainment** in the cafes and restaurants. Highlight is the two- or three-times daily (depending on the season) **spectacular show based around the galleon**, with roaring cannon, flashing cutlasses, pirate queens and ships boarded from the rigging. Some may say it's something of a poor-man's Disney,

others will delight in the low-key nature of the park and the lack of pressure to buy, buy, buy.

Pabellón de España Isla de la Cartuga. www.islamagica.es Info ☎ 902 16 17 16 Booking ☎ 902 16 00 00. Admission €23.50 (£15.75) adults, €16.50 (£11) children full day; 12 evening only high season. Opens 11am–11pm summer, until 10pm in spring, 9pm in autumn. Evening tickets allow entry from 3pm Children under 4 free. Free parking.

Barrio De Triana Stalls full of **fresh, multi-coloured fruit, vegetables and fish** in the municipal produce market, in the shadow of the Puente de Isabel II in the gypsy quarter, will keep the children amused. This combined with fantastic sweetmeats and cheeses, meats and herbs all contribute to a **sensory overload**. There's also a good little café where the orange juice and pastries are top notch.

Maestranza Bullring

MOMENTS >> **The Corridas of Power: Raging Bulls** <<

You may be poised to kit your youngster out in a top-to-toe matador costume, but think twice before taking him to see the real thing at Seville's noble **Maestranza bullring** on Paseo de Colón (📞 95-450-13-82, Easter – October, the best fights are during the April Fair). Even full-blooded, hoary, Hemingway-reading grown men can find the whole thing a little gruesome: watching six deaths on a Sunday afternoon, each ending with a still twitching hulk of prime beef, dragged belly-up from the blood-spattered sand ring, can be gruelling. If your heart is set on it, the advice from aficionados is to buy seats in the shade half way back in the arena and get sound advice on who you're going to see – pick a baddie and you'll have bought yourself a ringside seat to bloodshed, or, worse, bloody boredom set to a trumpet soundtrack, and will have a vegetarian child on your hands at the end. Tickets range from €10 (£6.70) to €40 (£26.80) available from either the ticket office (despacho de entradas) on Calle Adriano, beside the Maestranza or one of the many kiosks along Calle Sierpes. Bullfights take place every Sunday (every day during feria). There are various other routes into the important **Spanish culture of the bull**. The bullring, regarded as the most beautiful in the world – and not just by sevillanos – is a worthy sight in itself (Paseo de Cristóbal Colón 12 📞 *954 22 45 77* Mon – Sun 9.30am–7pm, *www.realmaestranza.com* **English speaking guides** lead tours daily, barring bullfight days) and entry €4 (£2.68) gets you into the Museo Taurino which will give you the chance of a closer look at the trajes de luces, the jazzy matadores' **'suits of light'**, and pictures of famous fans and matadors alike. Another option is to let Toros Tours take you to a **bull ranch**, or, more anodyne still, a stable for thoroughbred horses. *www. torostours.com* 📞 *95 566 42 61*. Or if you want your beef with popcorn, test the waters with an even more arm's length, screen version of events: **Adrien Brody** stars in **Menno Meyjes's film version of famous Spanish bull- fighter** Manuel Rodríguez Sánchez '**Manolete**' in a film due out this year (2007). Meyjes wrote *Indiana Jones and the Last Crusade* with George Lucas.

Triana was the centre of Seville's **azulejo (decorated tile) trade** and outlets like Ceramica Santa Ana on Plaza Callao, with its riotous façade and vast store of pots, plates, ornaments and toys are worth a detour. Calle Betis, along the river, is full of excellent bars and restaurants – great for a **family lunch**, equally good for a serious night out. At Triana's south-western borders lies the **Parque de los Remedios**, which is where the locals go, leaving Parque Maria Luisa to visitors. It's a lovely open space, with sports grounds, play- grounds and a **big duck pond**, and is flanked by ice cream kiosks and cafes where you can refuel while the children play in safety on the other side of the fence.

Sites If You Have More Time

Casa de Pilatos ★★ This **grand ducal palace** is the place to admire old carriages, **Greek and Roman statues** and paintings by Spanish masters but it's the overall feel of a grand palace that youngsters will go for. The 16th-century Andalucian palace of the dukes of Medinaceli combines Gothic, Mudéjar, and Plateresque styles in its courtyards, fountains, and salons. According to tradition, this is a reproduction of Pilate's House in Jerusalem. The museum's first floor is seen by guided tour only, but the ground floor, patios, and gardens are self-guided.

Plaza Pilatos 1. ☏ 95-422-52-98. Admission to museum €8 (£5.42), to patio and gardens €5 (£3.38). Daily June–Sept 9am–7pm, daily Oct–May 9am–6pm.

Torre del Oro Children will enjoy seeing this **12-sided Tower of Gold**, dating from the 13th century, beside the Guadalquivir River if only to count the number of sides. Once covered with gold tiles, it's now a **maritime museum**, the Museo Náutico, which holds drawings and engravings of the port of Seville in its golden heyday.

Paseo de Cristóbal Colón. ☏ 95-422-24-19. Admission €1 (£0.67). Tues–Fri 10am–2pm; Sat–Sun 11am–2pm. Free on Tues. Closed Aug.

Special Events Seville is literally mobbed during the **April Fair** – the most famous feria in Spain, with **bullfights**, **flamenco and folklore** on parade – and again during **Holy Week**, when wooden figures called pasos are paraded through streets by robed penitents. Both are spectacular and deserve their world renown, but hotels hike their prices, and navigating the city becomes very difficult. Semana Santa is a very spiritual, but pretty creepy spectacle which can be claustrophobic, even for adults. Your hotel can recommend broad places to stand so you don't feel too hemmed in. It's quite slow moving though, and children particularly might find it monotonous. The Feria is quite different and will appeal to children of all ages: there's **lights**, **horses**, **dances** and **pretty dresses** to get caught up in, but on the downside it's very much a local affair: like a load of private parties held simultaneously across the city.

April Fair

FAMILY-FRIENDLY ACCOMMODATION

Old world charm comes at a price in Seville, the best boutique hotels in the casco historico (particularly barrio Santa Cruz) are in restored 18th and 19th century buildings. Few, for this reason, have swimming pools, play areas or gardens, and most are quiet, but for the pealing church bells of the city, and in pedestrianised streets. During Holy Week and the Seville Fair, hotels often double, even triple, their rates. Further price increases are sometimes sprung on guests at the last minute. If you're going to be in Seville at these times, arrive with an ironclad reservation and an agreement about the price before checking in.

There are alternatives to staying in Seville: some of the historic outlying villages, which people staying in the city tend to visit on daytrips (Carmona, Italica, Cazalla de la Sierra, see listings below), have a handful of truly lovely upscale B&Bs where space is at less of a premium: so you can stay in the country but see the city too.

Santa Cruz District

surrounded by 16 hectares (40 acres) of olive groves and farmland. Basque-born entrepreneur Rafael Elejabeitia spent millions transforming the house into one of Andalucia's most charming hotels. The kitchen is now under the direction of Ferran Adrià, the famous Catalan chef whose El Bulli restaurant was voted best in the world again in 2006. The 33-course tasting menu promises to be an eating experience you'll never forget – though sausage and chips it definitely ain't. Even if you're not staying here, you might want to call for a dinner reservation. Chances are it'll be one of your finest meals in Seville, although probably not suitable for younger children or faddy eaters.

Calle Virgen de las Nieves s/n, 41800 Sanlúcar la Major, Sevilla. 📞 *95-570-33-44. Fax: 95-570-34-10. www.hbenazuza.com. 44 rooms. €310–390 (£207.70–261.30) double; €435–535 (£291.45–358.45) junior suite; €1,030–1,130 (£690.10–757.10) suite. AE, DC, MC, V. Free parking.*

VERY EXPENSIVE

Hacienda Benazuza/El Bulli Hotel ★★★

For families with children who like to play, explore and roam free, this legendary manor house on a hillside above the rural hamlet of Sanlúcar la Mayor, 19 km (12 miles) south of Seville, is

Sunday Shut-down

Spain, Seville included, still pretty much shuts down every Sunday, though there is a morning coin, stamp and collectors' market in Plaza del Cabildo. OPENCOR Paseo Cristina 3, is a 24-hour supermarket that is open on Sundays stocks nappies, baby food and utensils and a small range of children's clothes and toys.

Closed Jan. From Seville, follow the signs for Huelva and head south on the A-49, taking exit 16. Amenities: 3 restaurants; bar; outdoor pool; tennis court; 24-h room service; babysitting; laundry service/dry cleaning; limited mobility rooms. In room: A/C, TV, minibar, hair dryer, safe, dataport.

EXPENSIVE

Los Seises Right in the centre of Seville, this 16th century former archbishop's palace is crowned by a rooftop swimming pool with views over the Giralda. The comfortable, four-star rooms with terracotta tiled floors, and ochre bedspreads, offer every amenity. The in-house restaurant, La Cocina de los Seises, is set in a pretty patio. Roman and Arabic artifacts liven up the décor, although the atmosphere is a bit lacking.

Children under two are free or from two until 12 receive a 50% discount. One room in the hotel sleeps four and several of the double rooms are linked by interconnecting doors. The concierge will arrange babysitting at any time day or night.

Tercer Patio del Palacio Arzobispal, C/Segovias, 6, 41004 Seville, Spain. ☎ 95 422 94 95. Fax: 95 422 43 34. www.hotellosseises.com. 42 rooms including 37 doubles. Rates, low season (Jan to mid-March, July to mid-Sept, Nov to 31 Dec) €158 double (£106), €190 triple (£127.30), extra bed €30 (£20.10). Breakfast €16 (£10.70). Lunch or dinner €33 (£22.10). Parking €18 (£12.10) per day. All credit cards. 24-hour concierge. In room: AC, TV, minibar, hairdryer, safe.

Casa Imperial ★★★ This hotel near Casa Pilatos dates from the 15th century, when it was the home of the butler to the marquis of Tarifa. The interior is refined, and there are four Andalucian courtyards with exotic plants. The beamed ceilings are original, and sparkling chandeliers hang from the ceilings. All the guest rooms are large – 16 of them are suites and have small kitchens and ample terraces and can sleep up to four. For a bigger family go for rooms 4 and 24 which are connected. Children under 12 only have to pay for a half-price breakfast €9 (£6).

Calle Imperial 29, 41003 Sevilla. ☎ 95-450-03-00. Fax: 95-450-03-30. www.casaimperial.com. 26 rooms. €180–200 (£120.60–134) junior suite; €250–315 (£167.50–211.05) suites, for three person occupancy €315–395 (£211.05–264.65) including breakfast. AE, DC, MC, V. Limited free parking. Bus: 24 or 27. Amenities: Restaurant; bar; 24-h room service; babysitting; laundry service/dry cleaning. In room: A/C, TV, dataport, minibar, hair dryer, safe, shower and bath.

Taverna del Alabardero ★★

FIND This tavern, already famous for its food, is now one of the most charming places to stay in the city. Close to the bullring, it's a restored 19th-century mansion with a spectacular central patio and a romantic atmosphere. The rooms on the third floor have balconies overlooking street scenes as well as whirlpool tubs. The best rooms for families are the three junior suites, which have their own salon though all guestrooms, each decorated in a different regional style, are spacious and comfortable, and can take an extra bed.

Zaragoza 20, 41001 Sevilla. ☏ *95-456-06-37. Fax 95-456-36-66. 7 rooms. €130–150 (£87.10–100.50) double; €150–190 (£100.50–127.30) junior suite. Extra bed €45 (£30.15), children under-8 years free. Rates include continental breakfast. AE, DC, MC, V. Parking €12 (£8). Bus: 21, 25, 30, or 43. Amenities: Restaurant; bar; lounge; 24-h room service; babysitting; laundry service/dry cleaning. In room: A/C, TV, minibar, hair dryer, safe, shower and tub.*

MODERATE

Hotel Doña María ★ A rooftop

pool right in the heart of the old town is one of the main incentives here for families. Each one-off room is well furnished and comfortable, though some are rather small. A few have four-poster beds, others a handful of antique reproductions: the whole effect is a bit twee, but the hotel is still good value for a four-star and well located.

Don Remondo 19, 41004 Sevilla. ☏ *95-422-49-90. Fax 95-421-95-46.* **www.hdmaria.com.** *64 units.*

€241–276 (161.50–185) double. AE, DC, MC, V. Parking €12 (£8). Amenities: Breakfast room; 2 bars; outdoor pool; limited room service; babysitting; laundry service/dry cleaning. In room: A/C, TV, dataport, minibar, hair dryer, safe, bath and shower. Double with extra bed €289 (£193.65).

Las Casas de la Judería ★★

VALUE This 17th century palace, a short walk to the cathedral, once belonged to Spanish aristo the Duke of Beja, one-time patron of Cervantes. A hotel since 1991, it is now one of the best places to stay in Seville. The rooms are a good size, so can take an extra bed, and old-fashioned, some have four-posters. Each has a balcony, some of which face the street while others open onto one of the four typical Andaluz interior patios. The 24 junior suites have living rooms with space for an extra bed, or there are 17 triples. There's always a charge for extra beds.

Plaza Santa María la Blanca, Callejón de Dos Hermanas 7, 41004 Seville. ☏ *95-441-51-50. Fax: 95-442-21-70.* **juderia@casasypalacios.com.** *119 rooms. Triples €190–230 (£127.30–154.10), junior suites €155–190 (£103.85–127.30), extra beds €35–40 (£23.45–26.80). AE, DC, MC, V. Parking €15 (£10). Bus: 21 or 23. Amenities: Restaurant; bar; 24-h room service; babysitting; laundry service/dry cleaning; 2 rooms for those w/limited mobility. In room: A/C, TV, minibar, hair dryer, safe, bath and shower.*

AC Ciudad de Sevilla ★ A

great choice for families, this hotel has all the benefits of the innovative AC chain in a lovely, restored mansion just off the Avenida de las Palmeras, close to the Parque Maria Luisa and a 10 minute taxi ride from the centre. Classy modern interiors, great facilities including Playstation, big bedrooms and smart bathrooms, rooftop pool with a sundeck and fitness centre nearby. The staff are smart and friendly, the restaurant is excellent, the all-day coffee shop offers free drinks and snacks available and minibars are also free. You may never want to go into the city.

Avda Manuel Siurot 25. 41004 Sevilla. ☎ 954 230 505. Fax: 954 238 539. www.ac-hotels.com. 94 rooms. From €125 (£83.75) plus IVA. Breakfast €14 (£9.40) plus IVA (VAT) per person. No charge for extra bed (child). Parking €15 (£6) per night. Amenities: Restaurant, bar, pool, sun deck, fitness centre, Internet access, non-smoker rooms, 24-hour service, free coffee shop, 24-hour laundry service. In room: A/C, TV, Playstation, free minibar, hair dryer, bath, shower.

INEXPENSIVE

Hostería del Laurel ★ **FIND** A big food tavern first and foremost (downstairs has the typical Andalusian interior décor of hams and strings of fresh garlic) the Hosteria, just behind the Alcazabar, also has decent cheap rooms, three of which sleep three. It was here in 1844 that writer Don José Zorrilla created his famous character, Don Juan Tenorio. Guest rooms are simply furnished and immaculately kept, opening onto one of the barrio's time-mellowed, pedestrianized squares. The rooms are spread across several floors of restored old houses with tiny patios and bubbling fountains. Possibly not ideal for those who are light sleepers or have very young children as the square can be very noisy at night.

Plaza de los Venerables 5, 41004 Sevilla. ☎ 95-422-02-95. Fax: 95-421-04-50. www.hosteriadellaurel.com. 21 rooms all with bath and shower. €70–97 (£46.90–64.99) double. 3 triples €85–121 (£56.95–81). Rates include breakfast. AE, DC, MC, V. Bus: 21, 23, 41, or 42. Amenities: Restaurant; bar; 24-hr. room service for drinks; room for those w/limited mobility. In room: A/C, TV, hair dryer, safe.

Hotel Murillo Tucked away on a narrow street in the heart of Santa Cruz, the Murillo (named after the artist who used to live in this district) is just next to the gardens of the Alcázar. There's only one room in the main building that sleeps three, but the hotel also rents two apartments on a daily basis. One sleeps three (with one on the sofa-bed in the living room) while the second can house a family of five in two bedrooms, and has two bathrooms and a sitting room. Both have kitchens with utensils and crockery provided. Sitting rooms have nice architectural details and antique reproductions; behind a screen is a retreat for drinks. Cots supplied on request.

Calle Lope de Rueda 7–9, 41004 Sevilla. ☎ 95-421-60-95. Fax 95-421-96-16. www.hotelmurillo.com. 57 rooms, €81–106 (£54.30–71) triple; apartment A €81–99 (£54.30–63.30); apartment B €135–245 (£90.45–

166.15). AE, DC, MC, V. Parking
€14 (£9.50) nearby. Bus: 21 or 23.
Amenities: Breakfast room; laundry
service/dry cleaning; non-smoking
rooms. In room: A/C; tub and
shower; telephone, TV.

FAMILY-FRIENDLY DINING

As you'd expect in a major city, Seville offers plenty of dining options at all prices. A few top of the range establishments aside, the dining philosophy is simple: this is southern Spain, so **bring the family** and friends and turn your meal into a party. Unlike Britain, youngsters are **expected to be heard as well as seen**, so relax, let them run riot and have another glass of wine. If you're looking for picnic food, the **produce markets in El Arenal and Triana** are good hunting grounds and the basement supermarket in **El Corte Ingles** is reliable. Seville, like much of the rest of Spain and has a glut of simple, **inexpensive restaurants and pizzerias** ideal for families but if you want to explore the full range or have one **special evening**, the options below will help.

EXPENSIVE

El Burladero ★ CONTINENTAL

This restaurant in one of Seville's most prominent hotels is awash with the memorabilia and paraphernalia of bullfighting – so lots to keep older children interested. In fact, the restaurant is named after the wooden barricade behind which bullfighters dash to escape the charge of an enraged bull. The menu features poshed up versions of local country dishes, examples include bacalao al horno con patatas (baked salt cod with potatoes and saffron sauce).

In the Hotel Meliá Colón, Canalejas 1.
📞 *95-450-55-99. Reservations*
recommended. Main courses €14–22
(£9.40–14.75); fixed-price menus
from €35 (£23.45). AE, DC, MC, V.
Daily 1.30–3.30pm and 9–11.30pm.
Closed Aug. Bus: 2 or 43.

Hostería del Laurel ★ FIND

ANDALUSIAN Tiny Plaza de los Venerables is difficult to find, even by labyrinthine Barrio de Santa Cruz standards. Inside, amid Andalusian tiles, beamed ceilings, and more plants, you'll enjoy good regional cooking. Many diners stop for a drink and tapas at the ground-floor bar before going into one of the dining rooms. The hostería is attached to a well-recommended hotel; see 'Where to Stay' above.

Plaza de los Venerables 5. 📞 *95-422-02-95. Reservations recommended.*
Main courses €12–35 (£8–23.45).
AE, DC, MC, V. Daily noon–4pm and
8pm–midnight. Bus: 21, 23, 41, or 42.

MODERATE

Barbiana ★★

ANDALUSIAN/SEAFOOD Close to the Plaza Nueva, this is one of the city's best fish restaurants – the range of fish on display is an education for children in itself. In the classic Andalusian architectural tradition, a tapas bar is up front. In the rear is a cluster of rustically decorated dining rooms. The lunch special is seafood with rice (not available in the evening). Ortiguilla, a sea anemone quick-fried in oil, is worth trying, as are the tortillitas de camarones, latke-shaped chickpea fritters with bits of chopped shrimp and fresh scallions.

Calle Albaredo 11. 95-421-12-39. *Reservations recommended. Main courses €9–20 (£6–13.40). AE, DC, MC, V. Mon–Sat noon–4.30pm and daily 8pm–midnight. Bus: 21, 25, 30, or 40.*

INEXPENSIVE

Taberna Sol Y Sombra

Traditional Andalucian food in Triana served under the traditional Andaluz canopy of hanging hams. Sol Y Sombra has been a bullfighter's den since 1961, serving up excellent home cooking, fish, shellfish, and prized pigs fattened up on the hills of neighbouring Huelva province. Bull (buey) comes cooked in red wine. Great aged cheeses too, so is best for children with eclectic tastes.

Calle Castilla, 151 954 333 935 *www.tabernasolysombra.com 1pm–4pm, 9pm–midnight.*

Cafeteria Serranito SPANISH

This is a cheap, bustling workaday fast-food restaurant, Spanish style. Its position right by the bullring mean it's mobbed after bullfights so there's plenty of atmosphere. But Sevillana families flock here on other days too, coming for the pijotas (small fried hake), cazon en adobo (seasoned dogfish), pez espada (grilled swordfish) and

gambas al ajillo (prawns with garlic). If the interiors are too charmless (plasticky tables and chairs plus the odd stuffed bulls head aren't everyone's cup of tea) then pop around the corner to the simpler Freidura El Arenal instead.

Antonia Diaz 4 95 421 12 43. *No reservations. Mains €6–14 (£4–9.40). No credit cards. Daily noon–midnight.*

Río Grande ANDALUSIAN This

place would be popular for its views of the river and monuments alone let alone the sports events you can watch taking place on the water.

The food's good too, with dishes like stuffed sweet pepper flamenca, fish-and-seafood soup, salmon, chicken-and-shellfish paella, Andalusian-style bull tail, or garlic chicken. A selection of fresh shellfish is brought in daily. There's a snack bar, the Río Grande Pub, and a bingo room.

Calle Betis s/n. 95-427-39-56. *Reservations required. Main courses €15–21 (£10–14). AE, DC, MC, V. Daily 1–4pm and 8pm–midnight. Bus: C3.*

Cervecería Giralda SPANISH

The menu at this informal café and beer hall is as thick as a book, but just ask for what's fresh: white flakes of salt cod come drizzled in a shocking red slug of cream of pepper sauce with a layer of black squid ink on top. If your children want more muted food there are simpler, less colourful dishes like fast-fried boquerones. You have the choice of a street-side seat or at tables inside, but for something more substantial than the tasty tapas there's a sit-down restaurant where you can have proper meals, like Iberian ham stuffed with foie gras. Trade is brisk, and it's as popular with locals as with the many passing tourists.

Calle Mateos Gagos 1. 📞 *95 422 74 35. Tapas €2 (£1.35); meals 18. Daily noon–4.30pm and 8pm–midnight. AE, DC, MC, V.*

Freidura El Arenal SPANISH This is a proper old chippy, Sevilla-style. There's a fuzzy telly in one corner, a fan on the L-shaped marble counter, weighing scales and two big deep-fat fryers and little else. The shop's been in the Rey family since 1904 and the wood propping up the counter carries the scars. It all reeks of oil and bubbling boquerones. Dogfish (cazón en adobo) and squid (chocos) steeped in oregano, garlic and vinegar are the house specials, but there's hake, fish croquettes, and fresh potato chips and jumbo prawns too. It's all battered and fried and served up by the kilo in plain paper bags. Three tall tables out on the street corner are the only effort at accommodating their regulars, your fingers the cutlery. Over the street is a nice place serving ice creams.

Arfe 8, 41001 Sevilla 📞 *600858978. Times: 8.30–1030pm. Cash only. Closed Monday.*

El Rinconcillo Gerona 40 (📞 *95-422-31-83*), at the northern edge of Barrio de Santa Cruz, has a 1930s ambience, partly because of its real age and partly because of its owners' refusal to change one iota of the decor. It may actually be the oldest bar in Seville, with a history dating from 1670. It has dim lighting, heavy ceiling beams, and marble-topped tables, and the bartender will mark your tab in chalk on a well-worn wooden countertop. It's especially known for its tapas, salads, omelettes, hams, and selection of cheeses. Look for the Art Nouveau tile murals. Open every day from 1pm to 2am. A complete meal will cost around €20 (£13.40).

Some of the best seafood tapas are served at **La Alicantina**, Plaza del Salvador 2 (📞 *95-422-61-22*), which is always bursting with people, who mill around the bar and spill over the pavement. Come for generous portions of clams marinara, fried squid, grilled shrimp, fried cod, and clams in béchamel sauce. It's open September to June daily noon to midnight; July and August daily 10.30am to 4pm and 8pm to 1am. Tapas range upward from €2 (£13.40). At the northern end of Murillo Gardens, opening onto a quiet square with flower boxes and an ornate iron railing, **Modesto**, Cano y Cueto 5 (📞 *95-441-68-11*), also serves fabulous seafood tapas. Upstairs there's a good-value restaurant. Modesto is open daily from 8pm to 2am. Tapas are priced from €3 (£2).

Tapas

Tapas are said to have originated in Seville, and the old-fashioned **Casa Román**, Plaza de los Venerables 1 (☎ *95-422-84-83*), in the Barrio de Santa Cruz, looks as if it has been dishing them up since day one. (It's actually been around since 1934.) Open Monday to Friday 9.30am to 4pm and 7pm to midnight, Saturday and Sunday 11am to 4pm and 7.30pm to midnight. Tapas are priced from €3.50 (£2.35).

Shopping With Children

You will find all the major fashion labels such as Zara and Mango are here, most with extensive childrens' sections The most fertile ground for shoppers is the area centring on **Calle Sierpes** and **Calle Velazquez**, between **Plaza San Francisco** and **Plaza Duque de la Victoria**. All are a good **third cheaper than in the UK**. Seville is the city of a thousand shoe shops and the stores in **Calle Sagasta** (off Sierpes) in particular offer everything from flamenco shoes to Campers.

Ceramics Near the cathedral, **El Postigo**, Arfe s/n (☎ *95-456-00-13*), has a wide selection of Andalusian ceramics. Some of the pieces are much too big to fit into your suitcase; others – especially the hand-painted tiles and animals – make charming souvenirs that can easily be transported for children. It's open Monday to Saturday 10am to 2pm, Monday to Friday 5 to 8.30pm. Near the town hall, **Martian**, Calle Sierpes 74 (☎ *95-421-34-13*), sells a wide array of painted tiles and ceramics: vases, plates, cups, serving dishes, and statues, all made in or near Seville. Open Monday to Saturday 10am to 2pm and 5 to 8.30pm.

For a wider range (and lower prices) try crossing the river to Triana. There are dozens of outlets in the streets between the two bridges – Puente de Isabel II and Puente de San Telmo.

Department Stores El Corte Inglés, Plaza Duque de la Victoria, 13B (☎ *95-459-70-00*), is the best of the several department stores clustered in Seville's commercial centre. It features multilingual translators and rack after rack of every conceivable kind of merchandise for the well-stocked home, kitchen, and closet. It's open Monday through Saturday from 10am to 9pm.

Music El Corte Ingles (see above) has a good music section but the flamenco specialists are Allegro at Calle Dos de Mayo 38 (☎ *954 21 61 93*). They will be happy to talk about your likes and dislikes and explain a little about the mysteries of flamenco.

Performing Arts

Flamenco: Making A Big Song & Dance

Even the youngest souls can't help but be captivated by the vibrancy and passion of flamenco. It is everywhere here: as a soundtrack in bars, drifting from open windows in the whitewashed streets, being performed, impromptu, by anyone from pre-teen girls to old women on street corners and in the smallest of plazas and, of course, at organized events aimed at the thousands of tourists who want a taste of authentic southern Spain. Young children will particularly enjoy the pretty costumes as well as the castanets and colourful dancing. If you've got teenage girls, they may even want to have a go; there are dozens of flamenco schools in the city.

Seville – along with Granada and Jerez – is one of the focal points of this (originally) romany art form and where the other two cities remain sniffy about the 'purity' of their versions,

Seville's variation is acknowledged as the most accessible.

Old Spanish hands tend to sneer at the flamenco put on in the bars of the Barrio Santa Cruz as rehearsed tourist nonsense. But the search for authenticity and the urge for spontaneity become less pressing when you're pushing a baby-buggy. There are a number of giant corporate flamenco extravaganzas up for grabs in Seville, if you fancy something a bit RiverDance with castanets head for **El Palacio Andaluz** (Centro - c/Maria Auxiliadora, ☎ *18 954 534 720 www.elpalacioandaluz. com*) which is a razzle-dazzle floor show in a ballroom of a theatre with dinner thrown in. If your family has the concentration span for it, go instead for a more intimate, but strong flamenco puro performance at the **Tablao Los Gallos**, Plaza de Santa Cruz 11 (☎ *95-421-69-81, www.tablaolosgallos.com*, 8–10pm and 10.30–12.30am, €27 (£18.10) including a

Flamenco Dresses

Fan male

Carmen fluttered her fan and broke hearts – and your children can do their own fluttering too. The best place to pick up a traditional Andalusian fan is **Casa Rubio**, Sierpes 56 (℡ 95-422-68-72). It stocks one of the city's largest selections, from the austere and dramatic to the florid and fanciful. It's open Monday to Saturday from 9.30am to 1.30pm and 4.30 to 8.30pm.

drink). Since it was founded in 1966, this little club has launched some of the biggest names in today's flamenco circuit, and those that perform today divide their time between here, their own teaching academies and global tours promoting the art. Its leading competitor, charging roughly the same prices with more or less the same program, is **El Arenal**, Calle Rodó 7 (℡ 95-421-64-92 *www.tablao elarenal.com*), where you'll sit at tiny, cramped tables with barely enough room to breathe, let alone clap. If these two seem too tourist-trodden, try **Casa de la Memoria** (c/Ximénez de Enciso, 28, Santa Cruz), which has twice-nightly shows in an 18th century patio for just €12 (£8).

Museo del Baile Flamenco

Flamenco comes alive for children at this **new museum** situated in an 18th century building between the Cathedral and the Alcazabar. Opened in April 2006 this part dance school, part hang-out and part **interactive exhibition** offers **masterclasses** and **performances** as well as courses in **dance**, **singing** and **guitar**. The daytime snackbar by night switches into a café cantante, or flamenco stage. It was set up by the director and

choreographer of Ballet Flamenco de Andalucía, Cristina Hoyos, who has nearly 40 years experience on the flamenco circuit, half of which she spent as first dancer of the prestigious Antonio Gaddes Company. An on-site shop sells flamenco clothes and accessories, DVDs books and CDs.

Museo del Baile Flamenco, 3 Calle Manuel Rojas Marcos, Seville. ℡ 954-34-03-11, fax: 011-34-954-34-03-64. Detailed information in Spanish about performances and classes is on **www.museoflamenco.net**. *From April to October, open 9am–7pm and from November to March 9am–6pm. Admission is €10 (£6.70) for adults and €5 (£3.35) for children.*

Seville Province

Sierra Morena's Sierra Norte

The sheer vastness of the **Sierra Norte Natural Park** in the Sierra Morena north east of Seville, the mountainous northern border of Andalusia, will delight **active children** wanting to explore and run riot through its hills, ridges, thick forests of oak and chestnut and amazing landscapes such as the weird limestone labyrinths of **Cerro del Hierro** and the waterfalls and ponds of **Rio Hueznar**. Go on foot or bike or why not take to the saddle and explore the area on horseback? Try to get to **Constantina**, from where you can take one of the area's most **dramatic walks**. The tourist office has a list of a dozen walks from two to 11 km in length that even families with young children can explore. Big-lunged adventure – from fishing and hunting is available too.

Cazalla de la Sierra www. sierranortedesevilla.com Tiny little Cazalla de la Sierra 75 km from Seville is the **most central village** in the Sierra Norte and a good place for families to base themselves. Children of all ages will enjoy exploring the Neolithic caves nearby, whilst the picturesque village, with a population of only 5263, has a number of grand civic buildings, a chapel, hermitage, convent and the beautiful Church of the Consolacion, an architectural cross-breed of Islamic, Mudéjar and Reinassance styles, worth exploring too.

Getting there: Take the A- 432 from Seville by the regional highway. Cazalla de la Sierra Plaza Mayor, s/n ☎ *954 88 35 62 www.turismo sevilla.org.*

FAMILY-FRIENDLY ACCOMMODATION

Trasierra A 16th century olive mill and a real piece of Sierra Morenan utopia for families, who can take over any of the seven guest rooms, the cottage, or the whole place. It's relaxed but refined, and there are lots of activities nearby such as riding, walking, painting, yoga, massage, ping-pong, bicycles and flood-lit tennis court too. Babies stay free, but if you have young children it's best to take over the whole house.

☎ *95 488 43 24 www.trasierra. co.uk Singles €150 (£100.50), doubles €200–250 (£134–167.50), suites €300–350 (£201–234.50). Cottage €500 (£335) inc breakfast. Lunch €20 (£13.40); dinner €45 (£30.15). DC, MC, V, Private parking. Closed Jan, Feb, March apart from whole house bookings. No pets. Internet. CCR, TV DVD, Fax, kitchen, guest's kitchenette, fridges, coffeemaker, hairdryer, iron, laundry, no minibar. No phones.*

La Cartuja de Cazalla The prospect of spending a night in this former Carthusian monastery – however splendid – is not to every family's taste. A massive and hard-fought restoration project has preserved a church, its dome, two chapels, a belfry and the original cloisters from ruin: plenty for curious children to explore. They can then cool off in the swimming pool or natural spring-water pool. Today contemporary art is exhibited in the buildings. A bountiful organic vegetable farm yields lettuce, tomatoes, spinach and melons, plus the odd pig, all go into the home-cooked meals. Rooms in the new quarter are pared-down and functional. Families can also opt to stay in the comfortable self-catering cottage. Horse-riding and cycling are on offer nearby.

Monasterio de la Cartuja Cazalla de la Sierra, Apdo-46, 41370, Seville. 📞 95 488 45 16. Fax: 95 488 47 07. www.cartujadecazalla.com 14 rooms and a small cottage. Rates (€90 (£60.30) double, €120 (£80.40) suite). Prices include breakfast. 10% discount for stays of more than one night. Extra bed €15 (£10), cots €10 (£6.70). The cottage: €120 (£80.40) per night (two nights minimum), or €600 (£402) a week, breakfast not included. A 25% deposit is required to book. Meals €25 (£16.75) inc wine and coffee. Closed on Christmas Day. All credit cards. Pets welcome. Parking.

Las Navezuelas There are lots of farm animals for children to josh around with at this 16th-century olive mill which the Cicorella-Tena family have turned into great rustic choice for families. Upholstery is spartan (no pictures hang on the walls, instead the family calls their windows, which look out over meadows and mountain ranges, 'living murals'). There's a good shared sitting room, a swimming pool, nature rambles galore, and besides really rock-bottom single and double bedrooms (so there's no need to share) there are two apartments to sleep four and six respectively.

Apartado 14, Cazalla de la Sierra, Seville. 📞 34 954 884 764 Fax: 34 954 884 5944 doubles, 2 suites, 3 studio (for two plus kitchen), 2 apartments (for four in 2 beds plus kitchen) 1 apartment for 6 (three beds with kitchen). Doubles €65–68 (£43.55–45.55). Also four self-catering studios from €87 (£58.30). V, MC, Euro cards. Closed 2/1/07–25/2/07. Children under three free, extra bed €17–20 (£11.40–13.40), apartments €100–135 (£67–90.45). Dinner all year. Lunch provided in summer.

1 TV, trekking, cycling, riding, bird-watching. Salt water pool www.lasnavezuelas.com

Carmona and the Villages of the Campina

Much of Seville province is covered by a vast plain of rich agricultural land, its towns rising from fields of wheat or olive groves and visible from miles away. Carmona, to the east of Seville, is a veritable history book with a share of **grand fortresses and gateways** and a **Roman necropolis** complete with subterranean tombs you'll struggle to keep the children out of.

School history lessons will come alive in **Carmona** an ancient city dating from Neolithic times within an easy hour-long bus trip from the main terminal in Seville. Situated 34 km (21 miles) east of Seville, it grew in power and prestige under the Moors, establishing ties with Castile in 1252.

Surrounded by fortified walls, Carmona has **three Moorish fortresses** – one a parador, and the other two, the Alcázar de la Puerta de Córdoba and Alcázar de la Puerta de Sevilla. The top attraction is **Seville Gate**, with its double Moorish arch opposite St Peter's Church. The town itself is a virtual national landmark, filled with narrow streets, whitewashed walls, and Renaissance mansions. Plaza San Fernando is the most important square, with many elegant 17th-century houses and some pleasant little bars and cafes for little ones to rest their weary legs. In the area known as Jorge Bonsor (named for the original discoverer of the ruins) is a **Roman amphitheatre** as well as a Roman necropolis. On site is a **Museo Arqueológico** (📞 *95-423-24-01*) displaying artifacts found at the site. Hours are Wednesday through Saturday from 9am to 8pm, Tuesday from 3 to 8pm, and Sunday from 9am to 2pm. Admission is €1.50 (£1) for adults and free for students and children.

Casa de Carmona ★ ★ This property is one of the most elegant hotels in Andalusia. It was built as the home of the Lasso family during the 1500s. Several years ago, a team of entrepreneurs turned it into a luxury hotel but retained the marble columns, massive masonry, and graceful proportions of the original. Plaza de Lasso 1, 41410 Carmona (📞 *95-419-10-00*; fax: *95-419-01-89*; *www.casade carmona.com*). Rates are €120–270 (£80.40–180.90) for a double, and €500–900 (£335–603)

for a suite. AE, DC, MC, and V are accepted.

Italica and Aljarafe Students of Roman history and children will love scrambling over the ruins at Itálica (📞 *95-599-73-76*) an ancient city a couple of miles northwest of Seville on the major road to Lisbon, near the small town of Santiponce.

Two of the most famous of Roman emperors, Trajan and Hadrian, were born in the town founded by Publius Cornelius Scipio Africanus in 206BC after the battle of Ilipa. A small **museum** displays some of the Roman statuary found here, although the finest pieces have been shipped to Seville. Many mosaics, depicting beasts, gods, and birds, are on exhibit, and others are constantly being discovered. The ruins, including a Roman theatre, can be explored for €1.50 (£1). The site is open April to September, Tuesday to Saturday from 9am to 8pm and Sunday from 9am to 3pm. October to March, it's

Carmona

open Tuesday to Saturday from 9am to 5.30pm and Sunday from 10am to 4pm.

Hacienda de San Rafael This 300-year-old former olive farmhouse midway between Jerez and Seville, where the emphasis is on the great outdoors. Guests come here to relax and enjoy the big bougainvillea-filled patio, garden, infinity pool, paddle tennis court, 350 acres of land and big sweeping views of the Andaluz plains. There are lots of communal spaces too. You can sleep either in split-level bedrooms that are set around the patio in the main building (each of which has its own veranda) or, for extra privacy, opt instead for the thatched cottages or 'casitas' which are in their own garden, and have their own chozitas (sit-outs) and living rooms. All the rooms have rollaway beds, so can easily sleep one extra.

Apartado 28. Carretera N-IV (Km 594) Las Cabezas de San Juan, Seville – Spain. ☎ *34 95 5872193 Fax: 34 95 5872201 www.haciendadesan rafael.com 11 twin/double bedrooms, €225 (£150.75); 3 casitas all with tub and shower, pantry, living room, pantry, gallery 'siesta zones', €480 (£321.60) inc breakfast. Extra bed €105 (£70.35). Supper €55 (£36.85) per person. April–October. 2 outdoor swimming pools. Paddle court.*

HUELVA

Children will love Huelva's wide sandy beaches, which are relatively quiet even in high season, The district forms the

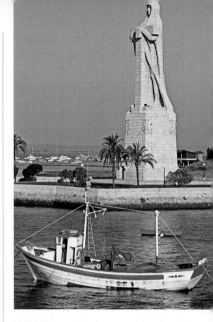

Huelva

northwestern segment of the **Costa de la Luz**, west of Cadiz, and is Andalusia's western **border with Portugal's Algarve region**. There are some beautiful unspoiled pockets of sand here and plenty to amuse youngsters: a ruined crumple left over from 16th century Berber defence lies in the middle of deserted **Playa de Torre Del Loro**, while 20 km of sandbanks crossed by streams, heaped up high in the dunes of Asperillo makes the monumental **Playa de Castilla**. If you are after a smash-and-grab look at Seville and Cordoba with some beautiful nature and impeccable gastronomy thrown in, a good loop would take you from Huelva up to the beautiful natural park of **Aracena** (with the Rio Tinto mines and nature trails the bait for the children), then get some bucket-and-spade action on this less Anglicized stretch of the Costa De La Luz before flying out from Seville again. History comes alive for children at **Palos de la Frontera** from where three caravels carrying 90 seafarers set sail on the 3rd of August 1492, little knowing that their journey would end with the discovery of America: there's lots of monuments to Christopher Columbus, and many of the buildings bear witness to the wealth the discoveries created for Spain. For foodies, the province is home to the prized black-footed Iberian pigs which produce **jamón Ibérico**. Jabugo is the centre of a big pig industry. It's not a lovely town, and the smell which pervades is not one which will have vegetarians drooling. But the quality of the ham is undeniable and it's worth a visit for curiosity's sake.

Essentials

Getting There

Although it is technically classed as the Costa De La Luz, Huelva's coast is awkward to get to from Sanlúcar de Barrameda, the closest town on Cadiz's side: the protected Doñana national park means you'd have to drive back into Seville to get down here. It's easy to get to from Seville, though: buses and trains from Seville take an hour and 90 minutes respectively. The bus station is at Avenida Dr Rubio (℡ 95-925-69-00), the Estación de Sevilla ℡ *902 24 02 02 www.renfe.es*, is on Avenida Italia.

Visitor Information

The **tourist office** is at Av. de Alemania 12 (℡ *95-925-74-03*; Mon–Fri 9am–7pm, Sat–Sun 10am–2pm). *www.turismo huelva.org*.

Coastal Huelva

Between Huelva city and the Doñana park, a long string of fine beaches is bookended by **Mazagón** and **Matalascañas**, all of them broad, sandy and good for children. Further west, the resorts of **Isla Cristina** and **Isla Canela** – heaving with Spanish holidaymakers in high summer, surprisingly empty for the rest of the year – have good beaches, marshlands to explore and, away from the slightly sterile apartments and beach front hotels, pleasant town centres with cheery bars and restaurants.

Inland Huelva

Gentle hikes, carefree horse rides, lush green valleys, ridges and plains and caves packed with stalactites and stalagmites await **active families** to the Huelvan extension of the Sierra Morena mountain chain, north west of Seville. The **Sierra de Aracena y Picos de Aroche nature park** is knoll upon knoll of acorn trees. One of the sweetest villages here is **Alájar**: tucked into a fold of cork trees, peeled of their bark at the base. The name is Arabic for stone and the quaint village's lovely narrow

Christopher Columbus

The great explorer is the main focus for children in Huelva, where a large statue on the west bank of the river commemorates the departure of his third voyage of discovery. About 7 km (4½ miles) up on the east bank of the Tinto River, a monument marks the exact spot where his ships were anchored while they were being loaded with supplies before departure. Children will have great fun scrabbling over the decks of the life-size models of Columbus's ships.

streets are duly paved with the marble that used to be excavated from local mines. Overhanging this pocket of 813 people is the **Peña de Arias Montano**, a rock cliff, there's a small hippy community living (organically, by solar power, from out of camper vans) nearby. Stay and eat here, but apart from nature trails, the best children's pursuit is in the bigger neighbouring town of **Aracena** (population 7000), at the **Cave of Marvels**: two whole kilometres of underground lakes and caves packed with stalactites and stalagmites.

Getting There & Around

Regular buses to Aracena leave the Plaza de Armas in Seville (one way, €6 (£4); round trip, €9 (£6)). Two major roads cross the Sierra: the east-west Seville-Lisbon N433 and the north-south Huelva-Badajoz (Extremadura) N435. There are twice-daily trains from Huelva to the Sierra's two stations: Almonaster-Cortegana and El Repilado. The best way to explore the villages is on foot or horseback.

What to See & Do

Gruta de las Maravillas – the Cave of Marvels Children will delight in exploring this chain of underground grottoes strung out across 2130 damp metres and showing how the organic designs of minerals can match any man-made cathedral. Underground chambers – 'Diamond', 'Great Lake', 'Chamber of the Nudes', 'the Shell', 'Emerald' and 'God's Glasswork' – have floors of sparkling water pools, and ceilings of mineral spears which will delight curious minds.

Pozo de la Nieve, s/n 21200 Aracena (Huelva) ☏ 34 959128355 ☏ 959128206/ Fax 34 959128355. 10am–1.30pm, 3–6pm. Adults €7.70 (£5.15). Groups of 25 or more €6 (£4) pax; pensioners and children 6–18 years €5.50 (£3.70). Discounts not valid Saturdays, Sundays and public holidays.

Museo Minero De Riotinto

What can be more fascinating for children than going back in time 5000 years on a tour of a mine. Put on a helmet and jump aboard the tourist train that goes along the rio, whose basin is the natural cleft running between

Caves at Aracena

Huelva's north and south. There's a contemporary art gallery and **corta atalaya**, one of the largest opencast mines in the world to explore too. There's also distinctly out of place **Bella Vista English quarter**, a slice of British Victorian village architecture created by the British engineers who pioneered the now multi-national company in the 19th century. Guided tours in English.

Villages Across the Sierra, from Zufre to Aroche, are dotted lots of little villages. The sweetest lie in the stretch between Cortegana and Aracena, taking in Linares de la Sierra, Alajar, and Almonaster La Real.

Step back in time at the castle of Cortegana dating from the 13th and 14th century Reconquest and grab some great views. It is challenged, though, for best sunset by Almonaster La Real's 10th century hilltop mosque, which is the last shard of Muslim architecture left in the area. What roads there are in the Aracena park are barely trafficked, and the hamlets here are mostly linked by tracks and trails. Los Madroñeros, though, is one where you really do step back into a world without cars.

'Sierra De Aracena – a Walk!' by David and Ros Braun (*www.dwgwalking.co.uk* £11.99) is a good guide with maps to trails and the Huelva tourist office does really spectacular, child friendly manuals.

Where to Stay

Huelvan Costa de la Luz

Accommodation is severely limited along the Costa de la Luz so it's crucial to have reservation in summer – and particularly so for families with young children. You can stay at a government-run parador east of Huelva in Mazagón (see below) or in the beach resort of Ayamonte, near the Portuguese border. Where you're unlikely to want to stay overnight is the dreary industrial port of Huelva itself.

Ayamonte's clean, wide, sandy beaches and calm waves are a favourite with children. Portions of the beaches are even calmer because of sandbars 50 to 100 m (164–328 ft) from the shore, which become virtual islands at low tide. The nearest beaches to Ayamonte are miles away at Isla Canela and Moral.

Parador de Ayamonte ★★

VALUE One of the leading in Ayamonte with a welcome outdoor pool for children to play in. Commanding a sweeping view of the river and the surrounding towns along its banks – sunsets are memorable here – the parador stands about 30 m (100 ft) above sea level on the site of the old castle of Ayamonte. It was built in a severe modern style and boasts Nordic-inspired furnishings. Most rooms are medium-size and comfortably appointed, with bathrooms with bath/shower combos.

Av. de la Constitución s/n, 21400 Ayamonte. ☏ 95-932-07-00. Fax 95-902-20-19. www.parador.es. 54 rooms. €89–110 (£59.60–73.70) double; €137–173 (£91.80–115.90) suite. Rates include breakfast. AE, DC,

MC, V. Free parking. From the centre of Ayamonte, signs for the parador lead you up a winding road to the hilltop, about 1 km (½ mile) southeast of the centre. Amenities: 2 restaurants; bar; outdoor pool; limited room service; babysitting; laundry service/dry cleaning; nonsmoking rooms; limited mobility rooms. In room: A/C, TV, minibar, hair dryer, safe.

Parador de Mazagón ★★

A great option for families wanting to stay outside Huelva and close to a beach. Situated on a pine grove cliff overlooking a sandy beach, this parador, which occupies a rambling 1960s structure, has comfortable, spacious rooms with balconies and terraces overlooking an expansive garden. Many prefer to stay in this village outside Huelva than at one of the more impersonal hotels within the city centre. Even if you're just driving and exploring the area, consider a lunch stopover here. The chef specializes in regional dishes of Huelva province.

Carretera de San Juan del Puerto a Matalascañas s/n, 21130 Mazagón. ☏ 95-953-63-00. Fax: 95-953-62-28. 63 units. €107–123 (£71.70–82.40) double; €142–168 (£95.15–112.80) suite. AE, DC, MC, V. Free parking. Exit from Magazón's eastern sector, following the signs to the town of Matalascañas. Take the coast road (Hwy. 442) to the parador. Amenities:

TIP ◁ **Jamon Jamon** ◁

Each pata negra (black leg) pig scoffs 1000 pounds of acorns in the three months from October before its slaughter to become jamón ibérico The best and biggest place to buy ham is from Mesón Sánchez Romero Carvajal (Calle San Juan del Puerto. ☏ *959 121 071*).

Restaurant; bar; lounge; limited room service; outdoor pool; indoor pool; gym; sauna; Jacuzzi; tennis court; babysitting; laundry service/dry cleaning; non-smoking rooms; 1 room for those with limited mobility. In room: A/C, TV, minibar, hair dryer, safe, dataport.

Family-Friendly Accommodation

Sierra De Aracena

Hotel La Posada Lucy, who's English, and Angel, her Sevillano husband, run a simple rustic B&B in sleepy little Alajar, and are brilliant people to tap for tips on activities like walking and riding locally and have a well-stocked library full of *National Geographics* and local walking guides. The eight rooms here, just refurbished and spotlessly clean, aren't massive but there's a lovely communal lounge with an open fire. The best place for families is the self-contained family rooms, in the attic, which sleep seven.

c/Médico Emilio González, 2. ☎ *959 12 57 12. Alajar www.laposada dealajar.com. Bar, café in room, games, reference library, TV shared lounge. V, MC (no Diners or AM). The family room is €110 (£73.70) for four people then an extra €20 (£13.40) per person.*

Family-Friendly Dining

If your children love ham, Jabugo, just around the corner, is known as making the best in Spain (no mean feat for a country in which every tasca dangles with ham haunches), the pig-food is in the forests all around you: holm and cork oaks. Pig dishes really are amazing here, and don't stumble over the price of Iberico. It'll be 10 times as steep for a plate at home. Other specialities include any recipe using one of the 200 different types of setas, or wild mushrooms.

La Botica de Alájar, calle Andalucía 9, ☎ *959 125 768; 660 147 366.* A simple rustic restaurant, wood beamed ceilings, white washed walls, Cruzcampo on tap, predictably incredible hams. A platter of Iberico is melt in the mouth. Other dishes are perfectly proportioned: breaded Iberico pork stuffed with ham and cheese, pork casserole, roast leg of suckling pig. The menu is translated into English. A menu del dia costs €10 (£6.70). Open Thursday–Sunday; 1pm till mid afternoon, depending on custom. 8.30pm till it closes.

4 Cordoba

CORDOBA

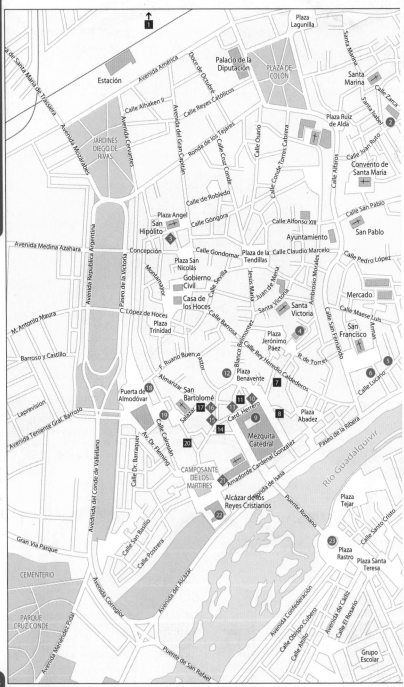

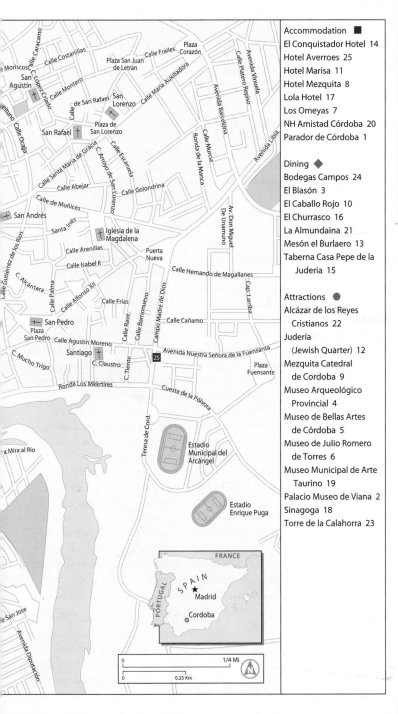

Accommodation ■
El Conquistador Hotel 14
Hotel Averroes 25
Hotel Marisa 11
Hotel Mezquita 8
Lola Hotel 17
Los Omeyas 7
NH Amistad Córdoba 20
Parador de Córdoba 1

Dining ◆
Bodegas Campos 24
El Blasón 3
El Caballo Rojo 10
El Churrasco 16
La Almundaina 21
Mesón el Burlaero 13
Taberna Casa Pepe de la
    Juderia 15

Attractions ●
Alcázar de los Reyes
    Cristianos 22
Judería
    (Jewish Quarter) 12
Mezquita Catedral
    de Cordoba 9
Museo Arqueológico
    Provincial 4
Museo de Bellas Artes
    de Córdoba 5
Museo de Julio Romero
    de Torres 6
Museo Municipal de Arte
    Taurino 19
Palacio Museo de Viana 2
Sinagoga 18
Torre de la Calahorra 23

Why visit Cordoba with children? The simple answer is atmosphere. A visit to Cordoba can bedazzle all members of the family and this is particularly true if you go in May for one of the festivals. Although at any time of the year, children who have studied Islam in RE at school will identify with the great Mezquita mosque/cathedral. The city is beautiful, with narrow streets, flower-filled patios and cobbled squares with splashing fountains for ice cream stops.

Ten centuries ago, when it was the capital of Muslim Spain and Europe's biggest city, Cordoba was a flourishing intellectual and cultural centre. Its 900,000 inhabitants had 300 mosques to choose between, and its architecture was on a par with that of Damascus, Constantinople and Baghdad. Infighting among its Muslim leaders led to the city's collapse in 1031, and the capital of the Caliphs moved to Seville. Greedy hordes sacked the city, tearing down its buildings and carting off its treasures, and it was taken back by the Christians in 1236.

The Mezquita, its interiors candy-striped red and white like a stick of rock for children to explore, is the main draw but there are heaps of other artistic and architectural riches to explore besides: the old Arab and Jewish quarters are a lovely chaos of narrow cobbled streets with whitewashed houses, pretty patios, and balconies.

Without doubt, the best time to visit is May, when there are three major festivals. The first, **Las Cruces de Mayo** sees elaborately decorated crosses raised all over the city, accompanied by festivity, dancing, outdoor drinking and partying and flamenco displays; it's a good chance to get a flavour of flamenco without having to sit through a long performance in a more formal *tablao.* Hot on the heels of the Crosses festival is the famous **Patio Festival**, when residents open up their carefully-tended patios to the public. This is a marvellous chance to snoop around private gardens; many of the houses are designed along traditional Moorish lines, with low-rise buildings encircling a shaded patio, often crammed with lemon and orange trees.

At the end of May is the major festival, **La Feria**, a great time for families to visit, although you'll need to book a long way ahead. The Feria takes place at the fairgrounds outside the city and includes nine days of horse displays, fairground rides, processions, competitions and general merrymaking. Each city establishment has a *caseta* – at least, a stall and at most, an elaborate exhibition structure akin to a large house, where food and wine are served and guests enjoy live music and entertainment. Buses run round the clock between the city centre and the fairgrounds.

ESSENTIALS

Getting There

By Train Cordoba is well connected by train: the **AVE** high-speed train to and from Seville takes 40 minutes, making it a feasible day-trip (one-way ticket €24 (£16.10). There are 12 trains daily from Malaga; the journey takes 2 to 3 hours and tickets cost €13 (£8.70) to €19 (£12.75). The station is at Glorieta de las Tres Culturas, off Avenida de América in the North of the city. Bus no. 3 runs between the rail station and the old city centre. For rail information, call ☏ 90-224-02-02; for AVE schedules or information, call ☏ 90-224-02-02. The RENFE advance-ticket office in Cordoba is at Ronda de los Tejares 10 (☏ 95-747-58-84).

By Bus Alsina Graells Sur (☏ 95-727-81-00) buses arrive at Diego Serrano 14 on the outskirts of the city near Paseo de la Victoria. The most popular routes are between Cordoba and Seville, with 10 to 13 buses per day. The trip takes two hours and costs €8.60 (£5.75) for a one-way ticket. 10 buses a day drive the three hours between Granada and Cordoba: €10 (£6.70) one-way.

By Car The city is 166 km northwest of Granada and 129 km east of Seville and is clearly signposted on the E5. The drive from Malaga is three hours, but you should stay the night, not attempt a day trip, as half the fun of this city is after dark.

Visitor Information

The **tourist office**, Calle Torrijos 10 (☏ 90-201-77; www.andalucia.org), is open Monday to Friday 9.30am to 6.30pm, Saturday 10am to 2pm and 5 to 7pm, Sunday and holidays 10am to 2pm.

Exploring Cordoba

Away from the main tourist attractions, Cordoba is a bustling city of verdant avenues, pedestrianised shopping areas and cheery plazas where the locals stand or sit and chat; in the heat of summer, which can exceed that of Seville, it's hard to do more. There are plenty of lovely old churches tucked into the streets up the hill from the Juderia (the Jewish quarter), as

FUN FACT ⟩ **Fun and Learning** ⟨

Cordoba was a place of extravagant lifestyles with pleasure palaces and huge harems and sophisticated learning (its library had 400,000 books and the city was where Europe's first university was founded) in the 8th to the 11th century, while most of Europe was languishing in the Dark Ages. It was then that a pilgrimage to the Great Mezquita (or Mosque) was said to have been as holy a journey as the Haj to Mecca.

Seneca the Elder, one of the greatest philosophers, lived in Cordoba in Roman times. He was a fan of work and patience, urging Romans to 'Toil to make yourself remarkable by some talent or other.', telling them that 'It is not because things are difficult that we do not dare; it is because we do not dare that things are difficult.'

well as a magnificent, part-restored Roman temple off Calle Claudio Marcelo. Everything in the modern city revolves around Plaza de las Tendillas, with its cafes and ice cream parlours. But for a sense of what Cordoba was like 500 years ago, make your way to the Plaza de la Corredera. Over the years it has been used for markets, inquisitions, trials, horse races and athletics.

Getting Around

Cordoba's sites are all within a compact area of labyrinthine cobblestone streets. You can walk everywhere, but there's also the family-friendly option of chartering a coche de caballo, horse-drawn carriage, from one of the streets around the Mezquita and Alcazar district.

WHAT TO SEE & DO

Children's Top 5 Attractions

❶ **Mezquita-Catedral de Córdoba** The red and white striped brick and stone arches are a forest for children to explore. The mix of architectural styles, intricate ceiling and mihrab will leave youngsters spellbound. See p. 90.

❷ **Alcázar de los Reyes Cristianos** It may be a wonderful example of military architecture but if you've got young children you know they'll be most engrossed by the gardens and fish ponds here. See p. 91.

❸ **Botanical Gardens** Children will enjoy the Ethnobotanical Museum exploring man's relationship with plants, plus the gardens offer a great natural environment to charge around for a while. See p. 91.

❹ **Museo Municipal de Arte Taurino** A bit of gore will appeal to teenagers and in this museum there's as much dashing or disgusting – depending on your standpoint – historical bull fighting nit bits to keep youngsters occupied. p. 92.

❺ **Torre de la Calahorra** There's plenty of strange and unfamiliar wax figures, instruments and models in here to attract all the family with the bonus of a panoramic view of the Roman bridge, the river, and the cathedral/mosque at the top of the Tower. p. 93.

Mezquita-Catedral de Córdoba ★★★ From the 8th century, the Mezquita was the crowning Muslim architectural achievement in the West. It's a fantastic labyrinth of red-and-white striped double arches. With typical tact, the Christians slapped a cathedral in the middle of the mosque in the 16th-century. Additional ill-conceived annexes later turned the Mezquita into an architectural oddity. Its most interesting feature is the mihrab ★★, a domed shrine of Byzantine mosaics that once housed the Koran. After exploring the interior, stroll through the Courtyard of the Orange Trees, which has a beautiful fountain.

La Mezquita

Wake children up with the climb up the 16th-century tower for a panorama of the city.

Torrijos and Calle Cardenal Herrero s/n (south of the train station, just north of the Roman Bridge). ☎ 95-747-05-12. Admission €8 (£5.40) adults, €4 (£2.70) children under 14. Mar–Oct Mon–Sat 10am–7pm, Sun 8.30–10.15am, 2-7pm; Nov–Apr Mon–Sat 10am–6pm, Sun 8.30–10.15am, 2–6pm. Check www.turismode cordoba.org for changes. Bus: 3.

Alcázar de los Reyes Cristianos ★

Commissioned in 1328 by Alfonso XI, the Alcázar of the Christian Kings is a fine example of military architecture. Ferdinand and Isabella governed Castile from this fortress on the river as they prepared to recon-quer Granada, the last Moorish stronghold in Spain. Columbus journeyed here to fill Isabella's ears with his plans for discovery.

Two blocks southwest of the Mezquita, this quadrangular building is notable for powerful walls and a trio of towers—the Tower of the Lions, the Tower of Allegiance, and the Tower of the River. The beautiful gardens (complete with fish ponds) and the Moorish baths are celebrated attractions.

Caballerizas Reales. ☎ 95-742-01-51. Admission €4 (£2.70) adults, free for children under 14 and all day friday. May–Sept Tues–Sun 8.30am–2pm and 6–8pm, Sun 10am–2pm; Oct–Apr Tues–Sat 10am–2pm and 4.30–6.30pm, Sun 9.30am–2.30pm. Gardens illuminated July–Sept 10pm–noon. Check www.turismo decordoba.org for changes. Bus: 3 or 12.

Botanical Gardens, Avenida de Linneo

This is an attractive site along the banks of the Guadalquivir River with gentle walking trails through displays of trees, shrubs and flowers from all over the world, ideal for children to let off steam. The Ethnobotanical Museum focuses on the relationship between man and plants and is unique in Spain.

DID YOU KNOW? >> **A Caliph's Pleasure Palace** FIND

Conjunto Arqueológico Madinat Al-Zahra, a kind of Moorish Versailles just outside Córdoba, was constructed in the 10th century by the first caliph of al-Andalús, Abd ar-Rahman III. He named it after the favourite of his harem, nicknamed 'the brilliant.' Thousands of workers and animals slaved to build this mammoth pleasure palace, which is supposed to have housed 300 baths and 400 houses. Over the following years the site was plundered for building materials; in fact, it might have been viewed as a quarry for the entire region. Some of its materials, so it's claimed, went to build the Alcázar in Seville. The Royal House, rendezvous point for the ministers, has been reconstructed. Just beyond the Royal House are the ruins of a mosque constructed to face Mecca. The Berbers sacked the place in 1013.

The palace is at Carretera Palma de Río Km 8 (📞 *95-735-35-55-07).* **www. juntadeandalucia.es/cultura.** *Admission is free for members of the EU, €1.50 (£1) rest of world. Hours are from May 1 to September 15, Tuesday through Saturday from 10am to 8.30pm, Sunday from 10am to 2pm; from October 1 to April 30, Tuesday through Saturday from 10am to 6.30pm, Sunday from 10am to 2pm. Buses leave from Paseo de la Rivera and Avenida de la Victoria (*📞 *90-220-17-74).*

Open 10.30am–2.30pm and 5.30pm–7.30pm, closed from mid July to mid Sept. Child / Adult: €1.20 (£0.80) / €1.80 (£1.20)

Museo Arqueológico Provincial ★

Cordoba's Archaeological Museum, two blocks northeast of the Mezquita, is one of the most important in Spain. Housed in a palace dating from 1505, it displays artifacts left behind by various conquerors who swept through the province.

Plaza Jerónimo Páez 7, Judería. 📞 *95-735-55-17. Admission Free for EU members, €1.50 (£1.00) rest of world. Tues 2.30–8.30pm; Wed–Sat 9am–8.30pm; Sun and public holidays 9am–2.30pm.*

Museo de Bellas Artes de Córdoba

As you cross the Plaza del Potro to reach the Fine Arts Museum, notice the fountain at one end of the square. Built in 1557, it shows a young stallion with forelegs raised, holding the shield of Córdoba. Housed in an old hospital on the plaza, the museum contains medieval Andalusian paintings, examples of Spanish baroque art, and works by the great Spanish master, Goya.

Plaza del Potro 1. 📞 *95-747-33-45. Admission Free for EU members, €1.50 (£1.00) rest of world. Tues 2.30–8.30pm; Wed–Sat 9am–8.30pm (June 15–Sept 15 8.30am–2.30pm); Sun and public holidays 9am–2.30pm. Check* **www.turismodecordoba.org** *for changes. Bus: 3, 4, or 7.*

Museo Municipal de Arte Taurino

This museum holds more attraction for children than the others. Memorabilia of great bullfights are housed here in the Jewish Quarter in a 16th-century building, inaugurated in 1983 as an appendage to the Museo Municipal de Arte Cordobesa. Its ample galleries recall Cordoba's great bullfighters with suits of light, pictures, trophies, posters, even stuffed bulls' heads.

Plaza de las Bulas (also called Plaza Maimónides). 📞 *95-720-10-56. Admission €3 (£2), free for children under 18. May–Sept Tues–Sat 8.30am–2.30pm and 5.30–7.30pm, Sun 9.30am–3pm; Oct–Apr Mon–Sat 10am–2pm and 5.30–7.30pm, Sun 9.30am–2.30pm. Bus: 3.*

Sinagoga In Cordoba you'll find one of Spain's few remaining pre-Inquisition synagogues, built in 1350 in the Barrio de la Judería (Jewish Quarter). The synagogue is noted particularly for its stuccowork; the east wall contains a large orifice where the Tabernacle was once placed. (The Tabernacle held the scrolls of the Pentateuch).

Calle de los Judíos 20. 📞 *95-720-29-28. Admission Free for EU members, €0.30 (£0.20) rest of world. Tues–Sat 9.30am–2pm and 3.30–5.30pm; Sun 9.30am–1.30pm. Bus: 3.*

Torre de la Calahorra The Tower of Calahorra stands across the river at the southern end of the Roman bridge. Commissioned by Henry II of Trastamara in 1369 to protect him from his brother, Peter I, it now houses a town museum where visitors can take a self-guided tour with headsets. One room houses wax figures of Cordoba's famous philosophers, including Averro and Maimónides. Other rooms exhibit a miniature model of the Alhambra at Granada, complete with water fountains; a miniature Mezquita; and a display of Arab musical instruments. Climb the tower for some panoramic views of the Roman bridge, the river, and the cathedral/mosque.

Torre de la Calahorra

Av. de la Confederación, Puente Romano. 📞 *95-729-39-29. Admission €4.50 (£3) adults, €3 (£2) children under 8. May–Sept daily 10am–2pm and 4.30–8.30pm; Oct–Apr daily 10am–6pm. Last tour 1 hr before closing time. Bus: 16.*

Shopping

In Moorish times, Cordoba was famous for its leather workers. Highly valued in 15th-century Europe, their leather was studded with gold and silver ornaments, then painted with embossed designs *(guadamaci)*. Large panels of it often served in lieu of tapestries. Today's market is mostly full of cheap imitations. An exception is **Artesanía Andaluza**, Tomás Conde 3 (no phone), near the bullfight museum, which features a vast array of Cordovan handicrafts, especially filigree silver from the mines of Sierra Morena, and some excellently crafted embossed leather, a holdover from the Muslim heyday. Lots of junk is mixed in with the good stuff, though, so beware. The shop is open Monday to Saturday 9am to 5pm.

Arte Zoco, Calle de los Judíos s/n (no phone), is the largest association of craftspeople in Cordoba and holds a good deal of fascination for children where you can see work in progress and see different skills on display. Established in the Jewish Quarter in the mid-1980s, it assembles on one site the creative output of about a dozen artisans whose mediums include leather, wood, silver, crystal, terra cotta, and iron. The shop is open Monday to Friday 9.30am to 8pm, Saturday and Sunday 9.30am to 2pm. The artisans'

Staying Cool in Cordoba

High summer really isn't an ideal time to visit because it's so stiflingly hot. But if you do, here are some tips for keeping cool:

- Get up early and go sightseeing before the heat becomes too intense
- Always carry bottled water for the whole family
- Use taxis, carriages and buses rather than walking
- Go native: Take a late lunch and then a siesta (bring a portable DVD player if your children are older and won't sleep – anything to keep them out of the sun). Go for an early evening stroll at sunset and eat late.
- Cool off by splashing in a fountain – lots of locals do
- Book a hotel with a swimming pool
- Consider staying in the hills out of town, where it's cooler, and driving in for sightseeing
- Check opening times – lots of shops and even museums sensibly close at lunchtime

Family-friendly Accommodation

Cordoba Bridge at Sunset

workshops and studios open and close according to the whims of their occupants, but are usually maintained Monday to Friday from 10am to 2pm and 5.30 to 8pm.

Alejandro and Carlos López Obrero run **Taller Meryan**, Calleja de Las Flores 2 (☎ 95-747-59-02), on one of the most colorful streets in the city. In this 250-year-old building you can see artisans plying their crafts; although most items must be custom-ordered, some ready-made pieces are for sale, including cigarette boxes, jewel cases, attaché cases, book and folio covers, and ottoman covers. Hours are Monday to Friday 9am to 8pm, Saturday 9am to 2pm.

FAMILY-FRIENDLY ACCOMMODATION

You'll want to stay within the city walls and ditch the car while you're here. The centre of the city is walkable, and though it may seem like there are plenty of accommodation options Cordoba has too few hotels to meet the demand of its peak summer season and May *feria*, so reserve as far in advance as possible.

EXPENSIVE

Amistad Córdoba ★★ In the heart of the Judería (old Jewish Quarter) a four-minute walk from the mosque, this hotel is one of the most desirable in town. The houses face each other and are linked by a small patio of beautiful Andalusian arches and colourful Spanish tiles. The spacious rooms come with modern comforts like excellent beds, and the decor is a tasteful combination of wood and fabric. An extra bed with a double room costs from €120–167 (£80.40–111.90).

Plaza de Maimónides 3, 14004 Córdoba. ☎ 95-742-03-35. Fax

95

*95-742-03-65. www.nh-hotels.com.
84 rooms. €140–153 (£93.80–68.35)
double. Parking € 14 (£9.40). AE, DC,
MC, V. Bus: 2, 3, 5, or 6. Amenities:
Restaurant; bar; 24-hr. room service;
babysitting; laundry service/dry cleaning; nonsmoking rooms. In room: A/C,
TV, dataport, coffeemaker, minibar,
hair dryer, safe (in some).*

Parador de Córdoba ★★

VALUE Found 4 km (2½ miles)
outside town in a suburb called
El Brillante, this parador, named
after an Arab word meaning
'palm grove,' offers the conven-
iences and facilities of a luxurious
resort hotel at reasonable rates.
Occupying the site of a former
Caliphate palace, it's one of the
finest paradors in Spain. The
spacious guest rooms have been
furnished with fine dark-wood
pieces, and some have balconies
where you can eat breakfast or
relax over a drink. The cost for
an extra bed in a standard room
is €22.50 (£15.10). There is also
an outdoor swimming pool, tennis courts and children's play
facilities.

*Av. de la Arruzafa 33, 14012 Córdoba.
☎ 95-727-59-00. Fax 95-728-04-09.
www.parador.es. 94 units. €113–130
(£75.70–58.30) double; €156 (£105)
suite. AE, DC, MC, V. Free parking.
Amenities: Restaurant; bar; outdoor
pool; tennis court; fitness centre;
sauna; limited room service; babysitting; laundry service/dry cleaning;
non-smoking rooms; room for those
w/limited mobility. In room: A/C, TV,
dataport, minibar, hair dryer, safe.*

MODERATE

Tryp Los Gallos Half a block
from a wide tree-shaded boulevard

on the western edge of town, this
aging 1970s hotel stands eight
floors high, crowned by an informal roof garden. The comfortable
but small rooms have balconies
and neat bathrooms.

*Av. Medina Azahara 7, 14005
Córdoba. ☎ 95-723-55-00. Fax 95-
723-16-36. www.solmelia.com. 113
rooms. €104 (£69.70) double; €127
(£85) triple; €140 (£95.20) junior
suite. AE, DC, MC, V. Bus: 5, 6, 8, or
9. Amenities: Restaurant; bar; lounge;
outdoor pool; laundry service/dry
cleaning; nonsmoking rooms.
In room: A/C, TV, dataport, minibar,
hair dryer, safe. No cots or babysitting; extra bed €20 (£13.40).
Breakfast €9 (£6).*

INEXPENSIVE

Hotel Mezquita This hotel faces
the mosque's east side and is the
lodging closest to the Mezquita.
The architecture is typically
Andalucian – arches, interior
patios, and hand-painted tiles,
along with old mirrors and
chandeliers. The small but
comfortable rooms are painted
in pastels to contrast with the
dark oak furnishings. The family
room sleeps up to four.

*Plaza Santa Catalina 1, 14003
Córdoba. ☎ 95-747-55-85. Fax 95-
747-62-19. hotelmezquita@wanadoo.
es. 31 rooms. €41–94 (£27.50–£63)
double. AE, DC, MC, V. Parking
nearby €14 (£9.40). Bus: 3 or 16.
Amenities: Breakfast room; rooms
for those w/limited mobility. In room:
A/C, TV, dataport.*

Lola Hotel ★★ Originally built
as a private home in 1888 just
behind the Mezquita a small but
cozy open air courtyard ringed

with stone columns serves as reception, breakfast room and bar. Guest rooms inside are large and plush. One of the best boutique hotels in Cordoba.

Calle Romero 3, 14003 Córdoba. ☎ 95-720-03-05. Fax 95-742-20-63. www.hotelconencantolola.com. 8 rooms. €76–109 (£53.90–73) double. Rates include breakfast. AE, DC, MC, V. Bus: 1, 3, or 7. Amenities: Large open-air rooftop terrace w/view over the city's core. In room: A/C. Children welcome but only one suitable room.

Los Omeyas ★ A place set slap in the cobwebbed heart Córdoba in the city's old Jewish Quarter, just steps away from the Mezquita. Arab history is still very much in evidence in white marble and latticework. There's a central colonnaded patio with tables, around which are comfortable, tasteful rooms; none are grand, but those on the top floor have great views. The best room for families is number 18, which sleeps four and has a huge bath – all for only €73 (£48.90) low season or €85 (£56.95) high. Otherwise the biggest rooms (numbers 108 and 206) can fit an extra bed for €10 (£6.70)

Calle Encarnación 17, 14003 Córdoba. ☎ 95-749-22-67. Fax 95-749-16-59. www.hotel-losomeyas.com. 33 units. €52–64 (£34.85–£42.90) double; €62–74 (£41.55–£49.90) triple; €72–84 (£48.25–£38.85) quad. AE, DC, MC, V. Parking €12 (£8). Bus: 3 or 16. Amenities: Hotel restaurant nearby; cafeteria; bar; lounge. In room: A/C, TV, safe.

FAMILY-FRIENDLY DINING

EXPENSIVE

Bodegas Campos ★★
SPANISH/ALUSIAN A local favourite on a narrow cobblestone street in a residential neighborhood that's 10 minutes walk from the Mezquita, the Bodegas Campos has been going strong since 1908. The tapas bar out front is always packed. Javier Campo runs his rustic joint as half wine cellar (bodega) half tavern. The walls are adorned with old fiesta posters. The Sacristy bar is tucked behind a wall of wine vats autographed by celebrity visitors.

Calle de los Lineros 32. ☎ 95-749-75-00. www.bodegascampos.com. Reservations recommended. Main courses €14–19 (£9–13). Gastronomic menu 37€ (£25). DC, MC, V. Daily 1–4pm; Mon–Sat 8pm–midnight. Closed Dec 25, Dec 31. Bus: 1, 3, or 7.

MODERATE

El Caballo Rojo ★★ SPANISH
Stop at the restaurant's popular bar for a pre-dinner drink, then take the iron-railed stairs to the upper dining room, where a typical meal might include gazpacho, a main dish of chicken, then ice cream and sangria. Try a variation on the usual gazpacho – almond-flavored broth with apple pieces. In addition to Andalucian dishes, the chef offers Mozarabic specialties, such as monkfish prepared with pine nuts, currants, carrots, and

cream. Children can tuck into lamb chops in honey.

Cardinal Herrero 28, Plaza de la Hoguera. 📞 95-747-53-75. Reservations required. Main courses €12–20 (£8–13.40). AE, DC, MC, V. Daily 1–4.30pm and 8pm–midnight. Bus: 2.

Taberna Casa Pepe de la Judería ★ `CORDOBAN` Around the corner from the mosque, this is one of the best-located restaurants in the ancient city. From May to October, tables are placed on the rooftop where meats such as chicken and pork are barbecued, and an Andalusian guitarist entertains. The fare is in the hearty regional style, both good tasting and made with first-rate ingredients.

Calle Romero 1 📞 95-720-07-44. Reservations recommended. Fixed-price menu €11–18 (£7.40–8). Mon–Thurs 1–4pm and 8–11pm;

Fri–Sat 1–4.30pm and 8.30pm–-midnight; Sun 1–4pm and 8.30–11.30pm.

`INEXPENSIVE`

El Churrasco ★ `ANDALUSIAN` Housed in an ancient stone-fronted building in the Jewish Quarter northwest of the Mezquita, El Churrasco serves elegant meals in five dining rooms. You can enjoy specials like grilled fillet of beef with whisky sauce, succulent roast lamb, grilled salmon, and monkfish in pine-nut sauce. The signature dish is the charcoal-grilled pork loin. There are also a few simple dishes on the menu such as ham, egg and chips for younger palettes.

Romero 16. 📞 95-729-08-19. www.elchurrasco.com. Reservations required. Main courses €13–25 (£8.70–16.75). AE, DC, MC, V. Daily 1–4pm and 8pm–midnight. Closed Aug. Bus: 2 or 6.

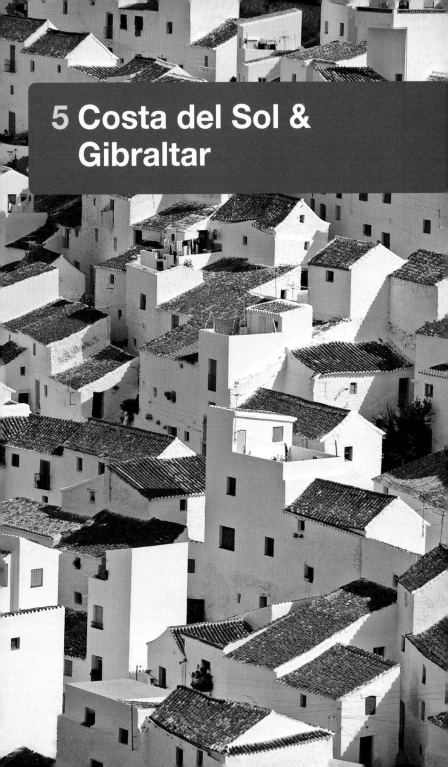

5 Costa del Sol & Gibraltar

COSTA DEL SOL

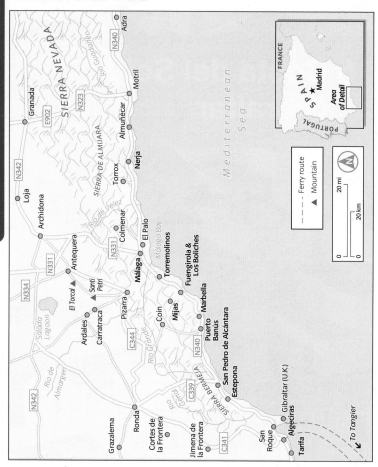

You'd have to have been living on Mars not to have heard of the
Costa del Sol, but do you really know what it's about? Ultra-hip
in the 1970s, it went downhill in the 1980s when it was regarded as a
bit naff and has enjoyed a resurgence throughout the 1990s and into
the 21st century thanks to endless villa developments which drape
themselves in candy colours over the brown, scrub-covered hills of the
Serrania de Ronda. The Costa del Sol extends from the border
between Spain and Gibraltar in the west, through the regional capital
of Málaga and to the east along the foothills of the Sierra Nevada as
far as the edge of Málaga province, after which it becomes the Costa
Tropical. The region bears little resemblance to the 'real' Spain until
you scratch the surface and the beaches are nothing special; but it does

have a fantastic climate, with a recorded 322 sunny days a year; golf galore; gorgeous mountains and villages within 30 minutes' drive; and a rapidly expanding expatriate population.

Marbella and its neighbouring marina, Puerto Banus, still retain an element of style and glamour, in a nouveau-riche kind of way, and there are several decent family resorts strung along the coast. Málaga itself is enjoying a much-deserved spell of popularity as a city break. But the Costa del Sol is best used as a base for exploring southern Andalucia, which holds great promise for families, from Moorish fortresses to mountain roads where bandits used to lurk, amazing views, colourful markets, lavish yachts with helicopters on their decks, all kinds of sport, water parks and great shopping.

If you go inland there's still much to be said for Málaga province. Gaucin, Ronda, Antequera and El Chorro Gorge (see Inland from Costa de Sol) are all some of the most striking places in the province. Gorgeous, exotic Seville, the magical sherry capital of Jerez, Cordoba (at a push, due to distance) and romantic Granada are all a day trip away and all have appeal for families. Children will also love a day in Gibraltar, with cable cars to ride, caves, English food and comical monkeys.

ESSENTIALS

Getting There

By Plane Málaga's **Pablo Ruiz Picasso** airport, two and a half hours flying time from the UK, is 8 km (5 miles) outside the city centre, just off the main A7 coast road and the AP7 Autopista Del Sol. All the major towns and resorts are clearly signposted. British Airways (📞 *0845 779 9977*; *www.british-airways.com*) and Iberia (📞 *0845 601 2854*; *www. iberia.com*) both fly from London to Málaga. Flybe (*www.flybe. com*) flies from Southampton, Birmingham, Exeter and Norwich. Thomson (*www. thomsonfly.com*) flies to 15 British cities including London Luton and Gatwick, Belfast, Cardiff, Glasgow, Edinburgh, Manchester and Leeds. Monarch (*www.flymonarch.com*) flies to Aberdeen, Blackpool, Manchester, Birmingham, London Luton and Gatwick. easyJet (*www.easyjet.com*) goes to Belfast, Glasgow, Liverpool, Newcastle, East Midlands, Bristol, London Luton, Stansted, Gatwick, Geneva, Berlin and Milan. Ryanair (*www. ryanair.com*) has flights to Shannon, Dublin and Brussels. As an alternative, don't forget the possibility of flying to Gibraltar if you're staying west of Marbella; GB Airways and Monarch both have services from the UK.

By Bus & Train There are both buses and trains that run every half hour from the main airport terminal, and a bus also goes

Beaches: The Good, the Bad & the Ugly

The Costa del Sol doesn't claim to be a paradise for swimmers, but its beaches crowd up just the same come the summer season with weekending locals and tourists. Crowding is at a peak on Sundays, May through October, when beaches are busy with family picnickers as well as sunbathers. All public beaches in Spain are free. Don't expect changing facilities. There might be cold showers on the major beaches, but that's it. The least enticing beaches – mainly pebbles and shingles – are at **Málaga** and **Almuñécar** to the east. Moving west, are the wide, somewhat gritty sands of **Torremolinos**. The best beaches here are at **El Bajondillo** and **La Carihuela** (which borders an old fishing village). Another good stretch of beach is along the meandering strip between **Carvajal**, **Los Boliches**, and **Fuengirola**. In addition, two good beaches – **El Fuerte** and **La Fontanilla** – lie on either side of **Marbella**.

Moving further west on the N340 and past San Pedro, **Playa del Padrón** is a fairly nice spot at the mouth of the River of the same name. Estepona, whose main traffic avenue is along the sea front, has two beaches: **La Rada** and **Playa del Cristo**. The former is the long, main beach still used by locals which has good cheap chiringuitos (beach bar/restaurants). Playa del Cristo is a cozier semi-circular cove closer to the night action of the port and with a few trees and reeds on its west end.

There are mostly dull but still popular beaches at **Casares** and **Manilva**. Further west, the geography gets more interesting just before you reach **Torreguadiaro**, with beaches featuring rocky promontories, clear water, and a host of fish. This stretch, including **Cala Manilva**, is accessible from various points off the N340, although you need to be travelling eastward to exit the road toward the beach. There is a roundabout before Torreguadiaro one of whose exits is to the beach, and about half a mile further east you'll find a tiny exit with a sign for the chiringuito **Sal y Sol**, which is on one of the nicest coves.

Finally, the beach at **Sotogrande** lies at the mouth of the **Rio Guadiaro**.

every 45 minutes from terminal two direct to Marbella. Taxi fares to Málaga cost €12 (£8), to Sotogrande at the far western end of the coast, €100 (£67).

Málaga is the gateway to the Costa Del Sol, although most of foreign visitors don't set foot inside its city limits, instead putting pedal to metal as soon as they land at Málaga airport and speeding to their resort.

By Car All of the beach resorts are linked by the infamous N-340 highway from Málaga to Estepona, which is a fast, six-lane road. A new toll expressway with four lanes – called **Autopista del Sol** – now runs exactly parallel to the N-340 and is a much

Fuengirola Beach

quicker way of getting around if you don't mind the tolls. The whole region is well signposted.

Visitor Information

The **tourist office** at Pasaje de Chinitas 4 (**📞 95-221-34-45; *www.andalucia.org***) is open Monday to Friday 9am–7.30pm, Sat 10am–7pm, Sun 10am–2pm.

Child-Friendly Events & Entertainment

Carnival in the Málaga province doesn't come close to the sophisticated extravaganza

Costa del Sport

The coast is known worldwide for the sheer quantity of its golf courses (over 40) catering to all playing levels and styles and including some highly prestigious competition venues. Some courses rent out children's clubs and have putting greens and driving ranges where children can have a go. From about the age of six upwards, children are allowed on driving ranges if they're well behaved and quiet. If you're a keen golfer, there's no better place to introduce them to the game. If you just fancy a round but don't want to encroach on family time, play nine holes at sunset, when the courses are quiet. Expect to pay high green fees on prestigious courses like **Sotogrande** and **Valderrama**, where the Ryder Cup was held.

Water-skiing and **windsurfing** are available in most resorts, and pedal boats or, sometimes, more adventurous vessels can be rented from kiosks at all the main beaches. Inland, there are **riding stables**, **walking** trails, **mountain bikes** for hire and **4x4 expeditions** into the hills.

of the celebration in Cadiz but the Entierro de la Sardina (the burial of the Sardine) on Ash Wednesday is a fun ritual. A local, dressed as the sardine, reads a testament full of political satire, then a giant sardine effigy, followed by 'weeping widows', processes through the streets, until finally, and confusingly at odds with the name of the event, ends up not buried but instead barbecued on a bonfire. In August, the feast of the Virgen del Carmen, patron saint of fishermen, is also spectacular: a statue of the Virgin is paraded at dusk on a boat and then dry land amidst great celebration, with fireworks at midnight.

WHAT TO SEE & DO

Children's Top 10 Attractions

❶ Cueva de Nerja (Cave of Nerja) Take a trip back to prehistoric Spain with a ramble through the stalactite and stalagmite coated caves. The stupendous galleries are over 70 m (200 ft) high at certain points. Awesome (see p. 122).

❷ Selwo Adventure Park, Estepona Hop onto trucks for the safari ride to spot a host of wild animals or check out the snake shows, bat cave or walk-in bird house. Crocs, monkeys and lemurs are kept safely behind bars (see p. 119).

❸ Gibralfaro, Málaga Trek up the steep vertical maze of steps to reach the castle at the top of this hill overlooking the city. Once there, children can scamper along the rampart walls before stopping for a juice in the shady café (see p. 107).

❹ Crocodile Park, Torremolinos A conservation and breeding centre to let the public get up close and personal with one of nature's snappiest creatures. Next door are two marine parks (see p. 111).

❺ Puerto de la Duquesa (near Estepona) For a day out with a difference, head to the real Roman baths – the Hediona sulphur spa (see p. 120).

❻ The TeleCabina Cable Car, Torremolinos, Benalmádena For stunning views of the sea, Gibraltar and Morocco hop on the car. You can either take it back down or for the adventurous hike or mountain-bike instead (see p. 111).

❼ Tivoli World, Arroyo de la Miel For a day of fun, take in the rides, restaurants, concerts and shows of all types at this permanent fun fair (see p. 111).

❽ Bodega el Pimpi, Málaga Spot the famous names chalked onto sherry barrels in this cheap eatery. A certain 'Antonio Blair' appears to have paid a visit (see p. 110).

❾ Born to be Wild, wildlife tour, Marbella A day's adventure through the Sierra de Las Nieves in a 4×4 will teach you all about local history, fauna and flora (see p. 114).

⑩ The Fuengirola flea market
Stock up on trinkets galore to take back home at the biggest market along the coast (see p. 111).

Málaga

Málaga Town The capital of Málaga is a charmingly scruffy, slightly down-at-heel city with an industrious but saggy, paint-peeling old quarter, a raft of brilliant spit-and-sawdust bodegas selling its trademark sweet wine, a couple of excellent museums, nice parks and character in spades. Swallow your prejudice: Málaga, capital of Costa del Sol, is culturally interesting, and downright cool and most children will find something to pique their interest on a day trip.

Old Quarter The tangle of streets around the old quarter are set around the cathedral, a 16th century structure that, as ever in Andalucia, was slapped down on the site of the old mosque. Its south tower was never finished, hence its local nickname La Manquita ('the little one-armed one').

Plaza Obispo. 📞 95-221-59-17. Admission €2 (£1.30). Mon–Sat 10am–6.30pm. Closed holidays.

Museo Picasso Málaga The collection at the new Museo Picasso Málaga is the art Picasso gave to his family or the art he wanted to keep for himself – since it was donated by his son Paulo's wife, Christine Ruiz-Picasso; and their son, Pablo's grandson, Bernard, and so the subjects are pretty personal and there are paintings of wives, *Olga Kokhlova with Mantilla*, and lovers, *Jacqueline Seated*. In all, there are more than 200 pieces of art. Arm your children

Museo Picasso

MÁLAGA TOWN

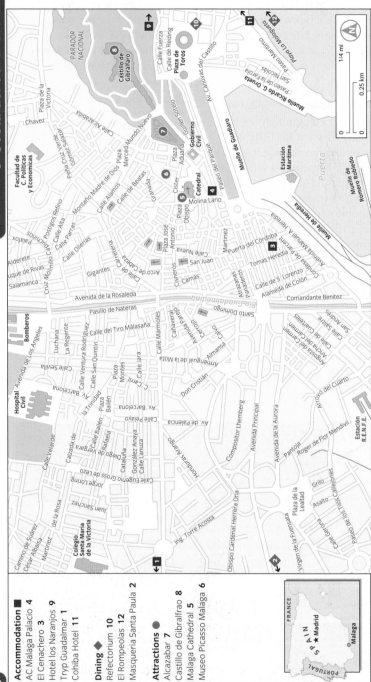

with crayons and paper and get them to draw their own Picasso as a challenge during the visit.

San Agustín 8. ☎ 95-129-600. www.museopicassomalaga.org. Combined permanent collection and exhibitions €8 (£5.35) adults; half-price for seniors, students, and children 10–16; free for children 9 and under. Tues–Sun 10am–8pm, Fri–Sat 10am–9pm.

Alcazabar Opposite is the Alcazabar, a fortress erected in the 9th or 10th century, surrounded by orange trees and purple bougainvillea and jasmine blossom, and brilliant views.

Plaza de la Aduana, Alcazabilla. ☎ 95-221-60-05. Admission €1.80 (£1.20). Museum Tues–Sun 8.30am–7pm.

The Castle Climb the vertical maze of steps winding through gardens to get to the entrance to the castle (Gibralfaro). You can run all the way along the rampart walls here, and there are yew and fig trees to cool off under. If you've packed a picnic, this is a good spot to enjoy it. A little museum at the top has a fashion show of military dress from the 16th the 20th century. For top nosh, Terraza del Castillo (10am–8pm summer, till 6pm winter), has a handful of tables under a veranda covered in cane, the best views in town, and serves simple food like spaghetti, tortilla, and ice cream milkshakes (€4–10 (£2.70–6.70) for mains).

La Malagueta If you can't resist a dip in the sea, La Malagueta is a proper city beach, with lots of restaurants serving similar Russian salads and mixed fish plates nearby. Although the suburban beaches are at Pedregaleo and El Palo where the sand has little patches of grass under the trees and the beaches are sheltered and shallow enough to swim in, Málaga is a working port so bear in mind that the water isn't the cleanest.

Shopping

Calle Granada, Calle Marqués de Larios, Calle Nueva and the Mercado de Atarazanas, hold the best of the city's boutiques – mostly it's just workaday stuff, pharmacies, clothes shops, handbags and family photographers. Miramar, though, on Calle Nueva, has rather an amazing selection of double painted '*abanicos*' – fans – packed into a grimy glass fronted shop.

The Big Feria

The most festive time in Málaga is the first week in August, when the city celebrates its reconquest by Ferdinand and Isabella in 1487. The big feria (fair) is an occasion for parades and bullfights. The major tree-shaded boulevard, **Paseo del Parque**, is transformed into a fairground.

Prices range from €5–100 (£3.35–67). Calle Nueva ✆ 29 626 071 842, open daily 10am–1pm; 5–9pm, closed Sun. V, MC.

FAMILY-FRIENDLY ACCOMMODATION

Considering it's the capital of one of the most heavily touristed regions in the world, Málaga has precious little to show for it. And that's no bad thing. Most visitors stay in the resorts along the coast so there aren't many hotels in town. Those that are tend more towards the functional than recreational or boutique. The hippest place to stay is **El Pedregal** in the suburbs, just a hop away from the centre, but right on the beach.

EXPENSIVE

AC Málaga Palacio ★ This is probably the town's leading hotel and almost certainly has the city's best views. The Palacio opens onto a tree-lined esplanade near the cathedral and the sea. Rooms are of a fair size.

Cortina del Muelle 1, 29015 Málaga. ✆ 95-221-51-85. Fax 95-222-51-00. www.ac-hoteles.com, mpalacio@ac-hotels.com. 214 rooms. €123–180 (£82.40–120.10) double; €147–324 (£98.50–217.10) suite. AE, DC, MC, V. Parking €21 (£14.10) nearby. Bus: 4, 18, 19, or 24. Amenities: Restaurant; bar; outdoor pool; fitness centre; sauna; 24-h room service; babysitting; laundry service/dry cleaning; nonsmoking rooms; room for those w/limited mobility. In room: A/C, TV, minibar, hair dryer. Extra bed €50 (£33.50); for under 12s free. Buffet breakfast €14 (£9.40).

Tryp Guadalmar ★ This nine-story modern hotel sits across from a private beach 3 km (2 miles) west of the centre of Málaga. Accommodations are spacious, airy, and simply furnished; each room has a private sea-view balcony. Lots of families here, but there is a prevailing air of anonymity.

Calle Mobydick 2, Urbanización Guadalmar, 29004 Málaga. ✆ 95-223-17-03. Fax 95-224-03-85. www.solmelia.com. 194 rooms. €168 (£112.55) double; €303 (£203) junior suite; €415 (£278.05) suite. Children under 12 stay half-price in parent's room. AE, DC, MC, V. Free parking. Amenities: 2 restaurants; bar; 2 pools (1 indoor); health club; Jacuzzi; sauna; limited room service; babysitting; laundry service/dry cleaning; nonsmoking rooms; rooms for those w/limited mobility. In room: A/C, TV, dataport, minibar, hair dryer, safe. Bath & shower. Breakfast €15 (£10.05).

MODERATE

Hotel Los Naranjos VALUE
Well-maintained Los Naranjos is one of the more reasonably priced choices in the city. It's 1.6 km (1 mile) from the heart of town on the eastern side of Málaga, past the Plaza de Toros (bullring), near the best beach in Málaga, Baños del Carmen. The hotel offers midsize rooms and serves only breakfast.

Paseo de Sancha 35, 29016 Málaga. ✆ 95-222-43-19. Fax 95-222-43-16. www.hotel-losnaranjos.com. 41 rooms. €98–150 (£65.65–73.70) double; €126–140 (£84.40–93.80) suite. AE, DC, MC, V. Parking €11 (£7.60). Bus: 11. Amenities: Restaurant; bar; limited room service; laundry

service/dry cleaning. In room: A/C,
TV, dataport, minibar, hair dryer, safe.

Cohiba Hotel The Cohiba
Hotel is a small three star hotel
in Málaga right on the achingly
hip but groovily low-key beachfront of Pedregalejo, the old fishing quarter 10 minutes east from
town centre. There are just 10
rooms here, and the bar downstairs is one of the coolest along
this beach, but the hotel has an
apartment nearby that's perfect
for families.

Paseo Marítimo El Pedregal, 64.
℡ 952 206 900. Fax 952 207 188
www.cohibahotel.com.

FAMILY-FRIENDLY DINING

EXPENSIVE

Marisqueria Santa Paula 365
days a year the marisqueria Santa
Paula opens at 7am with churros
(doughnuts) and hot chocolate.
Some 18 hours, and several hundred helpings of fish, *jamon*
(ham), cheese and wines later,
they close their giant doors for
six hours respite. Santa Paula is
the stuff of local folklore. All the
effort here has gone on sourcing
food and wine, rather than
shelling out on fancy interiors,
there's no music, past a faint whir
of the refrigerators, and there's
no Michelin star jiggery pokery
of the El Bulli school going on
either. Manchego is rich and
crumbly. The melting Joselito
hams are pulled down from
their hooks at a rate of 20 a
week, served in wafer slices with

tomato salad, and a mixed fish
plate of adobo, red mullet,
anchovies and calamaris comes
with fat, soaked red peppers.
You don't have to spend much,
scallops weigh in at €3.20
(£2.15) each, grilled salmon is
€11.50 (£7.70), veal chop,
€21 (£14.10).

Avda. de los Guindos, Barriada Santa
Paula Málaga. ℡ 952 236 557. V,
Amex, DC, MC. Seats 300. 7am–5pm
and 8pm–midnight daily.

INEXPENSIVE

Refectorium SPANISH Located
behind the Málaga bullring, the
testosterone-heavy Refectorium
fills up with aficionados and
often, after the fight, with the
matadors too. The food is old-
fashioned, portions are generous.
The typical soup of the Málaga
area is *ajo blanco con uvas*
(cold almond soup flavoured
with garlic and garnished with
big muscatel grapes). For a classic opener, try a plate of garlic-
flavoured mushrooms seasoned
with bits of ham. Very obliging
with regard to children.

Calle Cervantes 8. ℡ 95-221-89-90.
Reservations recommended on
weekends and at bullfights. Main
courses €6–18 (£4–12.10). AE, DC,
MC, V. Mon–Sat 1.30–5pm and
8.30pm–midnight.

**El Pedregal/El Palo El
Rompeolas** As the sun goes
down on the eastern suburbs of
Málaga, known as **El Palo**,
boat-shaped BBQs are fired up
on the beach outside most
establishments in preparation
for the nightly orders of sardines

on skewers and grilled bass. This casual and good value spot on the corner of the main pass does good coquinas (clams), boquerones fritos (fried anchovies) and dorada a la plancha (gilthead bream). Children can run off and play in the sand when they get tired of sitting at the table.

Puerto Maritimo, El Pedregal 89, 29017 Málaga. ℂ 952 299 752. 10.30am–4.30pm (winter), 10.30am–4.30pm and 8pm–midnight (summer).

Bodegas Head for La Posada Calle Granada 33 (no phone) to eat well and cheaply, portions are generous, so you'll only need a couple of tapas. Nearby, an all-pedestrian street, Calle Compagnía, and a square, Plaza Uncibays, are home to simpler, completely unpretentious tascas. You can sit and eat delicious cheap tapas variadas from giant upturned sherry barrels at many of the bodegas in Málaga, rinsing food down with the tangily sweet Málaga wine. Bodegas El Pimpi is beside the Picasso Museum. Salty meats (carne a la sal) are €9 (£6), also recommended are pimpi tostada (€5.50–8 (£3.70–5.35)), endives with Roquefort, and the salmorejo with ham. It's a big old place, an ivy-covered room with rattan chairs and low ceilings, and gets busy come sundown, but a cool mellow place to take young children if you get there before 8pm. Famous fans, whose names are in chalk on sherry barrels, include a certain Antonio Blair.

Cash only Calle Granada 62. ℂ 95 222 89 90 Seats 400. Noon–2am.

WEST FROM MÁLAGA: TORREMOLINOS, MIJAS & FUENGIROLA

Torremolinos Once a sleepy fishing village, Torremolinos (15 km or 9 miles west of Málaga) has long since been engulfed in cement-walled resort hotels. It's been the victim of great mockery over the years as a 'spam and chips' resort but has now settled into its niche as a budget destination on the Costa del Sol with great nightlife, a colourful gay scene and some of the coast's best sandy beaches. There are several family attractions alongside all this, including the incongruous **Crocodile Park**, which bills itself as a conservation centre and breeding programme open to the public (*www.crocodile-park.com*, ℂ *952 05 17 82*).

Calle San Miguel A smartly paved pedestrianised street, is the main drag of the town, lined with shops and always busy. The **Cuesta del Tajo**, at the end of San Miguel, leads down a steep flight of steps through the old fishing district of **El Bajondillo**. The seafront promenade, Paseo Maritimo, extends east to Playamar and west to La Carihuela, now continuing as far as Benalmádena Marina, merging all the resorts into one. It's a nice enough place for a family stroll when the heat of the sun has died down and you may still

Barbecue Style

Torremolinos is surrounded by forest and a fun thing to do, if you're self-catering, is to take off into the woods for a barbecue. It's here you'll find locals from Málaga at weekends and a much more 'Spanish' atmosphere. In September, there's a spectacular *romeria* in town, where locals emerge from the woodwork in stunning regalia, mounted on beautiful, prancing Andalucian horses and swigging *fino* from hip flasks. A statue of San Miguel (the town's patron saint, not related to the lager) is paraded through the streets to the pine woods for a massive cookout, dancing and feasting all night long.

see old men playing dominoes and drinking anis outside the original fishermen's cottages.

Benalmádena Torremolinos merges into Benálmadena Costa (many of the resorts have 'Costa' after the name, implying that the original town is up in the hills, safe from latter day pirates). Here, there's a swanky marina and lots of villas as well as high-rise hotels with much of the action in the lively Arroyo de la Miel area. This is one of the best bases on the coast for families as there's so much to do, including two marine life parks.

Selwo Marina This features shows employing dolphins, sea lions, penguins, and more (*www. selwomarina.com*, ☏ *902 190 482*). Sealife is a typical marine wildlife park with a touch pool and glass tunnels showing sharks on the prowl (*www.sealife.es*). The TeleCabina Cable Car is good for stunning views of the sea, Gibraltar, and the distant, hazy mountains of Morocco. You can return by cable car, or

hike or mountain-bike down. Arroyo de la Miel, Benalmádena, ☏ *902 190 482*.

Tivoli World Also in Arroyo de la Miel is the famous Tivoli World, an attraction park featuring rides, restaurants, concerts, and shows of all types. It's basically a permanent fun fair jazzed up with restaurants and concerts. You can buy several types of tickets to get in depending on how much you plan to see and do (*www.tivoli costadelsol.com*, ☏ *952 577 106*).

Fuengirola and Los Boliches
The fishing towns, and lower-budget holiday resorts, of Fuengirola and Los Boliches lie halfway between the more famous resorts of Marbella and Torremolinos (32 km or 20 miles west of Málaga). The flea market at Fuengirola on Tuesdays (near the Plaza de Toros) and Sundays (off the N340) is the biggest along the coast. There's also a zoo in Fuengirola, said to have a particularly humane way of keeping the animals (*www.zoo fuengirola.com*, ☏ *952 666 601*). Santa Amalja, Carvajal and Las

Gaviotas, the best beaches here are broad, clean, and sandy and moored at the Fuengirola marina is **The Dawn Approach**, an old Scottish wooden ship that will take you from the harbour on lunch, dinner, or dolphin sighting cruises, ☎ 952 665 607.

Mijas Mijas Pueblo At the foot of a mountain range 8 km (5 miles) inland from the coastal road turnoff to Fuengirola. The park at the top of Cuesta de la Villa is where you'll see the ruins of a Moorish fortress dating from 833 AD. There's a frequent bus service to Mijas from the terminal at Fuengirola, 30 minutes away. Don't confuse this with Mijas Costa, which is down on the coast.

Mijas Pueblo is gorgeous, and although it's very much filled with foreign residents, it's one of the original *pueblos blancos* (white towns). Drive up there just before sunset, when most of the coach parties have left and wander around the cobbled streets. If you've got very small children and aren't likely to make it to Ronda or any of the other white towns, this is an adequate compromise.

Family-Friendly Dining: Torremolinos

The cuisine in Torremolinos is more American and Continental European than Andalucian. The hotels often serve elaborate four-course meals, but you might want to sample more casual local offerings. A good spot to try is the food court La Nogalera

(☎ 95-238-15-00), the major gathering place between the coast road and the beach. Head down Calle del Cauce to this compound of modern whitewashed Andalucian buildings. Open to pedestrian traffic only, it's a maze of passageways, courtyards, and patios for eating and drinking. You can find anything from sandwiches to Belgian waffles to scrambled eggs to pizza.

If you want to get away from the high-rises and honky-tonks, head to nearby La Carihuela. In the old fishing village on the western outskirts of Torremolinos, you'll find some of the best bargain restaurants. Walk down a hill toward the sea to reach the village.

Casa Guaquin ★ FIND SEAFOOD serves staples like *boquerones fritos* sautéed fresh anchovies and market-fresh fish baked in salt on its terrace deck.

Paseo Marítimo 63. Reservations recommended. Main courses €20–31 (£13.40–20.75). AE, MC, V. Tues–Sun 1–3.30pm and 8–11.30pm. Closed Dec 15–Jan 15.

Casa Juan ★ SEAFOOD Try a *mariscada de mariscos* (shellfish), a platter of mixed fried fish, paella.

Calle San Gines 18–20, La Carihuela. ☎ 95-237-35-12. Reservations recommended. Main courses €10–22 (£6.70–14.75). AE, DC, MC, V. Tues–Sun 12.30–4.30pm and 7.30–11.30pm. Closed Dec.

Family-Friendly Dining: Mijas

El Padrastro INTERNATIONAL Part of the fun of dining here is to be

Mija's Donkey

had just getting there. You go to the cliff side of town and, if you're athletic, walk up 77 steps; if not, take the elevator to the highest point. The cuisine is international, served on covered terraces with panoramic views of the coast.

Paseo del Compás 22, Mijas. ☎ *95-248-50-00. Reservations recommended. Main courses €12–27 (£8–18.10). AE, DC, MC, V. Daily 12.30–4pm and 7–11.30pm.*

Villa Paradiso INTERNATIONAL

Lamb shanks are aromatically

Marbella

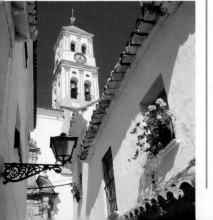

baked in the oven until fork tender and served with a fresh fruit sauce. Lubina or sea bass is baked in a salt crust, in the autumn venison is likely to appear on the menu.

Centro Comercial El Zoco, Mijas. ☎ *95-293-12-24. Reservations recommended. Main courses €8–27 (£5.35–18.10). AE, DC, MC, V. Daily 9am–1pm and 7pm–midnight.*

Marbella

Although it's packed with tourists and only slightly less popular than Torremolinos, Marbella (60 km or 37 miles west of Málaga) is still the nicest resort along the Costa del Sol and it remains what it always has been, a pleasant Andalusian town at the foot of the Sierra Blanca. Traces of its past survive in its palatial town hall, medieval ruins, and ancient Moorish walls. Marbella's most charming area is the **old quarter** of narrow cobblestone streets and Arab houses centred by Plaza de los Naranjos. The two beaches are

El Fuerte and La Fontanilla. There are other, more secluded beaches, but you need a car to get to them. Along the coast inland from Puerto Banus, the **Nueva Andalucía flea market** is every Saturday morning, selling everything from Spanish leather goods to local pottery and embroideries. The big shopping venue in Marbella is the la Cañada shopping centre.

Wildlife Tours Born to be Wild Tours (*www.borntobewild.es*, 📞 *952 781 006*) will pick you up in any hotel on the Fuengirola-Estepona stretch for day-long 4×4 rides into the Sierra de las Nieves above Marbella. Included are lectures in your language on the local history, fauna, and flora as well as lunch in a typical Spanish village restaurant. A similar company also operating principally in Sierra de las Nieves and offering guides who are qualified environmentalists is Monte Aventura (*www.monte aventura.com*, 📞 *952 881 519*).

Family-Friendly Accommodation

Some of the best hotels along the Costa del Sol are on Marbella's 'Golden Mile', an exclusive area with prices to match.

EXPENSIVE

El Fuerte ★★ One of the best hotels in Marbella proper. Set on a good, sandy beach it has some of the best-maintained and most beautiful landscaped hotel gardens along the coast. Sporty guests will find a body-building room, with aerobics, water gymnastics, and even a Turkish bath.

Av. El Fuerte, 29600 Marbella. 📞 *95-286-15-00. Fax 95-282-44-11. www. fuertehoteles.com/hotels/elfuerte marbella. 263 rooms. €197–265 (£132–177.55) double, €285–339 (£190.95–227.15) suite. Rates include continental breakfast. AE, DC, MC, V. Free parking outside, €6 (£4) inside. Amenities: 2 restaurants; bar; 2 pools (1 indoor); children's pool; nearby golf course; tennis court; gym; spa; sauna; children's playground; room service (8am–midnight); laundry*

Beach, Marbella

Marina, Marbella

service/dry cleaning. In room: A/C, TV, dataport, minibar, hair dryer, safe at extra charge. Children under 12 free; cots free.

MODERATE

Hotel Riu Rincón Andaluz ★

In a stylish area of Marbella 1 km (⅔ mile) from Puerto Banús, this four-star hotel was built to evoke a *pueblo andaluz* (Andalucian village). The resort lies in a park only 500 m (1640 ft) from a good beach. The low-level, rustic-style buildings form an ideal retreat. Rooms are large and each has at least a small living room (larger in the suites). Ground-floor rooms have direct access to the gardens; others open onto balconies.

Carretera de Cádiz, km 173, 29660, Marbella. 📞 *95-281-15-17. Fax 95-281-41-80. www.riu.com. 227 rooms. €100–137 (£67–91.80)*

double; €150–200 (£100.50–134) suite. Rates include breakfast. AE, DC, MC, V. Free parking. Amenities: Restaurant; 2 bars; 3 pools (1 indoor); 24-h room service; laundry service/ dry cleaning; nonsmoking rooms; rooms for those w/limited mobility. In room: A/C, TV, minibar, hair dryer, safe. Cots free; extra bed €100 (£67); babysitting.

INEXPENSIVE

El Rodeo VALUE Even though this modern hotel stands just off the main coastal road of Marbella, within walking distance of the bus station, the beach, and the old quarter, it is quiet and secluded.

Víctor de la Serna s/n, 29600 Marbella. 📞 *95-277-51-00. Fax 95-282-33-20. www.monarquehoteles.es. 100 rooms. €85–140 (£56.95–93.80) double. AE, DC, MC, V. Amenities: Restaurant; outdoor pool. In room: A/C, TV, safe.*

A Marbella Tasca Crawl

To really rub shoulders with the locals and experience a taste of Spain, take some of your meals in the **tapas bars**. You can eat well in most places, and Marbella boasts more hole-in-the-wall tapas bars than virtually any other resort town in southern Spain. Tapas actually translates as lids – in days gone by, it was traditional for a bartender to cover the glasses of fino on the bar with a little dish of olives or ham, to keep the flies off the rim. Very occasionally, you'll find a bar that still offers free tapas.

Prices and hours are remarkably consistent: The coffeehouse that opens at 7am will switch to wine and tapas when the first patron asks for it (sometimes shortly after breakfast), then continue through the day dispensing wine, sherry and, more recently, bottles of beer to accompany the food. On average, tapas cost €3–8 (£2–5.36) apiece; a *racion* is a bigger portion. *Platos combinados* are another option, offering more traditional cooked dishes with potatoes and one, two, or sometimes three meats.

Tapas served along the Costa del Sol are principally Andalucian in origin, with an emphasis on seafood. The most famous plate, **fritura malagueña**, consists of fried fish based on the catch of the day. Sometimes **ajo blanco**, a garlicky local version of gazpacho, is served, especially in summer. Fried squid or octopus is another favourite, as are

Accommodation Nearby

Castillo de Monda ★ FIND A transformed 8th-century Moorish fortress, which lies in a sleepy 'white' village 12 km (7½ miles) north of Marbella. Castillo de Monda adds a soothing note of calm and quiet to a region that grows glitzier by the year. Guest rooms are beautifully maintained and generous in size.

Monda, 29110 Málaga. ☎ *95-245-71-42. Fax 95-245-73-36.* www.castillodemonda.es. *29 rooms.* €113–136 (£75.70–91.10) double; €194–224 (£129–150.10) suite including breakfast. AE, MC, V. Free parking. Amenities: Restaurant; bar; outdoor pool; 24-h room service; babysitting; laundry service/dry cleaning; nonsmoking rooms; rooms

for those w/limited mobility. In room: A/C, TV, hair dryer. Extra bed €45 (£30.15); cots free.

Family-Friendly Dining

MODERATE

Casa de la Era ★ FIND ANDALUSIAN A rustic house, with internal patios of plants, trees, and flowers and a beautiful terrace. Wooden furniture adds to the old-fashioned look, along with hanging hams and decorative ceramics. Specials include filet of turbot with fried garlic, squid *a la moruna* (with hot peppers).

Finca El Chorraero-Noreste. ☎ *95-277-06-25. Reservations recommended.*

little Spanish-style herb-flavoured meatballs. **Tortilla** (an omelet with potatoes unless you specify 'francesa') is the most popular egg dish. Other well-known tapas are pungent tuna, potato salad, grilled shrimp, piquillos rellenos (red peppers stuffed with fish), octopus salad, bacalao (salt cod), mushrooms sautéed in olive oil and garlic, pork skewers, sausage (raw varieties prevail as tapas, including chorizo and blood sausage), and cured ham. The best bets for children are: croquetas (chicken croquettes); patatas bravas (sauté potatoes with a spicy sauce); slices of ham and manchego cheese; tortilla; and meatballs. Chunks of bread dipped in garlic mayonnaise are also good for filling up on.

Tapas bars line many of the narrow streets of Marbella's historic core, with rich pickings around Calle del Perral and, to a somewhat lesser extent, Calle Miguel Cana. In August especially, when you want to escape wall-to-wall people and the heat and noise of the Old Town, head for one of the shoreline restaurants and tapas bars called chiringuitos. All serve local specialties, and you can order a full meal, a snack, tapas, or a drink. **Los Sardinales** (Playa de los Alicates; 95-283-70-12) serves some of the best sangria in the area. You might return later for a succulent seafood dinner. Popular **Chiringuito La Pesquera** (Playa Marbellamar 95-277-03-38), is where you can order a plate of fresh grilled sardines.

Main courses €9–19 (£8–12.75). AE, DC, MC, V. May–Oct Mon–Sat 8–11pm and 8pm–midnight. Off season Mon–Sat 1–11pm.

Ciboca SPANISH In the heart of Marbella's historic medieval core, Ciboca occupies a 500-year-old building ringed with vines and flowers, whose tables are moved outdoors onto the historic square whenever the weather is balmy. A full roster of Spanish wines can accompany dishes that include virtually any kind of fish, especially sea bass, baked in a salt crust.

Plaza de las Naranjos 6. 95-277-37-43. Reservations recommended. Main courses €11–25 (£7.40–16.75). MC, V. Daily noon–11pm.

Estepona, Manilva, Caseres & Sotogrande

Beyond Marbella, a long string of resorts stretches along the coast to the Rock of Gibraltar, which brings an abrupt end to the Costa del Sol. There's less high rise down this end of the coast, the development focused on candy-coloured villas and expensive golf courses.

Estepona It may have once been of Roman origin but Estepona is now every inch the holiday town. Although less developed than Marbella or Torremolinos, it is still a rapidly expanding resort, in which the construction of homes and infrastructures is now taking place at a vertiginous speed. There's plenty going on here; the town hall is very active in promoting all manner of events like children's arts fair, exhibitions, theatre, motorcycle races, beach and seaside concerts. The town is dominated by the 1700 m (5000 ft) **Sierra Bermeja**, a natural haven for mongoose, wildcats, mountain goats, falcons, and chameleons as well as flora including the prehistoric Christmas-tree like Spanish Fir and the cork oak. The beautiful site of this 'Red Mountain' is at its most spectacular on the rare days in winter when its peaks are snow-capped, offering a dramatic contrast to the sea and warmth below. It's only a 40-minute drive to the summit, but you can walk or cycle up if you prefer. There are endless gentle hiking possibilities for young families and you can rejoin the famous Route of the **White Villages** from the valley behind

the mountain if you're trying to wear out teenagers and indulge in a bit of adventure.

For the best view from the summit go to the traditional mountain refuge, where food is sometimes served but where you can always bring your own and have a fire-side party alongside other groups. Also on the natural front, you can go on dolphin watching, fishing, or just touring trips with the Blue Dolphin Beach Club and Restaurant, both an adventure tour company and a restaurant on the east end of Playa de la Rada.

Estepona's port, both the traditional fishing and pleasure harbour, are also attractive as are its **beaches**: La Rada, 3 km (2 miles) long; and El Cristo, only 550 m (1804 ft) long. After the sun goes down, stroll along the Paseo Marítimo, a broad avenue with gardens on one side, beach on the other. **Selwo adventure park**, between Marbella and Estepona, is a typical 'safari' ride where you hop

Estepona

Casares

onto trucks to see a host of wild animals as well as enjoy some snake shows and a bat cave. Tickets are expensive, €73 (£48.90) for two adults and two children (*www.selwo.es*), ℂ *902 190 482* One unique Andalusian tradition, from Jerez, is that of the equestrian ballet using the pure-bred and stylishly dressed Andalucian horse. Estepona features a riding school, **Escuela de Arte Equestre Costa del Sol** so you don't have to go all the way to Jerez to get a taste of this spectacle. (On the N340 road at km 159, *www.escuela-ecuestre. com*, ℂ *952 808 077*).

Casares Just where the municipality of Estepona ends begins that of Casares, with a small stretch of coast, an uninteresting beach, and some luxury homes already standing or being built. The fun begins on the road up into the hills leading to the old village, bordered by cork oaks, olive, citrus, and avocado trees. If you're lucky you'll see a

cork oak farmer with a laden donkey or a goat herder making their way to the village. The road to the village from the coast is about 15 km (9 miles). Casares itself is a beautiful white village nestled in the mountains that once gave cover to bandoleros. Besides local flavour, Casares has accommodation and restaurants, stunning views all around, and wildlife. It is very close to an equally beautiful and historically important village: Gaucin (inland from Costa del Sol).

Manilva West of Casares and with a much longer coastal stretch is Manilva, another quaint village inland, a locally produced sweet wine, and a lot of Roman history and ruins. The coastal part of the municipality is just 15 minutes from Estepona, under intense development too, and somewhat less expensive. Don't miss the Sunday fleamarket: you'll find everything and anything you might need for your beach experience and maybe even some souvenirs worth taking home.

Castillo de la Duquesa Near to Puerto de la Duquesa is the Castillo, featuring both **Roman ruins** and an 18th century **Christian castle** now housing municipal buildings, a museum, and other attractions. Continuing inland on the same road as that of the flea market you will get to real **Roman baths**, the Hediona sulphur baths, in which **Julius Caesar** himself is said to have bathed. The Romans built a complex bathing chamber alongside the river and you'll be able to soak in the remaining warm dark rooms of the baths as well as in the cooler stream, although the whole site is in a depressing state of disrepair. For the full experience, follow the locals to the other side of the stream and apply clay mud over your body, leaving it there for a while before plunging again to the baths and rinsing it off. Children will love it.

The best part by far is going up the trail by the stream. You will pass by beautiful meadows and more **ruins**. It's well worth the effort: you will shortly arrive upon a series of **natural pools** and **cascades** frequented only by the more adventurous souls. You can swim, picnic, jump off the canyon walls into the water. If you go during the week, you'll have the place to yourself. You can finish off your day by returning to the beach at dusk or perhaps stay in the basic campsite/hotel that's upstream from the baths. You'll find it in a citrus grove: it consists of a swimming pool surrounded by rooms in US motel style. Another option for camping in Manilva is **Camping Chullera II**, on the N340 at km 142.8. ℂ *952 890 320*. Better not to attempt all this with a buggy, though.

Sotogrande A good 30-minute drive west of Estepona and in the municipal grounds of San Roque, in Cadiz province, Sotogrande was built in the sixties as a resort town for rich Spaniards from up north. The resort's permanent or seasonal population are now foreigners. The resort can be summed up in three words: luxury, golf, and family facilities. There are five golf courses onsite: Almenara, the Real Club de Golf de Sotogrande, la Cañada, Valderrama, and La Reserva de Sotogrande (itself containing two courses) as well as two courses adjacent or nearly adjacent to the resort: the San Roque Golf Club and Alcaidesa Links. For children there is also a sailing and kayaking club, a tennis club, a horse-riding academy and the beach, with its luxury chiringuito El Cucurrucho. The resort is divided by the N340 between Sotogrande Playa (Sotogrande beachside) and Sotogrande Alto (Sotogrande high side). The resort features limited shopping facilities but plenty of restaurants and hotels, none of them cheap.

Getting There

The main rail link is in Fuengirola. However, Estepona is on the bus route from Algeciras to Málaga. If you're driving, head east from Algeciras along the E-5/N-340. Algeciras-Granada, Algeciras-Cordoba, and Algeciras-Madrid line can be caught at a mountainous village called Cortes de la Frontera, accessible from Estepona via the Sierra Bermeja road in a 60 to 90-minute drive.

Visitor Information

The **tourist office,** Av. San Lorenzo 1 (📞 95-280-20-02; *www. infoestepona.com*), is open Monday to Friday 9am to 8pm, Saturday 10am to 1.30pm.

Family-Friendly Accommodation

Estepona has some of the most expensive and luxurious resorts along the coast.

Atalaya Park Golf Hotel & Resort ★★ Midway between Estepona and Marbella, this modern resort complex attracts sports and nature lovers. Its tranquil beachside location includes 8 hectares (20 acres) of subtropical gardens. Spacious rooms furnished in an elegant, modern style are well maintained and inviting. Guests have complimentary use of the hotel's extensive sports facilities, including two magnificent golf courses.

Carretera de Cádiz, km 168.5, 29688 Estepona. 📞 *95-288-90-00. Fax 95-288-90-02. www.atalaya-park.es.*

500 rooms. €166–284 (£111.20–190.30) double; €226–306 (£151.40–205) suite; €345–580 (£231.15–388.60) bungalow. Rates include breakfast. AE, DC, MC, V. Free parking. Amenities: 6 restaurants; 2 bars; nightclub (summer only); 6 outdoor pools; 2 18-hole golf courses; 9 tennis courts; health club; sauna; solarium; nautical sports centre; childrens club; car rental; babysitting; laundry service/dry cleaning. In room: A/C, TV, dataport, minibar, hair dryer, safe. Children under 12 free; cost of extra bed variable.

Family-Friendly Dining: Estepona

In summer, the cheapest places to eat in Estepona are the **chiringuitos,** little dining areas set up by local fishermen and their families right on the beach. Naturally they feature seafood, including sole and sardine kebabs grilled over an open fire. You can usually order a fresh salad and fried potatoes.

After your siesta, head for the tapas bars. You'll find most of them – called *freidurías* (fried-fish bars) – at the corner of Calle de los Reyes and La Terraza. Tables spill onto the sidewalks in summer. *Gambas a la plancha* (shrimp) are the favourite (but not the cheapest) tapas to order. Also try La Rada Restaurant, not right off the sea but known as one of the town's best places for fish.

A bit more upscale, three of Estepona's best restaurants are family friendly and next to one another, near the fountain at the west end of the pedestrian Calle Real: The Vines, El Rincón de

Pepe, and Rayuela. Rayuela's atmosphere can't be beat: it is run by an Argentine mother and son team who have decorated the minuscule place with a good dose of nostalgia and humour.

EAST FROM MÁLAGA

Heading east from Málaga, the Costa del Sol quietens down. Peaches, cherries, custard apples and pomegranates are cultivated in orchards and the land rises steeply upwards into the foothills of the mighty, snowy Sierra Nevada. The shoreline is dotted with old *atalaya*, or watch towers, from the days when Barbarian invasions were frequent and there's a more Spanish feel to the place.

Nerja This is a busy resort some 50 km from Málaga on the N340 coastal highway, the main tourist area of this stretch of coast. It's developed, but not as overwhelmingly so as the resorts west of Málaga. The town beach, backed by steep cliffs, is always packed but there are several smaller beaches within easy reach with soft sand and clear water. A big family attraction is the **caves**, 3 km from the town huge caverns with stalactites and stalagmites, the cave walls adorned with paintings 20,000 years old. Nerja is also reasonably close to Granada, so a day trip to the Alhambra with children is less punishing. The town is reasonably pretty, with a flower-filled

old quarter of narrow streets and whitewashed houses with wrought iron terraces. Of particular note – and where Spanish families take their nightly stroll – is the Balcon de Europa, a wide promenade along the top of a towering cliff.

Cueva de Nerja (Cave of Nerja) ★★ This prehistoric stalactite and stalagmite cave, 52 km (32 miles) east of Málaga and 3 km (2 miles) from Nerja, was inhabited from 25,000 to 2000 B.C. It was undiscovered until 1959, when a group of boys found it by chance. When fully opened, it revealed a wealth of treasures left from the days of the cave dwellers, including Paleolithic paintings. The archaeological museum in the cave contains a number of prehistoric artefacts.

Cueva: Carretera de Maro s/n (✆ 95-252-96-35). Daily 10am to 2pm and 4 to 6.30pm. Admission is €5 (£3.35) adults, €2.50 (£1.68) children 6 to 12, free for children under 6. Buses to the cave leave from Muelle de Heredia in Málaga hourly from 7am to 8.15pm. Return buses run every 2 hours until 8.15pm. The journey takes about an hour. If you're driving, head along the N-340/E-15 east 52 km (32 miles) from Málaga or take the N-340/E-15 168 km (104 miles) west from Almería.

Frigiliana The eastern Costa del Sol has its *pueblos blancos*, too, and 7 km north of Nerja is the gorgeous village of Frigiliana, voted many times as Andalucia's prettiest village. The best way to explore is on foot, climbing the **El Fuerte hill** to the ruins of a Moorish fort and a stupendous

Balcon de Europa, Nerja

view over the coastal plain. You'll find plenty of **ice cream stops** as well as several decent *ceramicas*.

Family-Friendly Accommodation: Nerja

EXPENSIVE

Paraíso del Mar ★ **FIND** This leafy little hacienda offers a panoramic view of the coast. It is a fantastically comfortable and kitsch set of villa rooms. Think 'ding dong' doorbells into the spacious rooms, marble floors, a spiral staircase to your roof terrace, Jacuzzi baths, fluffy bath robes and giant wide-screen satellite TVs. The hotel's terraced gardens lead past the swimming pool to a private walkway down to the beach below. The hosts are experts on how to the keep the children entertained.

Prolongación del Carabeo 22, 29780 Nerja. 📞 *95-252-16-21. Fax 95-252-23-09. www.jpmoser.com. 16 rooms. €77–125 (£60–83.75) double; €108–145 (£72.40–97.15) suite. Rates include breakfast. DC, MC, V. Parking €10 (£6.70). Amenities: Breakfast room (with highchairs); bar; outdoor pool; laundry service/dry cleaning.*

In room: A/C, TV, minibar, hair dryer, safe. Cot €7 (£4.70); extra bed €20–28 (£13.40–18.80). Min. stay 2 nights.

Family-Friendly Dining

Marisqueria La Marina The snappiest fresh fish at a brilliant stand up bar for all you can eat prawns, or sit down on the square outside for slightly fancier fish.

Castilla Perez 28, Nerja T 952 52 1299.

Meson de Antonio For a fun evening out, head to this tapas-bar-cum-restaurant and rub shoulders with the locals. There's a garden and terrace for balmy evenings.

Open 12–4pm, 7pm–midnight. Calle Diputacion Provincial, 1829780, Nerja. 📞 *0034952520033. Credit cards accepted.*

GIBRALTAR

Gibraltar is an intriguing sight. As you're travelling around the Costa del Sol, it's ever-present on the western horizon, rising out of the heat haze, a huge, sheer-sided, incongruous chunk of rock, the last piece of Europe before you hop across the Straits to Morocco.

Although it's a peninsula connected to Spain, Gibraltar is like a little slice of Blighty, with English food, English pubs, English brands in the shops, red pillar boxes and British public holidays.

The people, though, are unique to themselves, not like Brits, not like Spaniards, although they're descended from both. They speak English with a strong accent and Spanish with a local dialect.

Gibraltarians are reasonably hospitable but come across as peculiarly insular, a trait which stems from their suffering through history, from brutal sieges in the 18th century to more recently, when Spain closed the land borders between 1969 and 1985, leaving more than 20,000 people crammed into a tiny space, just 5.8 square miles, most of which is sheer rock face. They're highly political and well-informed. Never suggest that they are Spanish.

Gibraltar is an interesting day trip from the Costa del Sol

as there's a lot for families to see. Forget the fact that it's a tiny bit naff in places; for children, it's a combination of easily accessible history, action-adventure (remember the cable car scene with Jaws from the James Bond movie *Moonraker*?), cute monkeys, trips to see whales and dolphins and if you've over-done the tapas, fish and chips. Gibraltar is also incredibly cheap, as there's no VAT.

Essentials

Getting There

By Plane Flying in and out of Gibraltar is quite an event. The runway, built during World War II, juts out into the sea at both ends and runs parallel to the sheerest side of the Rock. The road from the Spanish border town of La Linea to Gibraltar's built-up area runs right across it and traffic stops frequently to allow landing and taking off air-craft to pass. It's mesmerising enough for adults, let alone for children.

There are daily direct sched-uled flights from Gatwick, Heathrow and London Luton, all less than three hours away, with British Airways (operated by GB Airways) and Monarch Scheduled, should you want to fly straight in to this end of the Costa del Sol. Alternatively, fly in and out of Málaga and rent a car. A new airline, Fly Gibraltar, started operation in April 2007 from London Stansted, Manchester, Birmingham and Bristol, as

Gibraltar Rock

Barbary Ape

well as Dublin and Cork in the Republic of Ireland.

British Airways, ☎ 0845 77 333 77, *www.ba.com*.

Monarch, ☎ 0870 040 5040, *www.flymonarch.com*.

FlyGibraltar, ☎ 0870 774 7411, *www.flygib.com*.

By Car Getting to Gibraltar from the Costa del Sol is easy – you can see it from pretty well anywhere west of Málaga. Simply take the N340 or the A7 motorway and follow the signs to La Linea, the grim and unappealing border town. The border is open 24 hours a day. The drive from Málaga airport, if that's your chosen gateway, should take about an hour and a half and you can take a Spanish car into Gibraltar.

Driving in Gibraltar Driving is on the right and the speed limit

is 50 kph. A couple of words of warning, though. The border crossing can be slow, depending on the volume of traffic and the mood of the guards on the Spanish side, so make sure you've got drinks and snacks for your children handy. Check the state of the queue by calling ☎ 350 42777 if you're in Gibraltar and wanting to leave, ☎ 9567 42777 if you're on the way there from Spain. (You have to dial ☎ +9567 instead of the country code of ☎ +350 when calling from Spain because Spain won't recognise Gibraltar as a country and prefixes all its five figure numbers with a local Spanish code.) Second, watch out for your rental car while driving around Gibraltar's incredibly narrow streets. It's a tight squeeze, buildings have irregular, sticking-out edges and parking is a challenge. Just look at the locals' cars – every one is dented and scratched. Think twice before taking a people mover into Gibraltar.

Car rental companies serving Málaga Airport include:

Andalucia Car, ☎ +34 605 93 00 15, *www.andaluciacar.com*.

Avis, ☎ 956 150 005, *www.avis.es*.

Málaga Car, ☎ + 34 952 59 25 01, *www.malagacar.com*.

e-Sixt, ☎ +34 902 28 76 00, *www.sixt.es*.

Taxi drivers will also take you from the airport as far as the border at La Linea for around €100 (£67).

By Bus There isn't any cross-border public transport but Spanish bus services from all over the Costa del Sol will take you to the bus station in La Linea, five minutes' walk from the border.

By Train From further afield, if you can get to Algeciras by train (there's an overnight sleeper service from Madrid, the Estrella del Estrecho, schedules at *www.renfe.es*), cross the road from the station to the bus terminal, from where buses leave every half hour for La Linea, some 30 minutes away.

Visitor Information

Gibraltar Tourist Board, Duke of Kent House, Cathedral Square, ✆*+350 74950*, tourism@gibraltar.gi, *www.gibraltar.gov.uk*.

Fast Facts: Gibraltar

Currency Exchange The unit of currency is the Gibraltar Pound, exactly the same as the Pound Sterling. English notes and coins are accepted, but not Scottish and Northern Irish ones. Gibraltar notes and coins are not accepted in UK, so either spend them or change them back. Euros are accepted in most places, but you may lose out on the exchange rate. Banks are generally open from 9am to 3.30pm, Monday to Thursday, and until 4.30pm on Friday. Bureaux de change open from 9am to 6pm. All major credit cards are accepted in shops, restaurants and hotels.

Consulate Gibraltar is a British Overseas Territory and as such is a tiny slice of Britain in the Med. The local authorities deal with issues that would normally be the duty of the consulate.

The Government of Gibraltar Civil Status and Registration Office (for passports, birth, marriage and death registration and other routine consular matters), ✆*+350 51725*); fax: +350 42706; *csro@gibnynex.gi*.

The Royal Gibraltar Police ✆*+350 72500* for general enquiries or ✆ *199* in emergencies.

Medical Emergencies Just show your passport (assuming you are British) and you will be entitled to free emergency medical treatment. It is, however, advisable to have a **European Health Insurance Card** (EHIC), for all the family, in case you need to be transferred to a bigger hospital in Spain. The main hospital is St Bernard's at Europort, ✆*+350 79700*.

Newspapers The main English language newspaper is the *Gibraltar Chronicle* and online, *Panorama,* a daily news service (*www.panorama.gi*).

Internet Café Cyberworld, Rooms 14–16, Ocean Heights Gallery, Queensway, ✆*+350 51416*.

Guided Tours & Excursions Blands Travel, ✆*+350 77012*.

Post Office 104 Main Street, ✆*+350 75714*.

Taxis Gibraltar Taxi Association, ✆*+350 70027*.

What to See & Do

The Rock

The British, the Spanish First, equip your children with a bit of history so they can put the rock into perspective.

The peninsula of Gibraltar used to belong to Spain but was captured by Britain in 1704 and ceded by Spain by the Treaty of Utrecht of 1713, which stipulates that the Crown of Spain has to be given first option on the territory if the Crown of Great Britain ever decides to surrender sovereignty.

Spain has made many efforts since then to recover Gibraltar, including a number of sieges in the 18th century. In World War II, the rock played an important strategic role for Britain and the civilian population was evacuated. Children will be thrilled to know that it's honeycombed with holes and tunnels, some of them still 'secret' and closed to all except the military.

Diplomacy In 1969, Britain gave Gibraltar a new constitution, granting the inhabitants of the rock a degree of self-government. At this point, the Spanish government closed the border in a huff, effectively isolating the Gibraltarians, who could only come and go by air, or by boat. This 1969 Constitution is not recognised by Spain, but then, nor is the Government of Gibraltar.

Things have, however, eased up due to continued diplomatic efforts. In 1982, the border partially re-opened (day-tripping Spaniards are by far the greatest proportion of visitors), although Spain still throws regular hissy fits about such issues as Gibraltar's football team and still refuses to play in tournaments where Gibraltar is allowed to submit a team.

The Upper Rock Take the cable car from Grand Parade up to the dizzying heights of the summit, and admire the incredible view, west towards Málaga, east towards Cadiz and south towards the High Atlas Mountains of Morocco. Most of the Upper

Enjoying the View

St Michael's Cave

Rock is a nature reserve, where you can spot many different species of migratory bird and some 600 types of plants and flowers. The cable car operates continuously, daily except Sundays, from 9.30am–5.45pm. The ride takes about six minutes. A cable car and apes ticket (including the Apes' Den, see below) costs £8 return, while a ticket including entrance to St Michael's Cave, the nature reserve and the Siege Tunnels costs £16. Entrance to each site costs £8 without the ticket. ☏ + 350 77826.

St Michael's Cave St Michael's Cave is a spectacular cavern of stalactites and stalagmites, deep inside the rock. On weekdays, there's a twice-daily sound and light show that describes the myths and legends of the rock, from the formation of the pillars of Hercules – it's only 15 minutes long and very child-friendly.

If you've got adventurous children over the age of 10, book one of the special tours into the lower cave, where there's an amazing lake and the cave is just as it was found in 1942. There's a fair bit of scrambling and use of ropes, so this is for the brave only, and you'll need decent shoes.

☏+350 56639000. Lower Cave tours take place weekdays from 6pm, Saturdays from 2.30pm and Sundays by appointment, and cost £5.

Great Siege Tunnels The Great Siege Tunnels were dug during the Great Siege of 1779 to 1783, as the defenders of Gibraltar were trying to get a better angle to shoot at the attacking French and Spanish armies. The Gibraltarians had to tunnel into the rock to align their guns to fire sideways at the trenches. You can visit the Upper Galleries of the tunnels on a trip to the Upper Rock. Open daily.

Apes' Den Children will probably be most anxious to visit the Apes' Den at the cable car

FUN FACT ⟩⟩ Nelson in a Barrel of Rum ⟨⟨

Children who have studied Nelson at school may be interested in Rosia Bay where his body was brought aboard HMS *Victory* (reputedly in a barrel of rum) after the Battle of Trafalgar at the western end of the Strait, as well as the unique '100 ton gun' – the Victorian 'Super Gun' which is nearby.

mid-station (where you can also buy a cuddly, screechy ape soft toy that will drive you mad in minutes). The 120 apes are in fact tail-less macaques, and roam free, although they are fed every day. Each one has a name. Their behaviour can be pretty lewd at times and you may find yourself answering questions about the birds and bees (and monkeys) that you'd prefer to save for later. Children shouldn't approach or feed the monkeys, which are wild. Don't stand around eating, either, as they may creep up on you and steal your banana or ice cream. There are more apes at the top of the cable car. Legend has it that when the monkeys leave Gibraltar, the rock will no longer be British.

World War II Tunnels These are a complete Boy's Own adventure, particularly if you take one of the tours. The tunnels were dug in 1940, when Gibraltar was surrounded by enemies and the only way to go was inwards. This warren of passageways, in total more than 30 miles of them, was partly opened to the public in 2005. Special tours of the tunnels are conducted by a guide from HM Forces and you'll need a torch and comfortable shoes. Minimum group size is six or seven, maximum 15, and the tours do take three hours, so are unsuitable for small children. WWII Tunnels, Princes Caroline's Battery, Upper Rock, ☎+350 45957. To book a tour, ☎+350 55820.

A balancing Barbary Ape

FUN FACT From Under the Sea

Gibraltar is an ancient piece of limestone, thrust up from the seabed and flipped over, millions of years ago, as the African continental plate collided with the European plate.

Dolphin Watching Several companies offer whale and dolphin-watching in the Straits of Gibraltar, often a prime spotting-ground. There are no guarantees but this is one of the best places in the Med; the dolphins are attracted to the schools of tuna and the deep water. It can get very choppy, so take a seasickness pill before you leave if you're susceptible. Most tours depart from the marina, which has a large car park nearby. If some members of the family choose to go and others stay behind, there are bars and cafes in which to sit all around the marina.

Dolphin Adventure, Marina Bay, ☎+350 50650. Adults: £20.00.

Children under 12: £10.00 (under 12 years).

Dolphin Safari, Marina Bay, ☎+350 71914, www.dolphinsafari.gi. Adults: £25.00 Children under 12: £12.00.

Main Street and Casemates Square All the shops are on Main Street and the alleyways either side of it. Good buys include glass, china, leather, electronics, booze, perfume and cigarettes, and British clothing brands. Casemates Square is another shopping/eating area, and the focus of Gibraltar's nightlife. There are lots of family-friendly restaurants and pubs around here and it's a good place to cool off and relax between sightseeing forays.

Main Street

Caleta Hotel

Family-Friendly Accommodation

EXPENSIVE

The Rock Hotel Gibraltar's poshest hotel, and a local institution. The hotel has 104 bedrooms and suites in colonial style, each with free Internet access, lollipops by the bed and ducks in the bathroom (toy ones). There's a saltwater pool, open April to October only, and a casino. As well as the main restaurant, there's afternoon tea in a panoramic lounge and tapas in the bar. The hotel supplies cots, high chairs, children's portions, babysitting and baby listening.

Rooms from £160 to £295 per night. Europa Road, ☎+350 73000, fax. +350 75313, rockhotel@ gibtelecom.net, www.rockhotel gibraltar.com.

The Caleta Hotel Four star hotel clinging to the rock face outside the old fishing village of Catalan Bay, looking across to north Africa. If you're staying more than a couple of nights, this makes a good base for a family as it has a pool; the only problem can be that it gets a bit overrun by conference groups. There's also a spa, a very good Italian restaurant, and outdoor grill, café and business centre. From £125 to £180 per room per night, room only. Family suites are available and babysitters can be arranged.

Catalan Bay, ☎+350 76501, Fax. +350 42143, reservations@caleta hotel.gi, www.caletahotel.com.

INEXPENSIVE

Continental Hotel A two-AA star hotel very close to Casemates Square. Rooms, all with private facilities, range from singles to quads, useful for families and there's a restaurant, bar and satellite TV.

From £52 for a single to £95 for a quad, per room per night including continental breakfast. Engineer Lane, ☎+350 76900; Fax. +350 41702, contihotel@gibtelecom.net.

The Marina

Family-Friendly Dining

The Star Bar The oldest bar in Gibraltar, open from breakfast time. Staple English food, from breakfast fry ups to steak and chips. There's a children's menu and outside seating. Parliament Lane (☎+350 75924).

Bianca's Restaurant One of the most popular restaurants, especially on summer evenings and for Sunday lunch, thanks to its large waterside terrace, overlooking the yachts. The menu is eclectic, with everything from Indian to spare ribs, pasta and Tex-Mex, with all manner of ice creams and sundaes for dessert. There's a children's menu, too.

6/7 Admiral's Walk, Marina Bay, ☎+350 73379.

Smith's Fish & Chips A traditional chippy – eat in or take away. There are pasties and burgers, too.

Open from 8am–6pm, daily. 295 Main Street, ☎+350 74254.

Buddies Pasta Casa Wide variety of pastas and other Italian dishes; ask for smaller portions for children. All the usual favourites are here – *fettuccine de formaggio, spaghetti alla carbonara* and *fusilli al salmone*.

Open Monday–Wednesday 10am–5pm, Thursday, Friday and Saturday 10am–4pm and 7pm–midnight. 15 Cannon Lane, ☎+350 40627.

Lord Nelson Bar Brasserie Famous and noisy pub/restaurant in old military building on Casemates Square. Children will love it because the interior is done out to represent Nelson's ship, complete with cloud and sky ceiling crossed with beams and sails. Daytime or early evening is better than late, as it gets overwhelmingly packed in the bar area and the music, though fun, is loud.

10 Casemates Square, ☎+350 50009, *www.lordnelson.gi.*

FUN FACT » **The Strait** «

The Strait was, in fact, once closed, as Gibraltar was connected to North Africa and the Mediterranean was a land-locked dust bowl – hard to imagine! Some five million years ago, a fissure opened where the Strait is today and the Atlantic gushed in, filling the basin in just one hundred years, with an awesome, 10,000 ft waterfall at the entrance to the Strait. Try getting your children to visualise that!

THE WHITE TOWNS

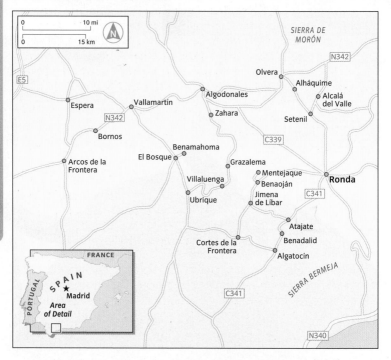

The pueblos blancos are, for many people, what Andalucia is all about: a string of white towns speckled across a mountainous green and brown landscape like polka dots on a flamenco dress. Purists may claim that the 'proper' white towns lie only in Cadiz province, but it's hard to argue against the inclusion of settlements like Ronda and Gaucin, set as they are in the same landscape, and undeniably white in colour. The *pueblos blancos* are spread across a couple of hundred kilometres connected by mountain roads, so it's possible to base yourself in one place and see everything you want to in a few days, although with children, it's best not to be too ambitious. Alternatively, this mountainous region is ideal for touring and most towns have at least a couple of good accommodation options.

History comes alive for children in this wild, hilly and once lawless region. Many of the towns have '*de la Frontera*' as their suffix, which means 'of the frontier', the frontier in question being the one-time edge of Moorish Andalucia. Bandits and highwaymen used to lurk on the mountain trails, mugging and sometimes killing travellers. Today, though, this is an area of stunning beauty and lends itself to walking, cycling, bird watching, even hang gliding and climbing, so you can be as active as you want depending on your children's ages. There are lakes, too, for cooling off in and sailing or kayaking on, and the towns themselves are full of things for children to see and do: ruined castles everywhere you look, labyrinthine centres to explore, the odd museum and any number of artefact shops to stock up on local goods. Even the smallest merits an hour or two for strolling and taking in the unique atmosphere of this area: part Spanish, part Moorish and totally geared to the hot summers and winters which can be surprisingly cold. Each town has its focal points and plazas where you can slip into the easy pace of life and linger over a drink or a long lunch, watching the locals come and go and gaining some insight into the way these communities run. The uniformity and beauty of these towns might at first glance seem austere but look further and all will reveal a great deal of charm.

ESSENTIALS

Getting There/ Orientation

The White Towns are a tight cluster of villages within easy driving distances to the international airports of Seville, Malaga, Granada and Jerez. To get the best of them and their surrounds you need to have a car, although once inside each is small enough to explore on foot. The biggest and most visited town is Ronda, which is 40 km (25 miles) from the coast, and 113 km (70 miles) from Málaga. It is the most easterly of the White Towns. Gaucin lies on the road between Ronda and Algeciras and Tarifa, and is only 30 minutes drive from the Costa Del Sol's Estepona. Arcos de la Frontera is the closest White Town to Jerez and Seville, and one of the most dramatic. Buses in the sierra are operated by Amarillos (956 704 977/956 329 347) who operate between Cadiz, Jerez, Arcos and Ubrique and all points in between and round about. Comes (902 199 208/956 342 174) also operate in the area. Trains go from Malaga to Ronda and on to Seville.

Towns & Villages

Ronda

Getting There
Ronda is around 97 km (60 miles) West of Málaga or 147 km (91 miles) South East of Seville. From the coast C344 you'll arrive first at the Barrio de San Francisco, where it's best to park and walk into the city through the Moorish gate Puerta de Almocábar.

Visitor Information

The tourist office is at Plaza de España 1 (95-287-12-72; *www.andalucia.org*; is open Monday to Friday 9am to 7.30pm, Saturday and Sunday 10am to 2pm. (*www.ronda.to*).

Getting Around
The town is small enough to get around on foot: on no account should you drive. It's a tiny place but there are horse-drawn carriages for hire.

WHAT TO SEE & DO

Children's Top 10 Attractions

❶ El Tajo Gazing at the gorge and the houses perched precariously on the edge of the chasm (see p. 137).

❷ Museo del Bandolero A must for youngsters into Cowboys and Indians type action and fascinating for teens, too. This is horrible history come to life (see p. 137).

❸ Casa del Rey Moro Gardens, a secret passage, slippery steps and a river, the Casa del Rey Moro is a little adventure children will really go for. The **Sala de Secretos** is a wonderful whispering wall (see p. 138).

❹ Cueva de la Pileta View the ancient paintings in this prehistoric cave system: see goats, horses, cows; and gape at the oddly shaped stalagmites and stalagtites (see p. 139).

❺ Parque Natural de Grazalema A biosphere with thick forests of holm oak, cork pines and wild olives. Birdlife includes griffon vultures, goshawk and the Egyptian vulture (see p. 140).

❻ Plaza del Cabildo Make your way to **Convento de Mercedarias Descalzas** for a sweet shop with a difference: a talking wall, a bell and a revolving contraption selling almond macaroons (see p. 143).

❼ Olvera bike track When large stretches of disused railway track in Olvera between Jerez to Malaga were turned into '*Vias Verdes*' or cycling tracks, the authorities really hit on a great idea (see p. 144).

❽ Alcazabar Walk from Antequera's small bullfighting museum up the alleyways of tall cypress trees to the Alcazabar, the ruined Moorish fortress (see p. 146).

❾ Lobo Park A must for children who will adore the captive bred timber, tundra and Iberian wolves roaming here (see p. 146).

❿ El Chorro Take to the water by El Chorro dam where on three lakes at Guadalhorce you can swim and canoe (see p. 146).

Puente Nuevo

El Tajo Ronda is home to the gorge that launched a thousand postcards: El Tajo. The bridge is an incredible sight for youngsters: a tiny Medieval garland to the heights of an isolated plateau split in two by the 150 m (500 ft) ravine. On either side of the giant cleft are cliff-hanging houses, crouched precariously close to the chasm. The gorge divides the town into an older part, the Moorish and aristocratic quarter of '**La Ciudad**' and the newer section south of the gorge, **El Mercadillo**. The old quarter is the more attractive of the two; narrow, rough streets and buildings with a marked Moorish influence. The two sides are joined by the 18th century **Puente Nuevo**.

Bullring Ronda has a magnificent bullring and is so associated with the bullfight it even has a street named after the sport's most famous American aficionado, Don Ernesto (who repaid the compliment by calling it his favourite Spanish town). The town was also home to the great Pedro Romero, one of Spain's most legendary matadors, who died in the ring here. Beyond bulls, the little town has rich historical sites, museums (particularly good for children is one on the area's banditry past), and nearby amazing nature and caves.

Museo del Bandolero ★ ★ ★

This small museum is an entertaining lesson in Horrible History for children. Consider yourselves lucky to be hitting Ronda's mean streets in the 21st century: back in the 19th tourists arriving in Ronda were uniformly held up, robbed, roughed up, and at worst murdered. In their heyday, some parts of Andalucia became total no-go zones for noblemen, even for those who were armed to the teeth. Poverty-stricken Andalucians lionized these highway robbers and cutthroats for their Robin Hood-like work redistributing the spoils from the rich land-owning classes to the needy. Very few deserved the praise: mostly the scoundrels emerged from their thieves' lairs to plunder and murder before disappearing back into the silent mountain passes, without any grand gestures of benevolence towards their fellow common man.

The small museum here contains a collection of historical documents, pictures, photographs, interviews, weapons and costumes to give a sense of the life of the bandits and the men who fought them bringing the bandits' story to life for children.

Calle Armiñán 65, 29400 Ronda, Málaga. ☎/Fax 952 87 77 85. Email: *museobandolero@hotmail.com, web-site: www.museobandolero.com. Admission €3 (£2), free for children under 7. Open every day. Spring–Summer 10.30am–8.30pm. Autumn–Winter 10.30am–7pm.*

Alameda De Tajo ★

This leafy park, in El Mercadillo, just by Spain's largest operational bullring, has improbably stunning views out across the sweep of the valley floor and the Ronda mountain range behind. It's Ronda's best place to picnic, packed with jungly vegetation and lots of benches in the shade. There are swings and slides by the brink of cliff face (and some dingy loos). There are also a few cages of peacocks, budgerigars and other 'exotic birds' which will keep little ones amused.

Plaza De Toros Nearby is the famous bullring, or Plaza de Toros, on the Plaza de Espana. The bullring dates back to 1785 and is where Pedro Romero, considered the godfather of modern bullfighting, evolved the style of fighting on foot instead of on horseback. He was painted by the artist Goya and in early September every year, the Goyesca takes place – a festival attended by the country's finest matadors, dressed in 18th century finery. There's a small museum at the bullring, which is a much better bet for children. (Open 10am–8pm in summer, 10am–6pm in winter.)

Sites If You Have Time

Casa del Rey Moro Marqués de Parada 17. This 'House of the Moorish King' was actually built in the early 1700s, long after the Moors had been kicked out. Through its gardens you get to the Water Mine, which is the secret route down to the river that Ronda's king Abomelik ordered his captive Christian slaves to dig in the 14th century

House of the Moorish King

in case a besieging army tried to starve the city of water. It's 300 slippery, badly lit steps to the very bottom but children will love it; the setting is like something out of a Scooby Doo adventure. **The Sala de Secretos** ★★ is where you can whisper secrets to each other by standing close to the wall, unheard by those standing in the centre.

Banos Arabes There's also the Banos Arabes in the Barrio de Padre Jesus, largely restored though not in working order. Beautiful, peaceful and worth the stroll down from the old town (and the hike back up, taking in some of the town's impressive fortifications).

Open Mar–Oct 10am–7pm daily; Nov–Feb Mon–Fri 10am–6pm, Sat, Sun 10am–2pm. Admission €2 (£1.34), €1 (£0.67) concessions, under-14s free.

TIP **Take a Hike**

There are lots of companies specializing in activity holidays in Andalucia, but you can easily arrange your own hikes, bike-rides or canyoning once you're in the area. **www.pasolargos.com** is the local walking club for Ronda. You can download walking route-maps from the website. Decent local routes include Tajo del Abanico in the Serrania de Ronda and Virgen de la Cabeza.

Near Ronda

Cueva de la Pileta ★ Some 25,000 years ago, palaeolothic men and women dug their way into 5 km of caves surrounded by a limestone mountain ridge called La Pileta and picked up their prehistoric paintbrushes to do a spot of painting and decorating. The ancient paintings they chose to embroider their walls with, of goats, horses, cows, and people, in the grottoes and galleries here now share space with crazy-shaped stalagmites and stalactites. It's well worth taking a tour, lit by paraffin lamps, around the cave system. The best part of the interconnecting cave system is the chamber of the fish, Sala Del Pez, which ends in a precipice that drops 75 m. El Pez itself is a 1.5 m-long fish drawn with both eyes on one side of the body. Also look out for the drawing of the famous pregnant mare.

The limestone entrance to the Cueva del Gato, Cave of the Cat, is supposed to look like a cat. It is a site of archaeological significance, but you can't go inside unless you're a skilled pot-holer. It does, however, make a great walk for energetic families, with an icy and crystal clear rock pool at the end. This isn't for small children, though, as you need to allow two hours in each direction from Benaojan.

Cueva de la Pileta, turn off the 4.5 km from Benaoján on the MA501 road to Cortes de la Frontera, the caves are at the top of the stone stairway. Daily 10am–1pm, 4pm–6pm. Obligatory guided tours last an hour.

Sierra de las Nieves (South and east of Ronda). El Tajo, the giant landmark ravine that draws visitors inland to Ronda from the Costa Del Sol, is not a one-off in this area, which is sliced in many places by deep gorges and mountain streams. The Natural Park of Sierra de las Nieves, a 20 by 30 km UNESCO biosphere reserve that's covered in Spanish firs, has beautiful mountain scenery to match El Tajo. The hills here are planted with firs, gall oak, yews, maples, carobs, chestnuts and holm oak. One is Calle of the Caina, which drops

FUN FACT **Dem Bones**

Well, more like a gruesome fact! Five fossilized human skeletons and two animals were unearthed when the caves were rediscovered in 1905.

over 100 m. Wildlife includes Spanish ibex, fallow deer, wild cat, golden eagle, owl and otter (the last at the río Verde or Green River).

Roads aren't tarmacked, and the only whole way across the park is in a 4×4, but you can drive a good way in and find some beautiful spots for picnics or playing in the woods. The San Pedro to Ronda road is your best entry point: turn at the A376 at km 136. There are also turnings at Tolox, Istan, El Burgo and Yunquera.

Valle De Genal Taking the river route between Sierra Bermeja and the road that connects the villages of Jimena and Ronda is like stepping back into a time-warp to a land of shepherds and donkeys. The landscapes are lovely, soft, and the whole area is pretty deserted.

Grazalema & The Natural Park

The Parque Natural de Grazalema is a rugged, limestone and dolomite massif full of crags, grottoes, caves and sinuous gorges west of Ronda. It was declared a biosphere reserve in 1975, and has the highest rainfall in the Iberian Peninsula, feeding thick forests of holm oak, cork pines, carob and wild olives. Birdlife (protected here since 1989) includes griffon vultures (there's a huge colony near the village of Zahara de la Sierra), goshawk and the Egyptian vulture. There are also huge bat colonies.

Wild walks

Rustic Blue (*www.rusticblue.com*) runs a number of self-guided walking holidays in the park. There are self-guided tours for the active family with older and energetic children: up to date walking notes and maps put together by Guy Hunter-Watts, who wrote the book *Walking in Andalucia* and has lived locally since the 1980s. Alternatively stay at El Tejar, which is the B&B that Guy Hunter-Watts himself runs just outside Ronda. Most of the guesthouses and hotels in Grazalema have information on walks.

Grazalema's tourist office is on Plaza de España (☎ *956 132 225*) and has information on walks, rock climbing, mountain biking, pot-holing and horse-riding.

Grazalema

The white town of Grazalema is not really about its monuments, it's about the town itself. The approach road from El Bosque leads you around the top of the town and as you look down on

---

FUN FACT 〉〉 **Making Rain** 〈

The limestone peaks of 1500 m around Grazalema are the first barriers that clouds from the Atlantic meet: hence the high rainfall here.

National Park, Grazalema

the tiled roofs and whitewashed houses the vista is spectacular, set as it is amid the mountains and with a lush valley stretching beyond. The town itself gets very busy at weekends with Spaniards out camping or just day-tripping or lunching here. But go out of season or in midweek and you'll find a lovely quiet town to wander around. Its tidy streets meander up and down, there are plenty of shops selling the

Grazalema

famous local blankets and up-market artefacts and lots of little restaurants and bars to eat in. Those on the main square, the Plaza de Espana, spread their tables across the pretty, tree-lined open space flanked on one side by the handsome Iglesia de la Aurora and the fare is good, hearty, country style stews and meat dishes. Wild mountain trout stuffed with ham is a delicious local speciality. Behind the Plaza de Espana is a Mirador with great views across the plain. The swimming pool is a bit run down and only open in high summer; a bit of a gamble but welcome on a hot day.

Gaucin

Brits may have been repopulat-ing the Costas for decades, but their influence in the village of Gaucin, perched high above the Costa del Sol, goes back more than 100 years. This was a stop-ping off point for British officers

Fiesta Fun!

In mid-July, around the Virgen del Carmen fiesta day of 16 July, the village holds its annual fiesta, with flamenco music, fireworks and a procession, culminating in an exciting mini-Pamplona, where a bull is released to charge through the streets. From a safe distance, this is a great spectacle for children to enjoy.

and their families en route from Gibraltar to summer quarters in cooler Ronda; nowadays it's home to a thriving, mostly arty community of northern European expats and wealthy second-homers whose villas are dotted around the hills that surround the town. The pretty, narrow streets are home to more British-plated Volvos and Range Rovers than locally-registered Seats, and the overall feel is like Hampstead-on-sea. The views of the coast and Gibraltar and across the straits to Morocco can be mind-blowing, especially from the **Castillo de Aguila** (Castle of the Eagle) which sits high above the town.

Arcos de la Frontera

Getting There

Turn off the A4 from Seville onto the A382. Don't be tempted to drive up to the Medina just because there's a car park in the Plaza del Cabildo: roads here are absurdly narrow and will challenge any estate car.

Visitor Information

The tourist office is on the Plaza del Cabildo (Mon–Sat 10am–2pm and 3.30–7.30pm, Sun 10am–2pm).

Orientation

Arcos de la Frontera is bigger than the other white towns – Ronda excepted – and enjoys a dramatic setting, clinging to the side of a cliff above the Guadalete river valley. The winding, sometimes switchback nature of its streets betray a Moorish past and though the fall away on the town's northern side is more gradual, no street in the *casco antiguo* (old quarter) is level. This up-and-down jumble of old, geranium-dressed houses and urban palaces has a charm you won't find anywhere else in the *pueblos blancos*.

What to See and Do

Arcos seems curiously uncommitted to tourism. Yes, there are

Arcos de la Frontera

souvenir shops, plenty of eating and drinking options and even a state-run Parador hotel. But Arcos life – in both the old and lower new town – revolves around the older concerns of agriculture and traditional building techniques. This seeming indifference to visitors may hark back to dark tales of witchcraft which abound locally – or it could just mean that the tourist euro is welcome, though not at any cost. Whatever, it provides visitors with a glimpse of a real Spanish countryside town – albeit one with a more spectacular outlook than most. It's worth spending a night in the Parador here in summer; on occasions, the town comes to life after sunset with bands playing in the main square and a generally festive atmosphere, children running around all over the place until midnight while parents dine al fresco.

Iglesia de Santa Maria Locals claim the bells of Iglesia de Santa Maria (St Mary's) (📞 956 70 00 06, open mid-March to mid-Oct Mon–Fri 10am–1pm, 4–6pm; Sat 10am–1.30pm. Mid Oct–mid March Mon-Sat 9.30am-2pm, 3.30pm–6pm; Sun 10.30am–1pm) are the most resonant in all of Andalucia. The church received the ultimate accolade from the Holy Tribune in Rome in 1764 when it was declared the most distinguished in Arcos. The nearby 16th century church **Iglesia de San Pedro** (St Peter's) (C/San Pedro 4, open Mon–Sat 10.30am–2pm).

San Pedro is probably more popular with children: you can climb its tower for even better views, and the paintings inside include Dolorosa by Pacheco, Velásquez's tutor, and works by Zurbarán and Ribera.

Plaza del Cabildo ★ The pretty, cobbled, Plaza del Cabildo, is at the heart of the old town. The south side of the square forms a stunning look out point (the *balcon de Arcos*) out over the cliffs and chequerboard of plains below.

To keep the family's energy up after climbing the steep streets to the old town and to give new meaning to drive-through, or walk-through, pay a visit to the Convento de Mercedarias Descalzas (c/ de loss Escribanos, 8.30am–2.30pm, 5–7pm daily). Here you'll find a vending machine with a difference. A sign on the wall invites you to 'press here for sweet things'. Ring the bell and a voice from behind an iron contraption in the wall asks whether you want sweets or cakes and how many boxes. The wares appear in front of you inside a revolving cage. The almond macaroons are €5 (£3.35) for a generous box.

There are guided walks around the old town (info from tourist office), a small Andaluz garden, recently created, and there's a pleasant, bar-lined *paseo*.

Lago de Arcos Just out of town the nearby lake, Lago de Arcos, is an excellent place to take a

Horsing Around

Horseriding: For horseriders, Centro Hípica Las Nieves is a spankingly clean stable with amazing horses. Instruction is for all levels. Only some of the staff speak English though. Carretera Arcos – Gibalbín km 1.5, Arcos, ☎ 658 855 825, **www.hipicalasnieves.com**. Hípica El Granero has 15 horses available for hacks, day long excursions or lessons ☎ 607 374 160, **www.andaluces.net**.

cooling swim. There is a municipal sailing club (☎ 956 70 30 11) on the banks and you can rent kayaks for a gentle paddle. Warm thermal breezes give 15 knots in the afternoon and you can even get RYA qualifications on Lasers, Optimists or Cadets. The water is safe, warm and flat. If you want an all-inclusive sporty holiday book through **www.spainsail.com** ☎ 020 7193 7368, which has 18 double bedrooms and bungalows for four people at El Hotel de la Molinera, a former olive oil mill powered by the windmill and a bus ride from Arcos.

Olvera

Via Verde de la Sierra: the Olvera bike track ★★ Olvera, a pleasant town on hill with amazing views of the sierra, a big church and castle vying for dominance on the skyline, has often been called one of the unsung *pueblos blancos* of Cádiz, but the town has been given new lease of life since the Spanish Railway Foundation (SRF) came up with a plan to turn large stretches of disused railway track into *Vias Verdes* or 'green ways'. At one stage Olvera was to become a stop on the Jerez to Málaga line,

but the line was never completed and the stations fell into disrepair and the track crumbled. Today, however, the old railway lines have been reconditioned and levelled and now provide a glorious 36 km (22½ mile) hiking and cycling route through delightful countryside. The track runs from Olvera to Puerto Serrano, cutting through mountains and neat olive groves via a series of viaducts and tunnels which light up when a cyclist whizzes through. There are no steep gradients, no traffic and the former stations at both ends of the route have been converted into simple hotels, so you can leave your car at one end, spend a night at the other end and cycle back the next day. Part of the track runs through the **Peñon de Aframagon nature reserve**, home to the area's largest colony of griffon vultures and there are plenty of excellent picnic spots. Derelict stations are being reborn as restaurants and bike-hire shops, catering for younger travellers.

Vias Verdes (☎ 911 51 1065). www. ffe.es/viasverdes. The Estacion Puerto Serrano (☎ 955 898190) double room €36 (£24.10). Estacion de Olvera (☎ 956 130802) double €48 (£32.15).

Other Towns

Setenil is pretty and pleasant to walk around, with streets diverging on the river which ate away the gorge and where the cave houses which the village is known for are built. There's a Moorish castle on a hill to one side of town, quite dramatic. Don't drive here – you'll never get out but you'll give the locals a big laugh.

Lovely **Zahara de la Sierra** sits above its reservoir, a pretty main street full of restaurants and bars and a Tugasa hotel at the far end, near the shrine to the Virgin. A steep but well made path leads to the spectacular castle with knockout views and where you can watch eagles and vultures flying below you. Even if you don't want to hike, drive the Puerto de las Palomas between Zahara and Grazalema; it's the highest mountain pass in Andalucia and weaves in and out of the pinsapo pine forests on the side of a sheer rock face. At the top, at 1350 m, the views are of rugged mountains, lush valleys and sun-bleached golden fields rolling towards the horizon.

Ubrique Ubrique has Roman ruins of Ocuri nearby. It is a leather town, famous for producing stuff for Italian designer labels, not ugly but not beautiful either. There are lots of retail outlets for bargain hunters but nowhere to stay. **El Bosque** sits at the foot of a sierra on a trout stream, famous for the fish farms, and has plenty of restaurants serving it up. **The parque natural Alcornocales** is very pretty and impressive but definitely one for serious nature lovers, has some of the biggest cork oaks in the world and is

Setenil

home to the gall and the holm oak as well as wild olive trees. Wildlife includes the Egyptian mongoose, the royal eagle, eagle owls, lion buzzards and the roebuck.

Antequera, El Torcal, Embalse De Guadalhorce (El Chorro)

Antequera isn't a white town – it lies on a plain, almost directly inland from Malaga, and combined with El Torcal and El Chorro makes a fun and undemanding day trip from the Malaga area with lots for children. You'll find a handsome, well-heeled, very Spanish town packed with history. Antequera has its own version of Stonehenge, Cueva de Menga, a huge dolmen (prehistoric tomb), which has been cut from rock and fashioned into a burial cave. Nobody knows how prehistoric man managed to do this.

Antequera also has an attractive bullring, the only one in Spain with a restaurant in it. If you missed the bullfighting museum in Ronda, there's a small one here, as well. You can also walk up the alleyways of tall cypress trees to the Alcazabar, the ruined Moorish fortress, and impress your children with the story of **Lovers' Rock**, a strange rock formation in the distance that looks like the face of a sleeping giant.

Lobo Park Just 8 km (5 miles) from Antequera is the fantastic Lobo Park, a 40-hectare reservation where captive-bred wolves roam in three huge enclosures. There are timber wolves, tundra wolves and Iberian wolves. Children will love it. There are guided tours, a wolf puppy enclosure, a petting zoo with pigs, ducks, geese, goats and a cuddly fox. At weekends, after 8pm, by appointment, you can go and observe the peculiar phenomenon of the wolves howling at the moon. The park also has some well-kept Andalucian horses and donkeys for small children to ride.

www.lobopark.com; open daily, Nov–Apr 10am–6pm, May–Oct 10am–8pm.

El Torcal Another spectacle a short drive from Antequera is El Torcal, an otherworldly natural park of strangely shaped limestone rocks. It's a truly wacky place and well worth wandering around. The central peak is 1370 m (4494 ft) high and is circled by a number of trails: three are signposted with different colours to indicate their level of difficulty. The green one is the easiest, at 45 minutes, but you can't do it with a buggy and it is essential to stick to the trail – it's too easy to get lost here.

El Chorro Further west, there are three lakes formed by the El Chorro dam at Guadalhorce where you can swim and canoe. The drive from Antequera is through tawny fields, through the triangular tops of mountains that look like nuggets of Toblerone. Bowlegged olive trees stand gnarled in the wind, and homes stand crumbling to dust. Back by the gorge take the signposts to Bobastro to get a truly matchless view of Malaga province. The Bar Restaurante El Kiosko serves up tourist price snacks and drinks, but better would be to visit a *fruiteria* in whichever town you're driving from and have a picnic in the shade of pines instead. There are campsites here, but otherwise your only options really are **La Posada del Conde Hotel Mesón Pantano del Chorro** (no 16, 18, 952 11 24 11, *www.laposadael conde.com*, *www.hoteldelconde. com*) 26 rooms, 22 doubles, 2 with Jacuzzi/sauna, 1 single, 1 suite. TV phone). **Estacion de El Chorro** (*952 495 101*, *www. refugioelchorro.com*), **La Garganta Aparamentos Restaurante** (*9524950000*, *www.lagarganta.com*) and **Finca La Campana**, apartments, double rooms, swimming pool, climbing wall, mountain bike lessons (*www.el-chorro.com*).

Garganta del Chorro While you're in the area, take the N337 road to Alora, to see the amazing spectacle of the Garganta del Chorro, a terrifyingly sheer-sided gorge with a rickety wooden catwalk clinging to the rockface.

Shopping

Ronda

Ronda has a busy knot of shops including some high street favourites and fashion stores, lots of knick-knack outlets, others selling anything from swords to heftily-priced antiques, pots and pans and probably a few straw donkeys. Ronda is by a long way the most commercialized of this generally tat-free zone, and there's very little that's actually aimed at children. Most shops along the main street of the old town sell identikit ethnic wares, sunhats, leather goods, table linen, and knock off classical paintings. However, for brilliantly misshapen ceramic cups and saucers and jugs that are half terracotta, half glaze, go to **Rondeña** at Plaza de España, 2 (*95 287 10 73*), which stocks the work of its owner's 70-something potter husband. If you want older pots, mainly shipped up from Jerez, go directly to the rag'n'bone style stacked shop of brothers Joaquín and Juan Muñoz Le Courtois.

10am–7pm Mon to Fri. Weekend openings longer in Summer. c/ Armiñán 48 95 287 30 69.

For a silly souvenir, duck just off the Plaza Espana to get a mock-up of an old fashioned self-portrait. Children can choose from bandit, flamenco, gypsy or bullfighter costumes and full colour, sepia or black and white.

Calle Rosario 3, next to the bridge, 952 87 80 13. 11am–10pm. First print €20 (£13.40), any copies €12 (£8) you have the choice of three. Five people max per pix.

Gaucin, Arcos, Grazalema

Grazalema's tourist office, on Plaza de España (*956 132 225*), sells a range of local handicrafts, like leather, ceramics and blankets, and local produce like honey, wine and cheese.

Grazalema is also famous for its woollen blankets (or mantas de Grazalema), a cottage industry in which production peaked in the 17th and 19th centuries. Artesanía-Textil de Grazalema (📞 956 132 008) still uses looms and carding machines blankets and sells the mantas and other textiles in its shop.

In Arcos, if you haven't got yourselves enough frilly skirts by now, Rincón de las Nieves (calle Boticas no 6 www.rincondelas nieves.com, 📞 656 886 256), sells flamenco outfits for little ones. Arcos also has several good local wine producers. Look out for Regantio Viejo, Viña Lucia and Tierra Blanca (the latter white). The whole area is excellent for olive oil, of course.

FAMILY-FRIENDLY ACCOMMODATION

The distances between the White Towns are small enough, by and large, to argue the case for using one as a base from which to explore the others and its surrounding scenery. The best options for high-end accommodation are Ronda, which has a number of top-end hotels in historic buildings in its old quarter and some lovely rural villas on its outskirts, and is midway between Sierra de Grazalema and Sierra de las Nieves and Gaucin, which has less in the way of sites in the town itself, but, as the bohemian haunt of long-staying British, has the lion's share of houses for rent,

and gets fewer daytrippers. Arcos has a lovely boutique hotel, and Grazalema is a good bet for the active family.

Ronda

EXPENSIVE

Finca La Morera (Mulberry Tree) Families searching for a slice of rural Arcadia, should take the narrow, winding country-track that leads to this immaculately restored farmhouse. Swishing through the iron gates past palm trees – a Moorish sign of welcome – visitors will find a cluster of sturdy whitewashed buildings, draped in jasmine and vines. A vast mulberry tree that sheds its sticky black fruit in the spring towers over the main house. Orchards of lemon, orange, fig and olive trees stretch down to the river and the organic gardens provide guests with armfuls of fresh vegetables. A vast dining room adjoins a country kitchen (one of two on the site) equipped with every gadget you can think of for self-catering with style. The six en suite double bedrooms each have their own terrace or balcony. Children can splash about in one of two swimming pools, curl up in the private cinema, or play table tennis, table football, pool, cards, or sing karaoke in the games room. The finca's charming caretaker couple, Paul and Ursula, can arrange a chef and maid service, and can get babysitters with 24 hours' notice.

Directions on request. Email: book-ings@fincalamorera.com. www. fincalamorera.com ☎ (from the UK) 01749 814 811. Rates vary from €2875 (£1926.25) a week throughout the year. The price includes: linen (except cot linen), all towels, air-conditioning or central heating, satel-lite TV, cleaning for three hours on three days per week, a broadband connection.

Parador de Ronda ★★

This parador is one of the best places to stay here. It's on the cliff-edge right on the gorge, next to the Puente Nuevo. The good-size guest rooms are beautifully fur-nished and many open onto views of the peaks surrounding Ronda.

Plaza de España s/n, 29400 Ronda. ☎ 95-287-75-00. Fax 95-287-81-88. www.parador.es. 78 rooms. €119–220 (£79.75–147.40) double; €184–240 (£123.30–160.80) suite. AE, DC, MC, V. Parking €10 (£6.70). Amenities: Restaurant; bar; outdoor pool; limited room service; laundry service/dry cleaning. In room: A/C, TV, minibar, coffeemaker (in some), hair dryer, safe, bath and shower.

Hotel La Fuente de la Higuera

The idea at this done-up old olive oil mill on the out-skirts of Ronda is that you'll feel like you're visiting some rather fabulous friends at their country house. Interiors are a mixture of 19th century Dutch art and con-temporary abstract. Every room can take an extra bed: standard rooms have terraces out onto the olive grove mountain, the three suites (9 and 11) have sitting rooms with open fires, your own garden or terrace with views, the three deluxe suites have even bigger living rooms and there's one double suite (number 7) which has room in its two twin bedrooms to sleep four adults.

Partido de los Frontones s/n Ronda ☎ +34 952 11 43 55 fax: +34 952 16 56 09 info@hotellafuente.com, www.hotellafuente.com, www. rise-resort.com. Standard rooms €135 (£90.45) (€908 (£608.40) weekly), suites €180 (£120.60) (€1210 (£810.70) weekly), deluxe suites €196 (£131.32) (€1320 (£884.40) weekly), double suite €260 (£174.20) (weekly €1747 (£1170.49)), junior suite and artist's suite €166 (£111.22), €1118 (£749) inc break-fast. An extra bed or cot costs €25 (£16.75) per night. Minimum stay two nights. Internet. Library. Restaurant. Bicycle for hire. Horseback riding.

INEXPENSIVE

La Española

This is a warm and welcoming place for a fam-ily wanting to stay in the centre of town on a tight budget. The hotel, run by an former banker from the UK, is tucked down a side-street leading off the bull-ring. The restaurant, serving up home-cooked traditional Andalucian dishes, has tables spilling out into the street. The rooms are comfortable and four of the 16 have views over out across Ronda's cliffs. All rooms have baths with showers. Right next door is the Michelin-starred Tragabuches restaurant.

Calle JoséAparicio 3, 29400 Ronda. ☎ 952 873488 Fax: 0034 952 879903 info@lasespanolahotel.com. www. laespanolahotel.com. Low season: Nov 1–Dec 20 and Jan 8–Feb 28,

Full-board €118 (£79.10) double or €148 (£99.15) suite; Half-board €99 (£66.30) double or €124 (£83.10) suite. Breakfast only €83 (£55.60) double, €100 (£67) suite. Extra bed €23–58 (£15.40–38.85).

Alavera de los Banos Ronda can be enjoyed from the terrace (and pool) of this hotel in the old tanners' quarter. Your young hosts are kindness personified and they have built their hotel in harmony with its surroundings. You are on the dramatic edge of the town with views across fields and meadows to the distant hills and mountains to the south.

San Miguel s/n, Ronda. ☎ 952 879143; fax: 952 879143. www. andalucia.com/alavera. 10 rooms. €85–105 (£56.95–70.35) doubles; €65–75 (£43.55–50.25) singles. AE, DC, MC, V. Free parking. Amenities: Restaurant, outdoor pool. In room: no phone.

Hotel San Gabriel ★ ★ FIND

This charming 1736 mansion stands in the historic core a short walk from the gorge. The building was painstakingly renovated by the owner and his sons and daughter, who give you Ronda's warmest welcome. Inside, all is stylish and homelike, filled with antiques, stained-glass windows, a Spanish-style billiard table, a cine salon (with seats taken from the city's old theatre), and even an old library. Each guest room is spacious and well appointed, all with exterior views, individual decoration. Try for no. 15, a cosy top-floor nest on two levels.

Marqués de Moctezuma 19 (just off Calle Armiñán), 29400 Ronda. ☎ 95-219-03-92. Fax 95-219-01-17. www.hotelsangabriel.com. 16 rooms. €78–90 (£52.25–60.30) double; €145–160 (£97.15–107.20) suite, €24 (£16.10) an extra bed. AE, MC, V. Amenities: breakfast room; bar; game room. In room: A/C, TV, minibar, hair dryer, safe, bath and shower.

Cortijo El Tejar Booking in to this cortijo gets you access to much more than a rather charming honeysuckle covered B&B: more crucially it gets you an appointment with Guy Hunter-Watts, an inveterate rambler and English author of *Walking in Andalucia*, who has lived locally since the 1980s. Make the most of him. The house has sweeping views of the Grazalema mountains. Every one of the four rooms comes with books and reading chairs. You are welcome to use the kitchen to fix yourself food all through the day (and there's an honesty bar too), but ask for home-made picnics for excursions too. The doubles have sitting rooms and annexes where extra beds can be set up for children, and there's a small cottage next door with a double and a small twin. There are cots, extra beds, a high chair, but it's unsuitable for toddlers because there are so many steps to all the different levels of the house.

El Tejar, Montecorto, near Ronda ☎ 952 184 053, 4 rooms, two twins, two doubles, all ensuite, swimming pool. B&B Sept and May €70–80

(£46.90–53.60) a night. Breakfast €7 (£4.70), picnic €7 (£4.70), dinner €25 (£16.75) inc. wine. Internet.

Grazalema

Plaza Pequeña has the four-star **Puerta de la Villa** (☎ *956 132 376*), with a tiny pool and good grub, but is maybe not the best option for children, there's a jacuzzi and gym; ask for a room with a mountain view. North of Grazalema is the **Villa Turística** (☎ *956 132 136*) with good views and a hotel, self-catering cottages, restaurant and a swimming pool – it's a bit rough and ready but perfect for families, especially the apartments. Five kilometres outside town in oak woods is the bunker style big four-star **Hotel Fuerte Grazalema** (☎ *956 133 000*), on the A372 to Ronda at km 53. Modern but good facilities. The town's campsite, Camping Tajo Rodillo, is on the C344 at km 49 to El Bosque.

Cortijo de Las Piletas Take an afternoon to ramble across this sprawling country estate, through wheat and sunflower fields and woodlands of oak and cork, past grazing cattle and a small, bubbling stream. Guests here are made to feel like one of the family. The comfortable, elegant and light rooms are uncluttered. The old farmhouse is now a drawing room, with a fireplace for cosy winter evenings. The small wooden-beamed dining room has a porch and large terrace for the warm evenings. There is a swimming pool.

Apdo 559, 29400 Ronda, ☎ 605080295. Fax: 951 230603. info@conrtijolaspiletas.com, *www. cortijolaspiletas.com*. 8 rooms. €79 (£52.95) double, breakfast is included. €15 (£10.05) extra bed. €21 (£14.10) dinner. Cots are free.

Arcos de la Frontera

The spectacular views which are the usual unique selling point of most *paradors* are, in Arcos, the rule rather than the exception: you'd have to go out of your way to find a room without one here. The only remaining reason to stay at Arcos's Parador here would be location and décor. On Plaza Cabildo, the former is excellent, but the latter is disappointing. Blandly furnished, with zip facilities for children, and a government approach to service, sleep elsewhere.

La Casa Grande Elena Posa worked in the ministry of culture in Barcelona and as an opera critic in Madrid before moving to Arcos to open this luxury guesthouse. The 1729 house she's carefully restored is correspondingly genteel and cultured: off the light stone plant-strewn patio where you take your generous continental breakfast, is a great library with illustrated books on Spanish history, and figures from art and music. The rooms are an elegant mix – bohemian with Moroccan embellishments – and come with personally mixed cassettes of Elena's favourite flamenco and classical music. The best for families are those at the top of the house, set back from the spacious roof terrace with its amazing views over the town – one suite has a kitchen.

c/Maldonado 10, 11630 Arcos de La Frontera, C ádiz. ℂ *956 70 39 30. Fax: 956 71 70 95. info@lacasagrande.net.* **www.lascasagrande.net.** *8 rooms (4 doubles, 2 suites for four). Triple €86–131 (£57.60–87.80), quadruple €114–126 (£76.40–84.40). Extra bed €25 (£16.75). Cot €15 (£10.05). Breakfast €8 (£5.36). AE DC MC V. Access is by foot. Parking in the main square. Closed last two weeks in Jan. Services: A/C, en suite (shower only), radio, TV and phone.*

Hotel Rural Cortijo Mesa de la Plata

4 km outside Arcos on the way to El Bosque is the family-centric *cortijo*, a traditional style ranch hotel which has horse riding on Andalucian horses, swimming pool, lounge and restaurant. The apartments have both kitchen and living room.

Maldonado 10, on the road from Arcos de la Frontera towards El Bosque. ℂ *956 703930; fax: 956 717095* **www.cortijomesadelaplata.**

Arcos de la Frontera

com. Doubles €77 (£51.80), singles €46 (£30.80) Inc breakfast. Apartment €96 (£64.32) Pool. Horseriding. Lounge. 1 restaurant. Internet. Rooms: TV A/C, safebox, minibar.

There is also a campsite near the lake: Camping Lago De Arcos, ℂ *956 70 83 33, email: lagodearcos@ campings.net, €3.60 (£2.40) per adult; €3 (£2) for children, caravans €4.25 (£2.85), tents from €3.60 (£2.40). Hot water and swimming pool free.*

FAMILY-FRIENDLY DINING

Ronda

Restaurant Almocabar

ANDALUCIAN Just outside the old city walls in the Plaza San Francisco, this excellent but tiny restaurant makes really decent hearty Andalucian gourmet food. Nothing special in the interiors, but you will eat very well: on dishes like rabbit stews, lamb chops or bacalao (and steak and

chips for something simpler). It's off the tourist trail but popular with locals, so it's worth booking one of the six tables in advance.

Calle Ruedo Alameda 5, ☎ 95-875-59-77. Seats 24. Reservations recommended on weekends. Main courses – €10–15 (£6.70–10.05); AE, DC, MC, V. Closed Tues.

Confitería Harillo The pastry chefs still turn out sweets based on centuries-old Moorish recipes. Fruit confections are made from ingredients grow in and around Ronda, including strawberries, lemons and oranges. Sugar cooked egg yolks is a typical pudding, as are lots of nougats and sweets made with a mix of almonds and pistachios. Some Arabic confections are really marzipan made with nuts that aren't almonds. Pastries start at €2 (£1.34) and cakes make good picnic fodder.

Carretera Espinel, 36, ☎ 95 287 13 60, 10am–9pm daily.

Del Escudero Sister restaurant to the Michelin-starred Tragabuches, Del Escudero is more affordable, almost as good, has incredible views over the mountains and a large garden for dining al fresco. Tucked behind the bullring, and built in a vast converted house, diners can chose from several rooms to savour the chef's modern Andalucian cuisine. Shellfish bisque is poured from a teapot over pasta parcel's of langoustine and crab. Hearty meat dishes include steak and *rado de toro guisado al vino tinto* (oxtail in red wine). The €31 (£20.80) tasting menu is excellent value. Palm trees in the garden lead down to a café for those wanting a lighter bite.

Restaurante del Escudero, Chalet del Tajo, Paseo de Lbas Infante 1,29400 Ronda, Malaga. ☎ 95 287 1367. Fax: 95 287 4532. Closed Sun nights.

Arcos de la Frontera

San Marcos San Marcos is an unassuming joint in the old town, just back from the Plaza de with just five tables of four chairs each and a long counter. Fill up on the bargain menu *del dia*, at €8 (£5.36), which gives you a choice of chickpea stew, salad and soup starter; meatball, tortilla, and pudding.

9am–11pm Mon–Sat. Simple bar with the telly on. Fresh coffee grinder and beer on tap. Pension c/ Marques de Torresoto 6, ☎ 956 700 721.

Meson de La Molinera By the lake is one of your best bets for children, as is nearby **Los Tres Picos**, a garden restaurant with good grills and some variations on the local favourite: pork and more pork.

☎ 956 708419, Avda de los tres picos s/n. Open lunch and dinner, every day in summer, closed Mon in winter.

7 Granada

ALHAMBRA

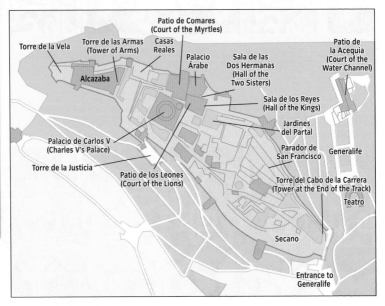

Patio de Comares
(Court of the Myrtles)

Torre de la Vela

Torre de las Armas
(Tower of Arms)

Casas
Reales

Palacio
Árabe

Sala de las
Dos Hermanas
(Hall of the
Two Sisters)

Patio de
la Acequia
(Court of the
Water Channel)

Alcazaba

Sala de los Reyes
(Hall of the Kings)

Jardines
del Partal

Palacio de Carlos V
(Charles V's Palace)

Parador de
San Francisco

Generalife

Torre de la Justicia

Patio de los Leones
(Court of the Lions)

Torre del Cabo de la Carrera
(Tower at the End of the Track)

Teatro

Secano

Entrance to
Generalife

For former Prime Minister Benjamin Disraeli, the Alhambra was quite simply, 'the most imaginative, the most delicate and fantastic creation that sprang up on a summer night in a fairy tale.' It may take quite some yarn to get your children's imaginations fired up on some of the finer points of Moorish history, but as you wander through the red fortress palaces and gardens, you can leave their eyes to feed and clothe their own imaginations.

The monument's romance has spilled over into Granada's broader old quarter, where wild-haired youths perform street theatre, ancient gypsy women clack their castanets and hum arias from *Carmen*, and modern day Arab traders have shops piled high with baboushes and trinkets of Morocco. Boabdil, the city's last Moorish ruler, was right to turn back and sigh.

Granada province, though, is not to be outdone by its capital: the natural world gives the Moorish architects a good run for their money here. The mountain backdrop that so defines the Alhambra is a natural fortress of the great outdoors. The fit can climb through its mountain air to camp overnight at Veleta, one of its highest peaks, waking to 360 degrees of Spain, the sea, and beyond, to Morocco's mountains. Lower down on the sierra's foothills lies the Alpujarra, little pockets of bucolic prettiness, natural springs and meadows, streams and country rambles. These are wedged between the wall of mountains and the Mediterranean 'Costa Tropical', shingle and pebble beaches of much more variety and far fewer English fish and chippies than the Costa del Sol.

Families visiting Granada will be spellbound by more than the mighty Moorish palace-citadel of Alhambra. Even the hardest heart can't fail to be swept away by the magic of this dusty city of fountains and gardens, rivers, souks and plant filled patios, peopled by Jews, Arabs, gypsies and gentiles, set against the snow-capped peaks of the Sierra Nevada. And if the hard-hearted are swept away, the romantics might just never leave.

ESSENTIALS

Getting There

By Plane Ryanair has flights to Granada from Stansted and Liverpool from £40 return *www.ryanair.com*. British Airways flies from Birmingham, Edinburgh, London Gatwick and Heathrow. Monarch and Avro fly from London Gatwick. Three planes a day land from Barcelona (one hour flight). The airport is 16 km (10 miles) west of the centre of town on Carretera Málaga in Santa Fé (℡ 95-824-52-00). There's a tourist information booth, ATM and restaurant/café in the airport. Buses run 7 times a day to and from the city centre (Palacio de Congresos). From the centre, buses leave at 9am, 12.45pm, 1.45pm, 5.20pm, 6.15pm, 745pm and 11pm and cost €3 (£2) and takes 30 minutes (℡ 958 490 164). Taxis cost €17 (£11.40) to the city centre, or €25 (£16.75) to the Alhambra.

By Train The train station is **Estación de RENFE de Granada**, Av. Andaluces s/n

(℡ *902 24 0202* to book or ℡ *93 490 112*; *www.renfe.es*), although the main ticket office is at Calle de los Reyes Católicos 45 (℡ *95-822-31-19*). Granada is not on the high-speed line but is well linked with the most important Spanish cities, especially those of Andalucia. Four trains daily from Seville (4–5 hours €17 single).

By Bus Most people choose the bus rather than the train from Malaga or Almeria, and Granada has bus links to virtually all the major towns and cities in Andalucia. The main bus terminal is **Estación de Autobuses de Granada**, Carretera de Jaén s/n (℡ *95-818-54-80*). The bus between Seville and Granada takes three hours, there are 10 a day, single ticket €16 (£10.70). To and from Córdoba is also three hours, costs €10 (£6.70) for a single. From the Costa del Sol it's two hours, €8.05 (£5.40) single (**Alsina Graells** at ℡ *95-818-54-80*).

Visitor Information

The tourist office is at Calle de Santa Ana 4 (℡ *95-822-59-90.*

www.andalusia.com), and open Monday to Saturday 9am to 7pm, Sunday 10am to 2pm. You can pick up the free *Where2* magazine from the tourist office with listings for the whole of Granada province every other month.

City Layout

Don't be put off by the industrial sprawl and giant ring-road on the outskirts of town. Granada's enchanting historic centre is laid out across three slopes. The Alhambra sits in a leafy quarter perched on the **al-Sabika hill** to the north-east of the city. On an opposite slope to the north-west you'll find the twisting, cobbled streets of the old Moorish quarter, known as the **Albayzín**, home to the city's fine clutch of boutique hotels and dinky Arabic tea rooms.

Follow the central thoroughfare, **Reyes Católicos** to the north, along the **Rio Darrio** and you'll reach **Sacromonte**, the beguiling gypsy quarter, where flamenco displays are still held in the hill-side caves. The centre of town is at the southerly foot of the two hills, past the Gran Via de Colón and the cathedral and is the best area for shopping. A stroll through the **Realejo**, the old Jewish quarter below the Alhambra, in the north east is the best place to get a feel for contemporary granadiño life.

Getting Around

Public Transport Granada has a good **bus system and taxis**

are plentiful (Radio Taxi ☎ 958 13 23 23 or Tele-Taxi ☎ 958 280 654, Taxi Paco ☎ 958 780 880 – which has 8-seater transport.) Taxis can be hailed in the streets, a green light signals it is free.

Without a doubt the best way to get around the relatively compact central and historic quarters is **on foot**. Even so, there's no avoiding hills, steep flights of steps or narrow, cobbled alleys. The city is not ideal for pushchairs. If you have a buggy, it is better to hop on one of the many public buses that connect all the various neighbourhoods with the city centre for little over €1 (£0.67). From the Albayzín, the 30 and 31 bus head to Plaza Nueva and into town every 15 minutes.

Driving & Parking in the Albayzín is a nightmare, but some hotels have spaces reserved in nearby public car parks. If not, park in a city centre car park and catch a taxi to your accommodation.

Hire Car companies include Europcar ☎ 902 105 030 or Hertz ☎ 902 402 405, Alquiauto ☎ 958 135 750. The Granada City tourist pass costs €24.50 (£16.40) (€22.50 (£15.10) if booked in advance) and includes nine public bus trips and one ticket, valid for 24 hours, for the Granada City sightseeing bus. It gives you access to five major sites (including the Alhambra, but you still need to book a time slot) at reduced ticket prices. You can buy the pass directly from the ticket offices at the

Alhambra, Royal Chapel or several branches of the Caja General de Ahorros bank. The bank charges a 12% extra booking service charge. Tickets are valid for seven days.

FAST FACTS: GRANADA

American Express Hotel Office at Called Reyes Católicos (📞 *958 22 45 12*). Mon–Fri 9am–1.30pm, 2–9pm. Sat 10am–2pm.

Babysitters The best way to find a sitter is to ask the concierge or receptionist at your hotel. They usually charge around €6 (£4) an hour. Alternatively try La Cabaña del Dormillón, Cortijo Argaz, Calle Alhami 6, Carretera de Huetor Vega (📞 *958 12 33 55*) which can send staff directly to your hotel. Open Mon–Fri 7.30am–9pm.

Airport See 'Arriving' earlier in this chapter.

Car Rentals See 'Getting Around', earlier in this chapter.

Consulate Honorary Consular Agent 669 895 053.

Emergencies Phone 📞 *112* for the police, fire brigade or ambulance. To report a theft (English spoken) call 📞 *902 102 112*.

Hospital Hospital Clínico, Av de Madrid s/n. 📞 *95 802 30 00*.

Currency Exchange Banco Santander Central Hispano, Gran Via 3. 📞 *958 21 73 00*.

May–Sept, Mon–Fri 9am–2pm; Oct–April Mon-Fri 9am–2pm.

Pharmacy Farmacia Zarco, Rios Puerta Real 2 (next to Hotel Victoria) is open 24 hours. 📞 *958 263 113*. Farmacia Tall ón, Recogidas 48. 📞 *958 251 290* is also 24 hours.

Internet Cafes Hecho Granada, Calle Mulhacen 9 📞 *958 26 53 42*, Internet Granada, Pintor Zuloago 29 📞 *958 53 50 25*, Madar Internet, Calderia Nueva 12, 📞 *958 229 007*.

Newspapers Spanish papers: *Ideal, La Opinión, Granada Hoy.* Pick up *Guíade Granada del Ocio* for listing (€1.50 (£1)) or *Where2* magazine is free.

Post Office Correos Granada, at Puerta Real s/n. 📞 *952 19 71 97*. Mon–Fri 8.30am–8.30pm. Sat 9.30am–2pm.

Toilets Public toilets along Paseo Violon, near Congress Hall (€0.20 (£0.13)). Otherwise duck into a café.

Telephones Local calls from one of the many payphones cost around €0.20 (£0.13) for 3 minutes. For international calls you can purchase an international phone card for €6 (£4), €10 (£6.70), or €20 (£13.40). Directory assistance is at 📞 *118118*.

Maps See 'City Layout'

Safety As with most European cities, petty crime and theft is commonplace: and the normal rules apply, keep your wits about you and don't invite attack by dangling cameras or purses or leaving possessions visible in empty cars.

WHAT TO SEE & DO

Children's Top 10 Attractions

❶ The Sacromonte Gypsy Caves, Granada A warren of homes wormed into the mountain-side, where many still live today in relative comfort with all mod cons (see p. 168).

❷ Calle Caldereria Vieja y Nueva, Granada Soak up the sights and sounds of souk-like streets at the foot of the Albayzín and pause at a terteria for refreshment and a sweet Arab pastry (see p. 176).

❸ An afternoon in the Sierra Nevadas Try the Genil, Monachil or Dilar valleys for a mountain walk or hire bikes for a day's cycling along the Vía Verde, 6 km of old railway line that is now a smooth track (see p. 181).

❹ Cathedral and Capilla Real, Granada Spot the burial place of some of Spain's most famous monarchs. See how small the coffins must have been. The Sacristia houses splendid jewels, a crown, sceptre and sword (see p. 169).

❺ Calle Cuesta de Gomérez Young music lovers will be particularly inspired by the guitar-making studios dotted along this street (see p. 172).

❻ Aquaola When the heat of the city gets too much head to Granada's water park, perched on a hillside outside town (see p. 170).

❼ Paseo del Salon, Granada Down by the banks of the Genil river, this wide boulevard is a great place to take the children. There's a merry-go-round, bric-a-brac stores and scores of cafes (see p. 169).

❽ Parque Carmen de los Martires, Granada An easy alternative to the Alhambra and just a bit further up the road, this private house has huge gardens where ducks and peacocks roam freely (see p. 165).

❾ El Triunfo fountains, Granada This magnificent fountain in the Triumfo gardens becomes a sea of light and colour at night (see p. 169).

❿ Parque de las Ciencias, Granada A tropical butterfly house, a maze, a watch tower and demonstrations of birds of prey in flight plus lots of interactive games and activities should be plenty to divert the little ones at this science park (see p. 170).

Granada Town

Day trips run from the Costa del Sol resorts to Granada but with children, it's a very long day involving coach journeys of two to three hours each way. The journey from the resorts on the Costa Tropical is, of course, much quicker. If you're based west of Málaga, seriously

A Little History

A little potted history helps to understand the great passion people feel for Granada. The city was the last Moorish stronghold to fall to the Catholic kings. Moors from North Africa invaded Al-Andalus and inhabited Granada from AD711. Throughout the 13th and 14th centuries, Christian armies worked their way through southern Spain, driving out the Moors. Granada managed to resist until 1479, when the dynastic marriage between Ferdinand of Aragon and Isabella of Castille proved just too powerful for the Moorish rulers. Ferdinand and Isabella marched on the city in 1491 and with the help of an enormous army, held it under siege for seven months. In 1492, the same year that Columbus sailed for the Americas, Boabdil, the last Moorish king, handed over the keys to his beloved city.

Legend has it that as he left Granada, he crossed a high mountain pass, looked back and wept. His mother, however, was unsupportive. She said, rather cruelly, 'Weep like a woman for what you have failed to defend like a man.' The mountain pass today is known as the Puerto del Suspiro del Moro – the Pass of the Sigh of the Moor.

consider staying the night in Granada. There's easily enough family-friendly action to fill two days and besides, you haven't lived until you've seen the Alhambra Palace glowing dusky pink in the sunset. There are some excellent restaurants and tapas bars for after dark and a wonderful buzz about the city on a balmy summer's night. Children may even enjoy a flamenco show, provided it's not too long.

Planning Your Outings

Granada has plenty of variety for a visiting family. Head to the gypsy caves, stroll through the river-side park, or take a tour of the tea shops in the old quarter. The Alhambra is on every itinerary, but families with younger children may want to be more selective about which areas they visit rather than take the recommended three hours to explore the palaces.

The Alhambra: A Chequered Past

250 years ago, this awesome 13th century Nasrid palace lay festering under a heap of dung, its salons used as taverns with a bawdy bunch of thieves and vagabonds clattering through its rooms. Many centuries after the palace's Muslim founders had been ejected from Granada and the Christian rulers, Charles V (1516–1556) and Philip V (1700–1746) had cleared out, the Alhambra was pretty much left to rot.

It was only in 1870 that work began to put the 'pearl set in emeralds' to rights.

GRANADA TOWN

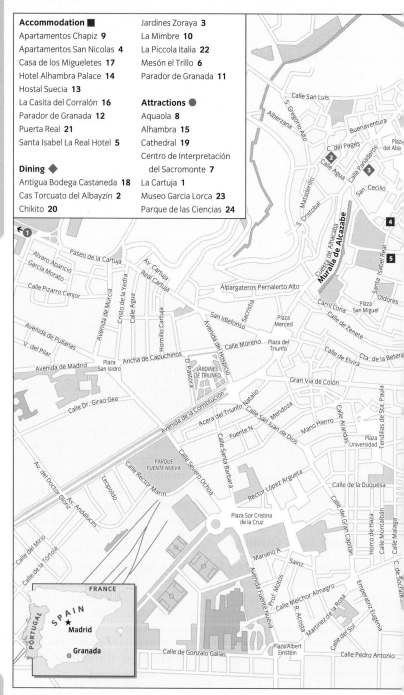

Accommodation ■
Apartamentos Chapiz **9**
Apartamentos San Nicolas **4**
Casa de los Migueletes **17**
Hotel Alhambra Palace **14**
Hostal Suecia **13**
La Casita del Corralón **16**
Parador de Granada **12**
Puerta Real **21**
Santa Isabel La Real Hotel **5**

Dining ◆
Antigua Bodega Castaneda **18**
Cas Torcuato del Albayzín **2**
Chikito **20**

Jardines Zoraya **3**
La Mimbre **10**
La Piccola Italia **22**
Mesón el Trillo **6**
Parador de Granada **11**

Attractions ●
Aquaola **8**
Alhambra **15**
Cathedral **19**
Centro de Interpretación
   del Sacromonte **7**
La Cartuja **1**
Museo Garcia Lorca **23**
Parque de las Ciencias **24**

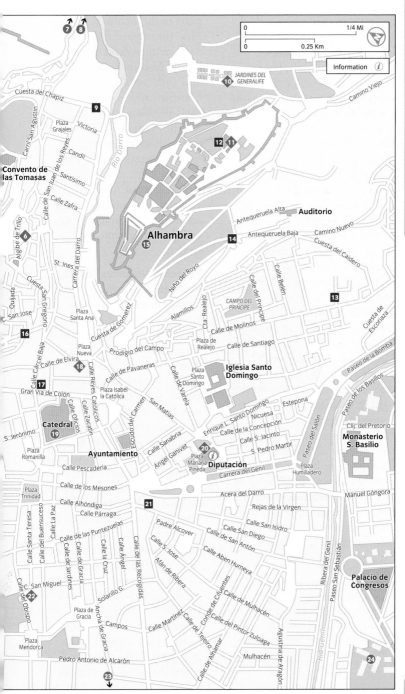

7 ↑ **8** ↑

0 _____ 1/4 Mi
0 _____ 0.25 Km

Information (i)

JARDINES DEL
GENERALIFE

10

Camino Viejo

Cuesta del Chapiz

9

Plaza
Grajales

Victoria

Carril San Agustín

Candil

Calle San Juan de los Reyes

Río Darro

12 **11**

Convento de
las Tomasas

Santísimo

Calle Zafra

Antequeruela Alta

Auditorio

Algibe de Trillo

6

St. Ines

Carrera del Darro

Alhambra

15

14

Antequeruela Baja

Camino Nuevo

Cuesta del Caidero

Cuesta San Gregorio

C. Quijada

C. San José

Niño del Royo

Calle del Príncipe

Calle Belén

Cuesta de
Escoriaza

16

Plaza
Santa Ana

Cuesta de Gomerez

Alamillos

Cta. Realejo

CAMPO DEL
PRINCIPE

Calle de Molinos

13

Plaza
Nueva

Prodigio del Campo

Plaza de
Realejo

Calle de Santiago

Paseo de la Bomba

Calle Cárcel Baja

Calle de Elvira

18

Calle de Pavaneras

Plaza
Santo
Domingo

**Iglesia Santo
Domingo**

Paseo de los Basilios

17

Gran Vía de Colón

Calle Reyes Católicos

Plaza Isabel
la Católica

Calle de Varela

Enrique L. Santo Domingo

Nicuesa

Estepona

Paseo del Salón

Clij. del Pretorio

**Monasterio
S. Basilio**

S. Jerónimo

Catedral

19

Calle Oficios

Calle Zacatín

Escudo del Carmen

San Matías

Calle Sanabria

Calle de la Concepción

S. Jacinto

S. Pedro Martir

Plaza
Romanilla

Ayuntamiento

Ángel Ganivet

Plaza
Mariana
Pineda

20 (i)

Diputación

Carrera del Genil

Plaza
Humilladero

Manuel Góngora

Calle Pescadería

Plaza
Trinidad

Calle de los Mesones

Acera del Darro

Rejas de la Virgen

Calle Alhóndiga

21

Calle Santa Teresa

Calle La Paz

Calle del Buensuceso

Calle Párraga

Padre Alcover

Calle San Diego

Calle San Isidro

Calle San Antón

Ribera del Genil

Calle de las Puntezuelas

Calle S. Jose

Calle Aben Humeya

Paseo San Sebastián

Calle de Gracia

Calle la Cruz

Calle Ángel

Calle de las Recogidas

Afán de Ribera

**Palacio de
Congresos**

Calle de Jardines

C. San Miguel

22

Solarillo G.

Calle del Pintor Zuloaga

Agustina de Aragón

C. del Obispo

Plaza de
Gracia

Ancha de Gracia

Campos

Calle Martínez

Calle de Tejeiro

Conde de Cifuentes

Calle de Mulhacén

Río Genil

Plaza
Mendorca

Pedro Antonio de Alcarón

Calle de Alhamar

Mulhacén

24

23 ↓

This was no mean feat. When the Christians moved in after the reconquest, they whitewashed over Arabic paintings and gilding damaging parts forever. Charles V then built, but never completed, his own palace in the centre of the complex, in majestic, but thoroughly incongruous, Renaissance style. To cap it all, Napoleon's retreating armies detonated mines under two of the palace's major towers and reduced the Torre de Siete Suelos and the Torre de Agua to rubble. Had it not been for the lone, invalid solider, José Garcia, who cut the hissing fuse when Napoleon tried to blow the building to bits, the Alhambra would not be here at all.

Inside the russet outer walls – that give the palace its name the 'Red Castle' – the Muslim rulers Yusuf I and Mohammed V sought to create a slice of paradise. Inscriptions etched on the light reflecting water basins in courtyards show that the Alhambra was indeed meant to be the physical realisation of Paradise from Islamic poetry. Fretted ceilings, stucco work of porcelain-like delicacy, hand painted tiles and splendid marble pillars and arches, are just some of the delights inside.

> **INSIDER TIP** ≫
> You can buy a great, illustrated book, the *Alhambra Told to Children* by Ricardo Villa-Real and Pilarín Bayès de Luna (Ediciones Miguel Sánchez) from the shops inside the complex.

The Complex: Light & Darkness

There are three main parts to the architectural complex, the original fort from the 11th century Zirid dynasty, the Nasrid Muslim palaces of 13th and 14th centuries and the Christian additions made after the 1492 Reconquest.

The Nasrid palaces are studded with water features and stucco to maximise the movement of light, which symbolizes the presence of Allah. Streams of water and heavenly pavilions are features of paradise along with bountiful fruit and flower gardens.

Palacios Nazaríes (Nasrid Palaces)

Mohammed V and his family's private quarters were arranged around the **Patio de los Leones** ★★★. There are 124 white marble columns, for children to count, holding up the gallery! But the keystone here is the alabaster basin, supported by 12 white marble lions. The illustrious poet Ibn Zamrak's inscription around the fountain describes the complex hydraulic system at work within the court. On the south side of the Palacio de Leones, the **Sala de los Abencerrajes** is known for its stunning, domed, mocarabé ceiling, designed to resemble stalactites. Water in the fountain reflects the image of the ornamental roof above. The **Sala de Comares or Salón de Embajadores** in the Palacio Comares is one of the most impressive in the complex. It is where the sultans carried out

Patio de los Leones

negotiations with Christian emissaries. The seven planes of the cedar wood ceiling represent the seven heavens of Koranic paradise, with Allah at the zenith.

The Generalife gardens were the pleasure gardens of the sultans, a network of fountains, patios and walkways carpeting the Cerro del Sol (Hill of the Sun). The Patio de la Acequia (Court of Water) has two long pools spouting rows of water jets in graceful arches, always good value for little ones.

Carmen de los Martires If you still have the energy after a trip round the Alhambra visit these meandering gardens, where children can see squawking peacocks, splashing ducks, spice gardens and an explosion of roses.

Paseo de los Martires, 📞 *958 22 79 53. Free admission. Mon–Fri 10am–1.30pm, 5pm–7pm. Sat–Sun, holidays 10am–7pm. Closed in August.*

Reservations for the Alhambra

The booking and reservations process is frustrating. The best way to organize a trip is to pre-book tickets, although you will still have to be at the site at least

The Writing on the Wall

The Nasrid battle cry 'Wa la ghalid illa allah' or 'No conqueror but god' is one of the many Arabic phrases inscribed in decorative cartouches across the walls. Verses of Kufic poetry eulogizing the sultans and the beauty of the palace and quotes of moral stricture from the Koran are also woven into the designs.

Sala Dos Hermanas

an hour before your allotted time – and queue – to stand a chance of getting in. Try to go early in the day, especially in the hot summer months. If you arrive later than 4pm you are unlikely to get in at all. Call the booking line on ☏ 915 37 91 78 to pay for tickets by credit card – the best method. Alternatively most hotels will reserve a ticket for you. The website at *www.alhambratickets.com* is slow and confusing. The BBVA (Banco Bilbao & Vizcaya) sells tickets at €10 (£6.70), plus an €0.88 (£0.59) charge. Visit a bank branch or call the BBVA on ☏ 90 222 44 60. You can also book through the administration office (☏ 958 220 912) and pick up the tickets on the day of visit at the entrance desk. **Visitar Granada** (part of Granavision ☏ 902 33 00 02 or reserves@granavision.com) offers 2½ hour guided tours in English with a pick up and drop off at your hotel. Prices, including entrance are €39.50 (£26.50) for adults, €25 (£16.75) for children aged 6–14 or free for children under 6, for the same price, **Central Servicio Turisticos**, Calle

TIP ≫ Tour Time

A full tour takes about three hours – by which point children under six will be crawling the beautiful stucco work walls. It is a vast site to cover on foot so make sure you are wearing comfy shoes and have your own supply of food and water, although there are cafes, toilets, loos and taps to top up water bottles. An English audio-guide costs €3 (£2). A passport or credit card is required as a deposit. Steer well clear of the mid-day slots during July and August when the heat is unbearable. The best time to see the complex is either first thing, or around dusk.

Estribo 2 ☎ *902 46 20 46* is also reliable. There are two museums in the grounds: The Museo de la Alhambra contains Hispano-Muslim art, including artifacts retrieved from the complex. Museo Bellas Artes displays religious paintings and sculpture.

Palacio de Carlos V. ☎ 95-822-09-12. Comprehensive ticket, including Alhambra and Generalife €10 (£6.70); Free for children under 8, with ID. €5 (£3.35) gardens only. Museo Bellas Artes €1.50 (£1); Museo de la Alhambra €1.50 (£1); illuminated visits €6.75 (£4.50). Mar–Oct: daily 9am–7.45pm, floodlit visits daily 10pm–midnight. Nov–Feb: daily 9am–5.45pm, floodlit visits daily 8–10pm.

Getting There

On Foot From Plaza Nueva take the Cuesta de Gomérez past the Puerta de las Granadas, the first of two gates to the Alhambra. Climb the shady tree-lined avenue past the 14th century Puerta de la Justicia (Gateway of Justice) and the fountain built for Charles V.

By Bus Routes 30 and 32 start at Plaza Nueva.

By Taxi €6–8 (£4–5.35) from the centre.

The Old Quarter

The **Albayzín** is the heart of the old Arab quarter, a village inside the city, narrow labyrinths of crooked streets and whitewashed houses, crammed together on the hillside. Twenty years ago it was a deeply undesirable part of the city. The quarter is being slowly gentrified. In Moorish Granada the Albayzín was a flourishing neighourhood and one of the wealthiest corners of the city. The Muslim population is slowly starting to increase again and a large new mosque (**Mezquita de Granada**) and garden now stand beside the lofty lookout point, Mirador de Sán Nicolás.

Generalife Gardens

Sacromonte ★ ★

Sacromonte is Granada's old gypsy district, a warren of homes wormed into the mountainside on the banks of the Darro river (sacro monte means 'the holy mountain'). Caves became a nifty – cheap, quick – way of solving the growing housing problem after the population boom that happened here at the end of the 19th and the first half of the 20th century, meaning the rural poor arriving to work in Granada could walk straight in to a walled abode. Plenty did, and the numbers living in caves swelled from 600 in 1900, to 3682 in 1950. Taking a wander down this bleached fold in the mountain is a good, rugged antidote to the haughty grandeur of the Alhambra and the pretty-prettiness of the Albayzín, but there will be lots of other tourists doing the exact same thing, particularly come dusk when the big American tour groups trail through in crocodiles to catch one of the many flamenco shows staged here.

Centro de Interpretacion

There's lots to be learned at the Centro de Interpretacion here, not just about gypsies but also about Granada's general history, and its terrain too, all packaged in really easily digested bite-size, interactive chunks. The interesting geological history of the area, which gives Granada its trademark hills, 'The Alhambra Formation', is demonstrated with all the different types of rock – hunks of quartzite, micaschist, dolomite and marble, put out for little hands to touch and feel.

Centro de Interpretation del Sacromonte €1 (£0.67) for the viewpoint, €4 (£2.70) for the museum. Barranco de los Negros Granada **www.sacromontegrandada.com** *Apr–Oct Tues to Fri 10am–2pm then 5–9pm, 11am–9pm weekends. Nov–Mar Tues–Fri 10am–2pm, 4–7pm; weekends 11am–7pm. Bus 34 from Plaza Nueva.*

River Darro

After Sacromonte walk down Cuesta Del Chapiz to the banks of the river Darro. The road bends right and if you cross over at the Puerte Del Rey Chico you come to a great little play park under the shade of the Alhambra and its tall trees. It's all pedestrianized on that side of the river bank, and the track goes all the way down to the river bed, where there are often big ducks waggling around.

Paseo de Los Tristes

Back on the Albayz ín side of the river are the fountains, cafes and bars along Po del Padre Manj ón (Paseo de Los Tristes): lots of restaurants and still lots of room to run around in – it's a general evening recreational area, making for lots of little curiosities. Senoras of a certain age whisk their fans and banter, grungy students lay about on benches, and street performers juggle and jump. If the shaded sit-outs at the restaurants here look too touristy, or you don 't fancy the fuss of a menu, go on to the fountain where there 's normally a baked potato stall (patatas asadas). Paseo De Los Tristes is the starting point for BurroTaxis, which can lead you and children of any age on one of four routes: up to the Alhambra, around the Albayzin, through Sacromonte, or forget about the sites, and trail the Darro river out of town instead on peaceful Fuente Avellano route.

Catedral & Capilla Real

(Burial place of the Catholic kings) Many years after forcing the Moors to relinquish Granada in 1492, Ferdinand II and Queen Isabella I commissioned the Capilla Real as their resting place. The couple saw the conquest as the crowning achievement of their reign. Little did they know that their sponsorship of Columbus's journeys into the new would eventually eclipse this somewhat inevitable triumph in the world's history books.

Children, with their natural ghoulishness, may observe that the coffins are very small – a reminder of how short the couple must have been – and their serene facial expressions moulded into the stone are accurate likenesses created using death masks. The Sacristia, behind two wooden doors contains Isabella's crown and sceptre and Ferdinand's sword. Capilla Real €3 (£2), children under 10 free. No credit cards.

Gardens & Parks

El Triunfo

This magnificently ostentatious fountain in the shady Triunfo gardens becomes a sea of light and colour at night. It's quite a feat of engineering and good excuse for a stroll out to the west of the town along Gran Via de Colon, where it meets Avenida de la Constitución or from the Iglesia de San Juan de Dios up Calle San Juan de Dios.

Paseo del Salon

Down by the banks of the Genil river this wide boulevard is a great place to take the children. Meander through the trees, let the children take a turn on a merry-go-round, while you browse through the tents selling bric-a-brac.

Outside the Centre

Lorca's Summer Home: Huerta de San Vicente

On the outskirts of town, García Lorca's familial home is now a museum surrounded by a well-manicured park named in his honour. The white mansion contains the ink-stained desk where the poet and dramatist wrote 'Blood Wedding' and 'Gypsy Songs'. 'There's so much jasmine and nightshade in the garden that we all wake up with lyrical headaches,' he wrote to a friend in 1926. Children might not find much to inspire them inside the house but the gardens are splendid for an afternoon stroll.

El Triunfo

€1.8 (£1.20) Children under six are free. ☎ 958 25 84 66. García Lorca Park, Calle Arabial) July–Aug: Tues–Sun 10am–12.30pm, 5pm–7.30pm. €1.8 (£1.20) (free on Wednesday if not a holiday).

Monastery La Cortuja FIND

The most lavishly decorated monastery in the whole of Spain – or the Christians' answer to the Alhambra – is barely visited. Inside the church you'll see twisted, multi-coloured marble columns, an explosion of gold, silver and ivory, stucco arabesques, the building's impossibly ornate ceiling and the baroque Churrigueresque fantasy that is the sacristy. Quite something. It's best to visit when leaving the city by car as the journey by bus is tricky.

€3 (£2), free under 8s. No credit cards. ☎ 958/161932 Camino de Alfacar, Cartuja, Granada, Spain.

Parque de las Ciencias

Granada's Parque de las Ciencias, an outdoor museum with 270 interactive exhibits. There's a 50metre observation tower. Don't shell out the extra €2 (£1.35) for the planetarium unless you understand Spanish. The Tropical butterfly house is probably the best bet for little ones, or the maze. The Regional council for the Environment houses animals from the Sanctuary for Injured Endangered Species and has flight demonstrations of day and night time birds of prey.

Parque de las Ciencias, Avda. Del Mediterraneo s/n, 18006, Granada. ☎ 958 131 900. Fax: 958 133 582. www.parqueciencias.com. Prices: museum €4.5 (£3) (€3.50 (£2.35) under 18s) planetarium €2 (£1.35) (€1.50 (£1) under 18s). Open Tues–Sat 10am–7pm. Closed Monday. Sunday, holidays 10am–3pm. Buses 1,5 (to the Park) or 4,10,11 to nearby Plaza de las Américas.

AQUAOLA: Water Park

Just out of the city and perched on a hillside this fun park offers nail biting water-chutes for older children and adults. For younger children there is a large pool and a private galleon to splosh through. It gets very busy at weekends.

Ctra de la Sierra, 4 km. Cenes de la Vega. 📞 *958 486 189. Restaurant* 📞 *958 486 186. Website www. aquaola.com. Open June–Sept every Mon–Sat 11am–8pm. Sun 11am–3pm, 6pm–8pm. A free bus service between La Parada stop for the 33 bus and the park. Adults €11 (£7.40) (€12.50 (£8.40) festival times) children €8.50 (£5.70) (€9.50 (£6.35) festival times). Free for children under 4.*

Favourite Family Experiences

City bus tours that take in the Convention centre, Camino de Ronda, Cathedral and royal chapel, Alhambra, the science park go from 10am to 8pm all year round. Adults €10 (£6.70), children 5–14 €5 (£3.35), under five travel for free.

Call 📞 *958 53 50 28 (Acerá del Darro, 2/3. 18005, Granada). For families with older children a walking tour of the historical centre, via the cathedral, through the Albayzín and along the Darro River costs €10 (£6.70) and takes two and half hours. Contact Cicerone Granada on* 📞 *600 41 20 51, or* 📞 *0034 670 54 16 69. www. ciceronegranada.com. Email: info@ciceronegranada.com. Tours leave from the Plaza del Carmen beside the town hall from 10.30am Mon–Sun. Children under 14 are free.*

Active Families

The snowcapped peaks of the Sierra Nevada (see separate section) offer a thrilling selection of activities for families from hiking, mountain-biking, trekking, gliding, skiing, canyoning, rafting – the list is endless. **Granada Activa** – the regional association of active tourism will source the right company for around 20 different activities (*www.granada-activa. com* 📞 *902 360 780*). Down by the coast, along the Costa Tropical (see separate section) water-sports enthusiasts will be equally spoilt for choice. You can take a balloon flight over Granada with **Glovento Sur** (📞 *958 290 316*. Mobile 📞 *670 596 770.* glovento@gloventosur.com *www. gloventosur.com*) departures are from Hermitage San Miguel to the West of the City, but it doesn't come cheap at around €720 (£482.40) for a family of four. Not suitable for children under five years old.

There are few parks and playgrounds in Granada for really small ones, but swings and slides have been set up in the leafy stretches along **Campo del Principe** and **Paseo del Salón**.

Shopping

Granada's main shopping area is centred just north of the cathedral. For a one stop shop and an incredible food hall, **El Corte Ingles** (Carrera del Genil 22, 📞 *958 22 32 40*) department store has it all. If you're in a self-catering accommodation and want to stock up on food, try the **Mercado municipal** (C/San Agustín) and the streets stalls heading from here to Plaza Pescadería. For a sweet treat while you are there, **Ora et Labora** (Plaza Pescaderia 7, 📞 *958 25 81 67*) sells cakes, sweets, honeys, wines and cheeses all made in monasteries and convents around Spain.

A trip to **Calle Cuesta de Gomérez**, a narrow and steeply sloping street that runs uphill to the Alhambra from a point near the Plaza Nueva, is the base for most of the guitar makers in the city – interesting even if you don't want to buy. Prices start at around €195 (£130.65) but for the best-crafted instruments you'll pay in excess of €2000 (£1340). The oldest studio, established in 1875 is **Casa Ferrer** on Calle Cuesta de Gomérez 26 (📞 *95 822 18 32*). Or try **Guitarrerí a Antonio Morales** along the road at number (📞 *958 822 27 41*), or **José López Bellido** at number 36 (📞 *958 822 27 41*). **Germá n Pérez Barranco** which maintains a cubby-hole on the street but really does the bulk of its trade from a shop on Calle Reyes Católicos, where you might be tempted buy one of the flamenco CDs on offer. For teenage fashion all the perennial High street favourites, **Zara**, **H&M**, **Mango**, and **Pimkie** are within striding distance along the central Recogidas thoroughfare.

Family Entertainment

Flamenco

In a 1930 homage to a flamenco dancer he admired, Lorca said that she was supreme at the art of 'inscribing the drowsy air with

that arabesque of blood and bone.' Although many think the Sacromonte flamenco performances have more to do with money than raw emotion, the shows still draw tourists in droves. These start at 10pm or 10.30pm so are not brilliant for really small children and it is best to avoid the usually over-priced packages including transport, free drinks and entrance to caves. Instead make your own way to Camino del Sacromonte to see if any of the clubs appeal. The zambras – as the shows are called – include one at **Cueva del Sacromonte** (📞 *958 12 11 83*) which charges €22 (£14.75) or **Cueva La Roc ío** (📞 *958 22 71 29*) with shows at 10 and 11pm for €23 (£15.40). Back in the centre of town, in the Albayzín area, Peña La Plateria (Placeta de Toqueros 7, 📞 *958 21 06 50*) is a restaurant by day and one of Granada's oldest flamenco clubs by night. On Thursdays (except from July–Sept) it throws its doors open to the public at 10pm.

Annual Events

Sacramonte Romeria is when every family takes a picnic out to the forested area at the far end of Sacramonte. Traditional food such as salaillas (a type of bread) and cod are served up in abundance.

Festival International de Música y Danza de Granada
In June and July, attracting top national flamenco stars and offers lots of free shows. **Holy**

Gipsy Caves, Sacromonte

Week: One of Granada's grandest festivities attracting an ever-increasing crowd of visitors each year. Highlights include the processions 'Christ of the Gypsies' (Cristo de los Gitanos) by torchlight and 'Las Anguastias'.

The Festival of the Reconquest

In Granada this celebrates the Catholic monarchs on 2 January. Throngs of people gather for the colourful processions of folk in period dress. The young of Granada climb up in pilgrimage the Terre de la Vela in the Alhambra to ring a bell. In the summer, on 3 May the Festival of Crosses brings the city to life with awesome floral displays spilling from the city's courtyards and houses. The biggest festival is the **Corpus Christi** fair, held between May and June. The streets are awash with folk in traditional costumes and horse-drawn carriages and you'll see plenty of dancing at the myriad stalls. On the last Sunday in September **Festival of the Virgen de las Angustias**, patron saint of the city, is celebrated with open-air dances, bullfights and colourful processions.

FAMILY-FRIENDLY ACCOMMODATION

Many of the city's hotels drop their prices in summer when the blistering heat sees tourists heading to the coast. On the flip side room rates during the spring and over the major festivals have been known to double, or even triple.

If you do visit in July and August, make sure your accommodation has **air-conditioning** and be warned that very few hotels have swimming pools unless you are willing to stay out of town.

Renting an **apartment** is a good bet for a family and good value. As well as plenty of room to spread out in, they usually come with well-equipped kitchens and a microwave for heating milk or food quickly. For a wackier stay that children will love there are several **cave-apartments** for rent in the Sacromonte.

Apartments

For families with young children, renting an apartment in Granada is a great idea. You'll have plenty of space and there are lots of mid-sized supermarkets dotted around.

Independent listings can be found at www.granadainfo.com (☏ 958 20 88 92). Babysitting can be arranged.

La Casita del Corralón in the Albaycín is a charming house and more reasonable than two rooms in a hotel. It has a lounge, kitchen, two twin bedrooms and a small patio and mini portable plunge pool in the summer.

Three to four people costs €102 (£68.35) a night (minimum three nights) or €609 (£408) a week. No pets. Cots provided for babies. Call ☏ 958 20 88 92. Web: www. granadainfo.com/corralon.

Puerta Real is a cluster of modern self-catering flats right in the centre of town. They are well equipped so popular for mothers with babies and sleep a maximum of six. There is an underground car park around three minutes walk away and department store El Corte Ingles with a food hall to rival Harrods.

Around €120 (£80.40) a night (minimum two nights). Call ☏ 958 20 88 92. Web: www.granada info.com.

Apartamentos Chapiz Apartments inside a large Andalucian house in the Albayzín. Rooms are spacious and light and sleep a maximum of four. There's an Internet connection and parking in the building for €6 (£4) per 24 hours. €105 (£70.35) a night (minimum two nights).

Cuesta Chapiz, 54, Albayzín, Granada. Call ☏ 958 20 88 92. Web: www. granadainfo.com.

Apartamentos San Nicolas Also in the Albayzín, these stylish, traditional apartments have a beautiful mosaic at the centre of the shared patio and stunning views over the town. The biggest apartment – 'Arrayán' – sleeps six.

Plaza St Nicholas, 3. Call ☏ 958 20 88 92. Web: www.granadainfo.com.

Casa Los Naranjos (Apartment cave) Pretend that you are a gypsy family and spend a few nights sleeping in the Sacromonte caves. Each comfortable, modern self-catering apartment sleeps four, and they share a sunny terrace. Inside, simple furniture rests on the terracotta floors and sitting rooms are draped with Moroccan hangings and rugs.

Barranco de los Naranjos 10, 18010 Sacromonte, Granada. ☏/Fax: 958 225 127. Email: info@granada-apartments. com. www.granada-apartments. com. Prices: For three people €86 (£57.60) a day, €485 (£324.95)

Countryside around Granada

a week, for four €100 (£67) a day, €550 (£368.50) a week (including tax).

Out of Town

Alojamiento Rural Cortijo del Pino For a bit of rural bliss, take the family to these grand old farmhouses just 15 minutes outside Granada. The house, topped with a tower and pigeon loft, is set around a stone patio and surrounded by a lush carpeting of lime, palm and cypress trees and rolling lawns. Super comfortable, high-ceilinged rooms are furnished with antiques. Two of the self-catering houses sleep four and one of them, Casa do los Naranjos, sleeps six.

E- 18194 Churriana de la Vega, Granada. 📞 *958 250 741. Email: info@cortijodelpino.com. Website: www.cortijodelpino.com. 4 self-catering apartments. Amenities: TV, firewood stove plus wood, fridge,*

gas cooker, coffee-maker. Prices (6 people €123 (£82.40) a night or €738 (£494.50) a week, 4 people €98 (£82.40) a night or €588 (£394) a week). Easter, Christmas and August €861 (£577) a week for six or €686 (£460) for four. Extra bed €12 (£8). Min stay two nights.

EXPENSIVE

Parador de Granada Actually inside Alhambra's grounds this parador is rich with mudéjar style, trickling fountains, wrap-around loggias and wisteria draped arches. Rooms in the old section are better. The bodies of Ferdinand and Isabel were held here while their tombs were being readied in the Cathedral.

Real de la Alhambra s/n, 18009 Granada. 📞 *95-822-14-40. Fax 95-822-22-64. www.parador.es. 36 rooms. €214 (£143.40) double. AE, DC, MC, V. Free parking. Bus: 30. Amenities: Restaurant; bar; limited* room service; laundry service/dry cleaning; currency exchange; room for those w/limited mobility. In room: A/C, TV, dataport, minibar, hair dryer. €337 (£225.80) for a triple or €737 (£493.80) for a king-sized suite that can sleep four. Cots are free. Babysitting on special request.

MODERATE

Santa Isabel La Real Hotel

Albayzín The 16th century house Santa Isabel La Real has taken six painstaking years to restore and is the latest boutique hotel to nestle into the increasingly chichi medieval Albayzín quarter. Cots are provided free and three room have double sofa beds so each can sleep up to two extra, for €35 (£23.45) extra per child under 12. Extra breakfasts charged at €4.50 (£3). Babysitting can be arranged too.

Santa Isabel La Real 19, 18010 Granada, Spain. ☎ 958 294 658 www.hotelsantaisabellareal.com Rooms 11. TV. A/C. En suite. Safe. Phone. Wifi. Hairdryer. Cards: Tariff: Standard double €90–160 (£60.30–107.20). Breakfast €9 (£6). There are extra beds in the three €130 (£87.10) rooms. Parking €12 (£8) surcharge.

INEXPENSIVE

Hostal Suecia

Hidden away at the foot of the Alhambra hill behind a profusion of green, The Suecia is good for families on a budget. There's a huge roof terrace, ideal for a balmy evening watching the light fade on the Alhambra, just a few minutes walk away. It has the feel of Spanish family home, with a sitting room downstairs and a pretty tree-flecked garden at the back. Rooms of several shapes and sizes are modest but clean with space for a maximum of three beds.

Guests can park in the cul-de-sac street right outside.

Calle Molinos 8, Huerta de los Angeles, 18009, Granada. ☎ 225044; fax: 958 225044. 11 rooms. Triple room (including extra bed) €70 (£46.90). Breakfast €4.50 (£3).

FAMILY-FRIENDLY DINING

Eating out in Granada can be as exotic or as basic as you like. Spicy Moroccan tagines, traditional Andalucian meat and fish dishes, tapas, crepes, crispy Italian pizza, hearty bowls of pasta and Moorish cakes and ice-cream sundaes are all in abundance. The banks of the Darrio River are an excellent place to prowl for drinks and snacks. Up in the Albayzín many of the best restaurants have leafy terraces and gardens, so children won't feel they are tied to the table all night. For a tapas crawl head down to the Campo del Principe where a lively cluster of tapas bars do a rollocking business in the evenings near the childrens' play area with swings and slides. Just west of Plaza Nueva, Calle Calderería Vieja y Nueva are at the centre of the Moorish tea and pastry shop revival: the pedestrianized streets here have lots of 'teterias', Arabic teahouses. Granada has a good spread of local mini-markets (as well its own food market) for picnic food. Try the Corte Ingles food hall for really gourmet food shopping.

MODERATE

La Mimbre ANDALUCIAN/GRANDINO
If you manage to time your trip around the Alhambra to start at around 10am you'll be able to pop into the Mimbre for a reviving lunch on your way out. Tucked right into the walls of the sultan's place, overlooking a garden with an old tinkling Andalucian fountain this eatery serves up a selection of traditional Spanish fare, fresh fish is the speciality. It can get pretty packed during the day but is a quieter in the evenings.

Ave del Generalife, Alhambra. 📞 *958 22 22 76. Main courses €12–20 (£8–13.40). AE, MC, V. Oct–Apr daily noon–4pm; May–Sept 8.30am–11.30pm. Closed part of Jan. Bus 1,6 or 7.*

La Piccola Italia ITALIAN
Families flock to this elegant Italian just south of Plaza Trinidad and the Cathedral for pizzas served straight from the oven. Pasta dishes such as ravioli filled with fresh spinach and a regional cheese are equally good. This is no casual trattoria however, tables are set and linen-covered although the atmosphere inside is relaxed.

Obispo Hurtado, 13, 18002, Granada. 📞 *958 259 678. Open 1.30pm–4.30pm and 8.30pm–midnight. Closed on Sundays. Main courses €12–24 (£8–16). Bus 2,7 or 11.*

INEXPENSIVE

Antigua Bodega Castaneda TAPAS One of the most popular tapas spots in Granada was actually divided in two after a particularly bitter family feud. The bodega with the stand up bar is heaving at weekends with tourists and locals. Staff serve up a mouthwatering array of

Granada Spice Market

snacks. Try the spicy chorizo sausages or jamón de Trevelez and de Bellota.

Calle Elvira 5. ☏ 95-822-63-62. Main courses €8–12 (£5.35–8). MC, V. Daily 12.30–5pm and 8pm–1.30am. Bus: 30 or 31.

Jardines Zoraya ★ ★ A natty haunt in the centre of the Albayzín near Plaza de Aliatar, with a palm tree sprouting through the ceiling of the dining room and a spacious garden terrace. Food is an eclectic mix of Italian, Spanish and modern European but most diners turn up for the truly excellent pizzas.

Jardines de Zoraya, Called Panaderos, 32, Albyzín, Granada. ☏ 958 29 35 03. Email: zoraya@ lingolex.com. All major credit cards except Amex. Open 12–5pm and 7.30pm until 1am 7 days a week.

Cas Torcuato del Albayzín. Andalucian This little rustic, Moorish-style restaurant serves up some of the best and most affordable dishes in the area. Its simple interior seating spills out onto terrace in the summer. Granadiños drop in for a gazpacho or garlic soup. Braver diners can sample recipes from days of old including a tortilla Sacromonte traditionally made with fried and breaded brain, lamb or veal testicles, potatoes, red peppers and peas.

Pagés 31, ☏ 95 520 2818. Reservations recommended. Main courses €6–12 (£4–8). Sun 11am–4pm. Mon–Sat 11am–4pm, 8pm–midnight. Closed Sundays in summer. Buses 3, 6 or 12.

Méson El Trillo Ring the bell at the gate and enter into the garden terrace overlooking the Alhambra in the distance. The chef here is happy to make special children's meals like spaghetti or chicken. Cod pil-pil with olive oil and garlic is good, and the spinach salads come with a tasty home-made yoghurt dressing. The lunch menu is excellent value.

Callej ón del Aljibe de Trillo 3. ☏ 95 822 51 82. Main courses €9–12 (£6–8). DC, MC, V. Wed–Mon noon–4pm, 8pm–midnight. Bus 1, 5, or 12.

Fast Food, Ice Cream & Arab Pastries

Lots of tapas to be had down by the Campo Del Principe and Carrera Del Darro: **Bar Amparo** (Campo del Principe 18), **En un Lugar del Alhambra** (Carrera del Darro 51) near the river and **Rabo de Nube** (Paseo de los Tristes) have great views of the Alhambra. The creamy smell of freshly melted chocolate should help you to locate **Fiorgelato** (Acera del Casion 3, next to Puerta Real). All the ice-cream sold in the shop is homemade in the basement. **Los Italianos** (Gran Via, near Plaza Isabel Catolica) is another scrumptious hang-out for a dairy-fix. Try the Cassita for €1.80 (£1.20). For the haute couture of lickable treats head to **Tiggani** (Bib Rambla) or for fancy sundaes try **Café Bar Futbol** (Plaza Marina Pineda). **Al-Andalús** (Called Caldereria Vieja 34, ☏ 95 822 46

41) is so bona fide its patrons even pass the water pipe. Stop by for tea, salads, or a honey-coated Moroccan lamb and pinchitos monunos (pork on a skewer with vegetables). Open 11.30am–2am. **López Mezquita Café Pastelería** (Calle de los Reyes Caólicos 3941, ☎ 95 822 12 05) 9am–11pm. Serves up meat pasties and pies. **Om Kalthum** (Calle Jardines) serves up chicken tagine, or try the pump-kin purée. Standing room only from 9pm. For a real indulgence try a chocolate con churros (doughnut sticks dipped in hot chocolate). Several cafes around the cathedral serve this choco-holic treat. Many locals head to **Monasterio de San Bernardo** (Called Gloria 2) for sweets and biccies. Pick up a caja surtida (a boxed selection) and take it to the nearest café to enjoy with a café con leche (milky coffee) or hot choc. Down in Calderia Baja you'll find a whole selection of shops offering sweet mint tea and honey pastries.

GAUDIX

East of Granada (58 km/36 miles) is one of Spain's oldest towns, the former mining cen-tre, Gaudix. It was a significant Roman colony and one of the first Visigothic settlements in the country. Today it is best known for its troglodyte cave houses, or casas cuevas, which are still home to almost half the town's 20,000-strong population.

Getting There

By Car The best way to get to Gaudix is by car. Alternatively take one of the 11 Maestra buses ☎ 95 866 06 57 leaving Granada from Mon–Sat (six on Sun) for around €4 (£2.70). It takes an hour.

By Train A train connection from Granada costs €5.25 (£3.50). The tourist office on Avenida Mariana Pineda ☎ 95 866 26 65 is open Mon–Fri 8am–3pm.

Cathedral Start your tour at the cathedral (built between 1594 and 1706) a melding of Gothic and baroque design with a spec-tacular façade. The doors are open Mon–Sat 11am to 1pm, 4.30–7pm, Sunday 10.30am–2pm. Free.

Palacio de Peñaflor Follow the streets south and you'll reach the Renaissance **Palacio de Peñaflor**, which stands next to the Gothic-Mudéjar church of **Santiago** and the 11th century Moorish **Alcazaba Arabe**. Unfortunately the Alcazaba is currently shut for restoration work.

Barriada de Cuevas ★★★
Back beyond the cathedral to the north, a 10-minute walk will take you to Barriada de Cuevas site of some 2000 cave dwellings, carved out of the soft sandstone mountains. Most are still occu-pied by families, although today, every cave has a TV antenna and most creature comforts of the modern world.

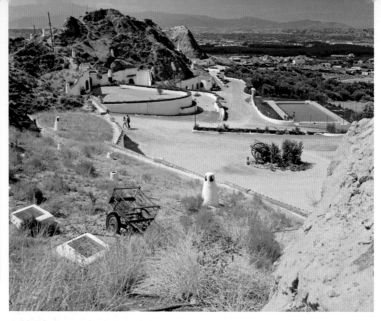

Cuevas Pedro Antonio de Alarcón

To see a completely preserved cave house, with artifacts, head to **Cueva-Museo de Costumbres Populares,** just off Calle Canada de las Perales (no phone). Open Mon–Sat 10am–2pm, 5–7pm, Sunday 10am–2pm. Admission €1.30 (£0.87).

Cueva-Museo de Alfarería

For a museum visit, call at the doorway to the Cueva-Museo de Alfarería, Calle San Miguel 467 (☎ 95 866 47 67), which contains a water well from the 17th century and decorative ceramics. Pedro de Mendoza, the conquistador who founded Buenos Aires lived here.

Family-friendly Accommodation: Gaudix

Apartamentos Cuevas Pedro Antonio de Alarcón: Cave apartments For the more

adventurous types wanting a night or two out of town, Gaudix offers the chance to stay in these rather luxurious self-catering cave-houses. The site of 23 caves is in the Barriada de la Estacion (railway station quarter) and the caves were built and lived by the railway workers. Rooms with large tiled-floors, decorated with Alpujarran hangings are certainly not primitive. 10 of the caves sleep 3–4 people and 8 sleep 5–6.

Bda.San Torcuato, S/n Guadix. ☎ 664 986. Fax 958 661 721. Website: www.cuevaspedro antonio.com. cavehotel@infogocio. com. Prices for 4 €87–97 (£58.30–65) or for 5 €93–107 (£62.30–71.70). Extra bed €10.50 (£7). Pets welcome. Amenities: Restaurant, big swimming pool, laundry, bbq. In rooms: TV, phone, hairdryer. Kitchens: microwave, electric stove, fridge.

Trips Out

Many Granadiños head to the alpine-style village of **Monachil** (10 km/6 miles south east of the city) for Sunday lunch. It can easily be reached by car or local bus. **Guejar Sierra** is a village in the lee of the Sierra Nevada just a 15 km bus ride from Paseo del Salón in the city centre. After exploring the narrow, sloping streets, take a stroll in the coutryside or a dip – or canoe – in the nearby reservoir. To get to **Jesus del Valle** start in the valley of Valparaíso in Sacromonte and head (on foot) up a leafy track along the meandering Darro River in the direction of two nearby villages **Huetor de Santillán** and **Beas de Granada**.

Sierra Nevada

The Sierra Nevada is 20 by 70 km of high altitude protected national park that runs parallel to Spain's southern coast. Within its bounds are the country's two highest mountains, La Valeta and Mulhacén, both of which, smudged with snow, shimmering against the bright blue ceiling of the clean high-mountain sky, give views across the glittering Mediterranean onto Africa and the Rif mountains. In winter, there's good learner skiing here for children, at Pradollano – also known as 'Solynieve' or 'sun and snow' thanks to its happy climate. Drive 15 minutes south from Granada and you are at the foothills of some of these sierras (Guejar, the Genil, Monachil and Dilar valleys), but if you head a little further, you'll reach the National Park's unofficial capital in the sleepy villages of the Alpujarra, part bucolic Shangri-la, part outdoor sports playground.

Sierra Nevada's West Side Story

The Granada portion of the Sierra Nevada gets relatively few footprints compared with the

Sierra Nevada Mountains

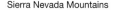

Alpujarra, but the Genil, Monachil and Dilar valleys do hold some fine mountain hikes, many of which you can undertake from your base in Granada: it can take as little as 20 minutes for you to get from locking the door of your hotel room to stretching your legs in the foothills of Spain's highest mountain range. An amiable family day out can be spent ambling down the **Vía Verde** of the Sierra Nevada, 6 km of old railway line that's been turned into a stunning walking and cycling track. The route runs parallel to the river so you can always slip in for a cooling swim. The route kicks off at pretty Güéjar-Sierra, 15 km east of Granada city, running past the Embalse de Canales reservoir to the Barranco de San Juan. You can walk and cycle all the way to San Juan, but when the route goes much deeper into the valley along the Vereda de la Estrella and the base of the highest of the 3000 metre peaks only serious, lycra-clad cross-country cyclists should apply. There are many more paths zigzagging the Genil, Monachil and Dilar valleys than there are corresponding signs, so on these routes it's usually best to go with a guide. Los Cahorros takes you through a stunning area where the Monachil river flows through a deep cut ravine. Some of the paths become quite narrow and you almost have to crawl under the overhanging rocks. The circuit leads into the gorge and across a long rope bridge. You can stop for a refreshing dip in the river and drink from a fresh water spring en route. The return leg of the trail follows an elevated track on the opposite side of the valley looking down into the ravine and passing through sparser, chalky landscape. The whole route is shady until the last three quarters of an hour. This is an ideal tour for families with either little or no experience of hiking and with younger children or a good way to start before tackling some of the steeper, more arduous climbs. Two to three hours.

By Foot Local outfit Sierra Essence can, at short notice, lead families across any of the above routes. Guiding rates start at €40 (£26.80) for up to 4 people. If all that sounds too pedestrian the company can also fix up quad biking, abseiling, canoeing, canyon descents, climbing, mountain biking or paragliding, and, even better for children, multiaventura: a day of mixing and matching some or all the above activities. From age seven and up. Guided walks from two to eight hours, all abilities, ☎ 646 178 406 *www.sierranevada.co.uk*.

By Car The switchback drive up to the Pradollano ski resort is a delight passing through tunnels of trees and brambles where orchards and stone cottages lie at the side of the road and the hedge rows are punctuated with wild poppies, where butterflies flutter.

If you head towards Granada at a cross-roads after climbing for 20 minutes or so, you'll find the El Dornajo visitors centre. Inside is an assortment of **information**.

The shop also sells souvenirs, reference books and maps.

A little further along the road and you come to the Mirador de Canales with stunning views over the resevoirs below (The Embalse de Canales).

Family-friendly Accommodation

Mirasierra This is basic but handy stop off point if you plan to spend more than a day out of town exploring the area around the Genil valley. The hotel is in the Gujar Sierra 20 minutes out of Granada or just 15 km away from the ski station.

There's a vast open plan lounge with views over the mountains and comfy sofas to sink into after a meal in the restaurant. Rooms sleep a maximum of 5 people and most have a private terrace.

Paseo de Mirasierra,18160 Guejar Sierra (Granada). ☎ 0034 958 484412, Fax: 0034 958 484415. 28 rooms. Prices for a double room, €37 (£24.80), includes breakfast Children under 12 are free, with a maximum of two children per room. Amenities: restaurant bar, pool table. In the rooms: A/C, heating, TV, phone. Parking €6 (£4) a night.

Alpujarra

Las Alpujarras, the southern flank of the Sierra Nevada, have deep ravines split by arid hillsides. The valleys here, of crop terraces, orange, mulberry and olive groves punctuated by pretty little whitewashed villages, are sandwiched between the massive haunches of the higher, snow-topped mountains, and the glittering of the Mediterranean coast. Well resourced, and under an hour from Granada and the coast of the Costa del Sol, it's arguably one of the best bases for a families wanting rural peace or high mountain expeditions.

By Car From Granada, head south along the A44 through the Puerto del Suspiro del Moro, the romantically named, but dreary-looking place where the departing Moorish King, Boabdil, took his last sigh, towards Motril, turning off on the A348 at Béznar. From Malaga go east along the coastal road, or Autopista Del Sol, turning inland just after Salobreña, onto the N323, E902, turning to the Alpujarra at Béznar. The A348 connects the main villages of the Alpujarra.

FUN FACT ≫ **No Moor** ≪

Las Alpujarras were the Moors' last toe-hold in Spain, but a rebellion in 1568 cost them their right to remain, and every Arab settler was thrown out, bar two families in each village who were kept on to teach the Asturian and Galician peasants who were parachuted in to replace them the ways of the local land.

Alpujarras

Visitor Information

Orgiva has the most facilities: Banco de Andalucia 9am–2pm Monday–Friday. Post Office (Correos) 9am–2pm Monday to Friday and Saturday 9am–1pm. Market: Thursdays till 2pm. There are two chemists.

Lanjarón

Lanjarón's spring is famous for its natural mineral properties so head for **Balneario de Lanjarón**, the town's spa. There are bath and shower therapies, massages, a sauna, steam room, gardens to wander through, a tennis court and a café. It's no Champney's: the atmosphere is more doctor's waiting room, but it remains a popular place, not least with the ageing Spaniards, so you'll need to book in advance. A package of treatments starts from around €29 (£19.45) for children between four and 10 years or €52 (£34.85) for an adult. Information and reservations ☏ *0034 958 770137* information@ balneariodelanjaron.com. *www. balneariodelanjaron.com* Av de la Constitución, Lanjarón.

Órgiva

The next village along is Órgiva, a sweet town that wouldn't be of much note but for its situation, plonked square in the valley of the Guadelfeo river between the haunches of the Alpujarra's two slopes of the Sierra Nevada and Sierra de Lújar. There is a sizeable

---

FUN FACT ❯❯ **Genesis of a New Life** ❮❮

Former Genesis drummer Chris Stewart is to the Alpujarra what Peter Mayle was to Provence: buy his whole literary trilogy – *Driving Over Lemons, A Parrot in the Pepper Tree* and *The Almond Blossom Appreciation Society* – to get the lowdown on every twist and turn in his decamping to these mountains (sold at many of the shops here). It's a colourful tale of survival with a young family in this beautiful but harsh place, and his subsequent success.

expat community so it has the best shopping and restaurants. As well as good international restaurants and hoteliers, you'll find English language babysitters, swimming teachers, bike rentals, paragliding teachers and walking guides here in abundance, making the rugged-looking mountains surprisingly easy access. Orgiva is lovely, but you can stay even further up the mountains: the Poqueira Valley is popular, and its villages of **Bubion**, **Pampaneira** and **Capileira** have lots of places to stay, from camping to self-catering luxury cottages, eco-lodges and proper hotels. At the top of the valley is **O Sel Ling**, a Tibetan Buddhist monastery founded by the Dalai Lama in 1982.

Walks

There's gentle walks following mule tracks cross the valleys of the Alpujarra, and if you just want a gentle amble, most guesthouses have maps or favourite rambling routes that start right from their gardens, many of which have rivers to swim in at the end.

Walking Guides

Rustic Blue stocks maps and walking guides, has local accommodation details and horse riding and hiking trips.

☏ *958 763 381 www.rusticblue.com.*

Other Activities

Alpujarra Experience, Orgiva, will rent you **mountain bikes**, and transport them to wherever you want to ride from, but can also arrange quad biking, paragliding and parapenting, canyoning, hot air ballooning, bunjey, archery, canoeing and death slides.

☏ *+34 651 614 494 hire@alpujarra-experience.com http://alpujarra-experience.com.*

Horizonte Vertical specializes in **paragliding**.

☏ *(+34) 958.30.82.91 Mobile: (+34) 689.11.86.66 info@horizonte-vertical.net http://horizonte-vertical.net/.*

Horseriding Dallas Love is one of the most experienced horse-women in the area. She only takes children over 12 when accompanied by an adult, there are four novice horses, whose riders must be comfortable at walk, trot and canter. Week-long rides cost €1192 (£799), with a 10% discount on groups of three or more. Sierra Trails Dallas Love Stables 18412 Bubion, ☏ *00 34 958 76 30 38 www.spain-horse-riding.com.*

For more: Turismo Deportivo Aventura Alpujarra *www.muli aventuraalpujarra.com*, *www. sierranevada.co.uk/Walking/ walking.html*; *www.naturexplorer. com/*; *www.viaverdeholidays. com/*; *www.austeroutdoor.com.*

Family-friendly Accommodation

EXPENSIVE

Casitas de Los Piedaos On a ridge just outside Orgiva is the organic olive, orange and lemon farm of the Cortijo de Los Piedaos. Four of the estate's ancient, thick-walled farm buildings have just been converted into lovely self-catering holiday cottages. It's very eco here too: water is recycled, there's solar-panels, and the swimming pool is chemical free. Each casita is quiet and private, but close enough together for big family groups to spill out over: there's lots of toys and games for children, and topnotch English language baby-sitting for €7.50 (£5) an hour, everyone – from toddlers and teens to grannies – is welcome here. All four cottages are safe and have space for children, but Villa La Rama is probably the best – it sleeps four in a double and a twin, and has its own washing machine. The other cottages share a laundry room. Book well in advance.

Orgiva, ☎ 958 784 470 www. holidays-in-southern-spain.com Holidays@LosPiedaos.com 4 cottages, double €485–785 (£325–526) weekly, Villa La Rama (sleeps four) €740–1040 (£496–697) extra bed £10. Sat TV, free Internet. Skype, TV, CD, DVD, kids channels on Sky, small play area. Pool, with toys, horseriding for novices.

Hotel Taray Botánico Three-star, hacienda-style (whitewashed walls, terracotta tiles) hotel with every possible comfort. It's a cosy place, the rooms are rustic and simple, and the biggest, and best for families, have lounges and open onto private rooftop terraces. It's surrounded by gardens and has two swimming pools in a belt of orange and palm trees, and there's a TV and music room. The hotel has its own trout farm, and the fish features large in the restaurant's good menu. Other ingredients come from local farms.

Ctra. A-348 km 18 Órgiva ☎ 958 784 525 Fax: (+34) 958 784 531 www. hoteltaray.com/i_en, tarayalp@ teleline.es 15 rooms. Standard double €75 (£50.25); with living room €97.50 (£65.35); double, living room and terrace; €102.62 (£68.75), extra bed €18.50 (£12.40) Breakfast €5.49 (£3.70). AE, DC, MC, V. Free parking. Laundry, room service, buffet breakfast, phone fax, Internet, WiFi, hairdryer. Shower & bath.

MODERATE

El Molino Slap on Orgiva's main road but tucked behind a huge wooden door is this rural B&B which used to be an olive mill. You're given the key to the front door, which opens onto a large patio with a full body-height plunge pool surrounded by flowers and trees and a barbeque. There are graded steps all the way around. Inside there's a giant living space, huge beaten-up TV (never on), massive saggy sofas, a few dining room tables and chairs, with lovely paintings from the area, for the real thing just head up the stairs to the great balcony with views across the valley to Sierra Nevada and Sierra de Lujar, and across the pretty market town's rooftops. The five rooms are all roomy, and three can hold an extra bed, breakfasts, are of fruit, yoghurt tea coffee, cake and toast. Family bedrooms have ensuite, satellite TV and AC.

*El Molino C/Gonzalez Robles 12
18400 Orgiva ☏ 00 34 958 785 745,
606 192373 www.lasalpujarras.
com/hotels/molino/molinoen.html
elmolino@casaruralelmolino.com;
5 doubles/twins, V, MC. Babysitting;
free cot; extra bed and breakfast
€18 (£12); double €54 (£36.20). No
parking.*

INEXPENSIVE

Las Terrazas De La Alpujarra

There's a guesthouse for 40 here,
but there are lots of self-contained
options with kitchen too in this
simple hotel in Busquistar. There
are apartments to sleep two, four
and six people, all of which have
living room, kitchen, TV and
terrace, and then there are two
houses, too: House of the Mill
has 10 bedrooms, two kitchens,
three big living rooms, and
Paco's House has five bedrooms,
three bathrooms, and a kitchen-
cum-living room.

*Busquisitar, Alpujarra ☏ 958 76 3034
www.terrazasalpujarra.com/ingles/
index.html Apartments €45 (£30.15),
10-bedroom apartment €180
(£120.60), five-bedroom apartment
€120 (£80.40).*

Camping

Camping Trevélez Spain's
highest campsite, also has cabins
for rent and a swimming pool.

*Ctra. Orgiva-Trevélez, km 32.5.
Open all year. V, M, MC. Rents bikes.
☏ 34-958858735 www.camping
trevelez.net.*

Camping Órgiva has a campsite
as well as farmhouses, bungalows
and a cabin for rent.

*A348 km18, 9. Open all year.
Swimming pool. B&B. ☏ 958 78 43
07. Restaurant (☏ 958 78 43 98) and
adventure sports (quad biking
included) ☏ 654 40 48 48, V, MC.
www.descubrelaalpujarra.com/.*

Refugios

Refugios are super-cheap high-
mountain accommodations that
offer beds and showers. There's
one in Refugio Poqueira, for
which you should book: ☏ 608
554 224.

*For more ideas go to lasalpujarras.
com; www.spainhouseoflight.com/
english/.*

Family-friendly Dining
(The Alpujarra)

**Restaurante Pizzería La
Almazara** **ITALIAN** Apparently
the Spanish restaurants in
Órgiva aren't a patch on home-
cooked mountain fare so when
locals eat out, they'd rather chew
on a rind of pizza instead. La
Almazara makes a fine choice:
rocket salad is €6.20 (£4.15),
cooled tomato soup with thyme
and Cordoba-style soup both
€4.50 (£3) while spaghettis and
spinach and pine nut lasagne
weigh in around €7.10 (£4.80).
The big, uncrowded garden, all
orange trees and pebbles, is
safely fenced off from Órgiva's
(already hardly threatening) high
street.

*Avenida González Robles 53 Órgiva
☏ 958 784 628. Closed Mondays.*

Café Libertad Half the menu
here at this popular expat café-
cum-restaurant is vegetarian,

but the dish that really flies out the kitchen is pork and chips. Sally and Andrew use organic produce where possible (the menu is seasonal) and are perfectly happy to serve half portions or make something from scratch (like pasta and cheese) for fussy littluns – everything's fresh. There's no ketchup, though, and no cola. They do great tea and cakes, all properly homemade.

Caprese salad is €4.50 (£3), pasta pesto, €9 (£6), calamari €12 (£8). Calle Libertad 36, Órgiva ☎ 958 785 800. Seats 30 Wed–Sun Cakes from 5pm; supper 7pm–last person leaves.

Mesón Casa Santiago At the town's main cross-roads, Casa Santiago is the closest Orgiva gets to a see and be seen joint, used by listless looking dreadlocked hippies, spruce daytrippers, hillwalkers and local Orgivans alike. The sopa de ajo is a pungent olive pool of sliced garlic, consommé and melted croutons. Service is lacklustre, but Orgiva's catering business isn't known for its cut-throat competition. Galindos, further up the road, does good tostados and pastries. *Plaza García Moreno, Órgiva ☎ 958 785 808.*

Baraka Set up by a Bilbao resident who converted to Islam and moved to this Muslim community pocket in the Alpujarra, Baraka provides Arabic favourites like falafel, halal schwarma, and veggie dips like houmous and babaganush, but Spanish fare too, like tortilla,

which they cook as thick as a car tyre here. The tea menu is vast and ice creams excellent.

Calle Estación 12 Órgiva ☎ 958 78 58 94 www.teteria-baraka.com Closed Mon. Open till 8pm.

Shopping

Órgiva Grocery The tiny supermercado Alpujarra (9.30am–2pm; 5–8pm Mon–Sat) is alarmingly well stocked, given the apparent remoteness of the mountains, you'll be ducking down aisles to escape the English expats flinging Heinz in their shopping baskets. Also stocks the local honeys and royal jellies and Alpujarra figs. For alfalfa sprouts, soya spreads and German breads, try **Camac Wholefoods**, run by Audrey and Steve Lee, c/ Real 23 Bajo Orgiva ☎ 958 784616 fax: 958 784 616 camacwholefoods@alpuwifi. com 10am–2pm Monday to Friday. **The Healthfood Shop**, by Nemesis I, sells handmade artisanal produce, local honeys, soaps, massage oils. The other thing to buy locally is jamon Serrano: Trevelez's name is synonymous with the stuff.

Beaches & Resorts

Costa Tropical This gentle stretch of coast just an hour's drive south of Granada is still defined by the Sierra Nevada behind: steep cliffs topped off with the ruins of ancient towers fall sharply into shingly and pebbly beaches and coves, stretching from La Herradura, a sleepy fishing village in the west to La

Rábita in the eastern border with Almeria province, whose borders are signalled by the corduroy lines of terraced tenting stretching up the bases of the province's market garden mountains.

Despite its proximity to the rough-and-tumble of the Costa del Sol the area is little-explored. It boasts many secluded beaches and the craggy cliffs, caves and coves yield picnic spots galore.

Almuñecar is the largest town along the coast but its highrise blocks and urban sprawl offer little of interest to passing visitors. Instead head west for La Herradura's water sports and family beach or east to Castello de Ferro, a pleasant, near-deserted resort town.

The sub-tropical climate, with average temperatures of 68°F (2°C), is ideal for growing avocadoes, mangoes, bananas and sugar cane.

La Herradura Touching the border with Malaga, the little pueblo of La Herradura (the horseshoe) is one of the prettiest bays along the costa. Its 2 km stretch of sandy beaches nestle between two natural promontories, the Punta de la Mona and Cerro Gordo. At one end of the main beach there is a camp site and a dive centre **Windsurf La Herradura** (Paseo Marítimo, 34. ℓ 958 64 01 43) and several good restaurants. **Dani's Esquí Náutic** at the easterly end of the beach front is a waterski centre. Further along, a small inlet behind a large rock known as

Peñón de las Caballas (Mackerel Rock) is the **Marina del Este** (ℓ 958 64 08 01. www.marinas mediterraneo.com), a port with around 220 yacht moorings – now some of the most expensive on the south coast. It's a lively corner in summer with an assortment of bars, restaurants and shops and the nearby Berengueles beach. If you're coming from Almuñecar, the best beach in La Herradura is **Cantariján** (also for nudists and semi-clad bathers), down a windy ¾ km coastal track signposted to Cerro Gordo just before the first tunnel on the main road. You'll find a cluster of **churringuitos** for coffee, ice-creams and seafood. To eat, pull up a chair at **La Gaviota's** (Paseo Marítimo ℓ 958 827 550) back at the westerly end of La Herradura beach and sit with your feet in the sand while sipping a tinto de verano and munching through a plate of grilled langoustine (€12 (£8)), paella or steamed mussels (€6 (£4)). Omelettes, soups and French fries are on the menu, so it's a fine spot to take children. **La Tartana** ★★ (Urbanización San Nicolás, ℓ 958 64 05 35. Open 7.30–11pm. Closed Sunday) is good for evening meals and is earning a reputation as one of the area's best restaurants. It's a favourite with children. The children's menu is €6.95 (£4.65). Choose from brownies, millefeuille with chocolate or white chocolate cheesecake. Book tables well in advance.

Family-friendly Accommodation

La Tartana Stepping through the heavy wooden doors of this Andalucían-style house set back (only just) off the main road in the hamlet of San Nicolás you'll find a charming stone patio around a fountain set in front of a bougainvillea draped terrace looking out across the Med. The eight rooms are spacious and comfortable, although it's best to avoid the ones overlooking the noisy N-340.

Hotel and restaurant La Tartana, Urbanizacion San Nicolas, 18697 La Herradura (Granada). /Fax: 0034 958 64 05 35. reservations@hotel latartana.com www.hotellatartana. com. 8 rooms, 3 possible triples. Prices: double with terrace €67–79 (£44.90–52.95) (including breakfast). An extra bed and break- fast is €20 (£13.40). Amenities: phone, TV, A/C.

Almuñecar

Almuñecar is big sprawling town ranged over the crests and troughs. The old quarter is a maze of narrow cobbled streets, crowned by the remains of a Moorish castle. Abd al-Rahman arrived here in 755, although the first settlers were the Phoenicians in 1000 BC. Today, the bustling Friday mar-ket attracts visitors from miles around, lured by stalls selling tropical fruits including lychees and the local 'chirimoyo' (cus-tard apples). There are 26 mainly pebbly beaches and an **Aquatropic** water park (Paseo Reina Sofia s/n. 9 ☎ 58 63 20 81.

Open June–Sept 11am–7pm. €12 (£8), free for under 4s) nearby.

Getting There

Regular buses shuttle between Málaga and Almeria. Almuñécar bus station has daily services to and from Granada. All services leave from the Almuñécar bus station, Avenida Juan Carlos. Timetables at *www.almunecar. com*.

Visitor Information

Almuñécar: Palacete de la Najarra, Avenida de Europa s/n (☎ *958 63 11 25. www.almunecar. info*). Open 10am–2pm, 4pm–8pm. La Herradura tourist office: Paseo Andrés Segovia. No phone.

Parque Ornitológico or Loro Sexi Bird Park ☆ is an aviary housing over 1500 doves, ostriches, macaws, swans and parrots and has the botanical gar-den **Parque del Majuelo** close by. If you don't mind a steep climb, take in the heady views up at the **San Miguel Castle** (No phone. Open daily from 10.30am–1.30pm and from 4–6.30pm. Entry for adults is €1.95 (£1.30)and for children and senior citizens €1.35) (£0.90) in turn a Phoenician, Roman and Moorish fortress or palace.

Plaza de San Cristóbel, ☎ 958 631 125 Open July–mid-Sept 11am– 2pm, 6pm–9pm daily, rest of year 11am–2pm, 4pm–6pm. €2.70 (£1.80) or €1.40 (£0.95) for children.

Salobreña & Around

You turn the corner from Almuñecar to be met by a broad sweep of flat plain at sea level, broken by Salobreña's beautifully dramatic cliff top castle, which rears up from the flat a few hundred metres from the shore. White-washed houses dotted along higgledy-piggledy streets tumble down the sides of this dramatic **Alcazaba**.

Nuestra Señora del Rosario

From the ruined Arab castle you can see the snowy peaks of the Sierra Nevada. Just below is the parish church Nuestra Señora del Rosario (Plaza de La Iglesia ☎ 958 61 03 14) built on the site of an old mosque.

Museo Histórico Down in the town the Museo Histórico (Plaza Antigua Ayuntamiento, Salobreña. ☎ 958 61 27 33. Open 10.30am–1.30pm, 5–9pm, July–mid Sept or 4pm to 7pm in the afternoons mid-Sept–June.

€1.30 (£0.87)) tells the story of the town's 6000-year history and why in the mid-1800s it became a centre for the production of sugar cane.

Azucarera del Guadalfeo

Today the Azucarera del Guadalfeo in the village of Caleta is the last remaining trapiche (sugar mill) to produce sugar in Europe. Down by the beach there are several little chiringuitos for a drink and a snack or take a walk along the **Peñon**, the imposing rock jutting out to sea that was a prison in the 1st and 2nd centuries and later a Christian burial site.

Castello de Ferro The road east, where the mountains grow more sulky – red and tawny rubble covered with scratchings of scrub, has azure waters hitting hard, cliff-backed coves. In the UK this would probably be as protected and well-trodden a

Salobreña

coastline as Cornwall's coast path, but Spain has more pragmatically slapped the dual carriageway alongside it. Castello de Ferro, identified by its watchtower, has two good, peaceful pebbly beaches, albeit with the same, slightly unsettling backdrop of intensive agricultural tents.

Family-friendly Accommodation

Casa de los Bates Built in the 17th century this Italiante villa is set back from the coast road and surrounded by lush gardens of palms, magnolias and cedars and fish ponds. Careful restoration has restored the home into a beautifully furnished gem. One of the rooms can accommodate two extra beds and another one extra bed.

Ctra. Nacional 340 km 3295. Apartado de Correos, 55, 18600 Motril, Granada; 📞 *958 349 495. Fax: 958 349 122. borjar@jet.es. www.casa delosbates.com. 5 rooms. €135 (£90.45) double, €180 (£120.60) suite. Extra bed €30 (£20.10). Dinner €25–45 (£16.75–30.15) à la carte and on request.*

8 Almeria

ALMERIA

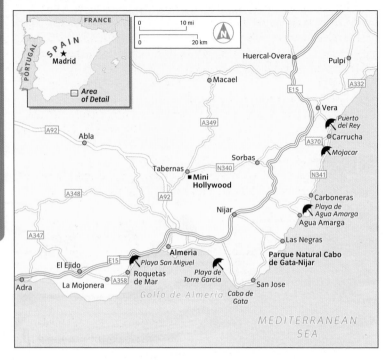

Families driving beyond the eastern reaches of the Costa
Tropical will find the scenery becomes arid and mountainous.
The easternmost city of the coastline, Almeria, around 162 km
(100 miles) from Granada, perches between the foothills of the Sierra
Nevada and the desert-like Sierra Alhamilla.

Almeria's name comes from the romantic Arabic '*Al-Mariyat*', or the
'mirror of the sea'. The city was a thriving Moorish port serving the city
of Granada until the mid-15th century, when Christian forces invaded
and drove out the Moors. Almeria fell into decline under the Christians
and suffered the misfortune of being rocked by several earthquakes. Its
luck didn't turn until the arrival of the railway in the 19th century,
which enabled entrepreneurs to exploit the area's rich mineral reserves.

Almeria itself, the provincial capital, has lots to look at, although it
is far from a museum piece. The Arab influence is very much alive
here and the hustle and bustle of street life will intrigue children.
Unlike the empty Moorish palaces and fortresses through which you'll
wander elsewhere, the trade between Spain and its African neighbours
is still a part of daily life. Almeria's messy streets are full of Moroccans
and Algerians, swilling mint tea and smoking in scruffy cafes. Arabs
and Christians have competed here for thousands of years – and the
two communities still bristle.

East along the coast, the slate-grey city of Cartagena, just beyond Andalucia's borders in Murcia, couldn't feel more different. It is a beautiful belle époque settlement that has history coming out of its ears, in museums, but also in its domestic and civic architecture, and in its port, still very much in action both for trade and defence, something else that will illuminate youngsters.

Between the two cities, the countryside is rich in archaeology. 'If you want to make the most beautiful museum in the world,' the researcher Siret once told Spain's minister of state education, 'all you need to do is cover the 90 kilometres between Cartagena and Almeria with a huge roof.'

All Mediterranean history is here: Paleolithic man settled in the caves of la Zajara; the Los Letreros cave paintings, just outside Velez Rubio, have earned a UNESCO World Heritage tag, while Los Millares's copper discoveries show the region once had a thriving Bronze Age culture. There's very much more contemporary family entertainment to be had here, too, either at the Spaghetti Western film-sets of Mini-Hollywood, deep in the desert, or over and under the water in the sparkling seas off the beautiful arid wilderness of Cabo de Gata.

ESSENTIALS

Getting There

Almeria airport is 9 km (5½ miles) to the east of the city centre on the AL-12 (carretera de Nijar ☎ 950 213 715) and the A7 coastal motorway is a couple of kilometres inland. BA, easyJet, First Choice, Flybe, GB Airways, Iberia, Monarch, Ryanair and Thomsonfly all operate between the airport and the UK, and there are regular domestic flights to Madrid, Barcelona, Palma de Mallorca and Melilla.

By Bus The number 14 bus runs to the city centre from the airport every half hour between about 7am–10pm. It costs €15 (£10) to get to town by taxi; Aguadulce is €19 (£12.75),

Cabo de Gata €23 (£15.40). Buses run from Almeria to Agua Amarga, La Isleta del Moro, Las Negras and Rodalquilar, San Jose, San Miguel de Cabo de Gata.

By Car The Autovía del Mediterráneo joins Almeria with Alicante and Murcia in the north and the rest of Andalucia to the south.

Visitor Information

Regional Tourism Board: Parque Nicolas Salmerón (s/n Esq Mtnez Campos), Mon–Fri 9am–7.30pm, Sat and Sun 10am–2pm ☎ 950 28 07 48. Provincial Tourism Board: Patronato Provincial de Turismo, Plaza Bendicho s/n., ☎ 950 62 11 17. www.almeria-turismo.org.

Indalo: A symbol for Almeria

You'll see this little fellow, the 'Indalo', all over Almeria. He may look just like a stick man with an arch over his head to you and me, but he is actually a symbol of good fortune and protection, bringing those who wear it good health, love and wealth. To see the original, head for the cave paintings in the village of Velez Blanco, well north of the city.

Getting Around

Almeria city is walkable, but most children would far prefer the **tourist train**, from the Plaza Circular, that runs Saturdays and Sundays at 11am and 12 noon, and daily at 6pm, 7pm and 8pm round the old quarter and the port: €3.50 (£2.35), *www. almeria-turismo.org*. To travel **by horse** go outside the Gran Hotel where Antonio sits, or lies, who drives, he says, the only horse-drawn carriage in Almeria. Thirty minutes costs €40 (£26.80). To **walk** the prettiest streets and stroll along when the heat of the day has died down go to *Las Ramblas*, the *Paseo de Almería*. A walk around the San Nicolás Salmerón park is also very pleasant. Las Ramblas go all the way to the port and the Almadrabillas beach.

Wandering through the city's Renaissance, Baroque and Neoclassical streets is nice enough but, once you've seen the Alcazaba and the Cathedral you should be ready to repair to the beach: which is lucky, because the city has precious little to recommend it in the way of overnight accommodation. Head east for Cabo de Gata, a huge terrestrial and marine natural park, with several lovely beaches and plenty of accommodation, instead.

Child-Friendly Events & Entertainment

Spring and early autumn are the best times to visit, although if you're here in August, you shouldn't miss the **Feria de Almeria**, usually held in the last two weeks. There are sporting contests, bullfighting, dancing, festivities and rides for children in the city's fairgrounds. Other interesting events include the **Carnival** celebrations with fancy dress, street bands and processions, should you be here just before Lent; the **Holy Week festivities** before Easter, again with processions and the '**Cruces de Mayo**' (May Crosses), usually held during the first three days in May.

WHAT TO SEE & DO

Children's Top 10 Attractions

❶ **Mini Hollywood, outside Almeria** Who shot the sheriff? Find out here on a one-time Wild West film-set with saloon

Almeria

bars, a sheriff's office and it's own bank. Stick around for the shoot-'em-up shows (see p. 200).

❷ Alcazaba, Almeria. The crowning glory of the city, a magnificent fortress built in 995 AD. Zig-zag through the jumbled streets of the medina before reaching the stepped pathway into the complex (see p. 198).

❸ Coastal drive to Mirador Amatista Drive through the stunning Cabo de Gata nature reserve to this look out spot for one of the most breathtaking views along the coast. Then take a dip in the crystal clear waters at the Peñon Blanco beach (see p. 204).

❹ Boat trip along the Cabo de Gata coast Jump on board a boat for a 90-minute tour of the coastline. Hire snorkelling equipment to see what goes on beneath the surface (see p. 207).

❺ Castillo de la Concepcion, Cartagena Walk past the park's peacocks for the best panoramic views of the city. Inside the Castillo is a centre with interactive aids to teach youngsters about the key historical sites in the area (see p. 209).

❻ Civil War Museum, Cartagena Interactive displays bring the civil war to life, while the 45m cylindrical elevator lends a little drama to the journey to the Castillo above. (see p. 210).

❼ Cartagena port boat trip Take the one-hour trip from Alfonso XII dock around the port. There's a commentary with stories and legends plucked from the city's two millennia of bumpy history (see p. 210).

❽ Salt Marshes (Reserva de las Salinas) Cabo de Gata. Drive down to the salt marshes to see the colony of flamingos carpeting the water's edge (see p. 203).

❾ Playa del Mónsul, Cabo de Gata One of the most beautiful, unspoilt beaches in Spain. Show the children where parts of *Indiana Jones and the Last Crusade* were filmed (see p. 204).

❿ Covered Market, Almeria Take the children to sample the Spanish food delights in this market. Ideal for preparing a slap-up picnic to take to one of Cabo de Gata's beaches (see p. 200).

Alcazaba ★ Try to visit this old Moorish castle at sunset, when children will be stunned by the views. Built at the behest of the Caliph of Córdoba in 995 AD, the Alcazaba is the city's crowning glory: a magnificent fortress towering over the old quarter with birds-eye views across the harbour. Zig-zag your way through the medina's jumbled streets, up Calle Almanzor to reach the stepped pathway into the complex. Inside it consists three massive, crenellated walled enclosures. The second area contains the remains of a mosque, later converted to a chapel by Ferdinand and Isabella, while the first Moorish palace is today filled with gardens. From this vantage-point you can also look over the cave quarter 'Barrio de la Chanca' and, on one side see

The Alcazaba

the antelope pens of the **Instituto de Aclimatación de Fauna Sahariana** rescue centre.

Alcazaba, c/ Almanzor s/n ☎ 950 17 55 00, Fax: 950 17 55 01. Free entry. Open July–Sept Tue–Sun 9am– 8.30pm. Oct–June 9am–6.30pm. No credit cards.

Catedral For a place of worship, this 16th century Catedral, built on the site of a former mosque, also looks like a fortress. It's no coincidence. When it was constructed in 1524, the southern Mediterranean was tied up fighting an unofficial war with Turkish and North African pirates. Its towers once held cannons.

For such an unpromising exterior, the church interior makes a graceful surprise. The nave of the Capilla de la Piedad contains works by Alonso Cano and Murillo.

C/Velasquez, 10am–4.30pm Mon–Fri; 10am–1pm Sat. €2 (£1.35), children €1.50 (£1). No credit cards.

FUN FACT ▶ **Sun City** ◀

Get children to look out for the image of the Sun of Portocarrero sculpted outside the entrance: it is one of the sunniest cities in Spain

ALMERIA TOWN

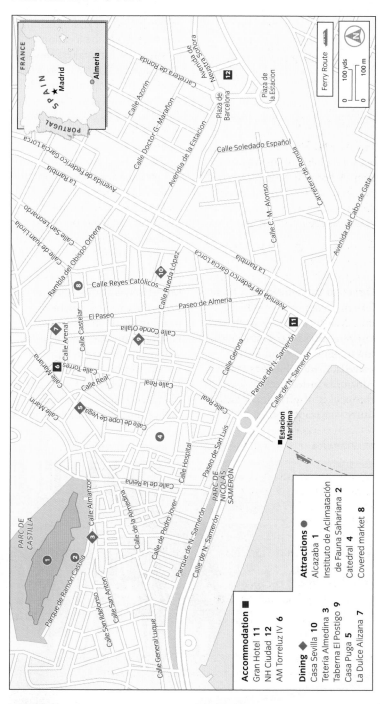

Ferry Route

0 — 100 yds
0 — 100 m

Accommodation ■
Gran Hotel **11**
NH Ciudad **12**
AM Torreluz IV **6**

Dining ◆
Casa Sevilla **10**
Tetería Almedina **3**
Taberna El Postigo **9**
Casa Puga **5**
La Dulce Alizana **7**

Attractions ●
Alcazaba **1**
Instituto de Aclimatación
de Fauna Sahariana **2**
Catedral **4**
Covered market **8**

Covered Market If the burgeoning global supermarket culture makes you despair, head down to Almeria's covered market where you'll find neat piles of Mediterranean vegetables, glistening fresh fish, huge cured hams and slabs of succulent meat for children to discover and pick out. There's everything for a slap-up picnic on Cabo de Gata's beaches: get some slivers of smoked tuna from Antonio Roque, Cuadro no 3, mesas 1, 2, 3, 4, for starters.

Mercado Central ☎ 950 23 16 34, Aguilar de Campo. Mon–Sat 7am–3pm.

Trips Out

Desierto de Tabernas A mere 20 km drive north of Almería takes you into a shock of **desert country**. It's as if the surrounding mountains of the Sierra Nevada, Gador, Filabres and Alhamilla furled back to leave this pocket of surreal, parched, dusty landscape in their wake.

Weird, eroded ravines, dry riverbeds, barren slopes and the endlessly beating and bleaching sun once made the location a favourite for filmmakers shooting spaghetti Westerns. Scenes from classics including the Clint Eastward greats *A Fistful of Dollars* and *The Good, The Bad and The Ugly* were shot here. For a panoramic view of the lunar landscape head to the astronomical observatory (Obervatorio de Calor Alton) north of Gérgel (around 23 km or 14 miles towards Granada from Mini-Hollywood): the site was chosen for the amazingly clear views of the skies.

Mini-Hollywood Before you reach the town of Tabernas heading north on the N-340, you'll hit this one-time film-set with a cast-list to die for. Orson Welles, Henry Fonda, Liz Taylor, Michael Caine, Sean Connery, Harrison Ford, Clint, Schwarzenegger, plus blockbuster

Mini-Hollywood

directors from Sergio Leone and Anthony Mann, Stone, Spielberg and Kubrick have all kicked up the dust around Almeria at some stage since the first reels were shot in the 1950s and 60s.

Today, the Wild West set with its saloon bars, sheriff's office and ripe-for-a-stagecoach-robbery bank have been turned into a fun, if slightly commercial tourist attraction which children will adore. Try and stick around for one of the twice-daily shows (12pm and 5pm) – or thrice daily between June and September with another at 8pm: a hammy but entertaining shoot-out. As a bit of an afterthought, there's also a large zoo at the back of the park.

Ctra. Nacional N-340, dirección Gaudix, Desierto de Tabernas, Almería. ☏ *950 36 52 36, Fax 950 36 28 84. poblado@playasenator.com. www.playasenator.com. Open Apr–Oct 10am–9pm. Nov–Mar 10am–7pm Sat, Sun. Wild West shows 12pm, 5pm (and 8pm in summer). Parrot show 1am, 3pm, 6pm. Price €18 (£11.40), €9 (£6) children. DC, MC, V.*

Texas Hollywood Further up the road is this slightly less glamorous, but maybe more charming rival outfit to Mini-Hollywood, also used as a film set, with either an 'Indian settlement', 'Mexican village' or 'Fort Bravo' backdrop. The set is still used today. In addition, children can enjoy shows, camels, bison and horses to provide plenty of entertainment. You can go trail riding in the desert on gentle horses in groups of five to ten,

and stay the night in one of the wooden cabins on the actual film set; details through *www.fort-bravo.com.*

Ctra Tabernas, A7. Paraje de Lunhay, Tabernas. ☏ *950 06 60 14. texas hollywood@topactive.com. www.fort-bravo.com. Call Rafael Molina in advance about times, but as a guide 10am–10pm on weekdays. Shows May–Nov 12.30pm, 2.30pm, 5.30pm, in the summer 7.30pm daily. €14.50 (£8.40), or €9.50 (£5) children. MC, V.*

Los Millares 17 km (10½ miles) north west of Almeria is Europe's largest Bronze Age settlement. The size of its fortifications – it has at least 13 protective outposts – is a good indication of its one-time prosperity and there is a cemetery with 80 megalithic passage-tombs on the site.

FAMILY-FRIENDLY DINING

The architecture wasn't the only thing that got steeped in all things Arabic: the cultural influence extended to the city's food too. There's a clutch of tapas bars in the city centre, but there is a fancy fish and seafood restaurant, **Club de Mar** (☏ *950 235 048*) excellent fish and seafood, Mon–Sat 1–4pm, 8.30–11.30pm, closed Tues; and **Bello Rincón** (☏ *950 238 427*) fantastic sea views good for fish and regional cuisine, open daily 1.30–4.30pm, not evenings. Both will cater for children.

Tetería Almedina NORTH AFRICAN

For a burst of North African cooking, pull up a cushion, huddle around the restaurant's low tables and try the chicken, date and almond tagine with a bowl of couscous. It's squarely aimed at tourists but since it's on the doorstep of the Alcazabar, it makes a handy stop for a cup of mint tea and some Arab sweets. There's a children's menu and for €3 (£2) the staff will throw in a henna tattoo.

Calle Paz 2, ☏ 629 277 827, restauranteteteriaalmedina.com). 1pm–6pm Tues, 1pm to midnight rest of week; closed Mondays. No credit cards.

Taberna El Postigo TAPAS

The menu is abbreviated at this simple joint on a laid-back pedestrianised side street, but what it lacks in choice it more than makes up for in mastery. If your family's used to burgers, this is a good place to try to wean them onto sausage rolls that are a cut above: the snacks here are of chorizo and Iberico. For the vegetarian there's *queso azul* – little slithers of blue cheese served with a couple of slices of *tostada*. It's shady and relaxed (€4.50 (£3)).

Calle Guzmán Number 1, ☏ 950 23 31 79. Mon–Sat 9.30am–12pm, 1pm–5pm, 7pm–2am

Casa Puga TAPAS

Right in the historic centre is the Casa Puga. Red prawns are done by weight (€10 (£6.70) for 100g), *Boquerones* are €7 (£4.70), Iberico ham 100g €15 (£10). Sit down for *raciones* or *medios*.

For meat there's *Solomillo con ajos* and *lomo en adobo*. For pudding there's chocolate cups, *copa de leche mergenada, trufas de chocolate*.

Jovellanos 7, Almeria ☏ 950 23 15 30. www.barcasapuga.es. 20 standing, 50 sitting. Mon–Sat 12–6pm and 8–midnight.

La Dulce Alianza

For some confectionary delights let your brood be lured in by the meringues and other sugary treats piled up in the window.

Paseo de Almería 8, 04001 Almeria. ☏ 950 237 379.

FAMILY-FRIENDLY ACCOMMODATION

Sadly, none of the accommodation here yet matches the nice atmosphere of the city. Push on to **Cabo De Gata** the same day if you can. If you can't, expect to shell out €60 (£40.20) a night to stay at one of the well-equipped business hotels: Gran Hotel.

NH Ciudad de Almeria www.nh-hotels.com; and Torreluz IV ☏ 0034 974-500-239.

CABO DE GATA-NÍJAR PARQUE NATURAL

This is one of the wildest and most isolated natural parks in Spain, clasped by one of the finest stretches of coast in the south. Searing temperatures and

Nijar Natural Park

the lowest rainfall in the Iberian Peninsula have created large swathes of semi-desert. Pimientos hang like beaded curtains round the doorways of whitewashed *cortijos* in the villages. Scrub and scree lie across the wilderness landscape, broken by big knolls of rock – just add tumbleweed. What few trees that make it through the desert heat here have seen the funny side: the comedic jujube sticks out at all sorts of improbable angles, having a Herculean stab at fecundity in the dry. Yet for

Cabo de Gata

such a superficially inhospitable landscape, Cabo de Gata is silently bubbling with natural riches. Agate, jasper and gold have been extracted from mines of **Rodalquilar** over the centuries, and there's enough nourishment in the park's dunes, salt marshes, gargantuan volcanic rocks and crystal waters to support a huge range of flowers and shrubs and wildlife, both on dry land and underwater. At the most westerly boundary of the park, on the route in from Almeria, the **Reserva de las Salinas** (salt marshes) is where flamingos flock to form a candy floss carpet by the water's edge, and conservationists are about to reintroduce the monk seal to this stretch of the Med. With all this, and beautiful driving terrain and walks and adventures to be had here, it's little wonder that the pristine waters and desert-strength sun attract a knowing clique of Spanish trippers.

Getting There

By Car From Almeria, follow the A7/ E-15 road east out of the town for 15 minutes, from where Cabo de Gata is first sign-posted – there are at least four routes off the motorway into the park. The first leads straight to San José.

By Bus Public transport is scarce in Cabo de Gata and to explore any of the beaches, caves or coves you will need a car. During the week Autocares Bernardo runs three buses a day from Almería to San José and four a day in the other direction. (☎ 950 250 422. *www.autocares bernardo.com*). On Sunday just two buses run.

Visitor Information

Tourist office: In San José, Calle Correos s/n, 04118, San José, Almeria. ☎ 950 380 299, info@ cabodegata-nijar.es. Fax *950 611055*.

On the most westerly road inside the park, the AL822, between **Retamar** and **San Miguel de Cabo de Gata Cabo**, the much praised visitor centre **Los Amoladeras** (☎ *950 160 435*) is only really rewarding if you speak Spanish, although some of the books, maps and leaflets are in English and show good walking routes (10am–2pm and 6–8pm. Oct–May, Tues-Sun 10am–2pm and 4–6pm). There are also information points at Las Sirenas on the southernmost tip of the Gata, La Isleta and Punta de los Muertos.

San José San José is the area's main resort. The town, which stretches around a shallow bay, is not particularly interesting but is the gateway to some spectacular beaches including **Playa del Mónsul** – featured in *Indiana Jones and the Last Crusade* – and the even better **Playa de Genoveses**, a one kilometre-long stretch of pristine white sand. Genoveses beach is long and sheltered. Without any tide, the water is flatter than pan-cakes. You'll need to bring your own refreshments and shade: it is as exposed as it comes.

La Isleta del Moro The next village that you come to heading east is La Isleta del Moro, a small fishing village. Octopi and fish are hung from houses to dry out in the sun. Stop at the **Mirador Amatista** (look out point) en route for a breathtaking vista. Then take a dip at the **Peñon Blanco** beach, which gets its name from the rock where local fishermen's wives used to stand to wave their menfolk off to sea. Or try the palm-fringed **Cala de los Toros** beach. At this point the road turns inland towards scruffy **Rodalquilar** – but there's no reason to stop. The main roads through the park do not always follow the coast, hence its many unspoilt coves and caves.

Las Negras Further along, Las Negras is something of a sleepy San José in waiting: sympatheti-cally built low-rise apartment blocks, and a sweet little beach, all hemmed in by big hills.

Follow signs to **La Caneta Camping** (see Family-friendly Accommodation) for a lovely cove with limestone cliffs to jump off. Take off on foot along one of the many trails and tracks for land-based adventures.

Agua Amarga At Las Negras the coastal road stops. To reach Agua Amarga (well worth the effort) a 10 km (6 mile) drive as the crow flies, drivers will have to head back to the motorway, to **Fernán Pérez** and take the road from there. This calm little village has an unexpected number of great places to stay and eat (see below).

Cortijo El Fraile Inland again, along a bumpy 4 km (2½ mile) track from the village **Los Albaricoques** is the abandoned Cortijo El Fraile. Federico Garcia Lorca's play *Blood Wedding* was inspired by a bloody crime of passion that took place on this barren farm more than 80 years ago when a bride-to-be ran off with her lover only to see him tracked down and shot by her betrothed.

A few kilometres inland and you arrive at **Níjar**, a white-washed town that is pretty enough in its own right, but which many visit for its handicrafts: jarapas (woven rag throws), esparto pieces and pottery.

Mojacar Leaving Cabo De Gata to the East is something of a crash landing: Mojacar is a burly, commercial beach. Its shop front should give you the picture: Thai restaurants, Indian take-aways, the Irish Rover pub, English language estate agents, pool maintenance companies and pine showrooms. The main road, and its curb-side parking, runs right along the coast. Still, the beach is nice and clean, every inch of it has its own bar, and there are banana boat rides.

Family-Friendly Accommodation

San José

Hotel Cortijo Solitto A ranch-style four star kitted out with South American rugs, right next door to a stable. Guests have the run of a tennis court, archery, a swimming pool, table tennis table and pool table. Rooms are decorated with local ceramic work and tiles. Most have white marble floors and come with their own terrace.

Carretera entrada a San Jose, 04118 San Jose, Nijar, Almeria. ☎ 950 611100; Fax: 950 611105. Restaurant reservations: ☎ 0034 950 380216. sotillo@a2000.es www.hotelsotillo. com. Prices (low season: double €90 (£60.30), suite €121 (£81.10), extra bed €18 (£12); mid-season double €103 (£69), suite €130 (£87.10), extra bed €26 (£17.40); high-season double €100 (£67), suite €157 (£105.20), extra bed €31 (£20.80). Includes breakfast. 20 rooms.

Hotel Dona Pakyta The building is no more imaginative than any of the others in San Jose, but every single room in this central sister hotel to the Cortijo Solitto has a sea view, and the whole place is phenomenally open to the light. There are two dormitories, which can sleep six, with a writing table, little sofa bed, a TV and sitting room. It's all scrupulously clean, rooms have giant beds, bare tiles, simple oil paintings, Steps from the bar lead straight down to the beach and terraces.

Calle Correo, s/n, San Jose, Nijar ☏ 950 611 175. Fax: 950 611 062, www.hotelpakyta.es. ADSL, A/C, TV, minibar, Restaurant, bar. There are 18 double rooms €110 (£73.70) double, €123 (£82.40) double w terrace in low season; suite €149.80 (£100.40) in low season, €162 (£109) in high season, with terrace. All inc. breakfast. Extra bed low season €18 (£12), high season €30 (£20.10). Cots free. 4 junior suites and 5 suites (€150 (£100.50) and €161 (£108)).

Agua Amarga

Charo's Houses Surrounded by prickly pears, palm trees and views of the mountains. La Joya is a small coastal fishing village. The two farmhouses here are an eco dream: made from natural products with solar power. Everything's biodegradable and recycled. Each *cortijo* has two bedrooms, a bathroom, large living room with open fire, kitchen, porches open to the west east and north give shade from sun and shelter from wind. They stand on 10,000 square metres of their own land in organic fruit groves, with lots of hidden corners to sunbathe and read or play about in. On-site are a swimming pool,

outdoor eating places, a barbeque and an Arab pavilion.

Directions: Exit the Autovia del Mediterraneo, at salida 494 to Carboneras, turn to Aguamarga. Barrio La Joy is signposted. Barrio La Joya, 04149 Aguamarga (Almeria). Contact Begona Garcia. ☏ 619 159 587 (from Spain) or ☏ 0039 0257602906 (from outside Spain). www.charoshouses.com. Prices on request.

Hotel Family Named after its sister hotel in Montepellier, France, this is a comfy spot, with welcoming owners and a great pool with a roped off shallow area. The nine rooms are traditional and rustic in style, with simple, rattan bedspreads and ceramic work for decoration. Rooms have lovely views out to sea. The restaurant (only open in the evenings) serves up a French/International menu. Fish soups, rabbit with mustard, pork Bourguignon, grilled fish. The children's menu costs €12 (£8), or the evening meal €18 (£12) for adults, including a glass of wine and cup of coffee.

Hostal Restaurant Family. Rene Y Michelle. Calle La Lomilla Aguamarga, Ando 23, Carboneras (Almeria) ☏ 950 13 80 14. Prices: (sea views – high season €85 (£56.95), low season €65 (£43.55). Downstairs – high season €55 (£36.85), low season €45 (£30.15). Breakfast is included. Extra bed €20 (£13.40).

Camping 'La Caleta' This camping is one of the most beautifully situated in all Spain and if you're in Cabo De Gata for its nature then there's no improving on actually sleeping out in it. There's nothing fancy to the facilities here: showers, shop, phone, etc., but it really is the lovely cove it's beside that makes this worth pitching camp for. It's a semi-private, secluded cove surrounded by beefy limestone cliff formations, all hollows and jags, with ledges to use as diving boards for those with the pluck, and clean water you'll share with schools of darting small fry. Popular with young people but still peaceful.

Electricity €3 (£2). Parking €6.50 (£4.35), €4.50 (£3) pax, tent €5.50 (£3.70), caravan €5.50 (£3.70), adult €4.50 (£3), child €4.20 (£2.80), dogs €2 (£1.35), cash only. Children's playground near the reception, bungalows, a garden and a swimming pool by the restaurant. Camping Las Negras. Las Negras-Nijar ☎ *950 525 237, Fax 950 16 51 16.* www.vaya camping.net/lacaleta; *camping lacaleta@arrakis.es.*

Family-Friendly Dining

La Palmera, Agua Marga. Beach front hotel and restaurant serving up a wide selection of seafood. Popular in the evenings. The outside terrace seats around 100. Best dishes are usually the fish of the day or paella to share. Prawns in garlic cost €13.40 (£9), clams for €14.50 (£9.70) anchovies and squid for around €12.30 (£8.25). Selection of salads and soups. Children will need to leave room for one of the 10 or so ice creams for dessert, including lemon, chocolate mousse and coconut flavour.

Open 12pm until 2am every day. V, MC.

For Active Families

Even relatively experienced scuba divers will find interesting underwater terrain around San José. Hidden treasures include the Vapor Arna, opposite the town itself, a steamboat almost 100 m long that sank in 1928, the Punta del Castillo at San José, ideal for night dives. Try **Centro de Buceo Alpha** (Puerto Deportivo San José – ☎ *609 912 641* or ☎ *951 380 321*) or **Centro de Buceo Isub San José** (C/Babor 8, ☎ *950 380 004 /609 015 172* or *630 506212*). The tourist office will also show you the best places to go: hiking, bird watching, caving, windsurfing, waterskiing, paragliding, cycle touring or kayaking.

Aventura Cabo de Gata offers daily 90-minute boat trips along the coast, for a minimum of six people at 11.30, 1.30, 4.30, and 6.30. Children €12 (£8), adults €20 (£13.40), or use it as a bus – leaving at 10.30am and returning at 8.30pm. Several shops also hire-out fins and snorkels for a few hours snorkelling.

At **Náutica Puerto San José** (C/Correos s/n, ☎ *950 611 088* or *667 78 63 30,* www.nauticapuerto sanjose.com) you can also hire, with or without captain, a boat to steer you through the cliffs and coves of the natural parks' coastline. If a kayak is more your thing try **Happy Kayak** (☎ *609644 722* or *636 280 767,* www.degata.com/ happykayak): there are five beginner's routes, which last three hours for €35 (£23.45), four intermediate routes lasting five hours, for €50 (£33.50), or top level excursions for a full day cost €60 (£40.20). A family excursion, for 90 minutes, from **San Jose to Cala Higuera** and back is €15 (£10.05) the family or €10 (£6.70) for children. Otherwise it's €10 (£6.70) an hour to do your own thing.

For Landlubbers the **Cortijo El Sotillo stables** might be more appropriate (San José Níjar, Almeria, ☎ *950 611 100*, *www. cortijoelsotillo.com*, 2.5 hours €45 (£30.15)).

Cartagena

CARTEGENA

Cartagena is a beautiful, belle époque, bite-sized city that holds all the ghosts of its very long past within an extremely easy tourist grasp. Plunge your children into more contemporary politics with a trip to one of the museums that reveals the city's maritime adventures or chronicles the fierce fascist reprisals it faced for its populations' unswerving loyalty to the Republican cause in the Spanish Civil War. For architectural buffs there are stunning eclectic and Modernist buildings to stroll past, the outward sign of a turn-of-the-century revival in the city's fortunes, and ancient ruined castles crumble on every tall hillside. For its ability to conjure up all sorts of pasts

alone it really does make the best stopover between Cabo De Gata and Alicante, the next major city to the east.

Visitor Information

Tourist office: Plaza A Bastarreche, s/n ☎ *968 50 64 83*, Fax 968 52 69 12. *www.cartagena. es*; *www.puertoculturas.com*. May–Sept Mon–Fri 10am–2pm and 5–7pm. Sat 10am–1pm.

Child-Friendly Events & Entertainment

Lo Ferro If you are in striking distance, definitely head for Lo Ferro, in the last week of August, when scores of the best new lungs and toes and heels and hand clappers in flamenco descend on this tiny Murcian

 Rocky Times

Cartagena's quarries, chock full of lime sandstone ('tabaire') have been constantly exploited from Punic times to today.

FUN FACT >> **Festivals: Carthaginians and Romans** <<

Come September the city re-enacts the conquest of the Carthaginian port by Scipio. There are processions and parades, and plays put on in the Roman circus.

village (population 300) to compete at the region's best regarded contest, the **Festival Internacionale de Cante Flamenco de lo Ferro.**

Peña Flamenco Melon De Oro, calle Morillo, 2, near Torre Pacheco Murcia 📞 968 589 469, www.festvial deloferro.org.

What To See & Do

Castillo de la Concepcion
Walk up through the park, with its flock of peacocks, for the best panoramic views over the historic city. Plaques marking out the rooftops of all the histor-ical sites will give you a good checklist for which landmarks along Cartagena's long historical road you want to visit. Inside the Castillo itself, the Interpretation Centre has some good teaching

aids for curious youngsters, including a cool computer generated rendering of key his-torical sites as they would have looked in their day, like the Roman amphitheatre and the types of ships that used to set sail from the harbour. There's also a much-boiled down potted history of succeeding rulers given with English subtitles. There are a lot of slopes and ramps, so bring a buggy.

Free for under 3, €2.50 (£1.70) under 12, €3.50 (£2.35) full price. Open 10.30am to 8.30pm daily July–Sept, Then Tues–Sun from 10am to 2.30pm and 4–7pm the rest of the year except Nov to Mar when it closes at 6.30pm.

Ascensor Panoramico A 45 m cylindrical elevator lends a little

Peacocks outside the Castillo

drama to the journey between the Castillo and the Refugio below.

C/ Gisbert, 10 daily July to Sept from 10.30am to 8.30pm from Tues till Sun 10am till 2pm reopening at 4pm the rest of the year to close at 6.30pm from Nov to Mar and 7pm other months. €1 (£0.67) adults, €0.80 (£0.55) concessions.

Refugio Museo Guerra Civil

In the sombre cool of a vault that 5500 Cartagenians used as their air raid shelter when German aerial attacks on the town began in earnest in October 1936, is this extremely family-friendly exhibition. It avoids finger wagging or the taking of sides in favour of showing what living through war felt like for the average man, woman or child in the street: disruption to school, social life, food are all

discussed using a series of well-edited display panels and first person recollections.

C/ Gisbert, 10 all year Tues to Sun 10am–2.30pm, reopening at 4pm to close at 8.30pm July to Sept (when it's also opened Mon), 6.30pm Nov to Mar and 7pm the rest of the year. €3.50 (£2.35), €2.50 (£1.70) under 3s free.

Centro Interpetacion Muralla Punica

The site where Quart-Hadast, as Cartagena was once known, had its defensive wall in 3rd century BC is now an exhibition centre charting some of the Mediterranean's most important civilizations, with sections on the legacies of Carthage and Rome, and portraits of the Greeks, the Phoenicians and the Iberians. There's a projection theatre, leisure zones for

Bus & Boat

The Tourist Office runs a one hour boat trip from Alfonso XII dock which will steer you around the very thing that has put Cartagena at the centre of so many civilizations: its port. There's a commentary on the coastal batteries, defence systems, and stories and legends plundered from the city's two millennia of bumpy history. The route takes you past the submarine base, and all the city's key outlying defensive buildings like Castillo de Galeras and the batteries of Navidad, Trincabotijas, San Isidoro y Santa Florentina, San Julian and San Leandro. There's also a half hour tourist bus to pique your interest in the rest of the town's sites: but you can easily explore Cartagena on foot. Muelle Alfonso XII, Cartagena Basin opposite to *Héroes de Cavite* June to September every day at 10.30am; 11.30am; 12.30pm; 3.30pm, 4.30pm, 5.30pm, 6.30pm, 7.30pm; Tuesday–Sunday the rest of the year from 10.30 till 1.30pm and March–June and September–October at 3.30pm, 4.30pm and 5.30pm. €5.50 (£3.70) and €4.50 (£3) concessions.

children, a crypt and both the excavated remains of the old city wall plus a modern day recreation of the city's ancient defences so you can see what it felt like to be kept at bay by a 10 m block of sandstone.

C/ San Diego, 25 Open daily 10am to 2.30 Mon to Sun July Aug and Sept, then 10am–2.30pm and 4pm–7pm Tues to Sun the rest of the year except Nov to Mar when it closes at 6.30pm. Adults €3.50 (£2.35); children under 12 €2.50 (£1.70), under-3s free.

Beaches & Resorts

The closest of much merit are the isolated nature reserves of found in the direction of Mar Menor at **Calblanque**, but if you're heading towards **Cabo De Gata** the road to Mazarrón will weave you through truly mighty, tawny country, burnt out *cortijos*, bits of wood twisted and bleached, mountains vanishing in multi-shaded layers, beyond which lie Isla Plana and La Azohia, two quite bustling Spanish holiday centres. They have reasonable campsites if you would rather stay near the beach than in Aguilas or Cartagena.

Nearby, is **El Portus**, two wonderful specks of pebbly beaches, kept apart by a mountain peak that you reach through stunning winding roads. The westerly beach (right on the approach road) is the nicer of the two, there are restaurants and bars, but neither has much in the way of facilities.

Playa Calblanque, Playa Negrete and Las Salinas del Rassall Calbanque beach is something of a secret and the shoddy state of its approach roads means it's happily likely to stay that way. But it's worth risking your sump tank for: the track cuts over hills that protect an area of deserted scratchy scrubland of bulrushes, wild lemon verbena plants, abandoned crunchy saltpans that are home to amazing birds, invertebrates, algae and aquatic plants, then lie giant sand dunes behind which are becalmed by glassy waters crashing on sand, pebbles or rock pools. It's part playa, part nature trail. Lifeguards, but no showers, shades or *chiringuitos*, and no sound apart from insects' rattling hind-legs. Birdlife includes herons (*garza real*), shelducks (*tarro blanco*) in summer or flamingos in the winter.

Directions: main road to La Manga, past Los Belones, to La Jordana.

Family-Friendly Accommodation

Cartagena isn't packed with hotels, but resign yourself to spending most of your time outside the bedroom instead. Because the city's tourist renaissance is in its infancy, there isn't yet much traffic and you can get bargains outside peak season (i.e. school holidays).

Hotel Cartagenera This is a slightly dog-eared place, worn down armchairs pack out its long jumble of an empty reception room. Bedrooms aren't exactly roomy, bedspreads are synthetic, service is hardly with a smile, but it's got a cracking location just at the top of the Calle Mayor, and is certainly tolerable for an overnight. €46 (£30.80).

Calle Jara 32, ☎ 968 502 504, Fax: 968 502 500. 44 rooms, a few of which can sleep three. €42–60 (£28.15–40.20) triple, double €47 (£31.50). Extra bed €60 (£40.20). No breakfast. Parking nearby. TV, phone, no A/C, bath and shower. Cash only.

La Manga ★ ★ ★ North of Cartegena on the Costa Calida (warm coast) is the well-known sports and leisure complex of La Manga. If you want a very family-friendly stay with everything catered for, this is it. There's an endless array of activities, more than 20 restaurants and bars, a children's club with junior golf, tennis and football academies, even karate. There are also children's menus, bikes with baby seats and babies pools. The high prices may be the only catch.

30385 Los Belones, Cartegena, Murcia. €348 (£233.15) ☎ +34 968 17 5000. Fax: +34 968 33 1235. www. lamangaclub.com.

Family-Friendly Dining

The **Calle Mayor** is the easiest place to get cheap, fresh Spanish food, it's basically one narrow, pedestrianised food shop-window full of babble, pulpo, chiperones and paella. Stock up on your savouries and you're never more than two paces from a *heladeria* (ice cream parlour). Probably best are the **Principal** and **La Mejillonera**, and just down Calle San Miguel is **Café Casa Miguel**, which is in a handy situation for children to investigate the outside *bas reliefs* on the walls of the Iglesia Santa Maria de Gracia in between

Ice-cream Kiosk

Like a Local

Plonk yourself at the port for the best views, or opt for the Calle Mayor for Belle Epoque atmosphere, but to live like locals head instead for the area round Jiménez de la Espada: Ikebana, Amsteleria, Gran Café are all good local dives.

mouthfuls. **La Tartana** (keep walking into town from the top of Calle Mayor) is opposite the town's McDonalds and has fast food done the tapas way instead – casual dining in wicker chairs outside a pink and white Modernist building (Puertas de Murcia, 14 📞 *968 500 011*). The port, around the yachting club, holds the pricier options, all of which are much the same here.

D'almansa Restaurante Café

The menu features 11 different types of rice: as well as amazing mains like creamy rice with monkfish and king prawns, foie filled with figs and a sweet red wine touch, the most popular dish being aubergine crisps with duck, ham and honey. Squid comes stuffed with Iberian ham and wild mushrooms in a sherry sauce. Mains are reasonable, at the €13 (£8.70) mark for most dishes, and puddings, like chocolate *coulant* with rose jam are €5.20 (£3.50). The bar menu is cheaper, simpler and snappier: croqettes, Iberico ham, *bacalao*, *queso* with Pedro Ximenez sherry at around the €8 (£5.35) mark.

Calle Sagasta 53 Cartagena. V, Amex, MC. 📞 868 099 666 almansaferrersll@ latinmail.com. 8am–midnight, daily, closed Sun evening.

9 Valencia

The true home of paella in Spain is a lively, breezy city that guidebooks often complain is skipped over. But since being picked to host the 32nd America's Cup it has been put firmly back in the spotlight. The 2007 sailing contest sent a new ripple of excitement through the place, evident in the frenetic activity along the port. Giant new architectural delights to rival the futuristic landscape of Valencia's Arts and Science Park have been constructed. This is a city committed to cutting edge design and looking good on the European stage. Some of the sites here will awe youngsters. Equally alluring, though for visitors, are the splendid Baroque and Gothic buildings of the old quarter, the blue-tiled church domes that punctuate the sky line, Art Nouveau mansions, medieval turrets, art galleries, museums and of course the plethora of beach-side paella restaurants, certain to win over even the most fussy youngsters. The whole lot adds up to create one of Spain's newest and hippest short break destinations.

ESSENTIALS

Getting There

By Plane Valencia has two international airports, Valencia and Alicante, and three ports, Valencia, Dénia and Alicante. The AP-7 Mediterranean motorway runs north to south, to Almeria and Catalonia

There are direct flights between all the major regional airports in the UK and Valencia Airport in Manises (96 159 85 00). Ryanair flies from Stansted, AirFrance, Lufthansa and Iberia all fly from London City and Heathrow, and Iberia from Gatwick. BA flies to Alicante Airport from Gatwick, along with Iberia, which also leaves from Heathrow. Thomson flies from Coventry and Bournemouth (96 691 90 00).

By Train There are two train stations, at Estación del Cabañal

Avda. Blasco Ibañez s/n, Valencia–Northern Railway Station at C/ Játiva, 24.

By Bus Valencia bus station is at Avda. Menéndez Pidal, 13, (96 346 62 66).

By Ferry Valencia is the main harbour for ferries to the Mallorca's Palma harbour (three and a quarter hours) from where you can get onwards ferries to Ibiza. (Denia down the coast has direct crossings). Operators include Balearia, (902 160 180/ (902 191 068 www.balearia.com.

Visitor Information

There are tourist information offices on the Plaza de la Reina, at the airport, and on Calle Paz, 48, (963986422; valencia. www.comunitatvalenciana.com, open Monday–Friday 9am–2.30pm, 4.30–8pm; Saturday 10am–6pm. Sunday closed.

VALENCIA TOWN

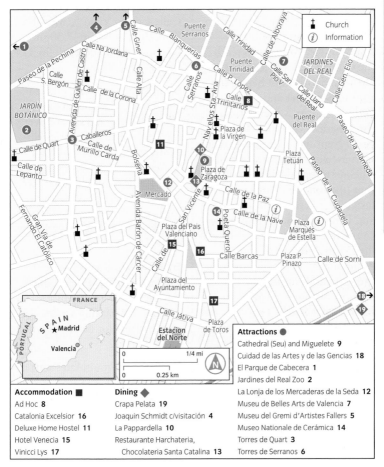

†	Church
(i)	Information

Attractions ●
Cathedral (Seu) and Miguelete **9**
Cuidad de las Artes y dé las Gencias **18**
El Parque de Cabecera **1**
Jardines del Real Zoo **2**
La Lonja de los Mercaderas de la Seda **12**
Museu de Belles Arts de Valencia **7**
Museu del Gremi d'Artistes Fallers **5**
Museo Nationale de Cerámica **14**
Torres de Quart **3**
Torres de Serranos **6**

Accommodation ■	Dining ◆
Ad Hoc **8**	Crapa Pelata **19**
Catalonia Excelsior **16**	Joaquin Schmidt c/visitación **4**
Deluxe Home Hostel **11**	La Pappardella **10**
Hotel Venecia **15**	Restaurante Harchateria,
Vinicci Lys **17**	Chocolateria Santa Catalina **13**

City Layout

Valencia is easy to explore on foot and distances are not great. There's enough colour and charm to appeal to children, with plenty of ice cream stops and street entertainment. Valencia's old quarter lies on the south bank of the city's dry river bed, the Antiguo Cauce Del Rio Turia. At it's heart are the Plaza

la Reina and Plaza de la Virgen and the main square, Plaza Ayuntamiento. The district's cirumference is marked by a series of gates – the north east border is marked by the Torres de Serranos and the river, the most westerly border is marked by the Gran Via, and the Punte de Ademuz, the south by the RENFE train station and the

Xativa gate, the most easterly is the Plaza Porta de la Mar, beside the Puente de la Exposicion. If you keep heading south-east from this last Porta you'll reach the Ciudad de las Artes y Las Ciencas. South from here is the road to Sidi Saler and L'Albufera, east is the Marina, the America's cup port, and paseo Neptuno, a beachside strip with excellent paella restaurants. The metro line 4 (there are only four lines on the metro) is the fastest link between the marina and Pont de Fusta (just over the river from the old town). The line 35 bus goes from Plaza Ayntamiento in the old town to the Ciudad de las Artes y Las Ciencas Autopista El Saler goes to Sidi Saler beach. The roads on either side of the river are one-way. The old town river bank takes traffic east, towards the sea, the north bank takes you inland.

Getting Around

By Bus The main bus company is EMT and covers all the central urban areas and suburbs. A 10 journey Bonobus card costs

€5.20 (£3.50). A bus map is available at the EMT office, Calle Correo Viejo 5 (Mon-Fri 9am–2pm, 4.30pm–7.30pm). For bus information call 96 315 85 15.

By Metro A modern, efficient, cheap way of getting about. There are four lines that traverse the city and all connect intelligently with the bus and train routes.

Prices for a single ticket start at €1.10 (£0.75). A 10 journey card costs €5.60 (£3.75). Trains run from 6am–11pm, or 10pm at weekends.

By Bike Valencia is flat, with vast parks suitable for cycling through – it certainly beats hunting for parking spaces. See 'tours' below for details of where to hire a bike.

By Taxi Minimum fares start at around €3.50–4 (£2.35–2.70). A trip to the airport from the centre costs around €14 (£9.40). The city is in the midst of issuing more taxi licenses to cope with a shortfall of cars.

FUN FACT **Fallas de San José**

Fallas de San José, is one of Spain's most famous – and fiery – festivals honoring the arrival of spring and the memory of St Joseph, is held 15–19 March. This is a wild street party with parades, street dancing, ground-shaking fireworks and bullfights. Every neighbourhood competes to see who can build the most spectacular, satirical papier-mâché effigy, or ninot. Some 300 ninots, many of them several stories high, then coast down the streets to be judged. The festival ends with la nit del foc, or 'fire night', when the caricatures are burned. Historically, this inferno was to exorcise social problems and bring luck to farmers in the coming summer.

VALENCIA OUTER TOWN

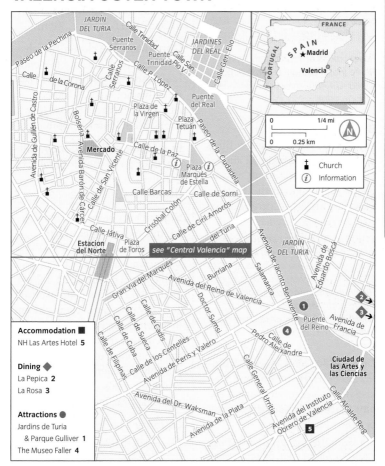

Accommodation ■
NH Las Artes Hotel **5**

Dining ◆
La Pepica **2**
La Rosa **3**

Attractions ●
Jardins de Turia
& Parque Gulliver **1**
The Museo Faller **4**

Planning Your Outings

Walking Tour This tour lasts
2 hours and takes in the central
market, silk exchange (Lonja de
los Mercaderes), Cathedral and
Plaza Redonda. English and
Spanish spoken.

Entrance via the tourist
office, Plaza de la Reina. Most
Thursdays and Saturdays from
10am throughout July and
August. Call to check times
throughout the rest of the year.

Tours can be booked in tourist
offices and through most hotels.
3½ hours including bike, guide
and drink €22 (£14.75).

*Paseo de la Pechina, 32, Valencia
46008. ☎ 963 851 740. www.valencia
guias.com. Adults €12 (£8), children
under 12 €6 (£4).*

Bus Tour Starts at Plaza de la
Reina and takes in the Modern
Art museum, the city of arts and
sciences, the fine arts museum.

Operates Mon–Sun 10.30am–7.30pm every hour (winter) or 10.30am–9pm every 30 mins (summer). Adults €12 (£8), children aged 7–11 €6 (£4).

Reservations at Tourist-Info Reina, Renfe (north station) and the airport. 963 414 400. www.valenciabus turistic.com.

Bike Tour/Rent Depart everyday at 10am from Valencia Bikes at Paseo do la Pechina 32 and takes 3 hours (minimum of two people) and takes in the Turia Gardens, historic centre and the City of Arts & Science.

€22 (£14.75) per person. Reserve at least one day in advance. Children's seats and bikes are available. 963 851 740. www.valenciabikes.com. Reservations at the tourist office, Renfe north station or the airport. Bikes with trailers or child seats on request.

DoYouBike rents bicycles from €2.50 (£1.70) an hour and also offers organized tours of the city. Corner Músico Magenti between Puebla Larga.

675730218. Fax: 963284911.Email: info@doyoubike.com. Before visiting the shop you must make an appointment by phone, fax or email. Open 10am–2pm, 5pm–8pm.

Coches Landós (horse and carriage) Departs from Plaza de la Reina. €30 (£20.10), carriage for 4.

FAST FACTS

Amex The local American Express representative is Duna Viajes, Calle Cirilo Amorós 88

(96-374-15-62). It's open Monday to Friday from 9.30am to 2pm and 6.30 to 7.30pm.

Consulate The closest British consulate is in Alicante (Valencia is an honorary consulate). Plaza de Calvo Sotelo, 1, 03001 Alicante. 96-521-61-90. Open Mon–Fri 8.30am–1.30pm.

In a Medical Emergency, call 112; or go to the Hospital Clínico Universitario, Av. Blasco Ibáñez 17 (96-386-26-00).

Signs Don't be surprised if you see signs in a language that's not Spanish or Catalán. It is Valenciano, a dialect of Catalán. Often you'll be handed a 'bilingual' menu in Castilian Spanish and in Valenciano. Many citizens of Valencia are not caught up in this cultural resurgence, and view the promotion of the dialect as possibly damaging to the city's economic goals. Most street names appear in Valenciano.

Laundry The self-service laundry Lavandería El Mercat, Plaza del Mercado 12 (96-391-20-10), is open Monday to Friday 10am to 2pm and 5 to 9pm, Saturday 10am to 3pm.

WHAT TO SEE & DO

Children's Top 10 Attractions

❶ **Paella by the sea** Valencia is the home of paella so take the family straight to the sea front along Avenida de Neptuno to tuck into a vast pan full of the colourful rice dish (see p. 226).

❷ **Dolphin show** at Valencia's City of Arts and Sciences Daily (and nightly in August) shows (see p. 222).

❸ **Zoo**, Jardins Real, natural science museum, Valencia. Picnic in the gardens, ride the reindeer train, check out the prehistoric skeletons in the museum and then visit the very much alive creatures from crocs, to hippos, monkeys, bats and tropical fish in the zoo (see p. 224).

❹ **Gulliver Park**, Turia Gardens, Valencia. Flopped on the floor of the gardens is a giant, prostrate statue of Gulliver that has been transformed into a huge playground for children (see p. 223).

❺ **Fallas museum**, Valencia Home to many of the giant, gaudy puppets or 'ninots' that are the main attraction in the city's annual festival (see p. 225).

❻ **Cathedral** (Seu) and Miguelete. Inspire your children with the tale of the Holy Grail and then take them to see the actual (so the cathedral has claimed for over 500 years) cup (see p. 223).

❼ **Cabecera Park**, Valencia Take a boat to row across the Cabecera lake in this lush green space, before scampering off to the playground (see p. 225).

❽ **Day trip** to El Saler & El Palmar Break from the city to wander around these nearby

Las Fallas

fishing villages. Go bird spotting in the Albufera National Park (see p. 226).

❾ **Sailing**, Charter your own for a few hours to escape the crowded summer beaches. Sailing schools also rent smaller boats, scuba diving and snorkeling gear (see p. 226).

❿ **Quart Tower**, Serranos Tower Scamper up the pentagon-shaped Serranos guard towers for some spectacular views over the Turia dry riverbed (see p. 224).

Walk Around the Old Quarter

The city's largest square is the **Plaza del Ayuntamiento**, to the west of the old quarter. The palatial town hall still dominates the square and overlooks a booming fountain. **Plaza de la Virgen**, beside the cathedral is a usually bustling pedestrian and pigeon-only square, with a dramatic fountain honoring the Turia river. **Plaza de la Reina**, round the corner is dotted with orange trees, bars and restaurants. The dinky **Plaza Redonda**, close by, has a special kind of charm. It's a circular square set around a fountain, surrounded by a clutch of slightly fusty, traditional shops selling lace, expensive baby clothes, ceramics and linen. On Sundays it plays host to an unusual market known as 'el clot' – the hole – selling a hotch potch of items from clothes to pets and religious knick-knacks. Spare some time to wander through the oldest part of the city – the **Barrio del Carmen** – packed with restaurants and bars.

Ciudad de las Artes y de las Ciencias (City of Arts & Sciences) ★★

A jaw-dropping futuristic urban complex fantastic for families designed to rival Seville's Expo and Barcelona's slick and modern port-development. The vast site to the south of the city, set in 90 acres (36 hectares) of landscaped park, aims to educate as well as entertain. You'll find four main buildings devoted to science, arts, the oceans and the natural world each offering shows, talks, and interactive displays.

L'Oceanographic To recreate the marine habitats of the world's oceans, the complex has been transformed into an underwater city. Above ground mini-wetlands, a dolphinarium and an Antarctic enclosure house sea-dwelling creatures from penguins to seals, sea lions and flamingos. The daily dolphin shows – plus an 8pm night show in August – allow the creatures to show off their many talents. There's even a 'Submarine' restaurant where you can enjoy a bite while gazing into the aquarium.

L'Hemisferic A stunning building designed by Santiago Calatrava, now houses a giant IMAX cinema screen with the soundtrack in four languages, plus other mini-screens showing documentaries about the natural world, from disasters to animal migration patterns.

Palacio de las Artes Another awesome Calatrava creation, with four state-of-the-art auditoriums – one outdoors – showing opera, dance, theatre and art.

Museo de las Ciencias Príncipe Felip Devoted to science and discovery. There's a planetarium bubble, displays about the human genome, plus a space academy simulating three stages in the preparation for a space launch. Visitors are invited to look, touch and feel in this hi-tech museum of sensations.

Avenida Autopista del Saler 1,3,5,7. ☎ *902 100 031 for info and booking. www.cac.es. Admission to L'Hemisferic €7.50 (£5), €5.80 (£3.90) for children aged 4–12 or adults over 65. All sites free for children under 3 years. L'Oceanografic €22 (£14.70), €16.60 (£11.10) children. Museo de las Ciencias Príncipe Felipe €7.50 (£5), or €5.80 (£3.90) children.*

Arts & Sciences Flyover

L'Hemisfèric open 10am–9pm daily. L'Oceanographic open Sun–Fri 10am–6pm low season (10am–8pm Sat), 10am–8pm mid-season everyday, 10am–midnight high season everyday. Ticket offices are open up to an hour before each site closes. Dolphin shows three times a day, four on Saturdays. Buses: 19, 35, 95 and 40.

Jardins de Turia & Parque Gulliver ★★★ These meandering lush, green gardens snake through the city along the dry riverbed of the old Turia, which was diverted to the south after devastating floods in 1957. They are known as the 'lung' of Valencia for their boost to the city's oxygen supply and for providing locals with a handy place to exercise. Fountains, flowers, cafes, tennis courts, jogging and cycling tracks make them a good spot for a stroll with the children or a workout. The Gulliver park, out towards the Ciudad de las Artes y las Ciencias in the south is a favourite with children. It contains a huge, prostrate statue of the fictional traveller tied to the ground by the little people of Lilliput, which has been fashioned into a giant playground.

Catedral (Seu), Museo de la Catedral and Miguelete ★ Da Vinci Code fans unite! For the past 500 years the cathedral has claimed to posses the Holy Grail – an agate cup with Arabic inscriptions around the lower portion. It is said to fit a description given by Saint Jerome of the cup used by Jesus at the Last Supper.

The Grail appears in Sir Thomas Malory's 1485 legend *Le Morte d'Arthur* about Sir Galahad, Tennyson's *Idylls of the King* and Wagner's *Parsifal* to name a few.

After visiting the cathedral, scale the 47 m (155 ft)-high Miguelet, a never-quite-completed octagonal bell tower offering panoramic views of the city. The museum contains paintings by Goya and Zurbarán. *Plaza de la Reina.* ☎ *96 391 81 27. Free admission to the cathedral. Miguelete 1. €20 (£13.40), Museo 1.*

€20 (£13.40). Cathedral open
7.30am–1pm, 4.30pm–8.30pm;
Miguelete Mon–Fri 10am–12.30pm,
5.30–6.30pm, Sun 10am–1pm,
5–6.30pm. Museo Mon–Fri
10am–4.30. Bus: 9, 27, 70 or 71.

Museu de Belles Arts de València

A real treasure trove
containing one of the best art
collections in Spain. The
museum's inventory lists over
3000 works of art.

Gruesome and fascinating
14th and 15th century Valencian
and Flemish 'primitives', a fantastical triptych of The Passion
by Hieronymus Bosch – or El
Bosco – plus works by Goya,
Velázquez, Morales, El Greco,
Ribera and Murillo are the shin-
ing lights of the collection.

San Pio V, 9, 46010 Valencia. ☎ 96
369 3088. Free admission. Tues–Sun
10am–8pm. Bus: 1, 5, 6, 8, 11, 18,
26, 29, 36, 79 or 95. Metro: Alameda.

Jardines del Reial, Museu de Cièncias Natural, Zoo de Valencia ★★

Once you have
taken a stroll, or enjoyed a picnic
in the delightful gardens – known
locally as the Jardines de Viveros –
take your little ones for a ride on
the park's reindeer train, drop
into the Natural Science museum
to see the prehistoric skeletons,
stuffed animals and selection of
fossils, or take a tour to meet the
very much alive exotic creatures
in the zoo. Among the lengthy
list of inhabitants are hippos,
crocodiles, monkeys, chimps,
giraffes, bats, tropical fish and
lions. The nocturnal enclosure is
a treat although the cages for

some of the larger animals in the
main enclosure are worryingly
small. There's a café on site.

At the time of going to press,
the zoo was scheduled to move
to Parque de Cabecera.

Zoo adults €6 (£4), children €3 (£2),
students 15% reduction. ☎ 96 360
08 22. Open everyday 10am until
sunset (times vary). Natural Science
museum, Jardines de Viveros,
General Elio s/n. ☎ 96 352 54 78 (ext
4313). museociencias@valencia.es.
Open Tues–Sat 9.30am–2pm,
4.30pm–8pm. Closed Mon, Sun and
festivals 10am–8pm. Adults €2
(£1.35), children under 16, €1
(£0.67). Free children under 7 years.
Free entrance Sat, Sun, festivals.

Torres de Quart and Torres de Serranos (part of the old city walls)

The Torres de Quart
were built in the 15th century –
Valencia's Golden Age – when El
Miguelete, La Loinja de la Seda,
El Palau de la Generalitat were
all constructed. Avenida Guillén
de Castro s/n 46003, Valencia.
☎ 96 391 90 70.

Marking the old northerly
gate of the city walls, opposite
the bridge of the same name are
the Torres Serranos. Wend your
way up to the top of these pentagon-shaped guard towers for
some spectacular views over the
Turia dry riverbed and the city.

Plaza dels Furs s/n, 46003, Valencia.
☎ 96 391 9070. Admission is free.
Tues–Sat 9am–1.45pm, 4pm–7pm;
Sunday 9am–1.45pm.

Museo Natcionale de Cerámica

This camp fantasy
in stone is pretty much the
Palacio de Dos Aguas, kept as

chocolate-boxy as it was when it was home to its owners, the Marquis of Dos Aguas. Things could not be much more ornate, alabaster entrance-ways give onto Carrera marble statues, outside chandeliered ballrooms. There's an ultra-elaborate chamber of faux-chinoiserie, and the dining room has dead ducks dangling as sculptures into its cornices in a show of abundance. Intriguing for children, terrifying for fans of flat-packed furniture.

Museo Natcionale de Cerámica y de las Artes Suntuarias Gonzalez Marti. C/ Poeta Querol 2 ☎ *96 351 63 92. www.mnceramica.mcu.es. €2.40 (£1.60), kids free, Mon–Sat 10am–2pm and 4–8pm. Sun 10am–2pm.*

The Museu Faller (Fallas Museum) ★★
The site is crammed with the gaudy, comical 'fallas' figures lampooning folk traditions, political figures and social ills. Artisans work on the giant caricatures – known as ninots or fallas – throughout the year in preparation for the spectacular festival in March when all but one of the figures are set aflame. The 'pardoned' figure is passed on to the museum.

Plaça de Montolivet 4. Town Hall ☎ *96 352 54 78 (extn 4625). www. fallas.com. Open Tues–Sat 10am–2pm, 4.30pm–8.30pm. Sun and holidays 10am–3pm. Closed Mondays and Jan 1st, May 1st, Dec 25th. Admission €2 (£1.35), or €1 (£0.67) for children under 16. Children under 7 are free. Buses: 13, 14, 18.*

Museu del Gremi d'Artistes Fallers (Fallero Artists Museum)
This site has a collection of sketches, photos and 'fallas' figures alongside the workshops of the artists and craftsmen who design the caricatures each year.

San José Artesano 17. ☎ *96 347 6585 for an appointment. Closed Sunday. For a tour of an artists' workshop call: 96 339 0390. Mon–Fri 10am–2pm, 4pm–7pm, Sat 10am–8pm, Sunday and festivals 10am–6pm.*

El Parque de Cabecera
Another of Valencia's lush green spaces, here the family can go boating, rowing or take a pedalo across the Cabecera lake. Choose one of three main walking routes through the park, or take the children to one of the playgrounds. Plans are afoot for a Bioparc or zoological garden and a Fun-Fair.

C/Pío Baroja s/n, ☎ *963 52 54 78.*

Beaches & Resorts

Las Arenas, Malvarrosa and Playa Cabañal beaches are just a few minutes from the city centre, north of the port. The sea-front promenade, Paseo Maritimo runs alongside this stretch of coast.

South of the port is the quieter beach of Playa Pinedo, awarded a blue flag for being in good environmental nick. It stretches out to become Playa del Saler – a 5 km long strip backed by pine forests which gets pretty crowded in summer. The Gabri wind that blows here in the summer

Malvarrosa Beach

evenings makes it a popular spot for windsurfing. Playa Devesa, further south still, is a good beach with a small nudist section at the most southerly end.

Boating Club Náutico Valencia, Camí del Canal 91 (📞 *96 367 90 11*) has a sailing school that rents out boats for scuba diving and snorkelling. It maintains a full yacht-service facility.

The Albufera National Park, El Saler and El Palmar One of Spain's largest nature reserves and home to more than 250 species of birds is just 12 km out of town. Unfortunately the large freshwater lagoon at the heart of the reserve has long-since been too polluted for swimmers or much of a thriving marine life.

Despite the pollution, the vast wetlands area still attracts many birds and the Valencian rice fields found in these parts ensure it has a thriving paella culture.

The villages of **El Saler** and **El Palmar** are among the best places to try the famous rice dish. The central square in El Palmar makes for a very pretty stopover on summer evenings, particularly when the local fishermen drag out tables for an evening's card-playing in the open air. The beaches in this area south of the port (El Saler and Devesa) are cleaner, wilder and have fewer facilities than those in town so you'll have to bring your own food, drink and umbrellas.

The park information office (Racó de 'Olla, 📞 961 627 345) is just off the main road between Valencia and El Palmar for maps, walking routes and hides. A car is essential. To reach El Palmar from Valencia take the Autocares Herca bus (📞 963 491 250) marked Valencia-El Saler-El Perellò for €1.45 (£0.95).

Shopping

The modernist central market, Plaza del Mercado 6, is truly vast and glorious, even if it's only architecture you're into. It is officially Europe's biggest fish market. Outside, on Calle de Ercilla, is where to pick up a quenching horchata and buy a paella dish. Vera Torralua (✆ 963 922 418) sells amazing full-length Catholic baby gets-ups from its outlet on the Plaza Redonda. Calle Colon offers high street perennials Zara and Mango. Calle Jorge Juan has all the most elegant boutiques. The city's largest department store, El Corte Inglés, Calle Pintor Sorolla 26 (✆ 96-315-95-00), sells a wide array of anything you might want, including local handicrafts, crystal and porcelain, and other luxury items.

The Mercado de Colón ★ In the heart of the city is a Gaudí-inspired fantasy and a hub of shops and cafes. The best food shop here is Manglano, 5 Mercado de Colón (✆ 96-352-8854), decorated in a Belle Epoque (turn-of-the-20th-c. style). Several streets around the market also attract the crowds, notably a locally famous chocolatier, Cacao Sampaka, 19 Calle Conde de Salvatierra (✆ 96-353-4062). Ever had a balsamic vinegar flavoured bonbon?

FAMILY-FRIENDLY ACCOMMODATION

Hotel Sidi Saler During the summer months, this resort hotel comes into its own, located as it is on one of Valencia's best sandy beaches just a few kilometres out of town.

Guests can loll around by the pool or take a stroll through the nearby sand dunes and pine forests in the national park. Rooms are midsize with balconies and could do with a bit of sprucing up. The junior suites, with a separate living room, are more suitable for families. The hotel restaurant is handy – albeit there is a dress code – and while there is no children's menu, the chefs are usually happy to prepare pasta or omelettes for young diners. In July and August the Piolin Miniclub looks after children from 10am–2pm and 4pm until 7pm. A free shuttle bus to the city centre runs throughout the day.

Playa del Saler, 46012 Valencia. ✆ 96-161-04-11. Fax: 96-161-08-38. www.hotelessidi.es. 276 rooms. €115–286 (£77–164.15) double; with breakfast €200–349 (£134–241.20) junior suite; €310–654 (£207.70–438.20) suite. AE, DC, MC, V. Amenities: 2 restaurants; 2 bars; 2 pools (1 indoor, 1 outdoor); fitness centre; sauna; 24-h room service; babysitting (summer only); laundry service/dry cleaning; nonsmoking rooms; room for those w/limited mobility. In room: A/C, TV, dataport, minibar, hair dryer, trouser press, safe. Extra bed €57 (£38.20).

Vincci Lys ★ Just a 4-minute walk from the train station, this centrally located hotel, is one of the best bets for those who want to drop anchor at the very heart of Valencia. Located on a pedestrian-only street lined with cafes, it offers modern functional space geared to holidaymakers and business guests. Rooms are light, airy, and spacious, with good-sized bathrooms. Nearly two dozen of the accommodations have private balconies opening onto cityscapes.

Martínez Cubells 5, 46002 Valencia. 96-350-95-50. Fax: 96-350-95-52. www.vinccihoteles.com. 101 rooms. €50–240 (£33.50–160.80) double; €223–360 (£149.40–241.20) junior suite; €323–590 (£216.40–395.30) suite. Extra bed €50 (£33.50). AE, DC, MC, V. Parking €18 (£12.10). Bus: 4, 6, 8, 16, 35, or 36. Amenities: Restaurant; bar; spa; sauna; room service (7am–midnight); laundry service/dry cleaning; nonsmoking rooms. In room: A/C, TV, dataport, minibar, hair dryer, safe.

MODERATE

Ad Hoc This little hotel has plenty of charm and is one of the best located places to stay in Valencia. The building dates from the 1880s and was restored by an antiques dealer. Rooms are soundproofed and blissfully quiet. Breakfast is served in a cosy room on the ground floor and there is a decent restaurant attached to the hotel. Parking is a problem, but there is an underground public parking place five minutes walk away.

C/Boix 4, 46003, Valencia. 96 391 91 40. Fax: 96 391 36 67. adhoc@ adhochoteles.com. www.adhoc hoteles com. 28 rooms, double or single. A/C. Restaurant (meant to be v.good) – 10 tables 'a la carte menu', modern market cuisine, Mediterranean touches. Extra bed costs €28 (£18.80), cots are free and there's no babysitting service.

NH Las Artes Hotel The hotel sits in an ultra-modern cluster of buildings near the City of Arts & Sciences. With one eye on the business traveller and another on passing families, children are well catered for in smart environment. There's play area with games at the weekends, Playstation, a babysitting service and free accommodation for under-12s sharing their parents' room. Rooms have big beds with well-spung mattresses. It's best to go for a back room overlooking a leafy square and the playground. Rooms overlooking the road are double-glazed to block out any noise from the busy street below.

Avenida Instituto Obrero de Valencia 28, 46013, Valencia. 96 3351 310, fax: 963 748 622. nhlasartes@nh-hotels.com. www.nh-hotels.com. 174 rooms (including 2 junior suites). Prices €115–130 (£77.05–87.10). Extra bed €45–50 (£30.15–33.50). Restaurant, café, fitness centre, pool, laundry/dry cleaning, cark park, 24 hour room service. In rooms: safe, A/C, minibar, hairdryer, satellite TV, Internet and wireless access.

INEXPENSIVE

Hotel Venecia ★ VALUE In the city centre you don't get frills here, but you are rewarded with an immaculate hotel with well-maintained and comfortable guest rooms. The rooms have a rather minimalist decor. Each comes with a small bathroom with shower stall. In spite of its simplicity, the Venecia has won several awards from Spanish hotel guides.

En Lop 5, 46002 Valencia. ☎ *96-352-42-67. Fax: 96-352-44-21.* **www. hotelvenecia.com.** *54 rooms. €59–100 (£39.50–67) double. AE, MC, V. Bus: 19, 35, 70, or 71. Amenities: Laundry service/dry cleaning; nonsmoking room. In room: A/C, TV, dataport, hair dryer, safe. Plaza del Ayuntamiento X/En Llop 5, 46002 Valencia.* ☎ *963 524 267. Fax: 963 524421. reserves@hotelvenecia. com* **www.hotelvenecia.com.**

Outskirts of Town

Mas de Canicatti For some serious pampering head 25 km west out of town to this luxury design hotel set in sprawling gardens and surrounding by more than 100 acres of citrus groves and pine trees. Dip in the gently bubbling swimming pool, or take one of the suites with a private pool. Play tennis, pàdel, or spend a few hours in the spa, soaking in the tropical pool. The main whitewashed hotel building is set around a pretty stone courtyard and fountain. The funkier new rooms are created using materials like zinc, glass and copper and have huge sealed cement floors and floor-to-ceiling windows. The kitchens of the El Càdec restaurant are supervised by a double Michelin starred chef. The botanical gardens are an excellent place for children to explore.

Cra.Pedralba km 2.9, 46191, Vilamarxant, Valencia. ☎ *961 650 534. (fax: 961 650 535) Email hotel@ masdecanicatti.com.* **www.masde canicatti.com.** *27 rooms (14 doubles, 2 junior suites, 5 suites, 6 royal suites). Doubles €191–228 (£128–153); suite €300–420 (£201–281). Breakfast €18 (£12); half-board €60 (£40.20) each, full-board €90 (£60.30). Extra bed €80 (£53.60) (adult) €52 (£34.85) (3–12 yrs). Breakfast included.*

Ad Hoc Parque Sweeping into the courtyard and around the fountain of this garden hotel and memories of the bustling city just 13 km away quickly start to fade. The traditional-style buildings, themselves set in fertile gardens have views over the Escorpíon Golf Club and are close to the Sierra Calderona Natural Park for a really green-fix. An outdoor pool, plus nearby riding centre are popular with children and there is a café with a garden terrace for snacks and drinks throughout the day.

FUN FACT ⟩⟩ ## Wot No Sea? ⟨⟨

Valencia is actually hosting the America's cup by default. It will be the first time, since the race began in 1851, that it has happened in Europe. Like the Eurovision song contest, the winning team hosts the next event. However, landlocked Switzerland shocked the sailing world by winning the prize last time round (in New Zealand), and so Valencia ducked in as surrogate host. The America's cup class boat holds 17 crew, is 24 metres in length and displaces 24 tonnes of water. Port America's Cup has been built, along with a super yacht pier. *www.americascup.com*

Parque – Urbanización Torre en Conill. C/Botxí 6-8, 46117, Bétera, Valencia. 📞 96 169 83 93, Fax: 96 169 81 91. adhocparque@ adhochoteles.com. *www.adhoc hoteles.com*. Prices: twin room €145–179 (£97.15–119.95) (€59–77 (£39.50–51.60) business rates). Extra bed €21 (£14). Breakfast €9 (£6). 24 hour room service, terraces in rooms. 41 rooms, 2 suites. Wi-fi, A/C, safe, hair dryers. Some rooms have balconies.

FAMILY-FRIENDLY DINING

Avenida de Neptuno is a bit awkward to get to from the town centre, but dotted along this South Beach style promenade, you'll find some the best paella restaurants in Valencia. For those willing to travel, the villages of El Saler and El Palmar south of the city put up good competition. They are the true home of paella and located beside the city's rice paddies.

Paella comes in many forms – with chicken, with rabbit, with seafood or with everything. Ask for a simpler version for small children – brightly coloured vegetables and chunks of chicken in perfect gooey rice are usually palatable to even the fussiest eaters. If you're self-catering, shop in the markets and have a go at making your own.

EXPENSIVE

La Pepica PAELLA La Pepica joins the long list of restaurants claiming Hemingway as an old regular, but the food continues

to be good enough to back up the claim. Fresh lobster is the priciest of the paellas, but there are grilled fishes and calamaris if rice isn't for you.

Avenida de Neptuno 6–8, La playa de las Arenas 📞 *96 371 03 66* €25–30 (£16.75–20.10). AE, DC, MC, V. Daily 1–3.30pm, Mon–Sat 8.30–11.30pm, Sun 1–3.30pm. Will cater for children.

MODERATE

Restaurante La Rosa PAELLA This is a restaurant that saves its energy on food, not interiors. 100 can sit at the air-conditioned tables inside, but outside on the coastal strip is where the action is. Denia prawns are €22 (£14.75), pescaditos de la playa €10 (£6.70), mojama all the way from Barbate €9 (£6). Most people come for the paella, which is €15 (£10.05) a head whether it's abanda, negro con chiperones or chicken and rabbit. To splash out though, have the Arroz Copa America, for €25 (£16.75).

Avenida de Neptuno, 70, 📞 *96 371 20 76 Mon–Sun 2–4pm; 9–11pm.*

INEXPENSIVE

La Pappardella ITALIAN A popular spot close to the Miguelete where you'll find tasty Italian fare in lively atmosphere with young, helpful staff and there's a great terrace.

Bordadores 5, (📞 *96 391 8915).* *www.viciositalianos.com. Pasta* €6–8 (£4–5.35). Menu del día €9 (£6).

Paella

Crapa Pelata ITALIAN Over 100 original pizzas with the finest Italian ingredients that you can combine to eat in the restaurant or takeaway with you.

C/del Mar 3, ☎ *96 392 3717. www. crapapelata.com.*

Restaurante Horchateria Chocalateria Santa Catalina
Step back from the main drag for an old fashioned ice-creamery. It's a lovely low-ceilinged café with painted tiles and colonnades and the temperature is as cool as a catacomb. It's a great place to dive into for a little pick me up. It seats about 100, American diner style, and has sausage shaped doughnuts and sponges, croissants, churros, whiskies and wine. They do proper savouries too, like paella for €16 (£10.70).

Plaza de la Reina 6 ☎ *96 391 2379.*

Ice cream, chocolate, churros and other sugary treats
There are several good quality gelaterias (ice cream parlours) and chocolaterias around the Plaza de la Reina, Plaza de Santa Catalina and Plaza de la Virgen. Take the children for a chocolate and churros – thick Spanish hot chocolate with a long doughnut (churros). Alternatively pick up a glass of sweet, milky horchata (orxata in Valencian) in one of the horchaterias – there is a good stand up stall near to the main market (see market listing). Locals dunk fartons (long sticks of dough into the drink. For sweets, head to the a popular Casa de los Caramelos chain.

BEACHES & RESORTS

Costa Blanca

The 'White Coast' might be one of the most developed resort areas in Spain, but its appeal for families cannot be under-estimated. Benidorm is the largest centre for package holidays in Europe and often scorned by people who have never been there, but if this is not to your taste there are several smaller resorts nearby where you can enjoy the best of both worlds.

Benidorm

If you enjoy being one of a crowd with some of the best beaches and entertainment in

Spain on hand, you should look closely at Benidorm and ignore the attitude of people who associate it with all the worst excesses of mass tourism. In the streets behind Levante beach you can certainly find British pubs selling British food and beer, with bars named after their owners' home towns in Britain and Union Jacks fluttering. But you may be surprised to learn that while one in three visitors is from Britain, the biggest contingent – 40% – is from Spain itself.

Like other Spanish resorts, which were first developed in the 1960s, Benidorm has had a make-over and re-invented itself as the **theme park capital** of Spain, tempting many families to visit for the first time or try it again after visiting other resorts. The Port Aventura theme park on the Costa Dorada might be better known, but Benidorm's range of theme parks, excellent beaches and warmer year-round climate give it the edge.

Benidorm is a sizeable city and if you don't like high-rise, give it a miss. The tower blocks of hotels and apartments that line both main beaches are here to stay, but at ground level there's been a lot of change. The streets are cleaner and the seafront along Levante beach has become a pedestrian-only zone, while six miles of greenery have been created by landscaping some of the main avenues and planting over 20,000 trees.

Costa Blanca beaches have 48 **Blue Flag** awards for cleanliness

and three of them are in Benidorm – quite some achievement when you consider that tens of thousands of people use them every day at the height of the summer.

As Benidorm faces south, both main beaches have sunshine all day. The busiest is **Levante**, where soft golden sands stretch for 2 km and visitors compete to create the best sand sculptures. In the last year the beach has been made more accessible with wooden ramps into the sea for wheelchair users and floating wheelchairs are also available. Levante is separated from **Poniente Beach** by a small part of the old town leading to Mal Pas cove. Poniente is the longest beach at over 3 km, with palm trees and less intensive commercial development than Levante. A small offshore island, **Isla Benidorm**, can be reached by boat from Mal Pas and is popular with divers.

Benidorm enjoys a micro-climate making it popular year-round, with families dominating in summer and during school holidays.

Terra Mitica As one of the new generation of theme parks it combines high-adrenaline rides with a more educational interpretation of Mediterranean civilisations. Divided into five zones – Egypt, Greece, Rome, Iberia and The Islands – the park's attractions are set around or within a lake and cover over one million square metres with a panoramic view of the Mediterranean. Each

COSTA BLANCA

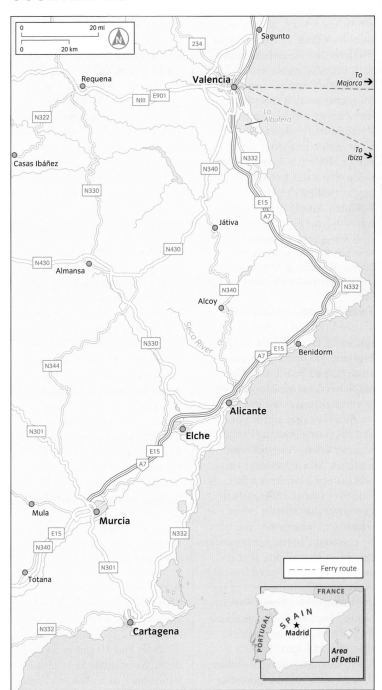

0   20 mi
0   20 km

Sagunto

234

Requena

Valencia

NIII   E901

N322

La Albufera

To Majorca →

Casas Ibáñez

N332

N340

To Ibiza →

N330

E15

A7

Játiva

N430

N430

Almansa

N340

N332

Alcoy

Seco River

N330

A7   E15

Benidorm

N344

Alicante

N301

Elche

E15

A7

Mula

Murcia

E15

N332

N340

N301

Totana

N332

Cartagena

- - - - Ferry route

FRANCE

PORTUGAL

SPAIN

★ Madrid

Area of Detail

of the five themed areas has shops and restaurants appropriate for the setting, and its own rides including 15 rides just for children that are rather gentler than the adult versions. Children particulalrly love go-kart racing (mitikarts) with a special circuit for younger children, and the Pyramid of Terror where Mummies come alive. Terra Mitica also has a series of shows using characters from mythology, including displays of Egyptian dance, Spanish horsemanship and Roman orators.

Terra Mitica, Ctra. de Benidorm a Finestrat, Partida de Moralet s/n, 03502, Benidorm. ☎ 902 02 02 20. www.terramiticapark.com.

Terra Natura The success of Terra Mitica led to the opening nearby of Terra Natura in 2005, bringing the first big animal attraction to Benidorm. The emphasis is on education as well as entertainment and it is based on America, Asia and Europe and the four elements: Pangea represents fire, America represents air, Asia represents earth and Europe represents water. The park boasts 1500 animals from over 200 species, 50 of which are endangered. You start by entering Pangea, a representation of earth millions of years ago which is dominated by a volcano. America is the land of the mythological feathered serpent of pre-Hispanic fame, inhabited by macaws, toucans, jaguars, monkeys and iguanas. Asia is home to the Kaziranga Wildlife Reserve with rhinos, leopards,

tigers, buffaloes, crocodiles and copious bird life. In the European zone you come face-to-face with not only deer, swans and domestic animals, but also a Greek village full of comedians. At Mare Nostrum you can swim safely with sharks and other species, and don't leave without seeing one of the shows including Flight of Quetzalcatl (birds and native dances), or the Magic of India.

Terra Natura, Foia del Verdader, 1, 03502, Benidorm. ☎ 902 500 414. www.terranatura.com.

Mundomar (Sea World) The success of Terra Mitica and Terra Natura has done nothing to undermine Benidorm's two more established family attractions. Mundomar is one of the largest marine animal parks in Spain, where you can watch shows with sea lions and dolphins. The dolphins' synchronised ballet is claimed to be the first such spectacle in the world, as dolphins perform with the Spanish Synchronised Swimming Team. Flamingoes, parrots, penguins and the obligatory Spanish Galleon add up to a busy family day out.

Mundomar, Sierra Helada s/n, 03503, Benidorm. ☎ 96 586 91 01. www. mundomar.es.

Aqualandia Adjacent to Mundomar is Aqualandia where the emphasis is very much on fun with 12 swimming pools, 17 slides and 10 games for children. Water attractions with names such as Kamikaze, Zigzag,

Niagara and Black Hole leave little to the imagination, and you can also swim with sea-lions.

Aqualandia, Sierra Helada s/n, 03503, Benidorm. 📞 *96 586 01 00.* *www.aqualandia.net.*

Altea

North of Benidorm towards Valencia are a string of smaller resorts where you can enjoy a less hectic ambience with the theme parks of Benidorm within easy reach for a day out. The nearest, Altea, is arguably the prettiest. The old part of town has genuine charm with impressive views of both sea and mountains but the beaches and coves are mainly of pebbles and shingles so don't expect to be building sandcastles. The old town of whitewashed buildings is enjoyable if you don't mind a steep stroll, with a church with blue and white dome. Altea's bay has wide beaches and small coves, the busiest being the beach beside the marina where you can try water-sports and sailing. Other beaches include Olla, with sand, pebbles and rocks, and pebbly Cap Negret. You'll find plenty of Spanish people on the beaches and you certainly won't feel it's a home from home or a smaller version of Benidorm.

Calpe

Looking north from Altea you will see one of the most dramatic features of Spain's eastern coast, the rock known as Peñón de Ifach. Below it is the resort of Calpe, which is more developed

Altea

than Altea but still appealing mainly to Spanish rather than international visitors. Calpe could not be described as a pretty resort but has a wide choice of beaches to suit most tastes. La Fossa and El Arenal beaches are sandy and busy, with facilities for windsurfing, pedaloes and jet skis. Levante also has fine golden sand and an open-air cinema, while Les Bassetes to the north of town is an example of a small, rocky cove where you can learn to sail and dive. The Peñón de Ifach rises sheer out of the sea to over 300 metres, and the chances are that someone in your family might want to climb it! You won't need mountaineering equipment to do that, as you can take a two-hour walk through a tunnel and up the gentler slopes on the seaward side. The views are fantastic with Ibiza, 70 km distant, visible on a clear day.

Javea

Often referred to by its Valencian name of Xabia – is along a stretch of coast where there has been much villa and residential development. The old town of narrow streets and whitewashed houses gives it a character lacking in some Costa Blanca resorts, but it is mainly devoted to the sea with a good choice of beaches and coves. The rocky coast south of the port attracts divers, while the long

beach of fine sand further south offers windsurfing and boat hire. The coast between San Martín and La Nao has escaped major development, an ambience no doubt appreciated by the villa owners whose properties are mainly in the hills.

Denia

A larger resort at the north end of the Costa Blanca, and also a port with ferry services to the Balearic Islands. The best beaches are north of the town stretching for about 10 km. These beaches are ideal for windsurfing as there is usually a brisk wind, especially in the afternoon. The coast to the south of the port is characterised by cliffs and rocky inlets, and inland is the Montgó nature reserve where the Cueva del Agua (cave of the water) has Roman inscriptions dating from the 7th Century.

Javea

Denia

Torrevieja

The one major resort on the Costa Blanca to the south of Alicante – Torrevieja – has been constructed more recently with a much higher concentration of privately owned property rather than hotels or apartments to rent. The atmosphere here is very international, with Locos and Cura beaches both having fine sand stretching below a busy promenade. The port includes a yacht club, marina, two diving centres, a sailing school and charter boats available for pleasure or fishing trips. Torrevieja is notable for two enormous saltwater lagoons which are now a nature reserve, where it is possible to see flamingoes and migrant birds. Another popular excursion (boats depart from Alicante or Santa Pola, between Torrevieja and Alicante) is the Island of Tabarca, a former pirate haven now popular with divers and day trippers where the walled village dates from the 18th Century.

Getting Around

If you don't want to depend on a car and don't mind some walking at your destination, a popular way of getting around is on the narrow-gauge railway between Denia, Calpe, Altea, Benidorm and Alicante. It runs along the coast in sections and is a good way of 'going local', with 40 stations and halts along the 93-km route. It is operated not by national rail operator RENFE but by Ferrocarril de la Generalitat Valenciana (FGV) – look for the signs.

Alicante

Alicante is the major city and gateway to the Costa Blanca, but many visitors see nothing other than the airport. It's a very Spanish city with a good choice of shops and restaurants, a few hotels, its own beaches and some historical interest. Santa Barbara Castle is a medieval fortress with fine views out to sea, with a lift from the seafront. Alicante's main beach Playa del Postiguet can be very crowded and lacks the facilities of Benidorm, but here you'll certainly meet the locals.

Inland

Inland from the Costa Blanca is a mountainous region with nature reserves and historic towns, the most interesting of which is Xativa with its castle and Romanesque church. Guadalest has a 16th Century Moorish castle, but being a popular day trip from Benidorm, it can be very crowded. Elche (Elx in Valencian) is renowned for over 300,000 palm trees which surround it, including the garden Huerto del Cura.

10 Barcelona

COSTA BRAVA

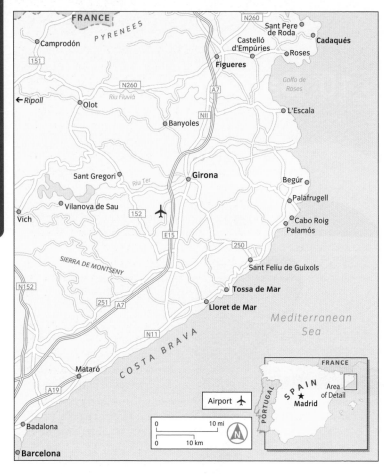

Both Costa Brava and the lesser-known Costa Dorada, a string of golden beaches extending south from Barcelona through resorts like Sitges, stretch along Spain's eastern coast. Both areas have wonderful attractions for families and like Costa Blanca further south present the opportunity to combine a beach and city holiday in one – Barcelona with the Costa Brava or Costa Dorada just as Valencia combines with the Costa Blanca.

The coastal cities are brilliantly diverse cultural capitals. At the southern end of the Costa Dorada, is the city of Tarragona, narrow streets packed with antiques-shops and the immaculate Roman mosaics of Medusa to vie for your attention with the bright lights of Port Aventura, Spain's biggest theme park.

For many people, Barcelona is synonymous with its chief architect Gaudi, whose wavy, lifelike buildings will appeal to even the youngest visitor, spotting a dragon on a roof, or a bony face in a facade. Finally, close to the border with France sits Girona, a laid-back city you can use as the jumping off point into the rocky coves and rugged walks of the Costa Brava, or from where you can make a pilgrimage to the surrealist mecca of Figueres and the mind-bending Salvador Dali theatre museum, after which art classes at school will never be the same. The inland jewels here are the peaks of the Pyrenees, a region of rolling valleys and sheer rock faces with gorges for anyone with teens itching for rafting.

The capital of Catalonia (Catalunya) is cosmopolitan and avantgarde. Experimentation in the arts, architecture and even in individual identities is celebrated and, aside from the obvious attractions for children such as aquariums and amusement parks, the city as a whole could be considered one vast playground – for adults and children alike. The Catalan people have great affection for children and you can take youngsters pretty well everywhere, as the locals do.

Among the many unique attractions in this exuberant city the maze-like gothic old town, the colourful, bustling Las Ramblas and the fantastical creations of architect Antoni Gaudi stand out as mustdos on any family agenda.

The northern coastline of the Costa Brava is rugged, whereas the Costa Dorada is flatter, with miles of sandy beaches as well as a mild, sunny climate. Pilgrims may go to Montserrat for its scenery and religious associations, and history buffs to Tarragona for its Roman ruins, but sun-lovers head for the Costa Dorada for good old bucket-and-spade fun. One popular stretch is La Maresme, extending from Río Tordera to Barcelona, a distance of 64 km (40 miles). Highlights along this coast include Costa de Garraf, a series of creeks skirted by the corniche road after Castelldefels, Sitges, and Tarragona. One of the coast's most beautiful stretches is Cape Salou, south of Tarragona in a setting of pinewoods.

The Monestir de Poblet in Tarragona is the other major monastery of Catalonia, another world-class attraction. Nearby the tiny medieval city of Montblanc boasts that St George slayed the dragon at one of its gates. So that happened in Spain, did it? 'No,' say locals haughtily, 'in Catalonia.' The two are not the same, and woe betide anyone who forgets it.

ESSENTIALS

Getting There

By Plane Barcelona's three-terminal airport at El Prat de Llobregat (☎ *93 298 38 38*, *www. Barcelona-Airport.com*) has connections with all of London's airports carriers such as easyJet, British Airways, Jet2, BMI and

Iberia. There are also direct flights to Coventry, Leeds, Bristol, Liverpool, Cork, Dublin and Belfast. The airport lies 13 km (8 miles) to the southwest of the city, a journey that takes 15 minutes by car on the Autovia C-246 once you're out of the city limits. Car hire companies Europcar, Hertz, Avis and Sixt all have offices at Barcelona airport. There are taxi ranks in front of each terminal and fares to the centre should be between €15 (£10.05) and €20 (£13.40). The blue Aerobús (A1) runs to the Plaza de Catalunya every 12 minutes between 6am and midnight from bus stops in front of each terminal, and departs Plaza de Catalunya between 5.30am and 11.15pm. Tickets cost €3.45 (£2.30) and the journey takes 35 minutes. A train runs to Barcelona's Estació Central de Barcelona-Sants every day from 5.38am to 10.11pm. It takes 30 minutes and costs €2.25 (£1.50). Those interested in a short visit to Port Aventura or the Costa Dorada might want to consider using Ryanair's cheap flights into Reus Airport, 45 minutes south of Barcelona, or Girona Airport, traditionally one of the cheapest Spanish routes from the UK, for easy access to the Costa Brava's northern beaches.

By Train The Spanish state railway network RENFE's main train station is Sants Estació. Within realistic striking distance by train are Valencia (15 trains daily taking three hours) and Madrid (six high speed trains daily taking five hours). There

are also express night trains to Paris Zurich, Milan and Geneva (*www.renfe.es*; ☎ *902 240 202*).

By Car You're likely to arrive via one of the coastal roads: the N11 coastal road from the north or the C32 from Valencia and the south. The city centre is well sign-posted. In 2008 the high-speed AVE train will connect Barcelona with Madrid and the rest of the European train network.

Visitor Information

The main city tourist office is at Plaza de Catalunya, 17-S (*www.barcelonaturisme.com*) and is open daily from 9am to 9pm. As well as providing tourist information, it sells the discount sightseeing Barcelona Card, tickets to Barcelona's tourist bus and handles booking of city walking tours and the regional, Catalunya tourist bus. There is also a second branch at the Sants Railway Station.

Neighbourhoods in Brief

The Barri Gòtic This is what people really mean when they talk about Barcelona. It is the jumbled, medieval quarter that's sandwiched between the sea, the Passeig de Colon's Columbus Monument to the south, and the Ronda de Sant Pere and Plaça de Catalunya to the north. Running between the two is the famous mile-long boulevard **Las Ramblas**, which is also the Barri Gòtic's western border with its seedier neighbour, the Raval.

TIP **Catalans**

As many Catalans will be quick to tell you: 'Catalonia is not Spain'. Despite stereotypes of grumpiness and reserved personalities, the Catalans will warm to you in an instant if you acknowledge their language. A simple 'Bon Dia', 'Adeu' and 'Merci' will score huge points and make you many friends.

The whole district is basically Barcelona's answer to the few square miles that are together London's Soho, Oxford Street and Leicester Square with all the sleaze, squalor, shopping, eating and sheer fun that a Catalan version of London's centre might conjure. Ancient buildings, the ruins of a Roman temple dedicated to Augustus, stores of antiques, bric-a-brac and tack, plus restaurants, cafes, museums, hotels, bookstores and street performers fill its streets. It can get a bit edgy late at night, but is full of eye-popping fun for children the rest of the time: each section has its own focus: caged birds, flowers, artists dashing off dodgy caricatures and there's a craft market on Sundays. It makes a lot of sense to base yourself in this throbbing centre of Barcelona, although few of the hotels have pools. La Boqueria, is the city's fantastic market and an Aladdin's cave of dazzling fruit and veg, glistening, grumpy-looking fish, hams, sausages and cheeses and huge stalls devoted entirely to sweets.

El Raval You wouldn't want to wander down some of its less salubrious southern streets at night, but it's a rough diamond of a district, and if you stick to Carrer de L'Hospital and the area around the MACBA (Museu d'Art Contemporani) you'll be in its vigorous, dynamic cosmopolitan hub. A great new designers market is held at weekends on the new palm tree lined Rambla del Raval – the bustling thoroughfare of Barcelona's immigrant population. Streetwise teenagers who are happy in Hoxton will thrive in this quarter's offbeat edge.

Barri de la Ribera and Born
These two districts on the eastern side of the Barri Gòtic have moved faster towards gentrification than El Raval. Art galleries now cluster around the brilliant Museu Picasso, housed in the 15th-century Palau Agüilar on Carrer de Montcada, and trendy boutiques are tucked into the quarters' mediaeval streets and arches. Quality shopping, eating and drinking are the mainstay of this quarter. The Born is a spic and span, safe base that's still right on the borders of the Barri Gòtic and close to the lovely Ciutadella Park, a good location for letting off steam after the Picasso museum.

La Barceloneta, the Harbour Front and Vila Olímpica The waterfront promenade, Passeig del Moll de la Fusta, is a hive of activity with a commercial centre, the Mare Magnum, built out over the water, housing, among other things, the aquarium and an IMAX cinema. This whole area is packed with families at weekends and on summer evenings, promenading and people-watching. To the east is a mainly artificial peninsula that La Barceloneta (Little Barcelona) is built on. This is a lively residential quarter and as the route to the city's seafront and beaches, it has a number of decent seafood restaurants. Further east is the Vila Olimpica where there is a five star hotel and the Port Olimpica, a busy marina, packed solid with restaurants and bars, many of them serving the kind of fast food children love. The place is hopping in summer and completely dead in winter.

The Eixample To the north of the Plaça de Catalunya is the Eixample, or Ensanche, the section of Barcelona that grew beyond the old medieval walls. Avenues form a grid of perpendicular streets, cut across by a majestic boulevard – **Passeig de Gràcia**, an imposingly posh shopping street. The area's main traffic artery is Avinguda Diagonal, which links the expressway and the heart of the congested city. The Eixample was the centre of Barcelona's modernismo movement, and it holds some of the most original buildings any architect ever designed: **Gaudí's Sagrada Família** is one of the major attractions. The unfinished cathedral's façade looks like something out of a Disney movie, with animals and birds adorning concrete dripping like melting icicles from a façade of puffy clouds. Take the lift to the top of the spires for an amazing view of the city. Eixample is probably the most glamorous address in the city, and hotels here reflect that fact. You can plot a short walking tour that takes in **Casa Battlo**, the famous Gaudi house inspired by St George and the dragon, and La Pedrera, with its wavy façade and wonky chimney stacks.

Montjuïc & Tibidabo Barcelona is encircled by mountains, two of which hold a particular presence in the city. Montjuïc is a leafy hillside to the west of central Barcelona that looks out over the shipping harbour. There are landscaped gardens, water features, a Greek theatre and a castle all with fabulous views of the city. There is also the city's world-class Olympic swimming pool, the **Joan Miró museum**, and the slightly peculiar **Poble Espanyol** (Spanish Village), which is a showcase for Spanish art and architecture built in the 1920s. On the northern side of Montjuïc are several grand palaces and pavilions, which look out over the **Plaza de Espana**. The **Miró Foundation** is a beautifully light, airy building with some fabulous, child-friendly features including **Alexander Calder's mesmerising Mercury Fountain**, as well as lots of brightly coloured Miró sculptures and paintings. Don't miss the museum shop for funky

Joan Miró Foundation

notebooks, pencils and rubbers for school, as well as **Miró** mugs and umbrellas. Tibidabo, to the north, provides the highest point from which to observe the city at 503 m (1650 ft). Sitting atop this peak is an eclectic amusement park giving families that added incentive to get up on to the city's limits.

GETTING AROUND

Barcelona has the advantage of being a human sized city and most attractions can be seen on foot. Walking the narrow streets of the old town, even with a buggy, is manageable. If your feet get tired, you can always hail one of the city's eco-friendly versions of the Indian rickshaw, the **electric VeloTaxi**, from the bottom of Las Ramblas or outside the Gothic Cathedral (€6 (£4) for 15mins, €10 (£6.70) for 30mins and €18 (£12) for 1 hour). The human-powered three-seater bicycle carriage

(which can carry two adults and one child), will take you anywhere you want to go. (*www.velotaxi.com*). **Horse drawn carriage** routes are pre-planned (also found at the bottom of the Rambla – €25 (£16.75) for an hour – but try haggling). If your children are a bit older, there are several places to hire bikes.

Metro Barcelona's Metro has six main lines. Two commuter trains run to the city suburbs. It runs from Monday through Friday from 5am to midnight, Saturday from 5am to 2am, and Sunday and holidays from 6am to 2am. The one-way fare is €1.10 (£0.75). Each Metro station entrance is marked with a red diamond. The major station for all Metro lines is **Plaça de Catalunya**. To get beyond the old city centre, you can hop on Barcelona's very efficient metro system, but it's worth bearing in mind that taxi prices are still relatively low and a much quicker option. You also get to see Barcelona's beautiful buildings.

By Bus Barcelona has over 100 km (63 miles) of bus lanes, bringing those parts of the city that the metro doesn't cover into quick, easy reach. They run daily from 6.30am to 10pm; and some night buses navigate the main arteries until 4am. Red buses do the city centre route by day, yellow ones at night. The one-way fare is €1.15 (£0.75). Buy tickets from the front of the bus.

> **INSIDER TIP**
> Use your T-10 metro card within an hour and a half of your underground ride and the two journeys will only count as one.

Bus Tour If you don't have long, Barcelona's open-topped Bus Turistic is an easy way of getting round all the key sites including Camp Nou, Sagrada Familia and Parc Güell. It leaves every 5–25 minutes from Plaça Catalunya and costs €18 (£12) a day or €22 (£14.75) for a two day pass (4–12yr olds: €11 (£7.35) or €14 (£9.40) respectively. 10% discount if you book online at *www.barcelonaturisme.com*.

> **INSIDER TIP**
> To save money on public transport, buy a carnet for 10 trips. Tarjeta T-10, for €6.10 (£4.10) is good for the Metro and the bus. Passes (*abonos temporales*) are available at Transports Metropolita de Barcelona, Plaça de la Universitat. It's open Monday to Friday 8am to 5pm, Saturday from 8am to 1pm.

By Taxi You can tell when the yellow and black city cabs are free when their green roof-light is lit and you can see the libre sign in the window. Fares start at €1.30 (£0.85) but check that the meter is zeroed at the start of your journey and what supplements might apply – €0.85 (£0.55) for a large suitcase placed in the trunk, for instance. Rides to the airport carry a supplement of €2.10 (£1.40). For a taxi, call ☎ *933 30 08 04*.

By Car Navigating busy Barca at the wheel of a car is no fun, there's little chance of finding a place to park, and foreign plates will single you out as a target for vandalism and theft. The decent, inexpensive trains out of the city are viable alternatives to car hire: north and south coastal routes to Sitges or the Costa Brava are a mere €3 (£2) or so and Barcelona Turisme arranges decent day-trips (*www.barcelona turisme.com*: €60 (£41) (free for children under 8yrs). Destinations include the monastic mountain of Montserrat, Sitges and a winery or Girona and the Dali Museum in Figueras.

By Funicular & Cable Car A family excursion to the hilltops of Tibidabo or Montjuïc (or both) gets you amazing panoramas of Barcelona. A train called Tramvía Blau (Blue Streetcar) goes every 20 minutes from Plaça Kennedy to the bottom of the funicular to Tibidabo from 9.05am to 9.35pm (weekends only). The fare is €2 (£1.35) one-way, €2.90 (£1.95) round-trip. On weekdays, buses run the route between 10am and 9.30pm. The bus costs €1 (£0.65) one-way.

The final leg to the 503 m summit is via a funicular, which only operates when the fun fair is open. Opening times vary, but during peak visiting hours it runs every 15 minutes. The fare is €2 (£1.35) one-way, €3 (£2) round-trip. The **Tibibus** (☎ 93-211-79-42) goes from the Plaça de Catalunya (in the city centre) to Tibidabo from 24 June to 15 September on Saturday and Sunday. It runs every 30 minutes from 11am to 6.30pm and sometimes 8.30pm, depending on when the park closes. The one-way fare is €2.30 (£1.55).

To reach Montjuïc take the **funicular** (☎ 93-318-70-74) from Parallel, which runs daily, from 9am to 10pm in summer or 8am to 8pm in winter. The round-trip fare is €2.40 (£1.60); one-way is €1.50 (£1). A **cable car** links the Montjuïc funicular with **Castell de Montjuïc** (daily, 10am to 7.30pm). The one-way fare is €3 (£2); the round-trip fare is €4.20 (£2.80) for adults. From 28 June to 15 September and holidays, it operates Monday to Friday 11.15am to 8pm, until 9pm on weekends. The **Montjuïc teleferic** (cable car) runs from Barceloneta, across the port to Montjuïc. Service from June 20 to September 15 is offered daily from 10.30am to 8pm. In winter it's offered daily from noon to

5pm. The fare is €7.50 (£5) one-way, €9 (£6) round-trip.

Bike Tours For three hours of easy-paced pedalling escorted by fun guides go for **Bike Tours Barcelona** (*www.biketours barcelona.com*, ☎ 932 68 21 05 – info@biketoursbarcelona.com). The tour meets at Plaça Sant Jaume every day at 11am and also at 4.30pm from Friday through to Monday in summer (April–15th Sept). The slant is historical but entertaining (pack your swimming togs). Price is €22 (£14.75) including bike rental, tour guide and drink. To explore independently, Bike Tours will also simply rent you a bike: €7 (£4.70) for up to three hours, €10 (£6.70) for between three and six hours and €15 (£77) for over six hours.

The tourist office also runs a hire service, **Barcelona Bici**, with great tour advice thrown in. You can rent for a half-day, full day or weekend picking the bike up at one point and returning it at another. Pick-up and drop-offs are at Placa Catalunya, Mirador de Colom and Passeig Joan de Borbo. An hour costs €4.50 (£3), a half day €1 (£0.67) 1, full day €15 (£10.05) and two days €21 (£14). **AGES 7 AND UP** . info@barcelo naturisme.com, Turisme de Barcelona: *www.barcelonaturisme. com*, ☎ 932 85 38 32.

Boat Rides Barcelona from the sea is an impressive but often overlooked pleasure. **Orsom** (*www.barcelona-orsom.com*, ☎ 934 41 05 37) offers 90 minutes

BARCELONA TOWN

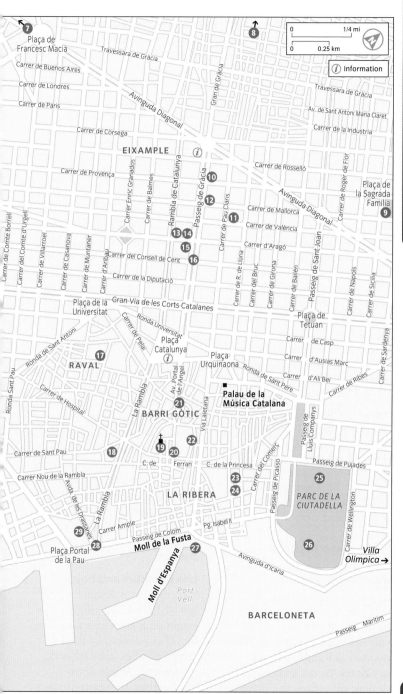

7 Plaça de Francesc Macià

Travessara de Gràcia

Carrer de Buenos Aires

Carrer de Londres

Carrer de Paris

Avinguda Diagonal

Gran de Gràcia

Travessara de Gràcia

Av. de Sant Antoni Maria Claret

Carrer de la Industria

Carrer de Còrsega

8

0   1/4 mi

0   0.25 km

i Information

EIXAMPLE **i**

Carrer de Rosselló

Carrer de Roger de Flor

Plaça de la Sagrada Família

Carrer de Provença

Avinguda Diagonal

9

Carrer Enric Granados

Carrer de Balmes

Rambla de Catalunya

Passeig de Gràcia

10

12

Carrer de Pau Claris

Carrer de Mallorca

Carrer de València

11

Carrer del Comte Borrell

Carrer del Comte d'Urgell

Carrer de Villarroel

Carrer de Casanova

Carrer de Muntaner

Carrer d'Aribau

Carrer del Consell de Cent

13 **14**

15

16

Carrer de R. de Lluria

Carrer del Bruc

Carrer de Girona

Carrer de Bailén

Passeig de Sant Joan

Carrer de Napols

Carrer de Sicilia

Carrer d'Aragó

Carrer de la Diputació

Plaça de la Universitat

Gran Via de les Corts Catalanes

Ronda Universitat

Carrer de Pelai

Plaça de Tetuan

Carrer   de Casp

Carrer   d'Ausias Marc

Carrer   d'Ali Bei

Carrer de Sardenya

Plaça Catalunya **i**

Plaça Urquinaona

Ronda de Sant Pere

Carrer de Ribes

RAVAL

17

Ronda de Sant Antoni

Ronda Sant Pau

Carrer de Hospital

La Rambla

Av. Portal de l'Àngel

Via Laietana

■ Palau de la Música Catalana

BARRI GÒTIC

21

19 **20**

22

Carrer de Sant Pau

18

C. de   Ferran

C. de la Princesa

23

24

Carrer del Comerç

Passeig de Picasso

Passeig de Lluis Companys

PARC DE LA CIUTADELLA

25

Passeig de Pujades

Carrer de Wellington

Carrer Nou de la Rambla

Avda. de les Drassanes

La Rambla

LA RIBERA

Carrer Ample

Pg. Isabel II

29

28

Passeig de Colom

Moll de la Fusta

27

Plaça Portal de la Pau

Moll d'Espanya

Avinguda d'Icaria

26

Villa Olímpica →

Port Vell

BARCELONETA

Passeig Marítim

Petty theft is routine here: bags and phones are snatched with grim inevitability, so be vigilant. Restaurants and cafés are favourite targets, so hook handbags over your leg or tie them to chair, and don't leave valuables lying out on the table. Rucksack pockets will be opened as you walk through a crowd on the Ramblas: don't put anything valuable inside. You're not immune in your car either: keep doors locked at traffic lights. The police station under Placa Catalunya (entrance opposite Caja Madrid) will deal with any reports.

on a luxury catamaran complete with live jazz saxophonist for only €14 (£9.40). *Las Golondrinas* (*www.lasgolondrinas.com*, ☏ *934 42 31 06*, Portal de la Pau) is classic wooden boat leaves from the old port at the bottom of Las Ramblas and travels the whole seafront up to the Forum Universal de Culturas (11.30am–6.30pm. 90 minutes Adults €9.70 (£6.50), children €4.10 (£2.75), Barcelona Turisme: *www.barcelonaturisme. com*, ☏ *932 85 38 32*). Check the city out from a yacht and learn basic sailing skills while you're at it. The two-hour trip is €28 (£18.75) for Adults and €16 (£10.70) for children (7–14yrs). Admission to **Barcelona's Maritime Museum** and onto the 1918 schooner **Santa Eulàlia** are also included.

First-Time Visitors

Montjuïc day out Fix yourself up with some fine fresh Spanish produce from the back of the **Boqueria Market** and then take the funicular from the bottom of Las Ramblas for a picnic in **Cactus World**. In between swallow dives from the **Olympic**

pool's soaring boards (the location for the music video for Kylie Minogue's pop song *Slow*) check out the amazing views of Barcelona. Clock the **Mercury Fountain** in the Fundacio Miró then stay around in the **Poble Espanyol** for supper, rounding off with the spectacular sound and light show at the **Palace fountains** in the evening.

Tibidabo day out Again, hop on board the funicular, then head for **Cosmocaixa**, a science museum full of interactive fun for children, from electro-static balls to swinging pendulums. Tibidabo has a whopping fairground, the **Parc D'Atraccions de Tibidabo**, with a giant Ferris wheel. Hire some wheels to bike about **Collserola** (the city's friendly green mountain) for brilliant views of Barca miles away from all the city's smoke and din.

Las Ramblas and beyond Start the day at **Boqueria market** where you can glug down a bright pink grapefruit juice for breakfast followed by fried creepy crawlies (they really do sell insects). Amble down Las Ramblas and commission a portrait or caricature, then zip up the **statue of Christopher Columbus** for views across Barceloneta before crossing the footbridge to get to the **Maremagnum Mall** for a retail fix. Grab a tapas lunch here then run the gauntlet of the shark tunnel at the **Aquarium** before finishing off with a 3D movie at the **IMAX**.

Ciutadella Park Ciutadella is a real under-sung joy in Barcelona's cityscape. Right on the fringes of the buzzy Barrio Gòtic it is a lovely landscape of palm trees and tropical hot-houses, with a **lake** you can row boats across and a **zoo** with a marine show. Pack your own table-tennis bat and ball and take advantage of one of the free courts that are dotted about the grounds. Walk through the Olympic village for a sight of Barcelona's twin towers (look out for the huge gold fish in its ponds) then head for lunch in the marina before volleyball or bat and ball on the beach and a sunset boat ride.

INSIDER TIP
Get tickets to a Barca match and your teenage son will forgive you anything.

FAST FACTS

Amex Oddly, the nearest office is in Tarragona. Worldjet Viatges (Fortuny 10, Tarragona, Spain, 43001. ☎ *977 250099*. Email: *worldjet@worldjettarragona.com*) is a licensed Amex operator.

Consulates The British Consulate, Av. Diagonal 477, 08036, Barcelona. ☎ *933666200*. Email *barcelonaconsulate@ fco.gov.uk*. It is open Monday to Friday 8.30am–1.30pm.

Currency Exchange Most banks exchange currency Monday to Friday (8.30am–2pm). There is a major *oficina de cambio* (exchange office) at Estacio Central de Barcelona Sants, the main railway station. It is open Monday to Sunday 8.30am–10pm, ☎ "la Caiza" *933 307 009*. Exchange offices at Barcelona airports are open daily.

Emergencies Fire *080*, police *092*, ambulance *061*, duty pharmacies *010*.

Hospitals Barcelona has many hospitals and clinics, including Hospital Clinic ☎ *932275400* and Hospital de la Santa Creu i Sant Pau, at the intersection of Carrer Cartagena and Carrer Sant Antoni Maria Claret ☎ *932919091*, *www.santpau.es*. Metro: Hospital Sant Pau.

Internet Access Electric Lounge, a café, lounge and gallery just in front of the main Cathedral. Calle Misser Ferrer 1, ☎ *933041616*. *www.electric-barcelona.com*). Cost €1 (£0.67). Open daily 9am–midnight.

Charging only €1.30 (£0.87) per hour, head to Easy Internet Café. Las Ramblas 31. ☎ *933 017 507*. *www.easyinternetcafe. com*; Metro: Liceu. Open 8am–2.30am.

Pharmacies The most centrally located one is Farmacia Manuel Nadal I Casas, Rambla de Canaletes 121, ☎ 933174942. Metro: Plaça de Catalunya. Open 9am–10pm.

Post Office The main post office is at Plaça d'Antoni López ☎ 934868050. Metro: Jaume 1. It is open Monday to Saturday 8.30am–9.30pm for sending letters and telegrams.

Telephone Dial 1003 for information in Barcelona. For elsewhere in Spain, dial 1009. Local calls cost €0.40 (£0.27).

WHAT TO SEE & DO

Children's Top 10 Attractions

❶ Aquarium, Barcelona An 80 m-long viewing tunnel is a great way to up close to gilt-heads, morays, exotic rays and sharks. (See p. 256.)

❷ Tibidabo Mountain, Barcelona Zip up the elevator to look out over Barceloneta from the Sierra de Collserola range. (See p. 258.)

❸ Chocolate Museum, Barcelona Children between 3–12 yrs can join in a chocolate making and designing workshop as well as learn how to make traditional Catalan cakes and walk away with a chocolate plaque. (See p. 254.)

❹ Parc Güell, Barcelona Fabulous fairy story houses designed by one of Spain's greatest artists, Gaudí are the reason for a trip here. (See p. 257.)

❺ Horse drawn carriage ride, Barcelona Let the horse do all the work while you sit back and enjoy the sites of the city. (See p. 245.)

❻ Poble Espanyol, Barcelona Pack your sense of irony at this 1929 representation of Spain's many architectural styles, beyond which are splashing fountains, restaurants, museums and Olympic swimming pools. (See p. 255.)

❼ Steam engine ride One for the boys (or dads). Take a ride from the historic town of Martorell to the Monastery of Montserrat. (See p. 261.)

❽ Port Aventura. Buckle up and head an hour south to Tarragona for one of Europe's top amusement parks. (See p. 286.)

❾ Trip to Tarragona Stroll through shaded gardens along the ancient ramparts – or Passeig Arqueològic – built on giant boulders. (See p. 283.)

❿ Cable Car ride to the Olympic swimming pool, Barcelona A family outing to the hilltops of Tibidabo or Montjuïc get you amazing panoramas of the city. (See p. 246.)

Barri Gòtic (Gothic Quarter) Barcelona's biggest draw is really the entire neighbourhood or more extensively the **Ciutat Vella** (Old City) ★★. Its narrow streets and squares continue to form a

Gothic Quarter

vibrant neighbourhood with buskers and street artists outside the cathedral for children. Start by walking up the Carrer del Carme, east of Las Ramblas. The buildings are austere for the most part, the cathedral being the crowning achievement. **Roman ruins** and the vestiges of 3rd-century walls add further interest. This area is intricately detailed and filled with many attractions that are easy to miss. It's filled with bustling, cosmopolitan youth, loads of trendy shops and cafes have sprung up.

Catedral de Barcelona ★★★
With its three naves, large bell towers, high altar and Gothic arches, Barcelona's cathedral ranks as one of the most impressive in Spain. The particularly

beautiful cloister, which surrounds a garden of magnolias, medlars, and palm trees, is the final resting place of Santa Eulalia, the patron saint of Barcelona.

Plaça de la Seu s/n. ℂ 933 15 15 54. Free admission to cathedral; to museum €1 (£0.65). Global ticket to museum, choir, rooftop terraces, and towers €4 (£2.70), €3 (£2) for groups. Cathedral daily 8am–12.45pm and 5.15–7.30pm; cloister museum daily 9am–12.45pm and 5–7pm. Metro: Jaume I.

Las Ramblas
The main thing to do on Las Ramblas is just walk. Start at the top, at Placa de Catalunya. You'll soon be on the **Rambla dels Ocells** (of the birds) where pretty well everything with fur, scales or feathers

is on sale. Next is **Rambla dels Flors**, fragrant and colourful, where you can buy anything from a Venus flytrap to a bonsai tree, before entering the section called **Rambla dels Caputxins**, lined with cafes and street entertainers, and people posing as statues. Next, the **Rambla de Santa Monica** is home to craft stalls, cheap costume jewellery and other bling on which children can spend their holiday Euros. **Boqueria Market tour:** *www.boqueria.info*, ☎ *933 04 02 70.* Get to know the history and hidden gastronomic delights (€12 (£8)).

Museu Picasso ★ Most parents think their children are early developers, but have a look at what little Pablo's doodles looked like age nine to see what a real child prodigy leaves in his wake. Picasso (1881–1973) donated some 2500 of his paintings, engravings, and drawings to the museum in 1970, three years before he died. He was particularly fond of Barcelona, where he spent much of his youth.

Montcada 15–19. ☎ 932 56 30 00. www.museupicasso.bcn.es. Admission to permanent exhibits €6 (£4) adults, €8.50 (£5.70) to both permanent and temporary exhibits; €3 (£2) students and ages 16–25; free for children under 16. Tues–Sun 10am–8pm. Metro: Jaume I (line 4).

CosmoCaixa ★ The recently opened science museum is now one of the most popular museums in Barcelona. Cosmocaixa caters for people of all ages and will keep you entertained all day.

The museum is beautifully designed with the curators going for quality over quantity and artful presentation of the objects. Children become instantly immersed in the active nature of many of the displays – from electro-static balls to swinging pendulums – and there are specific areas where they can participate in experiments and explore fundamental scientific phenomena. One of the best features of the museum is **The Flooded Forest** – a recreated rainforest complete with towering trees, exotic birds, pre-historic-looking fish and even alligators.

CosmoCaixa Teodor Roviralta 47–50. Bus: 17, 22, 58, 60, 73, 75. ☎ 902 22 30 40. Hrs: Tue–Sun: 10am–8pm.

Children from 3–7yrs have their own place at the **Museu de la Ciéncia**, Teodor Roviralta 47–51 (☎ *932 12 60 50).* '*Clik del Nens'* is a science playground just for them where they can walk on a giant piano, make bubbles, lift a hippopotamus, and enter an air tunnel. They observe, experiment, and examine nature in a specially created environment. *www.lacaixa.es/obrasocial.*

Chocolate Museum Children between 3–12yrs can participate in a 1-hour chocolate making and designing workshops as well as learn how to make traditional Catalan cakes and walk away with a chocolate plaque!

Comerç, 36. Free entrance. Activity: €6.30 (£4.20) Open 10am–7pm Mon–Fri and until 3pm on Sunday. Closed Tuesdays. www.pastisseria. com, ☎ 932 68 78 78.

Museu d'Art Contemporani de Barcelona ★ is to Barcelona what the Pompidou Centre is to Paris. The building is a work of art itself, manipulating sunlight to offer brilliant, natural interior brightness. Luminaries like Tàpies, Klee, Miró, are all on display. The museum has a library, bookshop, and cafeteria. They also often have very creative and forward thinking workshops for children. Check the website for details: *www.macba.es*.

Plaça dels Angels 1. 📞 *934 12 08 10. Admission €7 (£4.70) adults, €5.50 (£3.70) students, free for children under 14 and seniors over 65. Wed–Sat 11am–7.30pm; Sun 10am–3pm. Summer closes 8pm. Closed Tues except bank holidays. Metro: Plaça de Catalunya.*

Parc Zoològic ★ Modern, with bar-less enclosures, this ranks as Spain's top zoo. The setting itself is interesting in a century-old garden spread over 13 hectares (32 acres) of **Ciutadella Park**. The splendid park contains 7500 animals belonging to some 500 species from all over the world. There are a number of other species of primate, all in danger of extinction, including *titis*, the world's smallest monkeys. Themed family mornings are held on Sundays at 10am–12.30pm where hidden aspects of the animal kingdom are revealed (€11.50 (£7.70), child non-member and €15.50 (£10.40), adult non-member). Sign up the previous Wednesday to assure a place.

Parc de la Ciutadella. 📞 *932 25 67 80. www.zoobarcelona.com.*

Admission €14.95 (£9.40) adults, €9 (£5.50) students and children 3–12, €8 (£5.40), free for children under 3. Summer daily 10am–7pm; off season daily 10am–6pm. Metro: Ciutadella, Barceloneta, or Arc de Triomf. Buses: 14, 29–41, 42, or 141.

Poble Espanyol ★ This facsimile of a Spanish village was built for the 1929 World Fair, and is a walk through of the country's regional architectural styles. From the Levant to Galicia, 115 life-size reproductions of buildings and monuments represent developments in the building design world from the 10th to the 20th centuries. There's a café and lots of shops selling provincial crafts and souvenir items, and in some of them you can see artists at work – printing fabric or blowing glass. You can also go to shows, games and storytelling sessions held in the village's streets and squares.

Av. Marqués de Comillas 13, Parc de Montjuïc. 📞 *933 25 78 66. www. poble-espanyol.com. Admission: Family entrance (2 adults + 2 children 7–12yrs) €15 (£10.05), €7.50 (£5) adults, €4 (£2.70) children 7–12, free for children under 7. Mon 9am–8pm; Tues–Thurs 9am–2am; Fri–Sat 9am–4am; Sun 9am–midnight. Metro: Espanya. Bus: 13 or 50.*

Camp Nou FC Barcelona Football stadium: With over 1,160,000 visitors a year the **football museum** at Camp Nou is considered the original and best of its kind. The main museum focuses on the club's 100-odd year history with photographs, trophies and audiovisual displays. There are also the **Collecció**

Futbolart, a private collection of memorabilia from football's origins to the present day on permanent loan to the museum, the club's own impressive art collection and regular temporary exhibitions. Entrance to the museum includes a tour of the stadium, taking visitors through the opposition changing rooms, down the tunnel and onto the pitch.

Avinguda Aristides Maillol, www.fcbarcelona.com, ☏ 934 96 36 00. Museum open from Monday to Saturday: 10am–6.30pm – Camp Nou Tour until 5.30pm Sundays and Bank holidays: 10am–2pm – Camp Nou tour until 1.30pm. Days with a Champions League at the stadium: 10am–1pm–No Tour. 1/1, 6/1 and 25/12, closed. Prices: Museum visit/ with tour: Adults: €11 (£7.40), Up to 13yrs: €5.50/8.50 (£3.70/5.70).

Aquarium Barcelona's Aquarium is a real feast for young minds. Its Mediterranean displays are of global importance and the spectacular **Oceanarium**, where visitors get to wonder through an 80m-long transparent tunnel beneath 4500 m³ of water and spot such species as giltheads, morays, sunfish, rays and sharks, is one of only a handful in Europe. The Aquarium puts a strong emphasis on children and education with the permanent **Explora!** display providing interactive ways of discovering the sea world while an ever-evolving series of workshops, story telling and games keeps learning fresh and fun. So far most activities are in Spanish or Catalan but watch this space. Call to reserve.

Better still: 8–12 year-olds can camp out overnight at the Aquarium (under supervision of two monitors, 8pm–10am Fri and Sat nights). The evening focus is on the sharks with breakfast being taken as the sea world awakes. Don't forget pyjamas, sleeping bag and your toothbrush! (€75 (£50.25)).

Moll D'Espanya del Port Vell, ☏ 932 21 74 74, www.aquariumbcn.com. Opening at 9.30am, closing at 9pm Mon–Fri, 9.30pm on weekends and 11pm in July and August. Adults €15 (£10.05), Children 4–12yrs €10 (£6.70).

La Sagrada Família ★★
Gaudí's incomplete masterpiece is one of the country's more idiosyncratic creations. Begun in 1882 and not expected to be completed for another decade or so, this incredible cathedral – the Church of the Holy Family – is a bizarre wonder. The languid, amorphous structure embodies the essence of Gaudí's style, which you could call Art Nouveau run amok. The two sides, very different in character, tell the stories of the New and Old Testament. Enjoy spotting these modern interpretations of familiar characters such Samson, David and Goliath. Although it's a long way up, the **spiral staircases** are an architectural delight and the **views** are well worth the climb. Or there's always the lift. Admission includes a 20-minute video presentation.

Entrance from Carrer de Sardenya or Carrer de la Marina. ☏ 932 07 30 31. www.sagradafamilia.org.

Admission €8 (£5.35), 7 and under free; video guide €3.50 (£2.35); elevator to the top (about 60m/200ft.) €2 (£1.35). Nov–Mar daily 9am–6pm; Apr and Sept–Oct daily 9am–8pm. Closed May–Aug. Metro: Sagrada Família.

Parc Güell ★★ Gaudí, who was run over by a Barcelona tram in his work overalls, went to the grave leaving a couple of projects unfinished. Like the Sagrada, though, it still packs double the punch of more pedestrian landmarks, even though he only got around to building two of the 60 planned houses here. They look like they've been airlifted straight from a Hansel & Gretel fairy story. One of them,

Casa-Museu Gaudí, Carrer del Carmel 23 (☎ 93-219-38-11), contains models, furniture, drawings, and other memorabilia of the architect. (Ramón Berenguer, not Gaudí, designed the house.) Admission to the house is €4 (£2.70). It's open October to March daily from 10am to 5.45pm; April to September daily from 10am to 7.45pm. The other public area look like a Disneyland on LSD, with a mosaic pagoda and a lizard fountain spitting water.

At the end of Carrer de Larrard. ☎ *932 19 38 11. €4 (£2.70) adult, €3 (£2) children, under 9 free. May–Sept daily 10am–9pm; Oct–Mar daily 10am–5.45pm, rest of year 10–7.45pm. Bus: 24, 25, 31, or 74.* **www.casamuseogaudi.org.**

What to See & Do

La Sagrada Familia

Montjuïc In the southern part of the city, the mountain park of Montjuïc has splashing fountains, gardens, outdoor restaurants, and museums, making for quite an outing. A re-created Spanish village, the **Poble Espanyol**, and the **Joan Miró Foundation** are also in the park. There are many walks and vantage points from which to view the Barcelona skyline. There's also a beautiful, but dilapidated **Greek amphitheatre**, which has performances during the amazing month long Greek festival which takes over the whole of Barcelona every July. Head for the castle to get great views of the working docks. In the summer there are open-air film screenings. One of the gardens has wooden sculptures cum musical instrument that have to be jumped on or walked on or blown into, the more people involved the more of a hippy din is made.

An illuminated fountain display, Fuentes Luminosas, is on view at Plaça de la Font Magica, near the Plaça d'Espanya. October to May, is shown from 8–11pm every Saturday and Sunday; June to September, it is shown from 9pm to midnight on Thursday, Saturday, and Sunday.

A bus (labelled 'Parc de Montjüic') runs from Plaça d'Espanya, but you can easily walk and there are lots of escalators zigzagging up the hill. Or you can get the Montjuïc funicular from Barceloneta, which is open from 13th June to 30th September daily from 11am–10pm. In winter it operates daily from 10.45am–8pm. The round-trip fare is €3.60 (£2.40).

Fundació Joan Miró ★ Born in 1893, Joan Miró was one of Spain's greatest artists, known for his whimsical abstract forms and brilliant colours. Some 10,000 works by the Catalán surrealist, including paintings, graphics, and sculptures, are collected here. The wonderful outside terrace filled with his sculptures has amazing views of Barcelona and his **mercury fountain** is worth a look. Parents could pop in here while their children are swimming happily at the Olympic-sized pool on the same Montjuïc Mountain. Since 1997, the Joan Miró Foundation has organized 8 shows (€4 (£2.70)) in Catalan for children every year (October–May), which are performed on Saturdays at 5.30pm and on Sundays and Public Holidays at 11.30am and 1.00pm featuring drama, magic and the circus. Visually interesting even if you don't speak Catalan.

Plaça de Neptú, Parc de Montjuïc. ☏ 934 43 94 70, www.bcn.fjMiró.es. Admission €7.50 (£4.80) adults, €5 (£3.35) students, free for children under 15. July–Sept Tues–Wed and Fri–Sat 10am–8pm, Thurs 10am–9.30pm, Sun 10am–2.30pm; Oct–June Tues–Wed and Fri–Sat 10am–7pm, Thurs 10am–9.30pm, Sun 10am–2.30pm. Bus: 50 (at Plaça d'Espanya) or 55.

Tibidabo Mountain ★ west of the city limits, has the best views of Barcelona. A funicular takes you up 488 m (1600 ft) to the summit (which is the top of the Sierra de Collserola range). The ideal time to visit is at sunset, when the city lights are on. **Torre de Collserola** does have pretty cool views. It costs €4.40 (£2.95) to go up the tower. From Plaça de Catalunya, take the subway to Penintents on Line 3 and then take bus no. 73 to Avinguda del Tibidabo, where you can board a special bus to the funicular. The funicular runs daily when the park is open, starting 20 minutes before the Fun Fair. The fare is €2 (£1.35) one-way, €3 (£2) round-trip.

Parc d'Atraccions (Tibidabo) On top of Tibidabo, this park combines tradition with modernity in rides dating from the beginning of the 20th century to 1990s novelties. In summer the place takes on a carnival-like atmosphere.

Plaça Tibidabo 3–4, Cumbre del Tibidabo. ☎ *932 11 79 42.* www.tibidabo.es. *Ticket for all rides: €22 (£14.75) adults, €11 (£6), seniors over 60 and children up to 1.2 m (4 ft) in height €9 (£6), free for children under 3. May to June Sat–Sun noon–9pm; July to Sept Wed–Sun noon–10pm; off season Sat–Sun and holidays noon–6pm. Bus: 58 to Av. del Tibidabo to Tramvía Blau, then funicular.*

> **INSIDER TIP ▶**
> CaixaForum has a room where children can be left to do their own paintings, screen printings under supervision whilst adults can check out the usually high quality exhibitions.

Parc de la Ciutadella

Barcelona isn't just museums; much of its life takes place outside, in its unique parks and gardens. Gaudí contributed to the monumental fountain in the park when he was a student; the lampposts are also his. The park is open March daily 10am to 6pm; April daily 10am to 7pm; May to August daily 10am to 8pm; September daily 10am to 6pm; and October to February daily 10am to 5pm. Admission is €14 (£9.40) adults, €8.50 (£5.70) children 3 to 12. Easy walking distance from the centre, or take the Metro to Ciutadella. You can hire a rowing boat for a punt on the park's lake, too.

Av. Wellington s/n (☎ *932 25 67 80).*

Parc de Joan Miró, near the Plaça de Espanya, has an esplanade and a pond from which rises a giant sculpture by Miró, *Woman and Bird*. Palm, pine, and eucalyptus trees, as well as playgrounds and pergolas, complete the picture. To reach the park, take the Metro to Espanya. It is open throughout the day.

Piscina Bernado Picornell If it's a pool you're after easily the best choice is the Olympic swimming pool, **Piscina Bernardo Picornell**, Av. de Estadi 30–40, on Montjuïc (☎ *934 23 40 41).* Adjacent to the Olympic Stadium, it incorporates two of the best swimming pools in Spain (1 indoors, 1 outdoors). They're open to the public daily from 6.45am to 11pm, and bank holidays 7.30am–4pm. Admission costs €8.50 (£5.70) adults, €5.30 (£3.55) kids. www.picornell.cat. Bus no. 61 makes frequent runs from Plaça d'Espanya.

Tibidabo Fair

FAMILY-FRIENDLY ENTERTAINMENT

Seasonal Events

Barcelona is festival central. There isn't a weekend that goes by when there isn't some kind of event, be it traditional or contemporary culture. There are a number of very helpful tourist information centres dotted around the city. The biggest and most central is under **Plaça Catalunya**. Alternatively, go to a news stand or '*kiosko*' or an Irish bar and check out the listings in free monthly English language guides like *Catalonia Today*, *Metropolitan Magazine* (*www.barcelonametropolitan.com*), *Barcelona Connect* (*www.barcelonaconnect.com*), *Guide Out* (*www.guideout.net*), *Love Barcelona* (*www.lovebarcelona.com*) or in the *Guia del Ocio* (with English section at the back – €2

(£1.35)) **Barcelona's City Council Website** (in English): *www.bcn.es*, is particularly good for traditional festivals as is *www.barcelonaturisme.com*. Look at *www.servicaixa.es* and *www.telentrada.com* for last minute deals and tickets.

Festivals

King's Day (6th January) is celebrated more than Christmas day when the three kings come to town on a huge float and spend their evening throwing sweets to eager children. The parades start at Parc Ciutadella, go up Via Laeitana, to Placa Catalunya.

Carnaval In February, 40 days before Easter: the big knees-up before Lent happens here with people dressing up in satirical costumes to eat, drink and frolic to their hearts' content. Barcelona's Carnaval is fairly tame compared to Sitges (see Sitges) and Vilanova i la Geltru.

Sant Joan (night of 23rd June and 24th June) Official beginning of summer with huge firework show on Barceloneta beach, be warned, bangers go off left, right centre all night. (And about 3 weeks prior!)

Fiesta de la Mercé (weekend around 23rd Sept) Patron Saint of Barcelona: also the unofficial end of summer celebrations. Free concerts in every square (**Plaça Sant Jaume, Plaça del Rei, Rambla Raval**), Parades of huge giant statues in Plaça Sant Jaume during the day and the highlight is most definitely the **Correfoc** (fire run) where fire spurts from dragons' mouths and families can 'dance with the devil' under sparklers and huge revolving fireworks. Be sure to wear damp long-sleeved clothes and bandanas to cover your face.

Steam Engines

Steam Train *www.fcg.net*, 932 05 15 15/933 66 45 53. A steam engine ride from the historic town of Martorell to the Monestary of Montserrat. With a museum at the departure point where younger guests learn about the working parts that make up a steam train, an entertainment group on board and a recreation area for children on arrival, this makes a great family day out. All original train woodwork has been restored. Departure Sundays from October to June. Reservations

from the FGC shop at El Triangle in Plaça Catalunya.

Waterparks

Aqualand Aqua Brava (Girona) Ctra.de Cadaqués – Roses (Girona) 972 25 43 44, *www.aquabrava.com*. Prices: Children over 1.20 m height and adults €18 (£12) day, €14 (£9.40) half day; Children smaller than 1.20m height €10 (£6.70) day, €8 (£5.35) half day.

Aquadiver (Girona) Address: Ctra. de Circumval.lació, s/n – Platja d'Aro (Girona 972 81 87 32, *www.aquadiver.com*. Prices: Adults €23 (£12.40); Children €13.50 (£8.40).

Illa Fantasia (Barcelona) Finca Mas Brasso, s/n Vilassar de Dalt (Barcelona) 937 51 45 53, *www.illafantasia.com*. Prices: Adults €11 (£7.40); Children €7.50 (£5).

FAMILY-FRIENDLY ACCOMMODATION

Barcelona

Barcelona is one of the most expensive cities in Spain, and prices in the first-class and luxury hotels are climbing all the time. High season is summer (April–September), Easter week and the odd big conference date when hotel prices can quadruple. Babysitting is usually on offer but should be sorted out in advance (ditto cots). English-speaking sitters are easy to find, and will even stay with the children in their hotel room. However, that's where the good news ends. Very few hotels have special facilities for children, and while some have outdoor pools, lifeguards are rare. Most places will add an extra bed or cot for a surcharge but very few can accommodate four people so you'll have to book two rooms. These are not usually interconnecting.

The cheapest hotels are around the **Barri Gòtic**, the more modern and pricey versions are further north in the safer Eixample district near Plaça de Catalunya and Universitat, whose charming wide boulevards do have the drawback of more traffic noise and old infrastructure. These hotels are only about 15 minutes away from the city's main attractions.

Further north still, above the Avinguda Diagonal, you'll enter the Gràcia area, which is Barcelona's little patch of bohemia. There's lots of *botellon* (outdoor drinking) in the squares here: all perfectly amiable but a bit noisy at night.

When parking is available at a hotel, the price is indicated; otherwise, the hotel staff will direct you to a garage. Expect to pay upward of €18 (£12) for 24 hours, and if you do have a car, you might as well park it and leave it there, because driving around the city is fruitless.

For a real taste of life in Barcelona and to avoid expensive hotels, consider renting a self-catered apartment. Many residents leave Barcelona in the baking hot summer months, particularly over school holidays in August, and will advertise their flats/rooms for rent at very reasonable prices. See *www.barcelonaconnect.com*, *www.loquo.com*, and *www.catalunya-classified.com* for English language ads.

Ciutat Vella

The Ciutat Vella (Old City) forms the monumental centre of Barcelona, and holds all the action and attractions but is a bit dicier at night. It contains some of the city's best hotel bargains. Most of the glamorous, and more expensive, hotels are in the Eixample.

EXPENSIVE

Hotel Colón ★★ The Colón is an appropriate choice if you plan to spend a lot of time exploring Barcelona's medieval neighbourhoods, as did the stellar former guests like Jane Fonda and Sophia Loren. Possibly the most dramatic location in the city, opposite the main entrance to the cathedral. Inside, you'll find, a helpful staff, and good-size guest rooms filled with comfortable furniture. Not all rooms have views, and the ones in back are quieter. Sixth-floor rooms with balconies overlooking the square are the most desirable.

Av. de la Catedral 7, 08002 Barcelona. 📞 *933 01 14 04. Fax 933 17 29 15, www.hotelcolon.es. 145 rooms. €245 (£164.15) double; from €375 (£251.25) suite. AE, DC, MC, V. Bus:*

16, 17, 19, or 45. Amenities: Restaurant; bar; limited room service; babysitting; laundry service/dry cleaning. In room: A/C, TV, dataport, minibar, hair dryer, safe. Extra bed €38 (£25.45); cot free.

Rivoli Ramblas ★ The Colón has more tradition and style, and the Meridien more modern comfort. The minimalist public rooms glisten with polished marble. Guest rooms are carpeted, soundproofed, and elegant. The most desirable accommodations overlook the Ramblas.

Las Ramblas 128, 08002 Barcelona. ☎ 934 81 76 76, Fax 933 18 87 60, www.rivolihotels.com. 131 rooms/ 210 rooms. €175–230 (£117.25– 154.10) double; €453–735 (£303.50– 492.45) suite. Triples (€19 (£12.75) extra person) or triples with cot (free). Rates include breakfast. AE, DC, MC, V. Metro: Plaça de Catalunya or Liceu. Amenities: Restaurant; piano bar; health spa; jacuzzi, massage, sauna; solarium; 24-h room service; babysitting, laundry service/dry cleaning; non-smoking rooms; rooms for those w/limited mobility. In room: A/C, TV, dataport, minibar, hair dryer, iron, safe.

INEXPENSIVE

Hotel Banys Orientals VALUE
This is one of the Old City's best buys, and it lies in the heart of Barcelona, off the major artery, Vía Laietana. The hotel is a league above your typical no-frills lodgings. It lies in the beautiful **Born** district, near the Santa Maria del Mar cathedral. Guest rooms are beautifully maintained, and there is every convenience from bathtubs to bedside tables. Downstairs is one

of the most recommendable and most affordable restaurants in the centre, Senyor Pareyllada, serving seafood and traditional Catalan food. Breakfast/buffet €9.90 (£6.65).

Carrer Argenteria 37, 08003 Barcelona. ☎ 932 68 84 60, Fax 932 68 84 61, www.hotelbanysorientals. com. 55 rooms. €95 (£63.65) (all year) double; €125 (£83.75) suite. AE, DC, MC, V. Parking €20 (£13.40). Metro: Jaume I. Amenities: laundry service; room for those w/limited mobility. In room: A/C, TV, dataport, hair dryer, iron, safe. €40 (£26.80) extra bed/ crib free.

Mesón Castilla ★ VALUE This government-rated two-star hotel, a former apartment building, has a Castilian facade with a wealth of Art Nouveau detailing. Charming and well maintained, and it certainly has a fantastic location, right in the centre of the city close to Les Rambles. The midsize rooms are comfortable and some open onto large terraces and are worth the extra pennies. The tiled bathrooms are equipped with bath/shower combos.

Valldoncella 5, 08001 Barcelona. ☎ 93 3 18 21 82, Fax 934 12 40 20, www.mesoncastilla.com. 57 rooms. €90–130 (£60.30–87.10) double. Triple €135–170 (£90.45–113.90) Free crib. AE, DC, V. Parking €20 (£13.40). Metro: Plaça de Catalunya or Universitat. Amenities: Breakfast buffet room; lounge; coffee machine, babysitting in rooms if arranged in advance; laundry service/dry cleaning; rooms for those w/limited mobility. In room: A/C, TV, minibar, hair dryer, safe. Breakfast included.

Gaudi Bus Tour

Eixample

MODERATE

Hotel Balmes Set in a seven-story structure built in the late 1980s, this chain hotel success-fully combines a conservative decor with modern accessories and a well-trained staff. Spacious guest rooms are vaguely English in their inspiration. If you're looking for a maximum of peace and quiet, rooms overlooking the back of the hotel – site of a small garden – are quieter and calmer than those facing the busy street.

Carrer Mallorca 216, 08008 Barcelona. ☏ 934 51 19 14, Fax 934 51 00 49, www.derbyhotels.com. 100 rooms. €90–195 (£60.30–130.65) double. AE, DC, MC, V. Parking €20 (£13.40). Metro: Diagonal or Paseo de Gracia. Amenities: Restaurant; bar; outdoor pool; limited room service; laundry service/dry cleaning. In room: A/C, TV, dataport, minibar, hair dryer, safe. Extra bed €42 (£28.15), cot free. Breakfast €13 (£8.70).

INEXPENSIVE

Hotel Astoria ★ **VALUE** One of our favourite hotels, and excellent value, the Astoria is near the upper part of Las Ramblas and the Diagonal. Built in 1952, it has an Art Deco facade that makes it appear older than it is. The high ceilings, geometric designs, and brass-studded detail in the public rooms could be Moorish or Andalucian. The comfortable midsize guest rooms are soundproofed. All rooms come equipped with private bathrooms containing showers. One of the only hotels with rooms large enough to have 2 extra beds.

París 203, 08036 Barcelona. ☏ 932 09 83 11, Fax 932 02 30 08, www. derbyhotels.es or www.derby hotels.com. 114 rooms. €60–200 (£40.20–134) double; €221–255 (£148–170.85) suite. AE, DC, MC, V. Parking nearby €20 (£13.40). Metro: Diagonal. Amenities: Bar; lunchtime restaurant; lounge; outdoor pool on terrace; limited room service; babysitting; laundry service/dry cleaning. In room: A/C, TV, dataport, minibar, hair dryer, safe. Extra bed €41 (£27.50), cot free – €20 (£13.40) depending on season. Breakfast €12 (£8.05).

Norte Diagonal

Gallery Hotel ★ FIND This is a winning, modern choice lying between the Passeig de Gràcia and Rambla de Catalunya. Guest rooms are midsize for the most part and tastefully furnished; each has a small bathroom with bath and shower. The on-site restaurant is known for its savoury Mediterranean cuisine. Rooms over-looking the gardens of the Palau Robert are worth asking for.

Calle Rosello 249, 08008 Barcelona. ☏ 934 15 99 11, Fax 934 15 91 84, www.galleryhotels.com. 110 rooms €134–280 (£90–188) double, €165–360 (£110.55–241) suite. AE, DC, MC, V. Parking €16 (£10.70). Metro: Diagonal. Amenities: Restaurant; bar; fitness centre; sauna; solarium; 24-h room service; babysitting; laundry service/dry cleaning; non-smoking rooms; rooms for those w/limited mobility. In room: A/C, TV, dataport, minibar, coffeemaker, hair dryer, safe. Extra bed €35 (£23.45), cot free. Breakfast 16 (£10.70).

Vila Olimpica

Hotel Arts ★★★ The only beachfront address in Barcelona and now one of the city's distinguishing landmarks/skymarks! (One of the two twin towers modernly mirroring the towers of the Sagrada Familia.) This hotel occupies 33 floors of one of the highest buildings in Spain and one of Barcelona's only sky-scrapers. The hotel is about 2.5 km (1½ miles) southwest of Barcelona's historic core, near the sea and the Olympic Village. Its decor is contemporary and elegant. The spacious, well-equipped rooms have built-in furnishings and sumptuous beds. The young staff are polite and hardworking. There's a children's club and summer activity programme of crafts, games, films, magic and much more. Special Family Packages: €290 (£194.30) Two adults and one child* in a Deluxe Room.

*Valid for children up to 12 years old. Children up to 12 years old will receive complimentary room and breakfast in Café Veranda when sharing room with parents. Packages available from 10 July until 31 August. Extra bed €121 (£81). Breakfast €26 (£17.40) + VAT.

Carrer de la Marina 19–21, 08005 Barcelona. ☏ 932 21 10 00, Fax 932 21 10 70, www.hotelartsbarcelona. com. 482 rooms. €370–500 (£248–335) double; €485–650 (£325–435) suite. AE, DC, MC, V. Parking €35 (£23.45). Metro: Ciutadella–Vila Olímpica. Amenities: 4 restaurants; cafe; 2 bars; outdoor pool; fitness centre; whirlpool; 24-h room service; laundry service/dry cleaning; non-smoking rooms; rooms for those w/limited mobility. In room: A/C, TV, dataport, minibar, hair dryer, iron, safe.

Apartments for Rent

Better than hotel and often at the price of a backpacker's hostel, rental apartments are a really great option for families on a budget.

BARCELONA DINING & ACCOMMODATION

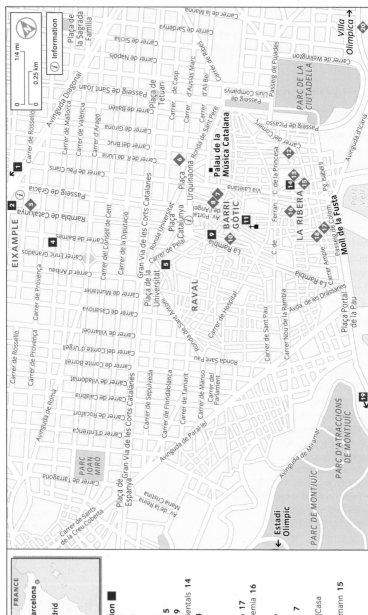

Accommodation ■
Gallery Hotel **2**
Hotel Astoria **1**
Hotel Arts **19**
Hotel Colón **11**
Mesón Castilla **5**
Rivoli Ramblas **9**
Hotel Banys Orientals **14**
Hotel Balmes **4**

Dining ◆
Agua **20**
Bodega la Plata **17**
Café de L'Academia **16**
Cal Pep **13**
Casa Alfonso **6**
Comerç 24 **12**
Els Quatre Gats **7**
La Rosca **8**
Las Campanas (Casa
Marcos) **18**
Restaurant Hofmann **15**
Tragaluz **3**
Dulcinea **10**

Many have great facilities like Wi-Fi, and DVD players, are self-catering. Drawbacks include endless flights of stairs and derelict buildings. There are several independent companies online, expect to pay about €100 (£67) per night based on two sharing, including **Vive Barcelona**: *www.vivebarcelona.com*. €100 (£67) high season: March – October, €90 (£60.30) low season*: November – February (except Christmas). *Prices for 1–2 persons/night Additional Person: Adults: €20 (£13.40), From 3 to 9 years old: €10 (£6.70). Under 3 years old: free. **Apartments Ramblas**; *www.apartments ramblas.com*. info@apartments ramblas.com, ☎ *933 01 76 78*. Tours also organised (e.g. €50 (£33.50) for 4 people); **ApartmentSi** *www.apartmentSi. com*, ☎ *+34 931 834 420*. Cheaper option (from €17 (£11.40) per person per night). Fun, bright coloured apartments. **Friendly Rentals**: *www.friendlyrentals.com*, ☎ *932 68 80 51*, Fax: *932 68 80 52*. Wide selection of stylish apartments starting at €90 (£60.30) a night for 2, some flats with pool, beach apartments, terrace and open plan lofts. **Rooms Barcelona**: *www.roomsbarcelona. com*, ☎ *934 42 36 69*, info@rooms-barcelona.com. Per night: for 4 people, only: €165 (£110.55) for 2 people, only: €90 (£60.30) for 1 person: €65 (£43.55). **Apt Barcelona**: *www.aptbcn.com*. Very inexpensive rooms (from €25 (£16.75)) and apartments. Holidays in Barcelona: *www.holidaysinbarcelona.com*.

☎ *609 68 94 73, 690 83 37 01* and *933 04 16 49*, reservations@ holidaysinbarcelona.com. €60–110 (£40.20–73.70) per night with last minute offers. **Rent 4 Days**: *www.rent4days. com*, ☎ *933 68 47 00*, info@rent 4 days.com. €100+ (£67+) a day with deluxe possibilities. **Barcelona for Rent**: *www. barcelonaforrent.com*. ☎ *934 58 63 40*, e-mail: info@barcelona forrent.com. **Urban Flats**: *www. urban-flats.com*, ☎ *932 15 01 96*. Have a look at *www.barcelona-tourist-guide.com/apartments/ barcelona-apartment-rental.html* for more.

FAMILY-FRIENDLY DINING

Children's menus, as in the rest of Spain, are rare here, and neither is there a culture of crayons at the table for Spanish children: they endure long lunches with the entire family without distractions. A book or a Nintendo may help if you're hoping for a long, lazy meal. The American fast food supremos have, with grim inevitability, made sure you're never more than 10 minutes from your nearest sesame seeded bun: MaccyD's Burger King, Kentucky Fried Chicken and Subways all have branches on Las Ramblas and Plaça de Catalunya. At the other end of the spectrum, if money is no object, you'll find some of the grandest culinary experiences in Europe here. Diverse **Catalán cuisine** reaches its pinnacle in

Barcelona, but you don't get just Catalán fare – the city is rich in the cuisines of all the major regions of Spain, including Castile and Andalusia. The top-end eateries that are too down-right awkward to get to, don't accommodate children, or where liver and snails are the only menu options, have not made the list below. Included are some very expensive options and even those that don't have high chairs, but are happy to accept offspring from infants to teens in case you do want to spend some real wedge on a gastronomic blow-out. There are huge numbers of innovative, characterful and trendy eateries springing up every day in Barcelona's old town. Since Barcelona also happens to be the most cosmopolitan of Spanish cities, there's a list of cheap and fast but nutritious food, taking advantage of Barcelona's cultural melting pot for a whole world of flavours.

The Districts

The **Ciutat Vella**, the old part of the city is full of great choices both for traditional and modern and creative cuisine. **Born** has cornered the trendy Mediterranean and fusion market, with lots of intimate and romantic restaurants in this chichi end of town with wine bars and outside tables particularly clustered around the **Santa Maria del Mar** cathedral. The **Barri Gòtic**, although it gets the most tourist footfall, still harbours a heap of totally authentic tapas taverns, particularly on Calle Mercé where local gents still sit to gossip with their '*compañeros*'. The nearby **Las Ramblas** is the opposite: you'll shell out a King's Ransom for mediocre tapas, paella and jugs of beer and sangria. Fun people watching, though. Next door, **El Raval** (the old Barrio Xines) has a large immigrant population,

Las Ramblas

Port Olimpic

although it's more North African than Chinese these days. Here's where to come for really bargain *scran*: predominantly kebabs, Lebanese, Pakistani and Indian. There are also some fine South American diners, particularly Argentine. **Poble Sec** is much less frequented by tourists than other areas: it does unstuffy, good value food, but don't expect much in the way of choice. **Eixample** is haute-Catalan cuisine's headquarters. The food is exquisite, but you pay through the nose for it and fussier taste buds are certainly not catered for. The **Olympic Port** holds an enormous array of outside seafood restaurants, which are pricey but worth popping in on for lunchtime menu del dia deals. The fish restaurants along the Barceloneta marina charge similar prices but have the edge in atmosphere.

Ciutat Vella

EXPENSIVE

Restaurant Hofmann ★★

CATALAN/FRENCH/INTERNATIONAL This Born bistro has three outside courtyards. German/Catalán proprietor Mey Hofmann turns out food with French ingredients like a fine tarte with de-boned sardines, a ragout of crayfish with green risotto, succulent pigs' feet with eggplant, and rack

Barcelona's opening times (as in all Spain) revolve around a long-lunch (2–4pm) and therefore dinner is rarely served before 9pm, though below are some that open earlier. If you are caught out, some all day food options are: **OVNI** (buffet salad, pizzas and free Internet) on Via Laietana, 32 or Ronda Sant Antoni, 11, open everyday from 12.30pm–1am or its equivalents, **FresCo** (*www.frescco. com* for your nearest branch, 12.30pm–1am) and **Lactuca**. Dinner options before 9pm are more limited but the main tourist tapas bars (located on or around Las Ramblas) will cater for early diners, though better avoided for their high prices and inauthenticity. Much better to do as the Spanish do and enjoy a '*menu del*'; a three course lunch at affordable prices can be found at even some of the higher class establishments which are otherwise out of price range at dinner time. These can come to as little as €6–15 (£4–10.05) including drinks.

of lamb with grilled baby vegetables and fondant of chocolate to finish. They are willing to adapt dishes to cater for children's preferences: just ask.

Carrer Argenteria 74–78. \ *933 19 58 89, www.hofmann-bcn.com. Reservations recommended. Main courses €16–36 (£10.70–24.10); fixed-price lunch €31 (£20.80) excluding drinks AE, DC, MC, V. Mon–Fri 1.30–3.15pm and 9–11.15pm. Metro: Jaume I.*

MODERATE

Comerç 24 ★ FIND CATALAN
Come here for food as adventure and art. Chef and owner Carles Abellan, a graduate from Ferran Adria's kitchen, has put his own twist on Catalonia's traditional fare using fresh seasonal ingredients, balanced sauces, and bold combinations. He believes in split-second culinary timing: his take on the traditional Spanish tortilla is supposed to be legendary. But to really get your children steeped in Catalan culture order what local children used to get instead of Marmite

on toast when they came home from school: a combination of chocolate, salt and bread flavoured with olive oil.

Carrer Comerç 24, La Ribera. \ *933 19 21 02. Reservations required. Main courses €7–14 (£4.70–9.40); tasting menu €48 (£32.15). MC, V. Tues–Sat 1.30–3.30pm and 8.30pm–midnight. Closed 10 days in Dec, 10 days in Aug. Metro: Arco de Triomfo, www.carlesabellan.com.*

Els Quatre Gats CATALAN The Four Cats is Catalan slang for 'just a few people'. But what people there were: this was the hang-out for some of Barcelona's key intellectuals and bohemians, a base for members of the *modernismo* movement, Picasso, Rusiñol and their peers took a shine to the place and started to hang their work on its walls. The fixed-price meal of unpretentious seasonal Catalan cooking is good value. Fish trumps meat here, especially the monkfish stew or loin of cod in a fiery pepper sauce. There are several child-friendly dishes and they

Els Quatre Gats

can rustle up a hamburger and chips.

Montsió 3. ☎ 933 02 41 40, www. 4gats.com. Reservations required Sat–Sun. Main courses €10–20 (£6.70–13.40); fixed-price menu (Mon–Fri) €17 (£11.40) (€21 (£14.10) on Saturdays excluding coffee). AE, DC, MC, V. Daily 8am–2am. Metro: Plaça de Catalunya.

INEXPENSIVE

Café de L'Academia ★ VALUE

CATALAN/MEDITERRANEAN This restaurant may look forbiddingly posh – brown stone walls, ancient wooden columns, 15th century building – but is pretty reasonable. Dishes of this quality could cost three times these prices elsewhere: the special is *codorniz rellena en cebollitas tiernas y foie de pato* (partridge stuffed with tender onions and duck liver). They are happy to adapt their dishes to children's taste buds and can turn out unfussy dishes like chicken and hamburgers, too.

Carrer Lledó 1 (Barri Gòtic), Plaça Sant Just. ☎ 933 15 00 26. Reservations required. Main courses €10–14 (£6.70–9.40); fixed-price menu (lunch only) €12.75 (£8.55) AE, MC, V. Mon–Fri 9am–noon, 1.30–4pm, and 8.45–11.30pm. Closed last 2 weeks Aug, Sat, Sun and bank holidays. Metro: Jaume I.

Dulcinea Established in 1930, Dulcinea, Vía Petrixol 2 (☎ 933 02 68 24), this is the most famous **chocolate shop** in Barcelona. The specialties are *melindros* (sugar-topped soft-sided biscuits), and the regulars who flock here love to dunk them into the very thick hot chocolate. Cocoa with cream €2.25 (£1.50), and a *ración* of *churros* for dunking goes for €1.35 (£0.90). No credit cards are accepted. Dulcinea is open daily from 9am to 1pm and 5 to 9pm; closed in August. Take the Metro to Liceu.

La Rosca CATALAN/SPANISH Don Alberto Vellve has been here for over 50 years and has built up some firm fans for his mix of Catalan and modern Spanish cuisine served from a small rustic house decorated with bullfighting posters and old photos of Barcelona. There are 60 unadorned tables, which fill up quickly for the cheap three-course lunch menu: hearty fare like veal stew or assorted grilled fish and shellfish, and baby squid in its own ink. Grilled monkfish is a good. Child-friendly dishes like pasta are also available on request.

Juliá Portet 6. ☎ 933 02 51 73. Reservations recommended. Main courses €6–12 (£4–8); fixed-price menu €8.50 (£5.70) (€13 (£8.70) on Sundays). No credit cards. Sun–Fri 1pm–4pm. Closed evenings except for group bookings. Closed Saturdays and last two weeks of Aug. Metro: Urquinaona, Catalunya, or Jaume I.

Sur Diagonal

Tragaluz ★ MEDITERRANEAN

Two contemporary beige dining rooms across two floors of this turn of the century building. The restaurant is refreshingly flexible and forward thinking for Spain: there are dishes for vegetarians and dieters, there's a sushi restaurant downstairs and 'Tragaluz rapid' which is open straight through from 1pm till 1am and serves cheaper and faster food from just €4.75–16 (£3.20–10.70) a dish. Homemade hamburgers are a safe bet. The main menu has things like terrine of duck liver, or beef tenderloin in a Rioja wine sauce. For afters there's a killer chocolate cake that's been deliberately under-baked.

Pasaje Concepción 5, Eixample. ℃ 934 87 06 21, www.grupotragaluz. com. Reservations recommended. Main courses €13–28 (£8.70–18.75). AE, DC, MC, V. Daily 1.30–4pm and 8.30pm–midnight; Thurs–Sat till 1am. Lunchtime set menu at €20 (£13.40) (Mon–Thurs) Metro: Diagonal or Provença.

Barceloneta

MODERATE

Cal Pep ★ FIND CATALAN
Set on 'Saucepan Street', Cal Pep lies close to the Picasso Museum and is a slice of local life. On a tiny postage-stamp square, it's generally packed, and the food is some of the tastiest in the Old Town. Pep is a great host, going around to see that everybody is one happy family. At the back is a small dining room which can hold groups of between 4 and 22 people but you need to book it three weeks in advance, and besides, it's more fun in the counter seats up front where you can watch all the dishes being freshly prepared. Try the fried artichokes or the mixed medley of seafood that includes small sardines. Tiny clams come swimming in a well-seasoned broth given extra spice by a sprinkling of hot peppers. Tuna comes with a sesame sauce, and fresh salmon comes with basil. **Passadis del Pep** (Pla del Palau, No.2: ℃ 93 310 1021) is Cal Pep's posher neighbour and serves amazing seafood.

Plaça des les Olles 8. ℃ 933 10 79 61, www.calpep.com. Reservations required. Non-smoking. Main courses €13–25 (£8.70–16.75). AE, MC, V. Mon 8–11.30pm; Tues–Sat 1.15–4pm and 8–11.30pm. Closed Aug and Easter. Metro: Barceloneta or Jaime I.

INEXPENSIVE

Agua ★ MEDITERRANEAN/ITALIAN

Well-prepared fish and shellfish in a hypermodern, hip setting overlooking the beach. Eat your pick of huge portions of meat and fish grilled on an open fire either on the outside terrace or in a big-windowed blue-and-yellow dining room. Huge display cases showing the catch of the day, and there's excellent

Agua

grilled chicken, fish, shrimp, crayfish, or stuffed squid. Most come with little culinary fanfare – sauces are shunned. Risottos are great and many are vegetarian. Highchairs and adapted children's meals are also available.

Passeig Marítim de la Barceloneta 30 (Port Olympic). 📞 *932 25 12 72, www.grupotragaluz.es. Reservations recommended. Main courses €15–35 (£10.05–23.45); lunch fixed-price menu €15 (£10.05). AE, MC, V. Daily 1.30–3.45pm (until 4.30pm Sat–Sun) and 8pm–11.30pm (till 12.30am Fri–Sat). Metro: Ciutadella/Port Olympic.*

Tapas

You can get good tapas all through the day from the chain bars on the **Passeig de Gracia**, where quality is high and you can watch the well-dressed world go by from their outside terrace tables.

Bodega la Plata TAPAS Late 1920s famous bodega with a no-nonsense attitude. Make a meal of two *raciones* of deep-fried sardine with the house's tomato, onion, and fresh anchovy salad.

Mercé 28. 📞 *933 15 10 09. Tapas at €1.50 (£1). No credit cards. Mon–Sat 10am–3pm and 6–11pm. Metro: Barceloneta or Drassaness. Closed Aug.*

Casa Alfonso TAPAS Jamón Jabugo is all they sell here. Whole haunches hang from steel braces. They're taken down, carved, and trimmed before you into paper-thin slices.

Roger de Lluria 6. 📞 *933 01 97 83. www.casaalfonso.com. Tapas €4–9 (£2.70–6)). AE, DC, MC, V. Mon–Tues 9am–midnight; Wed–Fri 9am–1am. Sat 11am–1pm Non-smoking area Metro: Urquinaona.*

Las Campanas (Casa Marcos) TAPAS Chorizo comes pinioned between two pieces of bread and there are all sorts of sausage, like *morcilla*, black sausage, or *chistorra*: thin red sausage best eaten with beer or red wine. Established in 1952, and hasn't changed much.

Mercé 21. 📞 *933 15 06 09. Tapas €1–7.50 (£0.67–5). No credit cards. Thurs–Tues 1–4pm and 8pm–2am. Metro: Jaume I.*

Picnics

Take advantage of beautiful weather, great fresh produce, and great parks overlooking some of the city's best monuments. Most good-sized supermarkets are in the Eixample area and the huge El Corte Ingles in Plaça de

Catalunya is open all day. Failing that though, there are Pakistani-run mini-markets on every corner of the old town selling most essentials with only slightly higher price tags than the big stores. Traditional Spanish ham and cheeses are the backbone of a good Spanish picnic so seek out some *jamon serrano* (dry-cured ham) or some semi-cured *manchego* to stuff in your freshly-baked loaf. There may not be many parks in Barcelona, but what the city lacks in quantity it makes up for in quality. Otherwise, the city is scattered with park benches and boasts a beautiful beach front. Montjuïc Mountain has a very peculiar cactus garden which makes a perfect picnic spot. Pick up huge, juicy peaches and big bags of cherries from La Boqueria and remember to pack the wet wipes.

SHOPPING

Bullfighting and flamenco are categorically un-Catalan pursuits. If you do buy souvenirs on Las Ramblas, one word: **barter**. The first price they quote will invariably be wildly inflated.

Barcelona is the street fashion centre of Spain. The city is full of beautiful young people writing their own style rules. Barcelona is packed with boutiques, but threads are pricey, even though the city has been a textile centre for centuries. Spain's well known high street shops such as **Zara**, **Mango**, **Bershka** and other international chains like **Benetton** and **Hennes** are well represented and prices in Spain are about two thirds of those on British high streets. Better still are Barcelona's **markets**, which make brilliant places to pick up both bargains and products unique to the city.

Camper the originally Spanish shoe brand has a big presence here and prices are cheaper than in the UK. Camper Carrer Elisebets, 11, *www.camper.com*.

The clothes shop British youth have dubbed 'high-street Prada' was also born in Spain. **Zara's** main branches are at Pg. Gràcia 16, 08007 Barcelona (℡ *933 18 76 75*) Pelai 58, 08001 Barcelona – (℡ *933 01 09 78*) and Av. Portal de l'Àngel 24, 08002 Barcelona (℡ *933 17 65 86*) 10am–9pm Mon–Sat. AmEx, DC, MC, V. Metro Catalunya. *www.zara.com*.

Ditto **Mango**, which has 12 branches in the city including Pg. Gràcia 12, 08007 Barcelona (℡ *933 18 00 78*) Pelai 48, 08001 Barcelona (℡ *933 18 87 90*)

 Sale Time

From June to August shops slash their prices by up to 70%. Your key piece of Spanish vocab here is *Rebajas*, or *Rebaixes* in Catalan. There are sales in January, too, but the Christmas shopping season is extended here until after the 6th of January: King's day.

Window Shopping

Canuda 28, 08002 Barcelona
(📞 934 12 08 52) 10am–9pm
Mon–Sat, AmEx, DC, MC, V
www.mango.com.

Mango 2 outlet on C/
Girona, 38: has last season's
stock at great prices.

For something a bit different
head for camel market on
Portaferrissa and **Rambla
Raval**, which is where young
designers show their wares. One
whole floor of the Plaça de
Catalunya branch of **El Corte
Inglés** is devoted to children,
while **Galeries Maldà** (no
phone, C/Portaferrissa 22, Barri
Gòtic) is a small shopping centre
with plenty of children's shops.
Larger branches of Zara have
decent children's sections.

Supermarkets Corte Ingles has
its own line of 24h supermarkets
called Open Cor (Gràcia 27,
08007 Barcelona 📞 932 38 60 85;
Ronda Sant Pere 33, 08010

Barcelona 📞 933 42 73 02; Ronda
Sant Pau 34, 08001 Barcelona
📞 933 24 85 24) Otherwise supermarkets tend to be in the
Eixample (e.g. Calle Comte
d'Urgell (metro: Urgell) has
Supersol), or bigger ones are
out of town.

The Shopping Scene For
snazzy window-shopping, stroll
along the Passeig de Gràcia from
the Avinguda Diagonal to the
Plaça de Catalunya, where
some of the city's most elegant
and expensive shops sit among
cafes and tapas bars in splendid
turn-of-the-20th-century buildings. Another prime spot is the
Ramblas de Catalunya (upper
Ramblas). In the old quarter not
far from Plaça de Catalunya, the
principal shopping streets are **all
five Ramblas**, plus **Carrer del
Pi**, **Carrer de la Palla**, and
Avinguda Portal de l'Angel.
Moving north in the Eixample,
you'll walk through **Passeig de
Catalunya**, **Passeig de Gràcia**,
and **Rambla de Catalunya**.
Even farther north, **Avinguda
Diagonal** is another major shopping boulevard. If you don't feel
up to that much pavement-
pounding, there is a blue bus
with luxury white leather seats
that you can jump on and off
called **TombBus** which leaves
every six minutes from 8am till
10pm from Plaça Catalunya. In
general, shopping hours are
Monday through Saturday from
9am to 8pm. Smaller shops may
close from 1.30–4pm.

Department Stores El Corte
Inglés ★ One of the local

representatives of the largest and most glamorous department store chain in Spain, this branch sells a wide variety of merchandise from Spanish handicrafts to high-fashion items, Catalán records to food. Open Monday through Saturday from 10am to 10pm. El Corte Inglés has other Barcelona locations: Av. Diagonal 617–619 (℡ 933 66 71 00; Metro: María Cristina), and Av. Diagonal 471 (℡ 934 93 48 00; Metro: Hospital Clinic). Plaça de Catalunya 14. ℡ 933 06 38 00. Metro: Plaça de Catalunya.

Food and Drink Markets A highlight of Barcelona's markets is the **Mercat de la Boqueria**, Rambla 91 (no phone), near Carrer del Carme has heaps of regional produce, like groceries, juices, breads, cheeses, meats, and fish and now, even a stall selling fried insects. Mon–Sat, 8am–8pm.

Shopping Centres

The retail landscape in Barcelona has exploded since the mid-1980s with the construction of several American-style shopping malls. Here's a description of some of the city's best, with a wide array of shops, food eateries, and children's play areas. All of these one-stop shop options are easy family shopping options.

Diagonal Centre (Lilla Diagonal) This two-story mall contains stores devoted to luxury products, as well as a scattering of bars, cafes, and simple but cheerful restaurants favoured by office workers and shoppers.

Open Monday to Saturday from 10am to 9.30pm. Av. Diagonal 557. ℡ 934 44 00 00. Metro: María Cristina.

Maremàgnum The best thing about this place is its position adjacent to the waterfront on Barcelona's historic seacoast; it's

Sweet Stall at the Market

also well suited to outdoor prom-
enades. It contains many shops,
12 cinemas, an IMAX, and a
wide variety of restaurants, pubs
and discos catering to a very
young crowd.

*Open daily from 10am to 10pm
(restaurants later). www.
maremagnum.es. Moll d'Espanya
s/n. ☏ 932 25 81 00. Metro:
Drassanes or Barceloneta.*

Sweets

Papabubble C/Ample 28, Barri
Gòtic (☏ 932 68 86 25, *www.
papabubble.com*). Metro
Barceloneta or Drassanes.

*Open 10am–2pm, 4–8.30pm Tue–Fri;
10am–8.30pm Sat; 11am–7.30pm
Sun. Closed Aug. Credit MC, V.*

Hot sugar candy is moulded
into sweets before your very eyes
at this shop that even Augustus
Gloop would envy. There are lol-
lies, humbugs, and rock made in
all possible flavours and you can
even ask for them to be person-
alized, for the sweet-toothed
prima donna in your flock.

Teenage Clothes Shopping

Most Spanish (and International
e.g.: Benetton, Hennes) high
street shops can be found on the
presincted **Portal del Angel** curv-
ing round to **Calle Portaferrissa**
where a huge papier maché
camel welcomes you into a two
floor trend heaven.

*Zara/Mango, Av. Portal d'Angel, 24 &
34 (though they can be found everywhere e.g. Passeig de Gracia and
Calle Pelai). Metro: Catalunya, www.
zara.com.*

Quick Fix Cafes

Hook A veritable ship's galleon
or treasure cave full of artefacts,
ships dangling from the ceiling,
treasure chests, fairy lights and all
things pirate. Open early (7pm)
and with a delicious kid-friendly
cocktail called *Niños Perdidos*
(lost children) consisting of
banana syrup, orange juice, milk
and cinnamon (€5 (£3.35)), let
Peter Pan and Wendy take you
away to this never never land.

Ample 35 Metro Jaume I.

NORTH FROM HERE TO THE COSTA BRAVA

The Costa Brava

The Costa Brava was one of the
first regions of Spain to be discovered by British tourists, and
its southern stretches of broad
white-sand beaches were also one
of the first to succumb to serious
tourism blight: resorts such as
Blanes, Lloret de Mar and Platja
d'Aro were intensively developed
and geared to the mass market.
They're easy choices for a family
holiday but, as one hotelier com-
mented, 'you might as well be in
Florida'. Head north beyond
these towards the border with
France and the countryside rears
up into a mountainous landscape
that has kept large-scale development at bay. Along this stretch
of coast small, sheltered beaches
and coves are ideal for families,
where atmospheric fishing villages have been given a touch of

sophistication by a selection of family-run hotels and restaurants. Calella de Palafrugell, Llafranc and Timariu are the beaches that provide the most idyllic images on the region's postcard stands, all grouped around the ancient hilltop village of Begur, and if you head further north there are more gems: Escala, where a chain of small beaches line the ancient Greco-Roman ruins of Empúries, Roses with its broad swathe of sheltered beach and trendy towns such as Cadaqués, infused with the edgy imaginative art of its most famous resident, **Salvador Dalí**. Dalí's art also sets the tone for the inland town of Figueres, though the region's capital, Girona, is much more rewarding, with an atmospheric medieval centre. Be warned however: the Costa Brava is seasonal. Many hotels, restaurants and even museums close for the winter.

Girona

This underrated gem of a city (97 km (60 miles) northeast of Barcelona) is a perfect introduction to Catalonia's long history and rich culture: in many ways better than its big, crime-ridden neighbour, Barcelona. The historic centre is set on the Riu Onyar, with a busy Rambla rising up to a beautifully-preserved old city, with a medieval Jewish quarter and a dramatic cathedral. Beseiged by France and repressed under Franco, only recently has the city started to

regain its former confidence, with a newly-founded university giving it a youthful buzz and shops and restaurants opening all the time.

Visitor Information

The **tourist office** is at Rambla Llibertat 1, (☎ *972 22 65 75*, *www.ajuntiment.gi*) Monday to Friday 8am–8pm, Saturday 8am–2pm and 4pm-8pm, Sundays 9am–2pm. The **airport** (☎ *972 18 66 00*) is 13 km (8 miles) south along the A7 autopista or the N-II toll-free road. The **train station** (☎ *972 20 70 93*) is southwest of the town centre, close to the bus station.

Family-friendly Accommodation

In the heart of the old city the **Hotel Europa** (☎ *972 20 27 50*, *www.hoteleuropagirona.com*, Juli Garreta 23, has family rooms with four beds for €100 (£67). More importantly, it keeps its doors open long after the rest of the city has packed off to bed for the night and is exceptionally friendly and welcoming. For many families a swimming pool is key: in this case choose the **Hotel Costabella**, (☎ *972 20 25 24*, *www.hotelcostabella.com*, Avda. França, 61), just outside the centre, where room prices range from €136–170 (£91.10–113.90) for a family room and there's a sunny pool (not monitored) with lovely city views.

Figueres

Dalí's legacy sets the tone for this provincial town (37 km (23 m) N. of Girona), with the

Teabro-Museu Dalí

hugely popular **Teatre-Museu Dalí** drawing a steady stream of visitors, who leave in their wake a good selection of places to eat and stay. From this focus at the north the Rambla runs southwards, with the old town dominated by restaurants and bars.

Teatre-Museu Dalí The second-most visited museum in Spain, this lavish homage to Surrealism's most populist exponent is always busy. Housed in a former theatre, it collects some of his most important creations and displays them effectively around a central courtyard. The bizarre drama of his art is very effective in enthusing children, and many of the exhibits contain interactive elements.

From June to the end of September it is open daily from 9am–7.45pm: at other times of year it is open only to 6pm and closes completely on

Mondays. Admission €10 (£6.70), children under 9 free. Further information ☎ 972 67 75 00 or see www.salvador-dali.org.

Visitor Information
The **tourist office** is at Plaça del Sol, (☎ 972 50 31 55, *www. figueres.com*). In July and August open daily 9am–9pm; for the rest of the year Monday to Saturday 9am–1pm and 4–7pm.

Family-friendly Accommodation
The three-star **Hotel Empordà** (☎ 972 50 05 62, *www.hotel emporda.com*, N11) is well located, a few minutes walk north of the main attraction and within easy reach of the Rambla. Rooms cost between €79 (£52.95) and €115 (£77.05) depending on season, and it has an excellent restaurant, though may be rather too stylish for many families with young children.

Begur

The hilltop town of Begur (144 km (90 miles) NW of Barcelona) is an ideal base for exploring the prettiest beaches and coves of the Costa Brava, where accommodation tends to be limited and much in demand, but is also well worth a visit in its own right. The pedestrianised centre is richly evocative of an earlier age, ringing with the sound of the central church bell, with a wide choice of bars and restaurants and a friendly, small-town atmosphere. For stylish accommodation in the city centre, the best choice is the **Hotel Rosa**, (☎ 972 62 30, *www.hotel-rosa.com*, Pi i Ralló), a small family-run hotel, rooms from €59–87 (£39.55–58.30) per double depending on season (closed from November to March). Beautifully restored accommodation includes some spacious suites ideal for families and the restaurant below is one of the region's finest.

Calella de Palafrugell

This large fishing village (16 km (10 miles) south of Begur) is set out in a languorous straggle along a whole series of small beaches, dotted with moored fishing boats and with a good selection of hotels, restaurants and bars. Accommodation is limited and often overpriced: a good choice is the **Hotel Portbo**, (☎ 972 61 49 62, *www.hotelportbo.com*, August Pi i Sunyer, 6), within easy reach of the beach,

with hotel rooms for €40–160 (£20.80–107.20) and apartments catering for four or six guests, from €60–228 (£40.20–152.75) depending on season and size.

Llafranc

The stately white-painted buildings that ring the beach give this village (10 km (6 miles) south of Begur) a genteel, almost Victorian atmosphere, with a yacht marina looking along a wide stretch of beach. Unfortunately the restaurants, hotels and bars are separated from the sea by a road, even if traffic generally moves slowly, which is not ideal for those who like their children on the beach while they enjoy a slow Catalonian lunch. Most visitors here tend to stay in private rental villas, but you can also find accommodation: a good choice is the **Hotel Llafranch**, (☎ 972 30 02 08, Passeig Cipsella 16, (£67–80.40) €100–120 per double) just across the road from the beach, where most of the rooms have separate sitting areas (ideal for cots) and balconies set over the restaurant below. Alternatively, look up **Llafranc Villas** (☎ 972 30 54 12, *www.llafranch-villas.com*) for a choice of family accommodation options.

Timariu

A small fishing village (8 km (5 miles) south of Begur) set around a deep sandy beach,

Timariu is one of the most attractive bays in the Costa Brava, with just a few restaurants and a small supermarket offering enough – but not too many – facilities. Parking is limited, especially in season, so it is well worth considering trying to stay locally. **Hotel Timariu**, (☎ *972 62 00 31*, *www.timariu.com*, **Calle Passeig del Mar** is centrally located a few car-free paces from the beach, with rooms from €95–136 (£63.65–91.10) per double, €26.60 (£17.80) per extra bed. More usefully for families it also has a small block of five three-bed apartments, just a block back from the beach, that cost from €155–210 (£103.85–140.70) per night, depending on season, complete with daily linen changes and washing machines in each flat.

The Far North: Escala, Roses and Cadaqués

Towards the French border the land flattens out but the coastline is still packed with attractions. **Escala** is a charming fishing town, set around a small harbour with its own sandy beach. To the south a rather soulless stretch of apartment blocks spread across a broad beach, but to the north the **Greco-Roman ruins** of *Empúries*, perhaps rather hot for most families, back a fringing shoreline of small beaches, all easily reached by a pedestrianised walkway from town. North of here the **Bay of Roses** leads up to **Roses** town,

most useful perhaps for the **Aquablava Waterpark**, (☎ *972 25 43 44*, Carretera de Cadaquez) where you'll find Europe's largest wave pool and more than 20 waterslides, pools, rapids flumes and other wet attractions: perfect for a long day out.

Open from the beginning of June to mid-September from 10am–7pm, entry fees range from €10 (£6.70) for those under 1 m 20 to €18 (£12) for those above this height.

Drive further north through the dramatic National Park landscape of the **Cap de Creus** and the town of **Cadaquez** is excellent for older children. The beach is shingle but the narrow streets are packed with art-shops, and the nearby fishing village of **Portlligat** is where Salvador Dalí built his private home, now the **Casa-Museo Dalí** (☎ *972 25 10 15*) showing his weird lifestyle and design sense in a domestic situation that will captivate older children with a nascent interest in art. In season you have to book your tours of his home, which take place at ten-minute intervals of small guided groups with surgical precision through the day.

Entry €10 (£6.70), children under 9 free, open through the summer week-long but closed on Mondays from mid-September to mid-June.

THE COSTA DORADA

Sitges

Sitges (40 km (25 miles) south of Barcelona) is the gay capital of Spain. Part of its charm is that its visitors are so eclectic; the wide promenade which splits the beach and the sea from a wall of restaurants and hotels is a parade of skateboarding youngsters, rollerblading 20-somethings, sedate cyclists, families, gay couples, straight couples and conservative looking pensioners all out to take a walk in the sea air. For years the resort drew largely prosperous middle-class industrialists from Barcelona, but those staid days have gone; Sitges is as swinging today as Benidorm and Torremolinos down the coast, but easily outclasses both. It's a fun place for a family day trip, or for a longer stay, and the beaches are gorgeous.

Essentials

Getting There

RENFE runs trains from Barcelona-Sants to Sitges; the 30-minute trip costs €2.50 (£1.70). Call 📞 *934 90 02 02* in Barcelona for information about schedules. Four trains leave Barcelona per hour.

Sitges is a 45-minute drive from Barcelona along the C-246, a coastal road. An express highway, the A-7, opened in 1991. The coastal road is more scenic, but it can be extremely slow on weekends because of the heavy traffic, as all of Barcelona seemingly heads for the beaches.

Visitor Information

The tourist office is at Carrer Sinea Morera 1 (📞 *938 94 50 04*; *www.sitges.org*). From July to

Sitges

September 15th, it's open daily 9am–9pm; September 16th to June, hours are Monday to Friday 9am–2pm and 4–6.30pm.

BEACHES & RESORTS

The Costa Dorada

The Costa Dorada ('gold coast') is little known in relation to Spain's other Costas, but has some beautiful beaches, wide arcs of golden sand, with fishing villages and resorts strung out along the entire coastline of the province of Tarragona. The Costa Dorada extends for some 211 km (131 miles) from **Cunit** as far as **Les Cases d'Alcanar**, a series of excellent beaches and impressive cliffs, along with beautiful pine-covered headlands. In the city of Tarragona itself is **El Milagre** beach, and a little farther north are the beaches of **L'Arrabassade**,

Savinosa, dels Capellans, and Llarga. At the end of the latter stands La Punta de la Mora, which has a 16th-century watch-tower. The small towns of Altafulla and Torredembarra, both complete with castles, stand next to these beaches and are the location of many hotels and urban developments.

Farther north again are the two magnificent beaches of Comarruga and Sant Salvador. The first is particularly cosmopolitan; the second is more secluded. Last come the beaches of Calafell, Segur, and Cunit, all with modern tourist complexes. You'll also find the small towns of Creixell, Sant Vicenç de Calders, and Clarà, which are backed by wooded hills.

South of Tarragona, the coastline forms a wide arc that stretches for miles and includes La Piñeda beach. El Recó beach fronts the Cape of Salou where, among its coves, hills, and hidden-away corners, many hotels and residential centres are located.

Continuing south toward Valencia, you next come to Cambrils, a maritime town with an excellent beach and an important fishing port. In the background stand the impressive Colldejou and Llaberia mountains. Farther south are the beaches of Montroig and L'Hospitalet, as well as the small town of L'Ametlla de Mar with its small fishing port.

After passing the Balaguer massif, you eventually reach the delta of the River Ebro, a wide lowland area covering more than 483 km (300 miles), opening like a fan into the sea. Here there are some beaches over several miles in length and others in small hidden estuaries. Two important towns in the region are Amposta, on the Ebro itself; and Sant Carles de la Ràpita.

The Costa Dorada extends to its most southwesterly point at the plain of Alcanar, a large area given over to the cultivation of oranges and other similar crops. Its beaches, along with the small hamlet of Les Cases d'Alcanar, mark the end of the Tarragona section of the Costa Dorada.

TARRAGONA

Getting There

By Car Tarragona is 97 km (60 miles) south of Barcelona by car. Take the A2 southwest from Barcelona to the A-7 then take the N-340, the fast toll road. The one-way toll to Tarragona costs around €8 (£5.35). The N-340 also connects with Tortosa and Valencia. Coming from Reus or Terol, take the N-420 carriageway.

By Train There are regular, daily trains from the Barcelona-Sants station that make the 1 hour trip to Tarragona. Take a Catalunya Express, Regional Express or Regional train – not the long-distance train which is far more expensive and no quicker. Regional trains leave every half hour during the day.

From Madrid, 5 trains a day make the 4-hour trip. The journey by train from Alicante takes 2½ to 3 hours. In the high season it is best to buy train tickets in advance. In Tarragona the RENFE office is in the train station at Plaza Pedrera s/n 90224 02 02.

By Bus From Barcelona there are 10 buses a day to Tarragona taking 1½ hours, or from Valencia the 10-buses a day take 3 hours. Contact Eurolines (℡ 977 22 40 00/ 902 40 50 40) or Alsa (℡ 913 27 05 04/902 42 22 42). Or call ℡ 977 22 91 26 in Tarragona for more information.

Getting Around

The best way to explore Tarragona is on foot, so ditch the car in one of the many public car parks, or find a spot in a 'blue zone' – designated on-street parking. There is a good network of buses linking the many hotels along Via Augusta to the new town centre and all other neighbourhoods. Alternatively take a taxi: Cucurull Deu (℡ 977 23 37 37), Sicart Polo (℡ 977 21 56 56), Andres Arfelis (℡ 977 24 23 77) or Agrupación Radio Taxi (℡ 977 22 14 14). A tourist train will take you around some of the city's highlights. You can pick it up at the top of Rambla Vella. Headsets offer information in English. Call ℡ 669 76 51 99. Cost €5 (£3.35) or €3 (£2) for children. Departs 10.30am, 1.30pm, 4.30pm, 6.30pm (7.30pm extra train In August). The tour takes an hour.

Visitor Information

Tourist office at Calle Major 39 (℡ 977 25 07 95, *www.tarragonaturisme.es)* Open Mon–Fri 9am–9pm, Sat 9am–2pm, 4pm–9pm, Sun 10am–3pm. Winter Mon–Sat 10am–2pm, 4pm–7pm (closed Sunday afternoon). Catalonia Tourist office: C/Fortuny, 4, 43001, Tarragona (℡ 977 23 34 15, *www.catalunyaturisme.com*) Open 9am–2pm, 4pm–6.30pm. Closed Sat afternoon, Sundays and bank holidays. **Tarrago! Card.** The card is sold in tourist offices, hotels and campsites and gives free admission to museums and sites, free public transport, discounts on the airport shuttle, the Port Aventura water park, spas and the casino. Passes of 24 hours to 72 hours are available for €10–20 (£6.70–13.40). (℡ 977 25 07 95). Website: *www.tarragonaturisme.es*.

About the Town

For an antidote to the big city sprawl of Barcelona, head for the little city sprawl of Tarragona just an hour's drive away to the south. Here you will find a sleepy port built atop a rocky bluff jutting out into the Mediterranean with wide beachfront boulevards, tree-lined streets and a clutch of charming beaches hugging the coastline.

New Town The new town has two main arteries, the fashionably wide boulevard Rambla Nova and, parallel to it, Rambla Vella. Excellent fish restaurants and beaches, plus spectacular views of the Med from the Balcony of the Mediterranean (**Balcó del Mediterráni**) make it an excellent place for a stop-over. For children, the big draws are the city's main bathing beach, the Platja del Miracle found along the Baixada del Miracle, just below the Roman Theatre, with two larger beaches, the Llarga, and the l'Arrabassada a bit further away. More importantly for children, Port Aventura, Spain's largest amusement park, 8 km (5 miles) south-west of Tarragona. Here five sections, China, Mexico, the American Far West, the Mediterranean and Polynesia, bring all the excitement they could wish for. See p. 286 for further details.

Amfiteatre Romà Audiences since the 2nd century have seen gladiators fighting for their lives against wild beasts, public executions and even – in 259AD – a bishop and his deacons being burned alive within its confines.

Parts of this elliptical structure at the foot of Miracle park have been carved out of the cliff that rises from the sea. Children who have studied the Romans at school should identify with the amphitheatre's gruesome past.

Parc del Miracle. 📞 *977 24 22 20. Admission €2 (£1.35) adults, €1 (£0.67) students and seniors, free for children 16 and under. May–Sept 26 Tues–Sat 9am–9pm, Sun 9am–3pm; Oct–Mar Tues–Sun 9am–3pm. Bus: 2.*

Passeig Arqueològic ★★
Dotted with shaded gardens, this walkway along the ancient ramparts is an ideal place to take the family for a stroll. At the far end of the Plaça del Pallol, an archway leads to the 8 km (5 mile) long passage built on giant boulders by the Romans.

El Portal del Roser. 📞 *977 24 57 96. Admission €2.20 (£1.45). Free under 16s.Oct–Mar Tues–Sat 9am–5pm, Sun and holidays 10am–3pm; Apr–Sept Tues–Sat 9am–9pm, Sun and holidays 10am–3pm. Bus: 2.*

Catedral At the highest point of the city is the 12th century cathedral built roughly on the site of a Roman temple and representing the transition from the Romanesque to Gothic styles of architecture. Highlights include the vast, vaulted entrance, fine stained-glass windows and Romanesque cloisters.

Plaça de la Seu. 📞 *977 23 86 85. Cathedral and museum €2.40 (£1.60), €1 (£0.67) for under 12s. Mar 16–May 30 Mon–Sat 10am–1pm and 4–7pm; June 1–Oct 15 Mon–Sat 10am–7pm; Oct 16–Nov 15 Mon–Sat 10am–5pm; Nov 16–Mar 15 Mon–Sat 10am–2pm. Bus: 1.*

Tarragona Cathedral

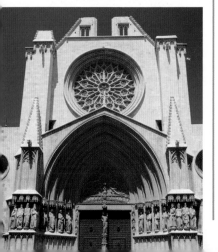

Port Aventura Amusement Park ★ Spain's largest amusement park is just 8 km (5 miles) out of town. Owned by Universal Studios, this appeals to adults and children of all ages and easily justifies staying for a couple of days in the area, or one of the resort's own hotels. It takes most pride in the **Dragon Khan roller coaster**, with 8 inverted loops, but there are plenty of quieter attractions to those whose tastes are less extreme. Divided into different cultural villages, there's the chance to take a canoe down a Polynesian river or sit and dine on Mexican food while mariachi singers play in the background. The cost of entry is €37 (£24.80) high season, €35 (£23.45) low season daily for adults, €30–28 (£20.10–18.75) for under-11s and over-60s, children under four go free. Prices reduce slightly if booking two or more consecutive days and if booking in advance. A part of the park is set aside as the **Caribe Water Park**, with wave pools, waterslides and flumes, many enclosed and heated: perfect for enjoying a full watery adventure whatever the weather. Tickets for this must be purchased separately, with prices for adults from €9.50–19 (£6.40–12.70), child prices from €8–15.50 (£5.35–10.40), depending on season. Current expansion plans already afoot will make Port Aventura the largest in Europe.

The park is fully open from mid-May till the end of September. Indoor areas only

Port Adventura

stay open till the end of October, and selected dates (including the Christmas and New Year holiday periods) through November, January and February, and then open again in late March: hours vary with season: in summer it is open daily from 10am until midnight, with reduced price tickets for entry after 7pm. In low-season it opens from 10am–7pm. For exact dates and details of what parts will be open check on their website at *www.portaventura.com* or call directly ℡ *977 77 90 90*.

Family-Friendly Accommodation

To make the most of the attractions and rides it makes practical sense to stay in one of Port Aventura's onsite hotels or partners nearby. Onsite there are three: the **Hotel El Paso**, the **Hotel Aventura** and the **Hotel Caribe**, each with special children's facilities such as a free children's club, supervised play areas, children's pools, children's menus in the hotel restaurants as well as lots of activities. All are four-star and include access to the park, with rooms designed to accommodate two adults and two children: prices are complicated and depend on length of stay and family size: best to call ☎ 977 77 90 90 or visit *www. portaventura.com* for a quote. Alternatively, the park has some large resort-type partner hotels nearby with good standards of accommodation and child facilities, but with little atmosphere: if there's any risk of theme-park fatigue setting in better to choose one of our Tarragona hotels and take Port Aventura a day at a time.

Getting There

Around half the **trains** along the Barcelona–Sitges–Tarragona line stop at port Aventura's own station (RENFE ☎ 902 24 02 02). From Barcelona the trip takes 50 minutes. A **taxi** from the centre of Tarragona costs around €13 (£8.70). If you know Port Aventura is a definte fixture in your travel plans the **theme park** is itself part of a substantial transport network and it may make sense to plan your **flights** in or out of Spain accordingly. Ryanair fly daily from London Stansted, London Luton, Liverpool, Glasgow and Dublin direct to Reus Airport, 10 minutes drive away, from where there's a regular airport shuttle. From Barcelona's El Prat Airport 13 buses daily go to Tarragona and then directly to Port Aventura so it's not always necessary to change. **Coaches** from all Spain's major cities also travel to Port Aventura: for details of routes and times call the park direct on ☎ 977 77 90 90.

Beaches & Resorts

Tarragona

Tarragona province boasts some pretty spectacular beaches along its 211 km (131 miles) of coast. Many are backed by stunning cliffs and situated along beautiful pine-covered headland. The city's own beach is **Platja Del Miracle**. Heading north out of town towards Barcelona are the beaches of **L'Arrabassada, Savinosa, dels Capellans** – a smaller beach – and **Llarga** – so named because it is 3000 m (9000 ft) long. **Cala Fonda** (north of Platja Llarga) this is a wilder, more remote beach without any of the usual facilities but much nicer for it. As it is secluded it attracts nudist bathers. For a rocky, rather than sandy beach try **Cala de La Roca Plana**. **Comarruga** and **Sant Salvador** – the more secluded of the two – both lie to the north of Platja Llarga and are well worth a visit. Alternatively, heading south out of Tarragona, you come to the beaches **La Piñeda** and then **El Recó** fronting the Cape of Salou.

Where to Stay

Heading north out of Tarragona along the Via Augusta you'll find a good selection of hotels that back onto the Del Miracle beach. Several have their own pools and rooms with terraces and of course, sea views. There's a grand dame of place in the centre of town for a different vibe or, if it's five star luxury you are after there's an extremely chic boutique hotel a 15 minute drive out of town.

EXPENSIVE

Hotel Husa Imperial Tarraco

This gigantic crescent of a modern hotel occupies the most commanding spot in Tarragona at the foot of the Rambla Vella on the tree-lined walkway, the **Passeig de les Palmeres**. Guests enter via a rather flashy, vast marble entranceway before sweeping upstairs to the one of 170 modern rooms—most with small balconies angled out to sea. Its central location, accommodating staff, pool and tennis court make it a perennial favourite with (mainly Spanish) families.

Passeig Palmeres s/n, E-43003 Tarragona. 📞 *977 23 30 40, Fax: 977 21 65 66. Email: hotelimperial tarraco@husa.es. Website: www. husa.es. 170 rooms. Suite €170 (£113.90); double €115–141 (£77.05–94.50) (including breakfast); 20 family rooms sleep four. AE, DC, MC, V. Babysitting can be arranged. Parking €13 (£8.70) per 24 h; casino, laundry/dry cleaning. In room: A/C, TV, minibar, hair dryer, safe.*

Family-Friendly Dining

L'Ancora The fact that this portside fish restaurant is usually heaving with locals at lunchtime says it all. It can be tricky to get one of the many outside tables, but if you sit at one of the wooden tables inside, the atmosphere is cosy and it's where most of the hustle and bustle takes place. Children can press their faces up against the fish tanks – one containing a jumble of terrapins. The waiters are sparky, chatty and quick. Clams or grilled fish are on the menu for €9.50 (£6.40) or sardines for €6 (£4). There's a good selection of tapas and paellas.

Trafalgar, 25 and 13, Puerto Pesquero, 43004 Tarragona. 📞 *977 24 28 06. Open 1pm–1am everyday. Closed Sunday.*

Sol-Ric Close to the beach out along Via Augusta, this is a lovely laid-back spot with large indoor and outdoor terraces with ample space for young ones to roam about. Décor is rustic, with a farm-house feel and the main house dates back to 1859. Staff are charming, the menu is extensive and there's a good selection of dishes for children. Muscles, prawns, lobster, squid and bacalao (salt cod) are among the best fish dishes. Or try the oven-baked hake with potatoes, tournedos with Roquefort or seafood stew. The €9 (£6) children's menu includes chicken breasts, cannelloni, macaroni, ice-cream.

Via Augusta 227, 43007, Tarragona. 📞 *977 23 20 32, Fax: 977 23 68 29. Open Tue–Sat 1–4pm, 8.30pm–11pm. Can seat 200. Fires, large indoor terrace in winter. Closed Dec 25–Jan 24.*

Appendix:
Terms & Phrases

LANGUAGE: USEFUL PHRASES

Spaniards are generally very patient with foreigners who try to speak their language and most understand a smattering of English. But even the most confident Spanish-speaking Brit might struggle with the country's regional dialects. Castilian (Castellano, or just Espanol) is understood everywhere. In Catalonia, they speak Catalán, or Euskera in the Basque country. It always helps to know a few basic phrases, so here's a list of simple Castilian Spanish to help you get by.

English	Spanish	Pronunciation
Good day	**Buenos dias**	bweh-nohs dee-ahs
How are you?	**Cómo está**	koh-moh es-tah
Very well	**Muy Bien**	Mwee byehn
Thank you	**Gracias**	grah-syahs
You're welcome	**De nada**	deh nah-dah
Goodbye	**Adiós**	ah-dyhos
Please	**Por Favour**	pohr fah-vohr
Yes	**Sí**	see
No	**No**	noh
Excuse me	**Perdó**	pehr-doh-neh meh
Give me	**Déme**	deh-meh
Where is?	**Dónde está?**	Dohn-deh es-tah
the station	**la estación**	lah es-tah-syohn
a hotel	**un hotel**	oon oh-tel
a gas station	**una gasolinera**	oon-nah gah-so-lee-neh-rah
a restaurant	**un restaurante**	oon res-tow-rahn-the
the toilet	**el baño**	el bah-nyoh
a good doctor	**un buen medico**	oon bwehn meh-dee-coh
the road to	**el camino ahacia**	el cah-mee-noh ah-syah
To the right	**a la derecha**	ah lah deh-reh-chah
To the left	**a la izquierda**	ah lah ees-kyehr-dah
Straight ahead	**Derecho**	deh-reh-choh
I would like	**Quisiera**	kee-syeh-rah
I want	**Quiero**	kyeh-roh
to eat	**comer**	ko-mehr
a room	**una habitacón**	oo-nah ah-bee-tah-syohn

English	Spanish	Pronunciation
Do you have?	**Tiene usted?**	Tyeh-neh oo-sted
a book	**un libro**	oon lee-broh
a dictionary	**un diccionario**	oon deek-syoh-na-ryo
How much is it?	**Cuánto cuesta?**	Kwahn-toh kwehs-tah
When?	**Cuándo?**	Kwahn-doh
What?	**Qué**	keh
There is	**Hay?**	Aye
What is there?	**Qué hay?**	Keh aye
yesterday	**Ayer**	ah-yer
today	**Hoy**	oy
tomorrow	**Mañana**	mah-nyah-nah
good	**Bueno**	bweh-noh
bad	**Malo**	mah-loh
better (best)	**(Lo) Mejor**	(loh) meh-hor
more	**Más**	mahs
less	**Menos**	meh-nohs
No smoking	**Se prohibe fumar**	she proh-ee-beh foo-mahr
postcard	**Tarjeta postal**	tat-heh-tah pohs-tahl
insect repellent	**Repelente contra**	reh-peh-lehn-the Insectos cohn-trah een-sehk-tohs

More Useful Phrases:

Do you speak English?	**Habla usted ingles?**	ah-blah oo-sted een-glehs?
Is there anyone here speaks English?	**Hay alguien aquí que hable ingles?**	eye ahl-gyehn ah- kee keh ah-bleh een-glehs?
I speak a little Spanish	**Hablo un poco de español**	ah-bloh oon poh-koh deh es-pah-nyol
I don't understand Spanish very well	**No (lo) entiendo muy bien el español**	hon (loh) ehn- tyehn-doh mwee byehn el es-pah-nyol
The meal is good	**Me gusta la comida**	meh goo-stah lah koh-mee-dah
What time is it?	**Qué hora es?**	Keh oh-rah es
May I see your menu?	**Puedo ver el menu**	pweh-do vehr el (la carta)? meh-noo (lah car-tah)?
The bill please	**La cuenta por favour**	lah kwehntah pohr fah-vohr
What do I owe you?	**Cuánto le debo**	kwahn-toh leh deh-boh

More Formal Phrases:

I want to see a room	**Quiero ver un cuarto**	kyeh-roh vehr oon kwahr-toh
	Or una habitación	oo-nah ah-bee-tah-syohn
for two persons	**para dos personas**	pah-rah dohs pehhr-soh-nas
with (without) bathroom	**con (sin) baño**	kohn (seen) bah-nyoh
We are staying here	**Nos quedamos aquí**	nohs keh-dah-mohs ah-kee
only	**solamente**	soh-lah-mehn-te
one night	**una noche**	oo-nah noh-cheh
one week	**una semana**	oo-nah she-mah-nah
We are leaving tomorrow	**Partimos mañana**	mah-nya-nah

NUMBERS

1	**uno**	(oo-noh)	17	**diecisiete**	(dyeh-see-syeh-teh)
2	**dos**	(dohs)	18	**dieciocho**	(dyeh-see-oh-choh)
3	**tres**	(trehs)	19	**diecinueve**	(dyeh-see-nweh-beh)
4	**cuatro**	(kwah-troh)	20	**veinte**	(bayn-tah)
5	**cinco**	(seen-koh)	30	**treinta**	(trayn-tah)
6	**seis**	(says)	40	**cuarenta**	(kwah-rehn-tah)
7	**siete**	(syeh-the)	50	**cincuenta**	(seen-kwehn-tah)
8	**ocho**	(oh-choh)	60	**sesenta**	(she-sehn-tah)
9	**nueve**	(nweh-beh)	70	**setenta**	(she-tehn-tah)
10	**diez**	(dyehs)	80	**ochenta**	(oh-chehn-tah)
11	**once**	(ohn-seh)	90	**noventa**	(hon-behn-tah)
12	**doce**	(doh-seh)	100	**cien**	(syehn)
13	**trece**	(treh-seh)	200	**doscientos**	(doh-syehn-tohs)
14	**catorce**	(kah-tohr-seh)	500	**quinientos**	(kee-nyehn-tos)
15	**quince**	(keen-seh)	1,000	**mil**	(meel)
16	**dieciséis**	(dyeh-see-says)			

USEFUL FOR TRAVELLING WITH CHILDREN

baby changing	**Mesa de cambia del bebe**	mhe-sa-de-camb-ia – del- bebe
baby equipment	**Equipo del bebe**	e-key-po-del-bebe
bottle warmer	**dispositivo para calentar**	dis-pos-it-teev-obotellas para cal-n-t-ar

buggy/pushchair	**cochecito**	co-she-see-to
child seat	**asiento infantil**	as-sien-to in-fan-til
children's Paracetamol	**paracetemol por ninos**	pa-ray-see-tem-ol pour los knee-nojs
dummy	**chupete**	chu-pe-te
formula milk	**leche de formula**	l-che-de-for-mu-l-a
follow-on milk	**leche de crecimiento**	l-eche de cre-ci-miento
highchair	**una silla alta**	uhn-a-sea-al-ta
nappies	**panales**	pa-na-les
playground	**Area de juegos**	Area-de-qhere-gos
seesaw/swing	**un balancin**	uhn-bal-uhn-cin
slide	**un tobogan**	uhn-tob-ogan
sterilising tablets	**tabletas de esterilizacion**	tab-let-as de ester-il-zasion
wet wipes	**los lingettes**	los-lunge-jets

In Your Hotel

family room	**habitacion tiene familia**	hab-it-acion-tiene-fam-il-ia
family suite	**suite de la familia/**	sweet-de-la- fam-il-ia
	appartamento de la familia	Appart-ment-o de-la-fam-il-ia
interconnecting rooms	**interconexion de cuartos**	inter-co-nexion de cuar-tos
extra bed	**cama adicional**	ca-ma add-dish-on-al
cot	**cuna**	cu-na
babysitting	**sesion de bebe**	session–de-bebe

FAMILY TRAVEL

Travelling as a family can be fun, exciting and create memories to savour, but a bit of preparation will go a long way in forging a smooth journey and holiday. There are plenty of sites providing parents with essential holiday information and even sites popping up for youngsters, too. From what to pack and coping with flights to childcare and accessories, the sites below will help give you a head start.

www.babygoes2.com: An innovative guide for parents travelling with babies and children with independent recommendations.

www.all4kidsuk.com: Links to tour companies offering family-friendly holidays, some of them in Spain.

www.youngtravellersclub.co.uk: Currently in its early days, this is a site for children themselves, which deserves to succeed.

www.deabirkett.com: The website of Guardian journalist Dea Birkett, who specialises in travelling with children. It includes a very useful Travelling with Kids Forum.

www.babycentre.co.uk: The travel section throws up some interesting articles on family holidays.

www.mumsnet.com: Set up by a journalist, TV producer and radio producer. Product reviews, interviews and planning help.

www.travellingwithchildren.co.uk: Comprehensive site with lots of handy tips for travelling parents.

www.travelforkids.com: An American site that has some good information on different countries with 'what not to leave at home' type tips.

www.familytravelforum.com: Lots of useful stuff on family travel in general.

www.travelwithyourkids.com: Easy to navigate with advice you feel comes from real experience of things having gone wrong!

www.thefamilytravelfiles.com: Heavily American, but with a section on Europe.

www.family-travel.co.uk: Independent advice on travelling with children: lots of sound general advice.

RESPONSIBLE TOURISM

Although one could argue any holiday including a flight can't be truly 'green', tourism can contribute positively to the environment and communities UK visitors travel to if investment is used wisely. Firstly, by offsetting carbon emissions from your flight, you can lessen the negative environmental impact of your journey. Secondly, by embracing responsible tourism practices you can choose forward looking companies who care about the resorts and countries we visit, preserving them for the future by working alongside local people. Below are a number of sustainable tourism initiatives and associations to help you plan a family trip and leave as small a 'footprint' as possible on the places you visit.

www.responsibletravel.com: A great source of sustainable travel ideas run by a spokesperson for responsible tourism in the travel industry.

www.tourismconcern.org.uk: Working to reduce social and environmental problems connected to tourism and find ways of improving tourism so that local benefits are increased.

www.climatecare.org.uk: Helping UK holidaymakers offset their carbon emissions through flying by funding sustainable energy projects

www.thetravelfoundation.org.uk: Produces excellent material on how to care for the places we visit on holiday. It also produces a special guide for children aged 7–10 and parents incorporating 'Hatch the Hatchling Hawksbill' with a play and puzzle book. Highly recommended.

www.aito.co.uk: The Association of Independent Tour Operators (AITO) is a group of interesting specialist operators leading the field in making holidays sustainable.

www.abta.com: The Association of British Travel Agents (ABTA) acts as a focal point for the UK travel industry and is one of the leading groups spearheading responsible tourism. It is launching a carbon-offsetting scheme with AITO and Federation of Tour Operators (FTO).

Index

See also Accommodations and Restaurant indexes, below.

General

A

Accommodations, 42–44.
See also Accommodations
Index
  best, 9–12
  money-saving tips, 21
  surfing for, 44–45
Agua Amarga, 205, 206–207
Airlines and air travel,
  35–37, 40
  checklist for, 30
Alájar, 79–80
Alameda De Tajo, 137–138
Albayzín (Granada), 167
Albufera National Park, 226
Alcazaba (Almeria), 190, 198
Alcazabar (Málaga), 107
Alcázar
  de los Reyes Cristianos
  (Córdoba), 90, 91
  Seville, 7, 59–60
Alcornocales, 145–146
Alcoy, 3
Alhambra (Granada), 7, 156,
  161, 164–167
Alicante, 238
Allegro (Seville), 72
All Saints' Day, 28
Almeria, 193–213
  events and entertain-
  ment, 196
  getting around, 196
  restaurants, 201–202
  sights and attractions,
  196–201
  travelling to, 195
  visitor information, 195
Almonaster La Real, 81
Almúnecar, 189–191
The Alpujarra, 182–188
Alpujarra Experience,
  184–185
Altea, 235
American Express, Seville,
  57
Americas Cup (Valencia),
  26, 229
Amfiteatre Romà
  (Tarragona), 285
Antequera, 146
Apartment or house rentals,
  42–43
  Barcelona, 265, 267
  Granada, 174–175
Apes' Den (Gibraltar), 129

April Fair (Seville), 26, 64
Aquadiver (Girona), 261
Aqualand (Roses), 261
Aqualandia (Benidorm),
  234–235
Aquaola (Granada), 170–171
Aquarium (Barcelona), 5–6,
  256
Aracena, 80
Arcos de la Frontera,
  142–144, 148
  accommodations,
  151–152
  restaurants, 153
Artesanía Andaluza
  (Córdoba), 94
Arte Zoco (Córdoba), 94–95
Ascensor Panoramico
  (Cartagena), 209–210
Azucarera del Guadalfeo
  (Caleta), 190

B

Babies and toddlers, checklist for, 29
Balneario de Lanjarón,
  183–184
Baños Arabes (Ronda), 138
Barcelona, 239–277
  accommodations,
  261–265, 267
  average temperature
  and rainfall, 23
  entertainment, 260
  festivals, 260–261
  getting around, 245–247
  neighbourhoods,
  242–245
  picnics, 273–274
  restaurants, 267–274
  shopping, 274–277
  sights and attractions,
  252–259
  travelling to, 241–242
  visitor information, 242
Barriada de Cuevas
  (Gaudix), 179
Barri de la Ribera
  (Barcelona), 243
Barri Gòtic (Gothic Quarter;
  Barcelona), 242–243,
  252–253
Barrio de Santa Cruz
  (Seville), 56, 59–61
Barrio de Triana (Seville),
  62–63

Beaches. *See also specific
  beaches*
  Almeria, 204, 205
  best resorts, 6
  Cartagena, 211
  Costa del Sol, 102
  Costa Dorada, 282–283
  Costa Tropical, 188
  Fuengirola area,
  111–112
  Huelva, 78, 79
  Málaga, 107
  Marbella, 114
  San José, 204
  Tarragona, 285, 287
  Valencia, 225–226
Bella Vista English quarter
  (Huelva), 81
Benalmadena, 111
Benidorm, 231–236
Bicycling, 144
  the Alpujarra, 184–185
  Barcelona, 247
  Valencia, 220
Bird-watching, 128, 140,
  144, 146, 190, 211, 226,
  234
Boating, 207
  Valencia, 226
Bocairente Festival of
  Christians and Moors
  (Valencia), 25
Books, recommended,
  45–47
Born (Barcelona), 243
Botanical Gardens
  (Córdoba), 91–92
Breastfeeding, 47
Bullfights
  Antequera, 146
  Málaga, 107
  Museo Municipal de
  Arte Taurino
  (Córdoba), 92–93
  Ronda, 137, 138
  Seville, 63
Bus travel, 38, 42

C

Cabo de Gata, 5, 9,
  202–204
Cadaquez, 281
Cala de los Toros, 204
Calblanque, 211
Calella de Palafrugell, 280

Restaurants

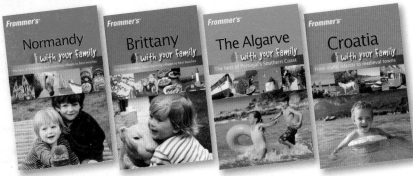

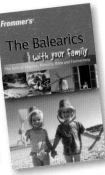

Notes